Cerealizing America

Cerealizing America

The Unsweetened Story
of American Breakfast Cereal

Scott Bruce and Bill Crawford

ff

Faber and Faber
Boston · London

First published in the United States in 1995
by Faber and Faber, Inc.,
50 Cross Street,
Winchester, MA 01890.

Copyright © 1995 by Scott Bruce and Bill Crawford
Foreword copyright © 1995 by Chuck McCann

Cataloging-in-Publication Data for this book
is available from the Library of Congress.

ISBN 0 571 19851 1

Jacket design by Mary Maurer
Cereal boxes reproduced on the jacket from the collection of Scott Bruce
Printed in the United States of America

For Mom, Beverly, and Nicholas
S. B.

For Antha Miller Crawford,
an American original
B. C.

Contents

Foreword

Cerealizing America is a book that had to be written. It is a wacky, wonderful celebration of breakfast cereal, the craziest link in the American food chain. Walk into any grocery store, stroll down the cereal aisle, and you'll realize that cereal is more than a food. It's an all-American form of entertainment.

I had my first encounter with the amazing world of breakfast cereal as a young comedian, just starting out in show business in 1962. Since I had a gift for doing voices and impressions, I naturally started doing commercials. One day, the Dancer Fitzgerald Sample agency in New York called me in for an audition. I was nervous. The ad business was competitive in those days and still is. But when the two ad men handed me a picture of a berserk bird with a loud-mouth attitude, I hesitated for only a few seconds before screeching out the call, "Wuuuwwk, I'm cuckoo for Cocoa Puffs, cuckoo for Cocoa Puffs, cuckoo for Cocoa Puffs!"

For the next eighteen years, I was the voice of Sonny, the Cocoa Puffs cuckoo bird. Over the years, I provided the voices for other cereal pitching characters as well, including Sugar Bear, Twinkles the elephant, and Bullwinkle the Moose, who needed me to supply his slogan, "the Big G stands for Goodness," on occasion.

It's strange, but after thirty years in the business and some forty films, I am still remembered by many people as the voice of Sonny. I get letters from fans almost every day who fondly recall the crazy squawk of the cereal munching cuckoo bird. It's like my big round glass house overlooking Los Angeles is the world's largest cereal bowl.

I have often wondered how a breakfast cereal character could become such a powerful icon of American popular culture. It wasn't until I read *Cerealizing America* that I realized the answer. The truth is, all of us look to cereal for excitement and fun. Down deep, everyone is cuckoo for Cocoa Puffs and other breakfast cereal. And everyone will be cuckoo about *Cerealizing America*.

Chuck McCann
The original voice of Sonny, the Cocoa Puffs cuckoo bird

Introduction

Breakfast cereal is the all-American food. Created by eccentric health reformers more than a hundred years ago, the strangely shaped bits of flavored grain have become a staple of the American diet, eaten by more than 80 million Americans every day. Cereal slogans such as "snap, crackle, pop," "koo-koo for cocoa puffs," and "silly rabbit," are better known than the national anthem, and are a lot funnier. Cereal characters, such as Tony the Tiger and Cap'n Crunch, are more recognizable than any American political leader, and at least as trustworthy.

In the words of economist Paul Samuelson, the saga of cereal is "one of those fascinating business stories that illuminate our lifestyles, history and economy." Indeed, only in America could the world's most sophisticated nutritional-industrial food processing complex earn more than eight billion dollars per year flaking, puffing, shredding, mashing, popping, and baking the most basic of foods—cereal.

Defined by Webster's dictionary as any edible grain, cereal was responsible for the rise of human civilization. When neolithic farmers figured out how to cultivate wheat, millet, oats, and other wild grasses some 10,000 years ago, they created the first steady food supply humankind had ever known. With cereal agriculture, humans no longer needed to spend their time wandering over the earth in search of wildlife or seasonally available vegetable foods. Instead, they could grow food in their own backyard and store it for later consumption. From Mohenjo-Daro to Babylon, from Ur to Memphis, the first civilized people on Earth thrived on cereal.

Of course, the Pharaohs didn't sit around on the pyramids munching on Sugar Frosted Flakes or Freakies. Porridge was the staff of life in the ancient world. The Greeks thrived on a grain-based concoction known as *sitos*, cooked cereal flavored with olive oil and perhaps a dash of lamb gravy. The Romans, whose *cerealia*, or festivals in honor of the goddess of agriculture, Ceres, gave us the word *cereal*, conquered the world on stomachs filled with *puls*, a gruel made from barley, millet, wheat, or oats.

From medieval times until the nineteenth century, Europeans ate rye or buckwheat gruel and slurped down *frumenty,* a boiled wheat-and-milk concoction. Native Americans munched on *hominy* and *samp,* porridges made from that unique North American grain product corn. It wasn't until the nineteenth century that a synthesis of American religious beliefs, scientific research, and technological innovation gave rise to the crunchy, crisp, snap-crackling foodstuff we now know as breakfast cereal.

Over the past hundred years, breakfast cereal has traveled from the North Pole to the South Pole, from the deepest jungles of equatorial Africa to the top of Mount Everest—even to the moon. One of the world's first health foods, cereal played an important role in convincing Americans to shape their lives to the rhythms of a healthy body. The crunchy foodstuff was one of America's first prepackaged and mass-marketed consumer products, helping to liberate homemakers from the drudgery of the kitchen while laying the foundation for modern advertising and food retailing operations.

More than just a food, cereal has also served as a barometer of the ever-changing trends in American dietary and popular culture. From All-Bran to Cap'n Crunch, from Babe Ruth to Michael Jordan, from Jack Armstrong to Super Mario Brothers, the cereal aisle is a true and accurate reflection of America's cultural psyche.

Ask octogenarians about breakfast cereal, and many will describe the china they collected from Quaker Oats boxes. Ask baby boomers about Tony the Tiger and stand back to hear the roar, "They're GR-R-REAT." Walk with four-year-olds along the cereal aisle and watch them lunge for Ninja Turtles or Fruity Pebbles. Like it or not, our stomachs and our brains are full of cereal. Luckily, the influence for the most part has been benign—and tremendously entertaining.

AMAZING CEREAL STATISTICS

★ Americans buy 2.7 billion packages of breakfast cereal each year. If laid end to end, the empty cereal boxes from one year's consumption would stretch to the moon and back.

★ In the last one hundred years, more than 1,000 cereal brands have been created in the United States alone.

★ The cereal industry uses 816 million pounds of sugar per year, enough to coat each and every American with more than three pounds of sugar. The cereal with the highest amount of sugar per serving is Smacks, which is 53 percent sugar.

★ Americans consume about ten pounds or 160 bowls of cereal per person per year. But America ranks only fourth in per capita cereal consumption. Ireland ranks first, England ranks second, and Australia ranks third.

★ Forty-nine percent of Americans start each morning with a bowl of cereal, thirty percent eat toast, twenty-eight percent eat eggs, twenty-eight percent have coffee, seventeen percent have hot cereal, and fewer than ten percent have pancakes, sausage, bagels, or french toast.

★ Breakfast cereals are the third most popular product sold at supermarkets in terms of dollar sales. The five most popular products are: 1) carbonated beverages, 2) milk, 3) breakfast cereal, 4) cigarettes, and 5) fresh bread and rolls.

★ In 1993, more than 1.3 million advertisements for cereal aired on American television, or more than twenty-five hours of cereal advertising per day, at a cost of $762 million for the purchase of air time. Only auto manufacturers spent more money on television advertising than the makers of breakfast cereal.

I

The Profits of Health

1

Manifest Stomachache

The late eighteenth and early nineteenth centuries witnessed a scientific, industrial, and religious awakening across America. The horizons seemed endless, bounded only by human energy and the ability to overcome the horrible consequences of the American diet.

Diagnosis: Dyspepsia

The young nation's appetite was enough to turn anyone's stomach. New Englanders breakfasted on "black tea and toast, scrambled eggs, fresh spring shad, wild pigeons, pigs' feet, tow robins on toast, oysters," according to one horrified journalist of the period.

British astronomer Francis Baily wrote in his diary that his landlord at a Virginia inn served a breakfast of "beefsteaks, sausages, stewed veal, fried ham, eggs, coffee and tea." His next diary entry noted simply, "whilst at the place, we buried the landlord of our inn."

Although Baily established no causal relationship between his landlord's death and breakfast, others decried "the established barbarisms of a public dinner." In keeping with the gluttonous spirit of the times, the standard rules of etiquette for breakfast, lunch, and dinner were "gobble, gulp, and go."

On the edges of the American frontier, the food was worse—much worse. Heading west from St. Louis, one writer commented that travelers soon struck "a region where the principal articles of diet are saleratus and grease, to which a little flour and pork are added." Saleratus was the nineteenth-century term for baking soda, but it was pork that filled the bellies of American pioneers.

Sliced, chopped, or torn from the bodies of the ubiquitous "rail splitter" hogs, most often salted so that it would keep, fried pork was served up in thick chunks for breakfast, lunch, and dinner. One adventurer, sniffing the breeze to discover the essence of the brave new land, came to the conclusion that "everything tastes and smells of hog's grease."

America in the nineteenth century had gone hog wild, nutritionally speaking, with all the anticipated consequences. As the young nation gulped down salt pork, whiskey, and coffee, a few wise men shook their heads in sadness over the state of the union's digestive tract. "Bilious complaints are now all the fashion at the 'Great West,'" wrote one chronicler. "Rapid eating almost always overloaded the stomach," wrote A. Combe in his 1842 work *Physiological Digestion*. "And when to this is added a total disregard of the quietude necessary for digestion, what can be expected to follow but inveterate dyspepsia?"

What indeed. Nineteenth-century America suffered from one huge, bloated, gaseous, painful, enormous bellyache. Defined in the mid-seventeeth century as "difficulty of digestion or fermentation in the stomach or guts," dyspepsia was the disease of the Steel Age. "All classes and all ages suffer from its attacks," noted the 1830 edition of the *Encyclopedia Americana* in its entry on dyspepsia. "Few are so happy to pass through a life of ordinary duration, without undergoing a protracted struggle with this malady." Dyspepsia was so much a part of the American lifestyle that one compiler of cookbooks referred to it as "Americanitis."

The problem of having too much to eat was a new one for previously hungry humanity. Though the calorie had been discovered by a Frenchman in the eighteenth century, most respected nineteenth-century physicians believed that all foods had the same nutritive value, one "universal aliment" that helped the body grow and repaired tissue. Bulk, not variety, was the only consideration, as dyspeptics looked outside the medical establishment for an end to their pain.

Put Back the Bran

Religious leaders were among the first to understand the relationship between good food and good health. Many of these fundamentalist healers took inspiration from various passages of the Bible, particularly Genesis 1:29: "Behold, I have given you every plant bearing seed which is upon the face of all the earth, and every tree with seed in its fruit: you shall have them for food."

No one in America believed in eating plants more fervently than William Metcalfe. "Father Metcalfe," as he was called, was a homeopathic doctor, a clergyman, and a follower of William Cowherd, the founder of the Bible Christian Church, England's only vegetarian congregation. Metcalfe transplanted the teachings of his mentor to the fertile spiritual soil of Philadelphia. In 1817, he founded the North Third Street Church, the first vegetarian organization in the United States, and began publishing *The American Vegetarian*, America's first magazine for non–meat eaters. "He that killeth an ox is as if he slew a man," argued Metcalfe and his pioneering group.

One of those lured by the vegetarian siren was Sylvester Graham. Ridiculed as the "peristaltic persuader" by some, heralded as the "prophet of bran bread and pumpkins" by Ralph Waldo Emerson, Graham was America's first bona fide health nut. It was Graham more than any other nineteenth-century individual who managed to convince a skeptical American public that diet and health were inseparably connected.

In thousands of words both published and spoken, Graham proclaimed the majesty of the simple raw vegetable. He warned that meat eating inflamed the "baser propensities," tea drinking led to delirium tremens, and mustard caused insanity. An ardent foe of sexual activity, Graham believed that meat eating led to masturbation, and masturbation made people stupid. As a cure for what he called the "vice," Graham recommended a diet devoid of meat. If indulgence in the "vice" still persisted, Graham recommended the application of handcuffs.

Trained as a Presbyterian minister, Graham began his health crusade in 1824, when he moved to Philadelphia to take up work as the spokesperson for the Pennsylvania State Society for the Suppression of the Use of Ardent Spirits. With the blessing of Father Metcalfe, the dogmatic thirty-four year old took up the cause of vegetarianism with equally unbridled enthusiasm. Scorned at first by the public, Graham's message began to hit home when a cholera epidemic swept through New York in 1832. Suddenly people were looking for a way to maintain their health, and Graham was there to guide them.

Eat nothing but fresh vegetables and fruits—raw, he urged the sickly masses. And chew them slowly with plenty of saliva. His radical ideas were safer than conventional medical wisdom, which relied heavily on the use of bleeding and leeches. As more and more people followed his dietary advice and the cholera epidemic passed, Graham's popularity surged, catapulting him to a level of national prominence that he was to enjoy for almost a decade. He became Jacksonian America's number one health spokesperson.

The Graham campaign to lead the nation out of its dyspeptic stupor focused on one particular item of the American diet—bread. "Put back the bran," he cried again and again, tracing the decline of the human physique to the refining process by which bran was taken out of whole-wheat flour. Graham's bran-filled hypothesis was simple—white bread will make you sick.

Graham accused commercial bakers of not only refining their flour to a sinful extreme but also growing their grain on debauched and exhausted soil, artificially stimulated with animal manure. Bakers did not take kindly to Graham's words and mobbed a Boston lecture hall where he was scheduled to speak in March 1837. Graham avoided any physical injury in the confrontation, but his reputation took a pounding after a later appearance, when the staff doctor of the Boston lunatic asylum declared that the reforming lecturer was obviously insane.

Insane though he may have been, Graham's speaking fees swelled to as much as $300 per night as he plunged into new areas of medical investigation. He preached against the dangers of feather beds and tight corsets, claiming that "folly in dress" killed 80,000 Americans each year. He criticized the schools, warning that the "disproportionate exercise of the brain" was dangerous for it "leads to a general debility of the nervous system, involving the genital organs."

Such eccentric opinions caused Graham's light to fade on the national stage. He retired to Northampton, Massachusetts, where he continued to pour forth medical and spiritual advice. By 1850, his health and status had declined to the point where one of his neighbors described him as "infirm, seated in a wheelbarrow, and clothed in a long dressing gown of bedticking, wheeled through the streets to the post office by a man-servant."

Despite his sad decline, Graham's message continues to thrive, embodied in the simple whole-grain snack that still bears his name, the graham cracker.

Water, Water Everywhere

Although Graham died in 1851, thousands of Americans continued the effort to purify the American lifestyle and find a cure for the nation's dyspepsia. The respected *Boston Medical and Surgical Journal* noted that "No man can travel by stage or steamboat, or go into any part of our country and begin to advocate a vegetable diet . . . without being immediately asked—'What. Are you a Grahamite?'"

Graham boarding houses sprang up in New York and Boston. More than eighty-five publications claiming Grahamite affiliation appeared in the mid-nineteenth century. Some of these pioneering vegetarians ate only raw food. Others ate only nuts and milks. Some avoided potatoes and other tuberous vegetables, while still others confined their diet to plants grown in virgin soil.

No matter what their individual vegetarian peculiarities, the Grahamites for the most part agreed with Dr. William A. Alcott. The author of dozens of popular self-help books, including *The Young Wife*, *The Young Housekeeper*, and *Vegetable Diet*, Alcott wrote, "A vegetable diet lies at the basis of all reform, whether, Civil, Social, Moral or Religious."

Dr. Alcott was one of the founding members of the American Vegetarian Society, the most influential vegetarian organization to arise from Graham's bran-filled theoretical compost heap. The guest list at the first meeting of the society held in New York City in 1850 read like a Who's Who of nineteenth-century reform. Sharing the toasts to "total abstinence, women's rights, and vegetarianism," were anti-slavery activist Harriet Beecher Stow; enemy of the corset Amelia Bloomer; journalist Horace Greeley; world-renowned phrenologists Orson and Lorenzo Fowler; and Dr. James Caleb Jackson, creator of the world's first cold breakfast cereal.

Jackson was an abolitionist, an editor, a lecturer, and a hydrotherapist, one of the many alternative-medicine practioners of the time who believed in the healing power of water. The "water cure," as hydrotherapy was called, first emerged in the 1820s when a Silesian peasant named Vincent Preissnitz broke his leg. Preissnitz treated his injury by wrapping his limb in water-soaked fabric. When the bone healed quickly, Preissntiz began to expose himself to water in any way he could. He sat in it, he doused himself with it, he wrapped himself in water soaked sheets, and he drank it—gallons of it.

In 1844, Dr. Joel Shew opened the first Priessnitz-styled water-cure establishment in the United States. Within ten years, sixty-two such water cures were in operation. "The water revolution is a great revolution," wrote Shew's colleague Dr. Jackson, "It touches more interests than any revolution since the days of Jesus Christ."

In 1859, James Caleb Jackson dove into the water cure business, transforming a run-down hotel in the small western New York town of Dansville into the Jackson Sanatorium, better known as "Our Home on the Hillside." Jackson treated his visitors to a strict regimen of exercise, fresh air, temperance, healthy foods, and plenty of pure (not mineral) water. For many, the hydropathic treatments were a unique experience. Most people in the 1860s simply did not bathe. At the very least, Jackson and the water cure craze did a great service to America by helping to clean up the country.

Jackson devised dietetic as well as liquid entertainment for his patients. Though he didn't insist on a vegetarian diet, he did his best to lure his visitors along the path of righteous consumption. In 1863, Jackson began a culinary experiment that would eventually revolutionize American eating. He took graham flour, as coarsely ground bran-filled whole-wheat flour was known, mixed it with water, and baked it. He then took the hard, brittle whole-wheat bricks, broke them up into the size of large beans or cherries, and baked them again. The resulting ready-to-eat food product he dubbed Granula, and he served it to his visitors for breakfast.

Granula could never compete with Cinnamon Toast Crunch. The first cold breakfast cereal was impossible to eat unless it soaked overnight in milk. Even then the bits of twice-cooked graham flour were tough and tasteless. Nevertheless, Jackson thought enough of his creation to found a commercial enterprise, Our Home Granula Company, and began to sell his breakfast concoctions. Jackson soon expanded his product line with Somo, a "health coffee," and ran ads in his publication, *The American Water Cure Journal and Health Reform Magazine*, encouraging his readers to order by mail so that they too could "Eat Granula, Drink Somo." Dyspepsia, by way of fundamentalism, temperance, vegetarianism, bran-filled bread, and cold-water bathing, had given birth to the first ready-to-eat cold breakfast cereal. But it took a message from heaven to turn Jackson's innovation into the crunch heard 'round the world.

DYSPEPTIC SHOPPING

Most nineteenth-century Americans grew or killed their own food. Those who were lucky enough to be able to shop for food in the days before the clean wide aisles of the supermarket had to endure an experience only slightly less grotesque than the slaughterhouse. In 1910, investigators from the Massachusetts Commission on the Cost of Living described a visit to an old-fashioned country store. "When one enters the door a bell rings, which calls the attendant from the barn. . . . He plunges his unwashed hands into the pork or pickel barrel, cuts cheese or butter, often drawing kerosene and molasses . . . and wiping the overflow on his coat sleeve. . . . The maple syrup bottles stand near by, and the keeper himself has been seen to take a swallow from them at different times, when his sweet tooth called."

2

Apocalypse Chow

A chill wind blew across the hilltop near Hampton, New York, on that fall morning in 1843 when the dedicated followers of the farmer-turned-prophet William Miller purposefully took their positions and waited for the second coming of Jesus Christ. The Millerites, as they were called, were convinced that their Lord was going to return to Earth on precisely that day and they were ready for the rapture.

Some clutched their Bibles. Some wore Ascension robes. Some sat in laundry baskets ready to ride to the promised land. Unfortunately for the Millerites, the creator did not appear. His tardiness was humanity's gain as some of the disappointed followers beat their laundry baskets into cereal bowls and created a revolutionary type of breakfast chow—one fit for the apocalypse.

A Vision of Health

Despite the Great Disappointment, as the Messianic no-show was called, a few truly inspired souls kept the millenial faith.

One of these true believers was Ellen Harmon Gould, the sickly daughter of a Maine hatter who was twelve years old in 1840 when she first heard William Miller speak. The spiritual fire Miller set in the young girl's soul blazed forth a few months after the Great Disappointment. "Glory, glory, glory," the fifteen-year-old cried. She saw a vision: twenty-four Millerites and four repulsive beasts gathered around a jasper throne canopied with a rainbow and floating on a sea of glass. The Lord, who sat on the throne, looked up and spoke to the young ecstatic: "Come in to a supper."

Thus began Ellen Harmon Gould's career as prophetess and leader of the religious organization that came to be known as the Seventh Day Adventist Church. Though she never had an official title, her divine communications directed the church during her lifetime and formed it into a strong organization that today boasts 6.2 million members worldwide.

Gould married Adventist brother James White and was known thereafter as Sister or Mother White. The two spent many years in the American spiritual wilderness, persecuted for their beliefs in temperance and in the importance of celebrating the Sabbath on Saturday, not Sunday. In 1855, they finally found a home for their church in a small community named for a brawl between two ornery surveyors and two stubborn Potawatomie Indians. The name of the town was Battle Creek, Michigan.

Seventh Day Adventistism wasn't the first spiritual movement to find a home in Battle Creek. Quakerism, Swedenborgianism, and spiritualism had preceded it to the area. As a nineteenth-century historian noted, Battle Creek had long been a place "where 'isms' take root and flourish."

Adventistism flourished in Battle Creek "like Jonah's gourd," and Sister White's visions began to define a pre-apocalyptic health-giving regimen in ever-greater detail. On June 6, 1863, an angel appeared to her and gave her a series of specific instructions. Eat two meals a day. Avoid meat, which strengthened the "animal propensities." Rely on graham bread, fruit, and vegetables. Eat little salt and no cake, lard, or spices. Abstain from coffee, tea, and tobacco. Drink only water. Do not pay physicians. Trust in the healing power of God.

Sister White's vision of health inspired her to explore the possibilities of faith healing, to study various water-cure journals, and to visit leading medical institutions such as Dr. James Caleb Jackson's Our Home on the Hillside. A savvy administrator as well as a prophetess, Sister White saw how lucrative health could be. "The health-food business is one of the Lord's own instruments," she later declared.

On the evening of Christmas Day, 1865, just after she returned from Jackson's institution, Sister White received divine instructions to establish an Adventist health maintenance organization in Battle Creek. The Western Health Reform Institute opened on September 5, 1866, with a staff of two physicians, two bath attendants, and one untrained nurse under the direction of Dr. Horatio Lay, an Adventist physician who formerly practiced his healing arts at Our Home on the Hillside.

The Institute was not an instant success. The few patients who did come sat in tubs of water and dined twice a day on saltless vegetarian fare prepared in a kitchen where "grease and spice took a back seat." The atmosphere, like the food, may have been healthy, but it was painfully dull. "Let the people complain of the vegetarian diet, if they will," scolded Sister White. "The Israelites always complained of Moses and God."

Despite her brave front, Sister White realized that a radical change had to be made at the Western Health Reform Institute if she was to avoid a bureaucratic Great Disappointment. What she needed was a new leader, someone who was not only a dedicated Adventist but also a brilliant, energetic man of medicine. She realized that the best way to get such a person was to create him. Her ambitious eyes fell on the son of an Adventist broom maker, a brilliant young man named John Harvey Kellogg.

John Harvey Kellogg, The Printer's Devil

John Harvey Kellogg was born in 1852, the fifth child of his mother Ann Janette and the tenth of his father John Preston Kellogg. John Preston was a true pioneer, a native of Hadley, Massachusetts, who gave up the comforts of the East Coast to carve out a living alongside the Chippewa Indians in the wilds of western Michigan.

A religious man by nature, John Preston Kellogg became even more so after suffering the trials of frontier life and the incompetence of frontier doctors. When his first wife got tuberculosis, doctors bled her and forced her to inhale resin fumes, hastening her death. When his daughter took ill with a lung infection, doctors treated her for worms, again bringing death to the Kellogg family. When John Preston himself suffered from a blinding eye infection, doctors prescribed a course of drugs that caused his tongue to swell up and stick out of his mouth.

It was no wonder that John Preston and his second wife Ann Janette converted to Adventism and became firm believers in the teachings of Sister White. "If there was in the land one physician in place of thousands," wrote Sister White, "a vast amount of premature mortality would be prevented."

Eventually, John Preston decided to spend less time farming the wilderness and more time working for the Adventist church. He moved his family to Battle Creek. To make ends meet, he started a broom-making factory, a skill that he had learned back East. As the business flourished, he became one of the most reliable supporters of Sister White's spiritual empire. When Sister White decided to create the Western Health Reform Institute, John Preston Kellogg was ready with the largest initial subscription for the establishment—$500, "a seed," he said, "to start the institution, sink or swim."

John Harvey Kellogg liked to say that his parents were so firmly convinced of the imminent end of the world that they considered it a waste of time for their children to go to school. He himself left school at the age of ten to work in his father's broom factory for ten hours a day, sorting the cornshucks from which the brooms were made. In 1854, James White visited John Preston and was so impressed with John Harvey that he offered him work as a printer's devil at the publishing operation owned by the Adventist church. John Harvey quickly learned to set type and read proofs. By the time he was sixteen, he was doing editorial work for the church's main newspaper, the *Advent Review and Sabbath Herald*. He spent a great deal of time with the Whites—so much so that the elder James White treated him as one of his own sons. Ellen White had a vision that John Harvey Kellogg was to have a definite place in the service of God, and began to groom him for a position at the Western Health Reform Institute.

After working briefly as a teacher and suffering a bout of tuberculosis, Kellogg was encouraged by the Whites to take up the study of medicine. Along with his older brother Merritt and the Whites' sons, John Harvey traveled to Florence Heights, New Jersey. The Battle Creek boys attended a course at the Hygieo-Therapeutic College, run by noted hydrotherapist Dr. Russell Trall, who believed that "three-fourths of all pulmonary and nasal difficulties that are attributed to the weather and climate, are really caused by overeating." After getting his degree (at a cost of twenty-five dollars), Kellogg continued his studies at State Normal in Ypsilanti, Michigan; the University of Michigan Medical School; and Bellevue Hospital Medical College in New York City, with the financial and spiritual support of the Whites.

An extraodinarily serious and hard-working student who read the latest scientific journals in French and German, John Harvey was a remarkable character in an era when even the Harvard Medical School did not give exams because so few members of its student body could read and write. After graduating from Bellevue, he briefly studied electrical-stimulation therapy and did some temperance promotional work before returning home on October 1, 1876. It was the hundredth anniversary of the American revolution, and the beginning of the health revolution in Battle Creek.

Kellogg's Club Med

Kellogg reluctantly took charge of the Western Health Reform Institute at the urging of the Whites. He agreed to stay for one year. He wound up staying for sixty-seven years. Surgeon, author, personality, and loveable crank, Kellogg became the best-known figure in late nineteenth-century American medicine. His work affected millions of American lives and continues to hold sway over the world's breakfast table.

Under Dr. Kellogg's guidance, the humble Adventist health institution was transformed into a Disneyland of medical marvels. "The University of Health" was a place where visitors could enjoy "rest without ennui" as they worked on "getting the stomach right." Its reputation quickly overshadowed earlier water cures, which could not compete with the scientific and promotional energy of the young Michigan medical man.

It was "the Battle Creek Idea" that did the trick, described as "the principle of healing through Nature's simple restorative methods." Kellogg's message was simple: avoid drugs, alcohol, and tobacco; get moderate exercise; and eat a low-calorie, low-meat diet. Simple though it was, it was revolutionary for the times and established Kellogg as the great-grandfather of the modern self-help movement.

Kellogg renamed the Institute the Medical and Surgical Sanitarium, a variant of the word *sanitorium,* which Kellogg hoped would come to mean a "place where people learn to stay well." "The San," as it was called, was a combination of medical boarding house, hospital, monastery, country club, spa, and revival camp, which eventually became the primary health address in America. In fact, by the turn of the century, its cable address was simply that—"Health."

What began as a modest farmhouse retreat evolved into a massive health complex—a 560-foot long, six-story tall modified Italian Renaissance edifice, complete with a solarium, a large gymnasium, half a mile of glassed-in halls, an Acidophilus Milk Bar, and a Palm Garden with banana and rubber trees. It was an environment suitable for what Kellogg called the "Aristocracy of Health," an all-inclusive medical establishment that claimed to offer "every facility and device known to modern therapeutics for the cure of disease."

Dr. Kellogg, who took no pay for his work at the San, considered his healing work to be a spiritual calling. He expected the same from his staff of eighty doctors and hundreds of nurses, cooks, masseurs, and bath attendants. Many members of the staff were Adventists whose belief in observing the Saturday sabbath made it difficult for them to find other jobs in the era of the six-day work week. Kellogg had no problem finding workers despite the low pay—no pay, in fact, for first-year nurses who received room, board, and a uniform for the privilege of thumping, twisting, jiggling, massaging, bathing, and feeding the thousands of patients who came under Dr. Kellogg's care.

Kellogg championed "biologic living"—holistic healing with a vengeance. Literature from the San described it as a regimen of "daily cold water and air baths, swimming, work in the gymnasium, wearing of light and porous clothing and frequent changes of underwear." Kellogg's specialty was not the grievously ill but victims of the fast-paced nineties (the 1890s, that is)—stressed-out men and women who just didn't understand why they felt so rotten.

Kellogg put his patients through their paces. They performed calesthenics at 7 A.M., followed by laughing exercises, Indian club demonstrations, and gymnastic classes. They withstood all manner of mechanical massage—pummelings with trunk rollers, poundings with chest beaters, and punches from stomach beaters. They stood on vibrating platforms to stimulate their inner organs, galloped on mechanical horses, or sat on Kellogg's patented vibrating chair. They bathed endlessly inside and out—with salt baths, steam baths, hot water baths, cold-water baths, showers, douches, fomentations, and a high-powered enema machine that could put fifteen gallons of water through the bowels in a matter of minutes. They glowed with infrared light baths, ultraviolet light baths, and plain electric light baths. They buzzed with oscillating current applied in a mild form of total-body electro-shock therapy, one of Kellogg's great enthusiasms. They were tested endlessly using the most modern equipment available—a dynamometer to measure muscle power, a pneumograph to measure lung power, and x-rays and chemical tests analyzed in the lab according to the most sophisticated statistical techniques.

Lest the mind be overlooked, the patients attended musicals, Shakespearean plays, and stimulating outings with well-known men of science. Exhausted, if not waterlogged or burned by the end of the day, patients concluded their activities with the "Grand March"—Dr. Kellogg's version of the Jane Fonda workout, during which all the guests of the Sanitarium marched as a drill team, weaving in and out to the tune of Samuel Siegel's "Battle Creek Sanitarium March."

Kellogg combined the finest talents of a physician, a hotelier, and a promoter. He never forgot a face, an enema, or an alimentary canal. He paid meticulous attention to every detail of the San's healing environment. He outlawed feather beds, because they underwent "slow decomposition . . . thus evolving foul and poisonous gases." He warned female patients that novel reading was "one of the most pernicious habits to which a young lady can become devoted . . . as inveterate as the use of liquor or opium." He even examined the wallpaper, noting that "many cases of poisoning, some of which are fatal, have been traced to the arsenic contained in several of the colors of wall-paper."

Though some of his ideas were off-the-wall, Kellogg had a reputation as one of the most talented surgeons of the time. He was a respected member of the American College of Surgeons, the American Association for the Advancement of Science, the Royal Society of Medicine, and the American Medical Association. Kellogg always claimed that surgery made him squeamish, yet he performed more than 22,000 operations in his lifetime and consulted with the greatest surgeons in Vienna, London, Paris, and Berlin. Kellogg perfected his surgical technique by sewing very small stitches during train trips. At one point Dr. Charles Mayo, one of the founders of the Mayo Clinic, astounded a patient by saying, "I see that Dr. Kellogg performed an operation for you." The patient asked how Dr. Mayo could tell. "That's easy. The scar is neat and small, just like a signature."

KELLOGG THE DOG LOVER

A firm opponent of vaccination, Dr. Kellogg did find animals useful for some of his scientific investigations. One of the subjects in which Kellogg had a keen professional interest was the effect of tight-fitting corsets on the female anatomy. At one point, the Doctor successfully convinced one of his patients to give up wearing a corset and displayed the abandoned pink undergarment in his office. When his pet collie came to the office one day for a visit, Doctor decided to test the effects of the corset on normal breathing patterns and dressed the dog in the restrictive lingerie. Doctor sat quietly pondering the frilly canine when a knock at the door interrupted his meditation. Embarrased to be seen in such a compromising position, Kellogg stepped into the outer office to greet his visitor. When he returned to the office, the collie had vanished. Doctor Kellogg ran out of the building, jumped on his bicycle, and chased the collie back to his home where Mrs. Kellogg reproached her husband for such flamboyant experimentation.

The only professional organization that ever challenged Kellogg's ideas was the Calhoun County Medical Association. In 1885, the Association accused Kellogg of violating its code of ethics by advertising his services through his publications and slandering the medical profession. Kellogg stood trial in front of the Association, won his case, and two years later was unanimously elected president of the medical group.

The list of "Battle freaks," as San enthusiasts were called, added glamor and excitement to the San's mystique. Visitors over the years included C. W. Barron; John D. Rockefeller; J. C. Penney; Montgomery Ward; Mrs. Walgreen; S. S. Kresge; Eleanor Roosevelt; Eddie Cantor; William Howard Taft; Calvin Coolidge; Johnnie Weismuller; Admiral Byrd; Roald Amundsen; Upton Close; Upton Sinclair; Harvey Firestone; Ruth St. Denis; E. T. Welch, the grape juice man; Billy Sunday; Lowell Thomas; William "Big Bill" Tilden; beturbaned rajahs from India; exotic-looking dignitaries from Turkey, Egypt, and China; and state governors, senators, and cabinet members too numerous to mention.

Sojourner Truth, the pipe-smoking ex-slave, was a regular fixture at the San, ready to regale visitors with down-home parables like "Every tub has to sit on its own bottom." Amelia Earhart visited the San and gave Doctor Kellogg his first aerial view of the vast health domain. Frequent visitor Henry Ford, who sometimes brought his square-dance orchestra with him, pronounced with finality, "I like Mr. Kellogg's philosophy."

The Perfect Flake

According to Dr. Kellogg's philosophy, the key to human happiness lay in the digestive tract. "If the whole truth were shown," he wrote, "it would appear that the causes of indigestion are responsible for more deaths than all other causes combined."

"Autointoxication," Kellogg called it—the process by which materials left in the intenstines due to constipation putrefied and caused disease. When Kellogg suggested that William Jennings Bryan might be suffering from autointoxication, the great orator asked, "Is that something that one gets from driving too rapidly in an automobile?"

To keep his own system flushed, Kellogg not only ate bran but enjoyed a daily enema, administered by a personal assistant right after breakfast. "The bowels should be emptied at least twice a day," he warned, "and three or four movements are still better." Kellogg believed that primitive people had bowel movements after each meal and that modern man should do the same. His interest did not end at evacuation. Kellogg even designed an indoor privy for use in pre-plumbing houses.

The kitchen practices at the beginning of the twentieth century terrified Dr. Kellogg. He called modern cookery "the greatest bane of civilization at the present time. . . . men and women are subject to few diseases whose origin may not be traced to the kitchen." He put the issue into historical perspective. "The decline of a nation commences when gourmandizing begins. Rome's collapse was well under way when slaves were thrown into the eel-pots to increase the gamy flavor of the eels when they came to the table."

Mustard, pepper, ginger, curry, and salt horrified him. "Every day a hundred thousand dyspeptics sigh and groan in consequence of condiments," he wrote. He looked upon vinegar as "a poison, not a food." "Coffee cripples the liver," he claimed, categorizing cola drinks as "insidious poison." Still, coffee was better than bouillon, which Dr. Kellogg described as "a veritable solution of poisons," or the oyster. "The oyster is a scavenger," Kellogg warned. "He dines on germs. His body is covered and filled with bacteria . . . and his slimy juice . . . is simply alive with wriggly worms."

Unlike Dr. William J. Bennett, Dr. John Harvey Kellogg believed the future welfare of America lay not in her moral education but in her bowel education. "It is of more consequence for a teacher to know whether a child's colon is evacuated regularly and frequently than to know that he is acquiring proficiency in mathematics," he wrote.

Kellogg worked to educate the American public by the mass media of the nineteenth century. He was one of the most popular authors of his time, churning out more than 220 articles and 81 books, some of which were published by Harpers and Macmillan and translated into Norwegian, Spanish, Chinese and other languages. Mahatma Gandhi, who had his own preoccupation with the bowels, once commented that Kellogg was probably better known outside of the United States than he was in his own country.

Kellogg's works included *Constipation: How to Fight It, What Is the Matter With the American Stomach?*, *The Art of Massage, Tobaccoism: Or How Tobacco Kills*, and *Plain Facts about Sexual Life*. Kellogg's *Itinerary of a Breakfast* took the reader on "a trip with a slice of bread along the most wonderful subway in the world."

As racy as they were informative, Kellogg's books were self-help bestsellers that earned him a a sizeable income. He dictated most of his works at a rapid clip and found that the hours just after midnight were his most productive. On many a Michigan winter night, Dr. Kellogg wrapped himself in blankets and lay on his front-porch glider, speaking his mind to a benumbed scribbling secretary.

In one of his more dramatic literary moments, Dr. Kellogg stripped off his western garb at an oasis in the Sahara desert, donned a loin cloth, and dictated an entire edition of his magazine *Good Health* to his secretary.

One of Dr. Kellogg's preferred tutorial platforms was the Medical Question Box, a lecture and discussion held at the San on Monday nights. Like a David Copperfield of the duodenum, Kellogg, who in his later years wore all white because of his belief in that color's health-giving properties, mesmerized his audience with lurid tales and stunning displays. He told the story of an American cavalryman who offered a pickle to a starving Indian only to be attacked for his misguided efforts. He showed lantern slides filled with enormous microbes to underscore the dangers of an improper diet. "Fresh meat is usually swarming with putrefactive bacteria," Doctor exclaimed to his astonished audience. "A bear kept at the Anatomical Museum at Gressen showed a quiet, gentle nature as long as he was fed on bread," he recalled, "but a few days . . . on meat made him vicious."

One of the regulars of the Monday night health show was a mean-tempered chimp. Once every month or so, Kellogg brought the chimp up to the front of the crowd and threw him a steak. Invariably, the chimp tossed the steak back, thereby proving his dietary sagacity. On other Monday evenings, Dr. Kellogg chose to display the preservative power of the "friendly bacilli" found in a Bulgarian food known as yogurt. After explaining to his audience that anything, even a steak, could be preserved by continuous immersion in a fresh bath of yogurt, Kellogg amazed his audience by pulling a string from a large bowl and displaying the fresh, yogurt-covered piece of beef. Kellogg used the same steak in his demonstration for seventeen years until a newly hired kitchen worker mistakenly disposed of it.

Each meal at the Sanitarium was a nutritional marvel. Entrées included stewed prunes, wheat gluten mush, avenola, wheatena, oatmeal crackers, graham rolls, and dyspeptic wafers—all washed down with caramel coffee, lemon oatmeal gruel, or tea made from South African kaffir grass. The dieticians at the San carefully weighed out every portion of food and began listing the protein, fat, and carbohydrate content of each item in 1904, shortly after such precise dietary measurement became possible.

"Fletcherize," said a sign cut into the arched entry of the Grand Dining Room, a reminder that patients were expected to follow the teachings of celebrity masticator Horace Fletcher and chew their food until it magically disappeared from their mouths. "Cannibals," Fletcher wrote, "always bolt their missionary." After each meal, an attendant swabbed the patients' mouths, brushed their teeth, and polished each tooth with a special paper polisher.

The dietary regimen for special patients was a bit more out of the ordinary. Kellogg ordered thin people to undergo twenty-six milk feedings a day and to remain motionless in bed with sandbags on their bellies to increase absorption of nourishment. For high blood pressure patients, he prescribed ten to fourteen pounds of grapes (peeled) every day. Period. "The joy of eating at Battle Creek," stated Kellogg's promotional literature, was that "every meal is a prescription."

Some who could not tolerate the menu snuck off to the Red Onion, a "meat speakeasy" that discreetly served up beer, onions, and steak. Even those closest to Dr. Kellogg, like Duke, his St. Bernard, sometimes lapsed from the strict regimen. Kellogg's comment on Duke and the other backsliders was simple: "They'll all come back to biologic living."

Kellogg understood the dietary dilemma only too well. He threw himself into the effort to develop new, tasty vegetarian foods with the same effort that he put into writing, lecturing, and performing surgery. His partner in this effort was his wife Ella Eaton Kellogg. Dr. Kellogg married his former hygiene and nursing student in 1879. During their honeymoon, Kellogg took time out to write *Plain Facts for Old and Young Embracing the Natural History and Hygiene of Organic Life*, a warning against the evils and dangers of sex. The young newlyweds practiced what they preached and chose a life of celibacy, though they eventually raised more than forty-two children, including some whose parents died as patients at the San.

While most of the Kellogg children grew up to be well-adjusted adults, there was one exception. When Dr. Kellogg read in the newspaper about a prostitute's son who was found foraging in a garbage can, he tracked him down, adopted him, and named him George. George never did take to biologic living. Instead, he became a drifter who frequently extorted money from his famous father.

Working elbow to elbow in the San's experimental kitchen, Dr. and Mrs. Kellogg created Caramel Cereal Coffee, a coffee substitute; Savit Gravy, a flavoring for soups; Protose, a nut product that Kellogg claimed "looks, tastes and smells like meat"; and dozens of other foods including peanut butter. Though Kellogg declared "There is no danger of food shortage, if we give the noble nut a chance," others were not so certain. One hungry visitor recalled that Kellogg's nut food Nutolene resembled "a good sized piece of shoe-maker's wax. . . . It was not unpleasant to taste, yet I did not find it appetizing. Rather, I should classify it in the broad category of uninteresting food."

One of Kellogg's greatest challenges was breakfast. As a youth, he had started every day with an unhealthy stack of pancakes and molasses. As a medical student in New York, he had breakfasted on apples and graham crackers supplemented by a weekly coconut or a side dish of potatoes. Thinking back to those days, he recalled, "It often occured to me that it should be possible to purchase cereals at grocers already cooked and ready to eat, and I considered different ways in which this might be done."

Kellogg's first efforts at creating a ready-to-eat cereal owed a great deal to the pioneering work of Dr. James Caleb Jackson. Kellogg and his wife began by mixing up a dough of wheat flour, cornmeal, and oatmeal. They formed the dough into biscuits, which they baked very slowly. They took the meal cakes, broke them up and offered the dried out cereal bits to patients for breakfast. They too called their concoction Granula.

Dr. Jackson didn't appreciate the fact that Kellogg had appropriated the name he had given to his own breakfast food. In the first of many breakfast cereal courtroom battles, Jackson sued Kellogg and won a judgment against him in 1881. Kellogg promptly chose another name for his breakfast concoction—Granola. By 1889, the Sanitarium Food Company, established by Dr. Kellogg, was selling more than two *tons* of Granola each week.

A visit to another food-technology pioneer led to Kellogg's most astounding culinary breakthrough. Hearing rumors of an innovative whole-wheat food, the peripatetic Dr. Kellogg traveled to Denver, Colorado, in 1894 and met with one Henry Perky, a dyspeptic lawyer-turned-food-entrepreneur who had invented something he called "shredded wheat." Kellogg was so impressed with the baked cereal filaments that he offered to buy Perky's company. The deal did not work out, but it inspired Kellogg's search for the perfect flake.

Kellogg himself never gave Perky the credit he deserved, but later maintained that the revolution in American breakfast started with a dream. "I prescribed zwieback for an old lady, and she broke her false teeth on it," Kellogg recalled. "I began to think that we ought to have a ready cooked food which would not break people's teeth. I puzzled over that a good deal."

Kellogg fell asleep one night in his puzzlement only to be awakened by a phone call. In that instant, he claimed, an idea came to him, the idea of a cereal flake. Kellogg boiled some wheat the next morning and

SEX AND CORNFLAKES

Dr. John Harvey Kellogg, the inventor of cornflakes and peanut butter, was a radical in the kitchen but an ultra-conservative in the boudoir. Kellogg believed that meat eating inspired dreaded animal urges, including the urge to masturbate. In his book *Man the Masterpiece*, Kellogg listed thirty-nine signs of the secret vice including bashfulness, unnatural boldness, and the desire to eat pencils and chalk. For some patients Kellogg recommended using cornflakes as an enema in the belief that constipation induced "abnormal excitement in the genital region." To cure the more dedicated male "devotees of Moloch," Kellogg recommended bandaging the hands or "covering the organs with a cage." For women, Kellogg's cures were more drastic. "The author has found the application of pure carbolic acid to the clitoris an excellent means of allaying the normal excitement," wrote Kellogg. In at least one case, the gifted surgeon wrote that he had been forced to remove the genital organs of a female masturbator "before the patient could be cured." Women who suffered from headaches and dyspepsia were much more fortunate. For them, Dr. Kellogg prescribed Womb Movement Treatment, a technique first used in Germany. As the patient reclined, an aide inserted a finger into the orifice nearest the womb and rotated. Blushing relief took as long as an hour to achieve, but many a skirted San regular swore by the practice.

ran it through a machine for making dough thin that Mrs. Kellogg had in the experimental kitchen. "I scraped it off with a knife and baked it in the oven," Kellogg later recalled. "That was the first of the modern breakfast foods."

Dr. Kellogg applied for a patent on "flaked cereals and process of preparing same" on May 31, 1894. The next year, he introduced his flaked cereal, dubbed Granose, at the General Conference of the Seventh Day Adventist Church held in Battle Creek. The breakfast flakes were an immediate hit. Dr. Kellogg set up the Sanitas Food Company, and hired his younger brother to ramrod the new health-food operation, which sold some 113,400 pounds of the leathery wheat morsels in its first year of production. Several years later, the Kellogg boys used their flakey expertise to create what would be their most lasting contribution to the American digestive system, the cornflake.

Though he was a magnificent egotist, Kellogg knew well enough to give credit to some of the flakes that had gone before him. "The Battle Creek food business began in New England about a century ago," remembered Kellogg, referring to the crusading vegetarian Sylvester Graham. "This was the real foundation of the Battle Creek food business."

And what a business it turned out to be.

3

The Original Grape-Nut

Four years before the discovery of the breakfast flake, a dyspeptic entrepreneur rolled his wheelchair into Dr. Kellogg's Sanitarium. Sporting a white Stetson hat, a *recuerdo* of his failed Texas real-estate ventures, the ailing visitor explained to Dr. Kellogg that he had tried to cure his condition with sea voyages, ranching, mineral baths, massage, gymnastics, and dieting, all to no avail. Dr. Kellogg immediately introduced him to the Battle Creek Idea, but after months of treatment the patient was no better physically and was financially much the worse for his visit. One can only imagine Kellogg's shock when his incurable patient, Charles William Post, turned biologic living into a multi-million dollar comestible empire.

The Road to Wellville

Post's "Road to Wellville," as he was later to entitle a popular cereal-premium booklet, led him from Illinois to Kansas to Texas to Battle Creek and beyond. He was born in Springfield, Illinois on October 26, 1854, just around the corner from the boyhood home of Abraham Lincoln.

The young Post was no Lincoln. An indifferent student, he seemed to be more interested in style than substance. He dropped out of his engineering course at Illinois Industrial College at Urbana after two years and joined the Springfield Zouaves, attracted in part by the bright red pantaloons worn by the ceremonial paramilitary force.

The call of the wild lured the teenage Post from his position with the Zouaves. He traveled west with a friend, worked as a cowhand for some time, then borrowed money from his parents to set up a hardware store in Independence, Kansas. The store made a little money, but Charlie decided to move back to Springfield in 1874 and marry his sweetheart Ella Letitia Merriweather.

The young couple settled down to family life and Charlie went to work for the Climax Corn Planter company as a traveling salesman. It was a romantic job seeing the country and swapping stories. Charlie, standing six feet, one inch tall with ramrod posture and immaculate bearing, made a good impression on the people he met, including Walt Whitman. "I thought today I would send you a little picture," wrote the author of *Leaves of Grass* to the future breakfast mogul, "to show you I had not forgotten you or those meetings in St. Louis."

After six years, Post quit the road and decided to go into business for himself. In the tradition of Edison and Marconi, Post threw himself into the world of invention. He patented a seed planter, a sulky plow, a harrow, a hay stacker, and various cultivators. He created a smokeless cooker, a water-powered electric generator, a bicycle, and a player piano for which he spent hours cutting out paper music rolls with a penknife on the kitchen table. Post's inventive lifestyle took a toll on his nerves. In 1885 he collapsed from nervous exhaustion. He was unable to work for six months and watched his business go into liquidation.

Like Davy Crockett, Sam Houston, and so many other energetic misfits, Charlie moved to Texas to get a new start. His health improved and he shifted into high gear. He bought land in Fort Worth, subdivided, and began peddling lots. He sowed some of his wild oats and acquired a "foster son." He invested in a woolen factory that made blankets. Annoyed by the fact that his pants didn't fit, he invented the "Scientific Suspender." He planned a nationwide ad campaign for his fashion product, and in November 1889 enthusiastically wrote to a friend, "The concern has been launched!"

The concern, and Post's health, crashed soon after launching. Once again Post found himself unable to work, and he developed a stomachache that left him weak to the point of death. Aware of the reputation of the Battle Creek Sanitarium run by the famous Dr. Kellogg, he set out for Michigan's medical mecca and checked into the San with his wife and three-year-old daughter on February 16, 1891—a bleak, raw day. "There is a taste of heaven in perfect health," Post wrote at about this time, "and a taste of Hell in sickness."

Light baths, diathermy, enemas, massages, not even Kellogg's patented vibrating chair did C. W. Post any good. The only thing that seemed to reanimate his active imagination was the cereal coffee served in the Sanitarium dining room.

While still a patient at the San, Post began conducting his own health-food experiments in the basement of a local jewelry store. Finally, his energy and his money depleted, Post realized he had to leave the care of Dr. Kellogg. "Ella, I think you should know that C. W. has very little time left," Kellogg told Post's wife, who paid for part of her husband's bills with blankets from the Fort Worth woolen mill. "He is not going to get well. I have done everything I know how to do."

On November 9, 1891, Ella Post pushed her husband's wheelchair out of the San and over to the home of her cousin, Mrs. Elizabeth Gregory. Mrs. Gregory was a follower of Mary Baker Eddy, the founder of the Christian Science movement, who believed that sickness was nothing more than a state of mind and that health was as contagious as disease. After talking with Mrs. Gregory for a few minutes, the exhausted Post caught a little good health and took his place at the family dinner table.

Incredibly, he was able to eat a fairly solid meal. Inspired by this miracle, he asked if he could spend the night. He awoke in the middle of night feeling a sensation that he had not felt for months—hunger. He went downstairs and raided the icebox, snacking on delicious cold chicken. The next morning he ate a hearty breakfast of pancakes and sausage. He began to walk around, and gained weight, marking the event with the pronouncement: "I am well!"

A rejuvenated Post set out to explore the path that led him to good health, "the road to wellville," as he came to call it. He read uplifting magazines. He explored the occult with fellow spiritual travelers. He became friendly with the esoteric Elbert Hubbard and the Roycrofters.

"Hold the health thought," he learned to say, convinced of the medical and fiscal benefits of mental healing. He approached Dr. Kellogg and offered to pray for the patients at the San for the modest sum of fifty dollars per week. Kellogg refused. He returned to the San once again, offering this time to market Kellogg's cereal coffee. Kellogg again refused.

Strapped for cash and rebuffed by the famous physician, Post borrowed some money from his wife and bought a ten-acre homestead on the east side of Battle Creek on March 23, 1892. Soon after, he opened his own version of Kellogg's health spa. Dubbed La Vita Inn, Post's healing oasis was a psycho-spiritual Sanitarium. He offered his own brand of positive thinking and a meat-eater's diet, at rates far less than those charged by his rival Kellogg.

"I simply treated patients by mental therapeutics," Post later explained. He encouraged them to "Kill off the old man (self) and let the new Being come up. Know yourself as Spirit, Mind, not Body . . ." In the New Age jargon of the 1890s, he convinced those suffering from disease that "there is a power within you that can and will work miracles." He even used mental suggestion at home, hypnotizing his daughter Marjorie so that she wouldn't feel any pain on her visits to the dentist.

Post summarized his mental therapeutics in a book entitled *"I Am Well!,"* *The Modern Practice of Natural Suggestion as Distinct from Hypnotic or Unnatural Influence,* published in 1893. He advertised that the work possessed "the peculiar power of healing the sick while being read." And he signed it "C. W. Post, worded for Plain People."

It was the idea of wording for plain people that was to make Post's fortune.

There's a Reason

Post's ambition reached far beyond the small income he earned from the guests at La Vita Inn. To make more money, he restarted his scientific suspender business and began a frenzied search for the product that he felt sure would make his fortune—a coffee substitute.

For more than a year, Post roasted various roots and grains on the family stove, ground them up, boiled them, and sipped. Most of the time he had to spit out the vile-tasting concoctions, but finally, with the help of a Swiss chemist, the memory of a Texas chicory beverage, and the nine recipes for *faux* coffee listed in Mrs. Ella Kellogg's cookbook, Post came up with a palatable drink.

To prepare for production, he moved his coffee experiments to the Greek Revival style horse barn located behind La Vita Inn. He invested $46.85 in a peanut roaster, a secondhand stove, and a coffee grinder, and another $21.91 in 2 bushels of wheat, 200 pounds of bran, cartons, and 10 jugs of molasses.

By January 1895, all was ready. Assisted by his helper Shorty Bristol, Post roasted the wheat berries, added the bran and molasses, and carefully brewed a beverage. He liked it. Shorty like it. His wife liked it. His daughter liked it. The patients at La Vita liked it. It was a major hit.

Post called his concoction Postum and founded Postum Cereal Coffee, Ltd., a subsidiary of La Vita Inn, legally owned and financed by his wife. He offered packages of Postum for $.15, selling them door to door from a pushcart in much the same way as he sold his orange embroidered suspenders.

After achieving a certain level of success locally, Post sought wider distribution for his noncoffee coffee beverage. He traveled to Grand Rapids and visited with a grocery jobber named E. J. Herrick. Post opened a package of Postum and leveled his gray-blue eyes at Herrick. In his well-modulated, quiet voice Post described the fortune that lay in the tiny grains of Postum spread before him.

Herrick was unimpressed. "Save your money, young man," he said, "have fun with it, or go into some business that there is some reason for. You simply cannot make anybody ask for an instead-of-coffee cereal drink." Post insisted that Herrick stock a case of Postum, on consignment, no cash involved. He promised to hold demonstrations and tastings in Herrick's store. Most important, he told Herrick that he would advertise the product—big time. Herrick reluctantly succumbed to the salesmanship of the suspender-inventor-turned-mental-therapist. He agreed to take a case. Post walked out of Herrick's office a satisfied man. He only had one problem. He had no cash to deliver the advertising he had promised.

Post entered the offices of the *Grand Rapids Evening Press* to convince the publisher to give him advertising space. He brewed up a batch of Postum and served it around the office. Everyone liked it. The editor was still dubious until he happened to notice Post's stationery. There in a corner was a small red dot. Beneath it was the statement, "It makes red blood." It was a mysterious slogan, slightly ominous yet intriguing. It made no scientific sense, but it was memorable, even vital. As he pondered the inscrutable slogan, the editor realized that Post had the advertiser's gift and granted him $10,000 credit. Post put his gift to work and launched an advertising barrage that was to earn him a reputation as "grandfather of American advertising."

In the late nineteenth century, respectable men of finance viewed advertising as little better than legalized gambling. This was understandable considering the fact that the majority of advertisements in America were designed to sell patent medicines such as Lydia E. Pinkham's Vegetable Compound, Microbe Killer, and Kickapoo Indian Sagwa—potions that promised "a positive cure" but delivered little more than alcohol. P. T. Barnum, who got his start writing ad copy for a baldness cure, eloquently described the attitude of the typical nineteenth-century advertiser when he made his famous observation, "There's a sucker born every minute."

Post, who wrote his own copy, reached right out from the pages of America's leading newspapers and magazines and grabbed those suckers by the eyeballs. "Lost Eyesight through Coffee Drinking," he warned in banner headlines.

"It is safe to say," advertised Post, "that one person in every three among coffee users has some incipient or advanced form of disease." He called coffee a "drug drink," containing "a poisonous drug—caffeine which belongs in the same class of alkaloids with cocaine, morphine, nicotine, and strychnine." He invented ailments like "coffee neuralgia," "coffee heart," and "brain fag." He urged his readers to try Postum, a "pure and natural food such as the Creator intended for man's subsistence" that provided "a rational method of dismissing sickness." Ungrammatically but convincingly he suggested, "If coffee don't agree—use Postum."

When he tired of the health pitch, Post played on guilt and self-doubt. "Is your yellow streak the coffee habit?" he asked accusingly. "Does it reduce your work time, kill your energy, push you into the big crowd of mongrels, deaden what thoroughbred blood you may have and neutralize all your efforts to make money and fame?"

Sometimes guilt gave way to mystery. One of Post's ads featured the picture of a fish, posing the question, "Only a live fish can swim upstream—which are you?" Post, described by some as the "hypnotic advertiser," thought back to the skeptical words of the wholesaler Herrick to develop one of the most effective advertising slogans in history, "There's a Reason."

Post knew the reason. He was reinventing American advertising to make a fortune. "Formerly we depended somewhat on the ability of the merchant to whom we sold to favorably represent our goods and secure an introduction and trade for them; but at this time, if we rely upon the old method, the business will fail," he wrote in a letter to his brother. "We are compelled to address advertising to, and place it before, the consumer, who, by his demand, compels the patronage of the dealer."

The going was nerve-racking at first. "My bills for advertising are enough to intimidate a man," he wrote to his brother in 1896. "Last month one bill was $981.78; but I am convinced it will repay me two-fold."

In 1897, Post sold $262,279.64 worth of product, and turned a handsome profit. But he didn't rest on his accomplishment. When asked what he was going to do with all his money, Post said, "I'm going to stick it all right back into advertising. After all, it's not enough to just make and sell cereal. After that you get it halfway down the customer's throat through the use of advertising. Then, they've got to swallow it."

In 1898, Post jumped on the breakfast table. He created what he thought was going to be his second coffee substitute. But when sales lagged, he sold the stuff as a cold breakfast cereal. He called it Grape-Nuts—"grape" because it contained maltose, which Post called "grape sugar," and "nuts" because of its flavor.

Post launched Grape-Nuts with the same advertising overkill that had made Postum a success. "Brains are Built by Grape-Nuts" he advertised. He claimed that they were good for brain workers because they contained the "natural phosphate of potash . . . used by the system in rebuilding and repairing the brain and nerve centers." The tiny flavor nuggets were "the most scientific food in the world." They made nerves steadier, blood redder, and cured consumption, malaria, loose teeth—even an inflamed appendix.

Post promoted Grape-Nuts with sample giveaways, in-store demonstrations, and free gift enclosures—including an eleven-page booklet, "The Road to Wellville," a condensation of his previous musings on mental therapeutics. "Get a famous little booklet in each package—'The Road to Wellville'—there's a reason. Think it over."

Sometimes he advertised Postum and Grape-Nuts together. Addressing his copy to "highly organized people," Post informed his readers, "you can recover from any ordinary illness by discontinuing coffee and poor food, and using Postum Food Coffee and Grape-Nuts." At first sales of Grape-Nuts were not spectacular, but after a few years the cereal outsold the coffee substitute two to one. And Post, who had been selling suspenders and running a New Age boardinghouse in 1895, was spending a million dollars a year on advertising and clearing a million dollars a year in profits just five years later. This was in the years before income tax, when a good wage for an unskilled worker was $2.50 a day. Never in American history had anyone gotten so rich so fast from selling a consumer product.

Asinine Views

The Postum Cereal Company didn't just grow quickly, it exploded. By 1900 it was the largest single consumer of molasses in the world. Post built his own power plant, his own paper mill, and his own box manufacturing company in Battle Creek. Thousands came to tour "white city," as the white-and-green trimmed Post plant built on the site of La Vita Inn became known. They gasped as they witnessed the creation of Grape-Nuts "never touched by human hands in the process of manufacturing" and gaped at the beautiful flowers growing nearby.

In addition to his Battle Creek headquarters housed in an Elizabethan style manor house packed full of art treasures, Post maintained offices in London and New York, a summer home in Greenwich, and a winter home in Santa Barbara. He socialized with European royalty and went on a Battle Creek building spree. He created The Post Addition, sometimes called Postumville—eighty-five acres of Queen Anne and Colonial Revival style homes available to Post employees for as little as $4 down and $4 per month. He built the Post Theatre, an office complex, and the Post Tavern, a six-story brick-and-stone hotel, one of the finest in the nation. Just down the street from the Kellogg Sanitarium, Post's establishment prided itself on its choice steaks and delicious cocktails.

It was all Dr. Kellogg could do to contain his indignation. "By ingenious advertising, much after the method of the medical quacks," he wrote, "some of these concerns have built up large business interests and have waxed rich by their ill-gotten gains. One party in particular has made some millions by the sale of a cheap mixture of bran and molasses."

"This work has not grown out of an original preparation by Dr. Kellogg," Post wrote in his own defense in 1903. "On the contrary, Dr. Kellogg made his food after an article manufactured by a Dansville, N.Y. Sanitarium, as evidenced by a suit brought by the Dansville people against Kellogg."

Kellogg was not above appropriating a good idea from Post either. In the late 1890s, the doctor introduced a breakfast cereal called Gran-Nuts. "We hereby notify you that the use by you of this compound word is a trespass upon our rights as granted by the United States Post Office," wrote Post in a memo dated June 30, 1899. "We propose to ask the proper court for relief and injunction and suitable damages." Gran-Nuts quickly disappeared from the market.

Others besides Kellogg imitated Post. Soon after the success of Postum, half a dozen other coffee substitutes hit the market—at cut-rate prices. Post characterized his competitors as "buzzards roosting on the fence waiting for some bones to lick," and then did some licking of his own. He poured Postum into packages labeled "Monk's Brew" and sold the product way below cost.

The price war cut the profit margins of the competitors down to zero, and they retreated from the retail battlefield. Post was surprised to find that even he couldn't sell Monk's Brew, priced at $.05 per package. When he poured the contents of the Monk's Brew packages into Postum packages and increased the price to $.15, the product sold much better. Consumers didn't really care about price. They bought the brand. "The imitators were ruined," Post gleefully recalled. "It was one of the most complete massacres I have ever seen."

Post's next product, called Dextro-Candy, made from "pre-digested sugar, known as Post Sugar, and very similar to grapes and raisins," was a flop. He followed it with a third product, a cornflake that once again relied on technology pioneered by Dr. Kellogg. He called his new breakfast sensation Elijah's Manna. The green-and-white box fea-

> ### CEREAL WAR
>
> The rivalry and resentment between C. W. Post and Dr. John Harvey Kellogg grew to legendary proportions in Battle Creek. While Kellogg referred to Post as "the original imitator," Post took every opportunity to annoy his former doctor. According to one tale, Post returned to the Sanitarium after making his first million. Dressed in black, to poke fun at the white-clothed Kellogg, Post entered the Sanitarium, lit up a big fat cigar, and stood smoking outside Kellogg's office. After some time, Kellogg appeared. Not wishing to give the interloper any satisfaction, the tobacco-hating medical man ignored the clouds of cigar smoke, invited a waiting patient into his office, and closed the door behind him. After three such appearances, an exasperated Post barked "Dog" at Kellogg as he whisked by. The doctor, without missing a beat, wheeled on his heels and hissed, "And you know what dogs do to posts."

tured the prophet Elijah resting on a rock, holding a staff in one hand while a raven dropped food into his other hand.

Churchmen in the United States were outraged and demanded that Post cease taking Elijah's name in vain. Post was outraged as well. He wrote, "Perhaps no one should eat Angel Food cake, enjoy Adam's Ale, live in St. Paul, nor work for Bethlehem Steel, nor could one have the healing benefits of St. Jacob's oil, one should have his Adam's apple removed and never again name a child for the good people of the Bible." By 1908 the controversy cut into sales and Post dropped the biblical name in favor of the secular Post Toasties.

But the brouhaha over Post's controversial advertising campaign was only beginning. In 1911 *Collier's* magazine attacked Post in an article entitled "The Great American Frauds." The magazine pointed out that Post used the endorsement of fictional doctors, and it called Post's advertised implication that Grape-Nuts could cure an appendicitis "lying, and potentially dangerous lying."

Stung to the quick, Post struck back. He spent $150,000 on newspaper ads saying *Collier's* editors were after him only because he would not buy advertising in their magazine. "When a journal willfully prostitutes its columns to try and harm a reputable manufacturer to force him to advertise," he wrote, "it is time the public knew the facts." *Collier's* sued Post for libel. After Condé Nast, *Collier's* ad manager, testified against Post, the magazine won a $50,000 verdict. But it took until 1951 for Post's Company, then known as General Foods, to reach an agreement with the Federal Trade Commission to alter its advertising so it would not imply that coffee creates ". . . divorces, business failures, factory accidents, juvenile delinquency, traffic accidents, fire or home foreclosures. . . ."

Inspired by his fantastic financial success and blessed with a cranky disposition, Post became less interested in the cereal business as the years went on. In 1902 he took partial retirement from his company and moved his residence to Washington. There he became the Ross Perot of his time, a feisty, glib conservative businessman who used his money to plaster his words across the nation's consciousness. In the spring of 1905 he became the first person to buy newspaper space for the sole purpose of expressing a personal opinion to the people. He attacked "sand-crab politicians" who "burrow in the sand at the sound of trouble." Though he himself was a card-carrying member of the Typographical Union, Post never tired of attacking "High Muck-A-Muck Unionists," and the "sociologists" who tried for years to organize Post's workers in Battle Creek and attacked him for what they called his "asinine views." John Fitzpatrick, the president of the Chicago Federation of Labor, told the press that "a recent wreck in Michigan showed that several cars were loaded with peanut shells consigned to a Battle Creek factory." The revelation ran under the headline, "Labor Leader: Breakfast Foods are 'Shell Game.'"

Post's political involvement fueled his other ambitions. He divorced his wife, whose money he had used to start his business, and married one of his "typewriters," as secretaries of the age were known, a beautiful Battle Creek girl some twenty years his junior named Leila Young. He bought thirty-three square miles of west Texas rangeland and created Post City. Post provided cheap housing and land for those who settled his agricultural utopia. The only thing he couldn't provide was adequate rainfall, though he tried. When drought conditions became particularly severe, Post ordered his managers to send up twenty-five kites, each packed with two pounds of dynamite, in hopes that the simulated thunder would shake rain from the heavens. The hopeful and thirsty residents repeated the experiment twenty-two times—with limited success.

Post had even less success conquering his own physical ailments. In the fall of 1913 he suffered a severe physical collapse. The rumor in Battle Creek was that the breakfast baron had paresis, better known today as syphilis. He convalesced at his home in Santa Barbara until March of 1914, when his condition took a serious turn for the worse. Even a visit to the Mayo Brothers Clinic in Rochester, Minnesota, didn't help.

The ailing health-food tycoon returned to his ranch at Santa Barbara and slipped into a deep depression. A life-long gun enthusiast, he ordered all firearms removed from his house. Unfortunately, one remained. On May 9, 1914, alone in his bedroom and dressed immaculately in a suit, Post ended his dietary, political, and meteorological experiments with a single shot to the head from a 30-30 caliber hunting rifle.

The fifty-nine-year-old president of the Postum Cereal Company left a corporate empire built on four products: Postum, Grape-Nuts, Instant Postum, and Post Toasties, and an estate worth $70 million. His twenty-seven-year-old daughter, who inherited the vast bulk of his estate, instantly became one of the richest women in the world.

Marjorie Merriweather Post was not intimidated by money, business, or anything else. Her father had taught her how to make herself look presentable, boxed with her, and explained to her every detail of his business. "I think I saw the manufacturing of every kind of product imaginable in those days," Marjorie later remembered. "And every kind of machinery and equipment was explained to me by Dad."

She took her father's Postum Cereal Company and ran with it, flourishing as one of the most flamboyant hostesses and savviest businesswomen the world had ever seen. Between throwing parties on the world's largest private yacht and building Mar Lago, the 123-room Palm Beach estate later purchased by Donald Trump, Ms. Post had time to teach her daughter Dina Merrill the art of skinning flamingos and to introduce the bureaucrats of Stalinist Russia to the delights of frozen foods.

Churning through E. F. Hutton and three other husbands, Marjorie transformed the Postum Cereal Company into America's greatest food conglomerate. She snatched up shiny brand names like Jell-O, Log Cabin Syrup, and Baker's Chocolate with the same enthusiasm as she purchased Fabergé eggs. Her biggest discovery was made during dinner on board her yacht one evening, when her cook served up a delicious goose. When Marjorie asked where the cook got such fresh fowl out of season, he replied that it had been frozen.

It took four years, but Marjorie finally convinced the Postum board of directors to buy the frozen-foods company founded by a former fur trapper named Clarence Birdseye. Postum took General Foods, the name of the Birdseye company, as its own corporate identity. Today the frozen goose has been transformed into a golden goose, as General Foods, the direct corporate descendant of C. W. Post's cereal coffee business, collects ten cents of every food dollar spent in America.

CLIFF ROBERTSON REMEMBERS

Cliff Robertson became part of America's cereal aristocracy when he married C. W. Post's granddaughter, actress Dina Merrill. Robertson, who won an Oscar in 1969 for his leading role in the film *Charlie*, traveled to Battle Creek to act in a company documentary about C. W. Post. During the filming, Robertson ran directly into the controversy still swirling around the creator of Grape-Nuts. Did C. W. Post steal Dr. Kellogg's recipes or not? "One of the original workers at the Post factory came up to me," Robertson recalled. "He was celebrating his seventy-fifth anniversary at Post, so he was quite old." Robertson got to know the old-time cereal hand between set ups. "Post got a job as the dishwasher in the Sanitarium kitchen," the old timer told him. "He stole the formula that had been developed by Dr. Kellogg and he simply changed the name to Postum."

4

The Great Cereal Rush

C. W. Post built a larger fortune faster than any other American in a legitimate enterprise, a fact that was not lost on equally ambitious entrepreneurs across the country. The process whereby a twelve-cent bushel of grain could be converted into a product retailing for six dollars seemed almost too good to be true. Hundreds of entrepreneurs flooded into the small Michigan city, turning Battle Creek into a breakfast cereal boomtown.

"Battle Creek has said: In place of disease we would give you health," the *New York World* newspaper reported in its September 7, 1902, special report on Battle Creek. "You have too long been called a nation of dyspeptics. Let us cure you." Others took the Battle Creek message to mean: "Let us make you rich."

Quacks and Flakes

Battle Creek, the frontier of American health food, attracted its share of rapscallions, many of whom were quacko-traditionalists, men and women who believed that a person could still make a dishonest dollar selling bogus medical concoctions. As one of these health hustlers boasted, "I can advertise dishwater and sell it, just as well as an article of merit."

Dr. A. Johnson prescribed his Malarial Antidote, Blood Purifier, and Female Elixer from his downtown medical dispensary. Mrs. M. E. Pendill, "The Celebrated Indian Doctress," specialized in female problems. "Men never have and never will understand a woman in health," she stated in her literature. "Why should you trust them in sickness?" The Old Indian Medicine Company, based in Battle Creek, offered pseudo–Native American cures in the form of a pile ointment and its best-selling Wahoo Bitters, while Mrs. Ellen Overholt forsook ancient wisdom for hi-tech paraphenelia. Billing herself as an "electrician," she promised to shock her patients back to health.

Most of these quacks were not successful enough to warrant

concern from the more established medical institutions in Battle Creek, but Frank J. Kellogg infuriated John H. Kellogg by marketing a thyroid extract called Kellogg's Safe Fat Reducer. Although Frank J. was no relation to John H., "Anti-Fat Kellogg" earned a national reputation by selling his elixer with the simple but effective slogan, "Don't Stay Fat." A few years later, "Anti-Fat Kellogg" introduced a new medicine to the market, an anti-thin concoction designed to help his customers gain the weight he helped them lose.

RAISING THE DEAD

Of all the mentalists, crystal gazers, neuropaths, and breakfast-cereal inventors who wandered through Battle Creek at the turn of the century, none was more brazen than Dr. James N. Peebles. The author of many spiritual self-help books, including *Hell Revised, Modernized and Made More Comfortable*, Peebles set up shop above a Battle Creek cigar store and started selling a "brain restorative" that he claimed could raise the dead. The seventy-three-year-old Peebles was arrested for fraudulent use of the mail and was tried in Detroit's U.S. District Court in 1901. When the prosecutor asked Peebles if he believed he had the power of Jesus Christ to raise the dead, the six-foot four-inch vegetarian stood up, raised his fist over his head, looked heavenward and cried, "I do! And may God strike me dead on this spot if I am not possessed of such power!" He stood stone still for a few moments, then turned to the jury. "Gentlemen, you see for yourselves." The jury saw only too well and promptly convicted him.

The smartest operators realized that cancer cures, Indian health nostrums, and other mail-order medicines were chicken feed compared to the big-money item, health food—most particularly the flaked health food invented by Dr. Kellogg. The profit-hungry cereal sharks found that they could imitate the flaking process developed by Kellogg without fear of prosecution and began churning out tons of poor-quality flakes.

There was Grain-O; Grape Sugar Flakes; Malted Zweiback; Malt-Too; My Food; Flak-Ota; Cocoa Cream Flakes; Cereola; Frumenta;

Norka (Akron spelled backwards); and Malted Oats, "Richer than wheat, better than meat." A former Battle Creek grocer produced Per-Fo, short for the perfect food. One man introduced a cereal made of dehulled beans with the advertisement "all the bean but the armor plate." The Fuller Brothers, two mechanics from Kalamazoo, came to Battle Creek to launch the Korn Krisp Company. Even those breakfast foods that didn't come from Battle Creek claimed a piece of the town's health giving-mystique. The Battle Creek Breakfast Food Cereal Company produced the cereal Egg-O-See in their plant located in Quincy, Illinois.

Perhaps the most unique breakfast product was the brain child of Chicago entrepreneur Dr. V. C. Price. In 1903 Price established a breakfast cereal factory in an old water mill located half way between "Cereal City" (Battle Creek) and "Celery City" (Kalamazoo). His creation was Tryabita, a celery-flavored cereal sold in a box depicting a cereal-munching girl framed by celery stalks and sheaves of wheat.

By 1902, at the time when the *New York World* profiled the breakfast cereal boom, Battle Creek was a breakfast cereal klondike. The town of 30,000 people was home to thirty wheat-flake companies, which spent close to $10 million per year promoting Battle Creek as "The World's Cereal Bowl," "The Cereal City," "The Health City," "Foodtown," "The Biggest Little City in the U.S.A.," "Cornflake Capital of the World," and "A Little Chicago."

Con men, investors, racketeers, gangsters, and peddlers choked the streets of the small town, creating a frenetic carnival of capitalism in which everyone from cowboys to accountants jumped in to make a buck from breakfast. The quickest money was made by stock hustlers. Taking investments from anyone they could buttonhole, these sharpies promised a cereal fortune but delivered nothing but worthless shares in limited liability partnerships with names like the Battle Creek Breakfast Food Company, the Battle Creek Flaked Food Company, the Battle Creek Flesh Food Company, and three different companies named the Battle Creek Food Company. One company promised that it would manufacture a health coffee as soon as it came up with a name. Lewis G. Stevenson, father of Adlai Stevenson, had a health food product called Javril, but no place to make it. He told his men to set up tents, complaining that Battle Creek was so full, "There are no houses to be had."

Most of the funds invested in these cereal companies quickly disappeared, along with the company organizers. Though the government in Lansing made some noises about cracking down on investment

MUSCLE HUSTLE

On Thanksgiving Day 1902, Michigan beat Minnesota in Ann Arbor to win the Western Conference (now Big Ten) football title. Cereal makers located just down the road in Battle Creek were quick to pick up on the gridiron action. "Mapl-Flakes always engenders brain and muscle, two elements of success in the game of football," proclaimed one upstart manufacturer. The Norka Food Company printed pictures of a gigantic football with the advertising pitch, "This is the way a team would look if it was fed on Norka Oats." In 1910, kids were knocking imaginary balls into the butter dish thanks to "the most realistic baseball game ever invented" printed on the inside of Kellogg's Corn Flakes boxes. To play, kids cut out the dice with kitchen scissors, assembled them with "mucilage" and then followed the rules of "Kellogg's World's Champions Cereal League." Jack Dempsey, the world's heavyweight boxing title holder scored a knockout during the 1920s by urging Americans to "Train with me on Rippled Wheat . . . a delicious whole-wheat breakfast food." Working with athletes presented peculiar challenges to advertising producers. Max Bryer, who directed scores of Post cereal television commercials in the 1950s and 1960s, recalled that many big league ball players' tobacco-stained teeth had to be "cleaned up" before the guys could be shot smiling over a bowl of flakes. Laughed Bryer, "We always had a porcelain jar for them to spit their tobacco juice into."

frauds, the action was developing too fast for regulators to catch up. The billboard opposite the Michigan Central depot that told people to "Better Yourself in Battle Creek," should probably have read, "Better Watch Out in Battle Creek."

The World's Fare Food Company, Ltd., had a different scam, an ingenious combination breakfast food, automotive, and real estate game. Promoter Benjamin F. Morgan advertised his cereal Golden Manna as "the invalid's delight" and "Battle Creek's best builder of blood, bone, body, brawn and brain." In each packet of Golden Manna was a ticket for a ride on the firm's three-seated fringe-topped automobile, which drove straight out to Morgan's real estate development, Morgan Park.

The more sensible folks around Battle Creek managed to keep the commercial hysteria in perspective. These jaded natives joked that the whole cereal commotion was a plot cooked up by the Michigan lumber industry to make use of all the leftover sawdust.

Sunny Jim

Not all turn-of-the-century breakfast entrepreneurs rushed to Battle Creek. Several of the most successful caught a whiff of the healthful business and put together cereal operations closer to home.

Edward "The Duke" Ellsworth started up his flake operation in Buffalo, New York. A tall, gray-haired, mustachioed entrepreneur, the Duke owned H-O Oats, makers of America's first quick-cooking oatmeal. The dashing Duke peddled his oats with a flamboyant advertising campaign featuring billboards on elevated train platforms around New York City with pictures of Oliver Twist holding up an empty bowl and the words, "I want some more!"

By 1900, Ellsworth was ready to jump into flakes. His first move was to hire Charles Rhoades away from Dr. Kellogg's breakfast cereal operation and set up a whole-wheat flake production line. Rhoades figured out how to create a good-tasting flake that was resistant to mold. Ellsworth figured out a brand name for the new product that reflected his dynamic personality—Force.

Ellsworth first advertised his cold cereal with the picture of an electric generator labeled "Force" above the Post-like slogan "Reason Why." When sales sputtered, Ellsworth adopted a new mascot, a personable dynamo named Sunny Jim.

Drawn by W. W. Denslow, the man who illustrated the first edition of the *Wizard of Oz,* Sunny Jim was a cross between Uncle Sam and Mr. Natural—a strutting grandfatherly gentleman in top hat, high collar, and red-tailed coat, who wore his hair in a pigtail and carried a walking stick.

"Good gracious! A breakfast food isn't all life, is it?" recalled writer Minnie Maude Hanff, explaining how she came up with her Sunny Jim ad copy. "People aren't going to take it nearly as seriously as an advertiser wants them to. . . . I thought far better to give them a minute's entertainment."

Her first jingle, widely printed in newspapers and magazines, told the origin story of the well-tempered consumer:

Jim Dumps was a most unfriendly man,
Who lived his life on the hermit plan;
In his gloomy way he'd gone through life,
And made the most of woe and strife;
Till Force one day was served to him—
Since then they've called him "Sunny Jim."

Sunny Jim became hugely popular. His pigtailed image appeared on billboards, newspapers, and magazines. He was promoted with postcards, coupons, chinaware, pocket watches—there was even a talking Sunny Jim doll equipped with an internal bellows so that when the chest was squeezed a voice-like sound emanated from the mouth. His popularity led others to celebrate his sunny personality in cartoons, songs, and even a Broadway play. "He is as well known as President Roosevelt or J. Pierpont Morgan," the magazine *Printer's Ink* declared.

The pervasive Sunny Jim campaign for Force had only one problem—it didn't boost sales. "The advertising absolutely sold 'Sunny Jim' to the public, but it did not sell Force," advertising pioneer Earnest Elmo Calkins later commented. "Humor, you see, is a very good servant but a bad master."

A hard-sell ad campaign succeeded where Sunny Jim had failed. By April 1912, Force was listed by the *Journal of Commerce* as one of the most popular ready-to-eat cereals in New York and New England, more popular even than Grape-Nuts. But the money that Force was producing could not keep up with the extravagant plans of the visionary Ellsworth. The Duke "plunged on an idea like a gambler on a lucky number," remembered ad man Calkins. "No sooner had one thing made good than all the profits were thrown on the board on another chance."

Ellsworth took chances with poor-quality cornflakes, a new type of oatmeal, and a self-rising cake flour, all of which were rejected by the public. By 1920 he was so overextended that he could not pay his advertising bills, and he lost the company. Under new ownership, Sunny Jim continued to grace grocery store shelves for many years, especially in England where the brand continued to truck right along into the 1970s under the name "Sunny Jim's Original Force Wheat Flakes."

Edible Linoleum

While Sunny Jim tickled the American funny bone, LaFayette Coltrin was more concerned with the section of the anatomy that so fascinated Dr. Kellogg. In 1907, the Omaha-based businessman was told by his doctors that he had at most six months to live. The sixty-seven-year-old bachelor suffered from acute abdominal ulcers aggravated by chronic constipation.

One doctor recommended two tablespoons of flaxseed mixed with warm water two times daily to relieve the pain of his stomach ulcer and ease his solidified bowel. Coltrin was skeptical. Flaxseed oil, also known as linseed oil, was a vile yellowish substance used as a drying agent in paints and varnishes and as one of the basic ingredients in linoleum. Coltrin knew that consuming full-strength linseed oil would make him vomit. To his great delight, he found that eating the flaxseed itself "was cathartic."

However spectacular the resulting bowel movement, there remained one problem with the flaxseed cure. The little laxative bits tasted terrible. A clever and able man, Coltrin began an exhaustive search for a more palatable alternative. After much experimentation, he sprinkled flaxseed over whole-wheat flakes and added celery powder to mask the taste of his botanical bowel-blasters. To his surprise he found the high-fiber blend not only quite delicious but even more effective than the original pure flaxseed prescription. Aware that his cereal could bring blessed relief to millions of constipated Americans, Coltrin decided to bring his product to market.

A tall, dignified man with a goatee, LaFayette Coltrin bore such a resemblance to the nation's fictional patriarch that he had long been known as "Sam" to his friends. It seemed only natural to christen his dietary invention "Uncle Sam Breakfast Food," and to decorate the box with his own image dressed in a black top hat and tie. "L. Coltrin, the inventor of this food, after years of suffering from stomach troubles was compelled to 'eat or die'," read a testimonial on the side of the package. "The result is Uncle Sam 'The Food for Health'."

Coltrin peddled the new health food to local merchants from his horse and buggy, which was plastered with the cheery words "The Friend to All Mankind . . . Banishes Constipation, No Matter What the Cause." His cereal proved so popular that he sold out the business within a year and moved to Long Beach, California, where he lived to an old age enjoying a certain notoriety as the father of "The Food That Glides!"

The new owner, Omaha businessman John M. McGowan, dropped Coltrin's visage from the cereal packages in favor of an Uncle Sam line drawing on a box festooned in patriotic colors. McGowan also had high hopes for the stuff, claiming that Uncle Sam "Does away with constipation, that arch enemy and stepping stone to so many ills of modern civilization."

McGowan was not disappointed. Within five years, the distinctive red, white, and blue Uncle Sam package was in major markets coast to coast. It was awarded highest honors for excellence by both the San Francisco and Milwaukee Pure Food Expositions. It even earned an endorsement from the American Medical Association. Endorsements poured in as Uncle Sam placed advertisements in many leading medical journals and sent full-sized samples to any physician who wrote in a request. "A dry bowel retains feces and the poisons which nature is trying to eliminate, are absorbed. This causes liver spots, and eruptions on the face," wrote Dr. J. F Cate in 1913. "Uncle Sam will remove all these conditions." Gushed W. E. Lyons, "I have a friend at Lodi, NY who has not had a natural operation for over 12 years until he ate your food."

In the 1920s the Uncle Sam Breakfast Food Company made breakfast history with Vanilla Sweeties, a vanilla-flavored whole-wheat flake, one of the first cereals targeted at kids. Though the Sweeties did not last long, Uncle Sam's next product did. In 1928, an Omaha macaroni manufacturer named Lloyd Skinner observed that his blushing bride enjoyed adding plump raisins to her wheat flakes in the morning. Skinner realized that a fruit and fiber cereal was a new and brilliant breakfast concept. The macaroni man promptly christened his invention Skinner Raisin Bran, registered the trademark, and teamed up with the Uncle Sam Breakfast Food Company for production. Sales of Skinner Raisin Bran took off and soon caught the eyes of the big boys in Battle Creek. By 1942, both Kellogg and Post were selling their own imitations. Skinner sued, claiming that Kellogg's and Post's use of the term *raisin bran* was an infringement on his trademark. Although his suit was unsuccessful, his name lives on in the recesses of the cereal aisle.

Uncle Sam also survives, although under a different owner. In the 1980s, the company that produced the laxative cereal was acquired by Erewhon, a Boston-based health-food distributor established by the man who introduced the macrobiotic diet to the United States. The company that popularized brown rice continues to distribute Uncle Sam cereal nationwide, relying on word of mouth to advertise the wondrous effects of the flaxseed cereal.

It's in the Shreds

The romantic roar of Niagara Falls provided the soundtrack for the manufacturing operation of the man who first brought shreds to the breakfast table, Henry Drushel Perky.

Born in Holmes County, Ohio, in 1843, Perky was a farm boy who, like C. W. Post, had unbounded energy that scattered itself across the inventive spectrum. He worked as a schoolteacher, a lawyer, a newspaper editor, an expedition organizer, and a promoter whose money-making schemes never quite seemed to take off. As he knocked around the country with his family in tow, he never lost his enthusiasm for life but he gained an incurable case of dyspepsia.

Perky became engrossed in the subject of food. He spent hours in the public library in Cambridge, Massachusetts, and conferring with doctors who recommended a diet of raw vegetables. Perky began to widen his culinary investigations with travel. In 1890, after his forty-seventh birthday, Perky was in Denver when he came up with a plan that he felt sure would cure his digestive problem and increase his bank account. The idea was dehydrated corn. Perky invited a friend who was an engineer and had a little machine shop in Watertown, New York, to come to Denver and work on the corn-drying project. The friend declined. Undaunted, Perky packed up his family and moved to Watertown.

Working together, the shade-tree food technologists left behind their plans to dehydrate corn. Instead, Perky and his partner created and patented a machine to "shred" cereal food. The machine was simple in design—two rollers that pressed against each other, one grooved, one not. The partners unsuccessfully tried to shred corn and a number of other food items until Perky thought back to a man he had met in a Nebraska café. The man confessed to Perky that the only thing he could digest was boiled wheat. After hearing the story, Perky's partner went out and bought a small container of seed wheat. The partners cooked it, ran it through the machine, piled the extruded wheat threads into a two-foot long mound, cut it up, and asked an obliging neighbor woman to pop it in the oven.

The two experimenters went berserk when they saw the final product. Perky's friend grabbed the hot pan and burned his hands, while Perky himself waved his arms and burst into song. They knew exactly what was going to happen. In a few years, no home in America would be without a wheat shredder. It would become the essential kitchen appliance.

After the initial enthusiasm wore off, Perky's friend decided to bow out of the shredding business while Perky moved back to the Mile High City, set up the Cereal Machine Company, and went on a promotional binge. He rented a small store in which he shredded wheat for anyone he could drag in off the street. He fitted out a magnificent gold-and-white horse-drawn wagon to carry bags of shredded wheat biscuits all over town. He opened up a restaurant in which every item on the menu, from the mashed potatoes to the coffee, featured shredded wheat.

Perky quickly came to realize that the secret was not in the shredder. "It's in the shreds," became the marketing pitch for his company, which he renamed the Natural Food Company in 1895. He set up a factory in Worcester, Massachusetts, and traveled around the country on a speaking tour. He explained to his audiences how shredded wheat, which he called the "naturally organized food," had cured his dyspepsia by "reorganizing my body into perfectly healthy condition." Like diet and fitness gun Susan Powter, he encouraged his listeners to stop the insanity and face the truth. "Mothers, do you know that children crave natural food until you pervert their tastes by the use of unnatural food?" he asked accusingly. "Unnatural food develops unnatural and therefore strong propensities and desires in children. Like begets like— pure food, pure minds." There was only one answer: "Shredded Wheat is the perfect food."

Perky purchased the Oread Collegiate Institute in Worcester, Massachusetts, and transformed it into the Oread Institute of Domestic Science, whose graduates dispersed around the country to demonstrate the practical benefits of shredded wheat.

At the Institute, Perky encouraged experimentation with his wheat packets. He recommended Welsh rarebit on shredded-wheat biscuit, chocolate jelly on shredded-wheat biscuit, escalloped celery à la shredded wheat biscuit, creamed oysters in shredded wheat biscuit baskets, and shredded wheat ice cream. He collected his baroque recipes in *The Vital Question Cook Book.* By 1902 grocers had distributed more than a million and a half copies of the culinary classic.

In the same year that Perky moved to Worcester, developers built an electrical plant to exploit the generating power of Niagara Falls. They invited Perky to come for a visit. The sight of the enormous, pristine falls inspired Perky. He set out to build the most astonishing commercial monument the world had ever seen, "a temple of cleanliness to house the purest and cleanest of foods." He bought a ten-acre site in the choicest residential neighborhood of the town, organized a $10 million stock company, and raised enough cash to open the "Palace of Light" in 1901.

The new plant not only produced two million shredded-wheat puffs per day, it became one of America's most popular tourist destinations. More than 100,000 visitors a year came from all over the world to take the free plant tour. The crowds marveled at the factory's immaculately clean white enamel and hardwood interior, its 30,000 glass lights, its 884 windows, its roof garden, and its complete air-conditioning system.

The visitors shook their heads in disbelief as they heard about the working conditions, the furnished "rest rooms," the free lunch, the "factory mother" who looked after the female employees, and, most astonishing, two fifteen-minute work breaks, one in the morning and one in the evening. "If only my life could be like this," sighed millions of visiting honeymooners, their nuptial memories forever entwined with the scent of shredded wheat. Marilyn Monroe even met the shredded wheat plant manager as part of her postmarital ritual in the film *Niagara*. "Probably the most rational scheme of social and moral better-ment that may be found in any factory in this country," was how Perky described his "Conservatory of Food."

Perky's enthusiasm couldn't be contained, even by his massive Niagara Falls plant. Obsessed with the desire to found an agricultural school, he sold his interest in Shredded Wheat for $150,000 and moved to Maryland. He died shortly thereafter, in June, 1906. Just twenty-two years later, the company that started with Perky's stomachache was sold to the National Biscuit Company, now known as Nabisco, for some thirty-five million dollars' worth of stock.

One of the people who missed out on the shredded wheat bonanza was Dr. Kellogg. In 1894, a visitor brought some of the crusty wheat pillows up to the Battle Creek Sanitarium. Though the gentleman thought that eating shredded wheat was like "eating a whisk broom," Kellogg was sufficiently intrigued by the product to travel to Denver and meet the inventor.

As Kellogg munched on the baked wheat, his ever active mind began to spin. The crusty snacks were palatable. They wouldn't break any teeth. They might be popular in Battle Creek. He offered Perky $100,000 for his business. Perky wanted more. Kellogg refused to raise his offer and headed back to Battle Creek. Years later, Dr. Kellogg confessed, "The greatest business mistake I ever made was in not buying Shredded Wheat when it was offered at a reasonable price."

5

Battle Creek Babylon

The decision not to buy Shredded Wheat was just one of many terrible business miscalculations made by Dr. Kellogg. Self-described as "high-headed and hasty, suspicious, stubborn and irritable, hypersensitive, morbid and fretful," Kellogg had too large an ego and too little respect for the world of commerce to cash in on the health-food products that he invented. In 1902, at a time when C. W. Post was netting a million dollars a year with products derived from Kellogg's recipes, Dr. Kellogg's own food company was losing money.

No one resented Dr. Kellogg's attitude toward money more than his younger brother, Will Keith Kellogg. The younger Kellogg managed his older brother's health enterprises. He kept the books, helped in the kitchen, at times even shaved his elder brother, blackened his shoes, and ran alongside him while John Harvey rode his bicycle to discuss business matters. A stout, bald man with round spectacles who looked like a grumpy Elmer Fudd, W. K. Kellogg collected a pitifully small salary and watched health-food fortunes pile up around him.

"It takes too much time to make and keep money," John Harvey complained. "The attempt to accumulate a fortune keeps a man from doing many other things that he wants to do." Frequent Sanitarium visitor and business publishing pioneer Clarence W. Barron remarked that his good friend Dr. Kellogg "should have been one of the richest men in the world, but he let money slip through his fingers." Younger brother W. K. Kellogg put the problem more succinctly. "My brother is the greatest disorganizer in the world," he sighed.

The Flunkey

Willie Keith Kellogg was born on April 7, 1860, eight years after John Harvey. Unlike his older brother, who dazzled his parents and friends with his precocious brilliance, Willie, who later changed his first name to Will, was thought to be something of a dullard by his teachers because he was unable to read from the blackboard. It was not until he was

47

twenty years old that Will realized his learning disability was caused by nearsightedness.

Will grew up taciturn and shy, as introverted as his elder brother was extroverted. About his only friend was the old family horse named Spot. When his father sold the horse, Will vowed he would own a whole stable someday.

At the age of thirteen, Will left school to join his father's broom business, selling brooms from a horse-drawn cart. Four years later he went to work in the broom factory owned by his half-brother Albert. When the broom factory failed, Albert refused to pay his seemingly slow-witted relative. Showing unexpected gumption, Will placed his trunk on his half-brother's front porch, sat on it, and refused to move until he got his money. Albert paid up.

After a brief stint managing Adventist Elder James White's broom factory in Dallas, Texas, Will Keith secured a bookkeeping certificate from the Parson's Business College in Kalamazoo, married, and went to work for the man he referred to as "The Doctor," his older brother John Harvey, in 1880.

For the next twenty-two and a half years, W. K. worked at the Sanitarium fifteen hours a day, seven days a week. He kept the books, bought the lumber, answered the correspondence, and handled the labor problems. He set the rates for operations and occasionally acted as an orderly. He arranged free care for indigent patients, special services for wealthy patients, and funerals for dead patients. When insane patients broke out of the Sanitarium, it was W. K. who roamed the streets and brought them back. "I kept account of the people who called on me one evening after 5:00," he later re-membered, "and they numbered 33." It seemed that the work never ended, and for W. K., who suffered from terrible insomnia, it in fact never did.

For all this, his older brother paid him a salary of six dollars a week plus room and board. Three and a half years after he had begun working at the San, John Harvey gave his little brother a raise—to seven dollars per week. To make ends meet, W. K. took another job taking care of a horse for three dollars per week. He waited seven years for his first vacation because the Doctor didn't believe in holidays. Struggling to make things comfortable for his sickly wife, the overworked father of two sons confided in his diary, "I feel kind of blue. Am afraid that I will always be a poor man the way things look now."

In the early 1890s the Doctor gave W. K. a chance to make a little extra money. He offered to let him manage his publishing and health-food businesses and keep 25 percent of the profits for his pay. W. K. was glad for the chance to make the extra money, even though it meant adding a new headache to his 100-hour-a-week workload.

It was a major undertaking to figure out just what Dr. Kellogg's companies were, much less how to run them. During his career, the Doctor created over two dozen business enterprises, including the Sanitary Supply Company, the Sanitarium Equipment Company, the Sanitarium Food Company, the Sanitarium Health Food Company, the Sanitas Nut Food Company, Ltd., the Sanitas Food Company, the Toasted Rice Flake and Biscuit Company, the Yoghurt Company, the Colax Company, the Noko Company, the Electric Light Bath Company, and the magazine *Bacteriological World.* Will Keith was in large part responsible for manufacturing, selling, and shipping a mind-numbing array of products—vegetable meats, cereal coffees, crackers, muscle beaters, flesh brushers, butter-dyed agar-agar, yogurt capsules, peanut butter, electrical light bathing cabinets, and the ever-popular vibrating chair. Will Keith realized that most of the products the Doctor thought up were not great sellers. He understood that to make money, the operation had to focus on one or two popular items. And the most popular item that the Doctor ever invented was the breakfast cereal flake.

None Genuine Without this Signature

While the Doctor claimed that the inspiration for flaked foods came to him in a dream, W. K. maintained that the crunchy foodstuffs were born of hard work. According to W. K.'s version of the story, the Doctor ordered him to come up with a digestible substitute for bread that would be, in W. K.'s words, "something better than the shredded wheat made in Denver."

W. K. tried turning the individual grains of wheat into tiny pieces of toast by cooking them and mashing them through a strainer with a plunger. He tried rolling the wheat out on a dough board. Eventually he set up two rollers in the experimental kitchen of the San and designed a knife blade to peel the grain flakes off the primitive smashing device. The Doctor's wife, Ella Kellogg, one of Kellogg's adopted children, W. K. and others spent hours feeding boiled wheat through the rollers and scraping off the pasty, shapeless blobs of grain mush.

Exhausted from their experiments, the flake crew left a batch of cooked wheat soaking in water overnight. The next day, when they fed the wheat through the rollers, they found that the moldy grain formed perfect individual flakes, crisp when baked. They had discovered the secret of tempering the wheat to equalize its moisture content. The first breakfast flake, Granose, was born.

The Doctor wanted to rub the flakes through a screen and sell them as crumbs, but W. K. convinced him that the whole flakes were more attractive and began production in a little barn behind the Sanitarium. In 1896, the first year of commercial production, W. K. sold 113,400 pounds of flakes, a huge amount considering that Dr. Kellogg restricted his younger brother's sales efforts to current Sanitarium patients, former patients, and ads placed in his publications *Good Health* and the *Battle Creek Idea*. The ads described Granose Flakes as "ready for solution by the digestive juice and for prompt assimilation." Interesting medical theory—lousy advertising.

In his own deliberate style, W. K. moved to take the wheat flakes big time. In 1898, he made an appeal to the board of the Sanitarium, asking them to fund the building of a proper factory for Granose production. "I recall having offered a suggestion that . . . the food company would develop in such a manner that the Sanitarium would be only a side show as to the magnitude of the food business," W. K. recalled. "I confess at the time I little realized the extent to which the food business might develop in Battle Creek."

The wheat flakes were such a hit that W. K., under the direction of his brother, began experimenting with the all-American grain, corn. Flakes of corn, called cerealine, were used widely in the brewing industry but it wasn't until 1898 that the Kellogg boys came up with a corn-flake suitable for the breakfast table. They called it "Sanitas Toasted Corn Flakes" and sold it in blue packages emblazoned with a picture of the Battle Creek Sanitarium. The only problem with the product was that it quickly turned rancid.

W. K. and the Doctor kept working on the cornflake. They narrowed their investigations to the corn kernel itself, which they later called "the sweetheart of the corn," and experimented with various malt flavorings. By 1902 the problem of spoilage was overcome, though for many years the Kelloggs recommended that consumers take corn-flakes from the box and "heat for a moment in an open oven to restore crispness."

Not content with the perfectly good but rather flat-tasting flake, W. K. kept experimenting. While his brother was touring Europe on a medical fact-finding mission, W. K. added a forbidden ingredient to the product—cane sugar. When the Doctor returned and examined the adulterated cereal, he was furious. Dr. Kellogg felt that sugar was unhealthy and argued vehemently against using it in cornflakes. His medical concerns were less persuasive than the opinion of cornflake consumers, who approved of the sugary addition. Sales of Sanitas Toasted Corn Flakes soared and the sugar stayed.

In 1903, Kellogg's application to patent the flaking process for breakfast cereal, which had been infringed by many, was finally turned down. W. K. responded to the legal setback by launching a massive advertising campaign, spearheaded by Arch Shaw, who was to become one of America's leading business theorists. In 1903 W. K. placed ads for "Toasted Corn Flakes" in newspapers. Placards on streetcars described the food as "A breakfast treat—that makes you eat." Pitch men paraded on streets across America, dressed up as ears of corn or boxes of corn-flakes. Canvassers went ahead of advertising and distribution, giving away small sample boxes of cereal, an industry first. In one town, the chalk *X*'s made on fenceposts by these door-to-door canvassers terrified the inhabitants, who believed they were marked for robbery or some-thing worse.

An insurance man from St. Louis, Charles D. Bolin, gave W. K. his next break. Staying and eating as a patient at the San, Bolin tasted corn-flakes and got the bug. He urged W. K. to start up a company to manu-facture the flakes. The two proposed the option to the Doctor, who was too absorbed by other distractions to leap into a new expensive food venture.

Bolin and W. K. changed their tack and offered the Doctor another option—separate the cornflake business from his other eclectic business interests and let W. K. and Bolin run the operation in exchange for a large block of stock. It took six months of convincing but finally Dr. Kellogg agreed. W. K. incorporated the Battle Creek Toasted Corn Flake Com-pany on February 19, 1906. The company that became the Kellogg Com-pany in 1925, and in 1992 earned $6.1 billion in revenue, started making cornflakes in a building that W. K. described as "an old fire trap."

There was conflict between the two brothers about what to call their cornflakes. The Doctor preferred the name Sanitas, which W. K. found distasteful. Finally, while the Doctor was again traveling, W. K. came to a decision. He called the breakfast-food creation "Kellogg's Toasted Corn Flakes." To differentiate Kellogg's cornflakes from the numerous knock-offs that appeared on the market, and to benefit from the health-giving resonance of the Kellogg name, W. K. left a signature line on each package in bold red letters, a line that he had actually started using on boxes of Sanitas Toasted Corn Flakes in 1903. It read, "Beware of Imita-tions. None Genuine Without This Signature, W. K. Kellogg."

Each box of cornflakes was W. K.'s declaration of independence from his nutty older brother. But before he could claim that independence, a revolution had to take place within the Kellogg kingdom.

FAKE FLAKES

In 1911, exactly 107 brands of cornflakes besides Kellogg's were being packaged in Battle Creek by entrepreneurs hoping to cash in on the cereal boom. According to the Kellogg Company newsletter, the *Kellogg's Square Dealer*, these brands included: Bon Ton Brand Corn Crisps, HoneyMoon Brand Corn Flakes, Korn-Kinks, Eureka Corn Flakes, Autumn Leaf Brand Corn Flakes, Maz-All, Squirrel Brand Corn Flakes, Child's Toasted Corn Flakes, Luck Boy Corn Flakes, Corn-O-Plenty, Sunbeam Corn Flakes, Sunset Brand Corn Flakes, Blue Bird Oven Baked Flaked Corn, Buffalo Brand Oven Baked Flaked Corn, White Bear Brand Corn Flakes, Elk Brand Corn Flakes, University Brand Daintily-Crisped Flaked Corn, None-Such Brand Corn Flakes Toasted, Indian Corn Flakes, Chief Corn Flakes, Jane Justice Brand Corn Flakes, Krebs Breakfast Flaked Corn, Cecelia Brand Toasted Corn Flakes, Hazel Brand Toasted Corn Flakes, Dr. Beltrand's Toasted Ready-to-Eat Corn Flakes, Dr. Price's Corn Flakes, and the generic-sounding Blanke's Toasted Korn-Flake. "It was a grand orgy of frenzied finance in luxuriant growth from which the small investor who lost sauntered down the road talking to himself," observed John K. Lippen, research food chemist with both the Kellogg Toasted Corn Flake Company and the original Postum Company.

The Flaming Sword

The Kellogg boys despised and adored each other, as only brothers could. W. K. referred to himself as "J. H.'s flunkey," a "bookkeeper, cashier, packing and shipping clerk, errand boy and general utility man." Dr. Kellogg, who was characterized by a close associate as "the kindest and the harshest man I ever knew," ridiculed his younger brother and often referred to him as a "loafer." Even when the Doctor tried to be nice it didn't work out. When he invited W. K. over to his house for a leisurely stroll in the garden, one of the Doctor's pet deer attacked W. K. and trampled him.

Their disagreements were numerous and heated, but the major eruption between the two brothers occurred in 1900. While the Doctor was in Europe consulting with Pavlov about his recent experiments with drooling dogs, W. K. raised $50,000 and invested it in the construction of a desperately needed food-production facility. W. K.'s financial accomplishment infuriated the Doctor. Claiming that his younger brother did not have the authority to approve such an arrangement, the Doctor ordered W. K. to pay back every penny. "I guess my father did not like that very well," mused W. K.'s son John L. Kellogg.

W. K. managed to scrape the $50,000 together but he was so fed up with his older brother that he quit his position at the San, a job he had slaved at for more than twenty years. Six months later, W. K. was drawn back temporarily to the San, like a moth to a flame.

Early in the morning of February 18, 1902, a fire broke out at the Battle Creek Sanitarium and burned America's premier health establishment to the ground. Some claimed that it was an accident. Others, like Sister White, believed that it had been ordained. Shortly before the fire, Sister White had had a vision of a "flaming sword" that engulfed and purified the church. She characterized the fire as punishment, both for the Battle Creek Adventist community and for Dr. Kellogg, who had gotten far too high and mighty. Still others believed the fire was set by angry Adventists. After all, there had been a fire at the Sanitarium Health Food Company in 1898, a fire at the Sanitas Food Company in 1900, and eleven other fires in the area of the Sanitarium in the preceding few years.

No matter what the cause, Sister White declared, "the Lord is not very well pleased with Battle Creek" and moved the world headquarters of Adventism from the Michigan town to Tacoma Park, Maryland.

W. K. Kellogg realized that he had given too much of his life to the San to see it go up in flames. Showing almost superhuman determination, he went back to work for the brother he detested and raised the funds to rebuild the health institution into an even more glorious temple to biologic living. With uncharacteristic feeling, he said of this experience, "These two and one half years which completed my work of twenty-five years with the San were the hardest of my life, and no amount of money would tempt me to repeat those years."

Fed up with his brother and the San, W. K. turned his attention to the Battle Creek Toasted Corn Flake Company. When it was set up,

W. K. owned only a third of the company's shares. His big brother owned the majority of the stock. But with characteristic business abandon Dr. Kellogg distributed a large block of his stock to the Sanitarium staff in lieu of payment and left for Moscow to discuss the latest breakthroughs in Russian psychology. In a deft corporate takeover, W. K. nibbled away at the stock, buying it in pieces here and there until he became the majority shareholder. At the age of forty-six he was finally his own man, the real power behind the cornflake.

The Battle of the Bran

Within six months of founding the company, W. K. was putting out 2,900 cases of cornflakes a day. The competition was fierce. Before 1912, more than 100 different companies tried to break into the cornflake business. Post used industrial espionage to limit W. K.'s expansion. In 1907, a fire burned down W. K.'s plant. "The fire is of no consequence," said W. K. with his usual abruptness. "You can't burn down what you have registered in the mind of the American woman."

W. K. put Kellogg's Toasted Corn Flakes in the minds of American women with a relentless advertising campaign. "This announcement violates all the rules of good advertising," he proclaimed to the four million readers of the *Ladies Home Journal* in his first full-page magazine advertisement. Kellogg stated that the supply of cornflakes was so limited that only 10 percent of the women in America could buy them at the grocer. This, of course, inspired the other 90 percent to send in the coupon included in the ad so that they wouldn't be left out of the latest food trend.

Other campaigns added spice to cornflakes. In 1907 W. K. promoted Wink Day. Wink at your grocer, Kellogg encouraged the shoppers of America and see what you will get. Taking a chance at being slightly risqué, winking women increased cornflake sales in New York City alone from two carloads per month to two carloads per day.

W. K. humanized the Sweetheart of the Corn and chose a midwestern girl picked from the secretarial staff to carry the title in a million-dollar ad campaign. He flashed the words "Kellogg's Corn Flakes" on an eighty-ton iron billboard atop the Mecca Building in Times Square. Another massive sign built at the corner of Adams and State Streets in Chicago showed a youngster's crying face with the words "I Want Kellogg's," changing to a smile with the words "I got Kellogg's." W. K. even courted the press. He conducted the first ever airborne taste test, serving cereal to a group of reporters as they flew in a plane. Sales of cornflakes soared to over a million cases a year.

W. K. Kellogg put a large chunk of his funds into one proven product mover, the premium. In 1851 Benjamin Talbott Babbitt introduced Americans to the commercial premium when he offered a full-color lithographic "panel picture" for twenty-five wrappers from his Sweet Home Laundry Soap. Soap sales soared, Babbitt became a millionaire, and premiums began to inundate the American consumer. Kellogg's most popular premium was the "Funny Jungleland Moving Picture Booklet," a colorful publication with dozens of costumed animals pictured on split pages, allowing children to mix and match the heads, bellies, and legs of the critters. From 1909 to 1933, grocers distributed more than 43 million copies of the booklet to customers who bought two boxes of cornflakes.

W. K. proved to be an astonishingly good, if reserved, manager. His memory was as remarkable as his older brother's. Instead of being fascinated by scientific data, W. K. was riveted by business statistics—sales, car loadings, the price of grain, cash reports. In his wallet, where most men carry pictures of their family, the cornflake baron carried a consolidated statement of company earnings. He toured his facilities constantly, taking particular notice of the odd radiator that was left on too high or the lamp that was burning needlessly. "That is wasteful," was one of his most severe reprimands. An insomniac who always kept a notebook by his bed, Kellogg reported to the office one morning with forty new advertising, sales, and production ideas.

Dr. Kellogg was jealous of his little brother's success and felt betrayed. After all, he reasoned, it was his genius and his reputation that had given rise to his sibling's fortune. When W. K. changed the name of the Battle Creek Toasted Corn Flake Company to the Kellogg Toasted Corn Flake Company, the Doctor responded by changing the name of his Sanitas Nut Food Company to the Kellogg Food Company.

There was tremendous confusion between the two Battle Creek Kelloggs. Even the post office had a hard time telling the companies apart. Rumors circulated that W. K. had defrauded his older brother, causing W. K. to write the following words to the Doctor. "For twenty-two and one-half years, I had absolutely lost all my individuality in you. I tried to see things through your eyes and do things as you would do them. You know in your heart whether or not I am a rascal. You also know whether or not I would defraud anyone under any circumstances."

The battling brothers ended up in court. In 1910, W. K. sued his older brother to enjoin him from using the Kellogg name either as a corporate name or as a descriptive name of food. The Doctor claimed that he had only given his brother permission to sell one product in one

---

W. K. KELLOGG'S LAST LAUGH

Raised in the shadow of his brilliant older brother, W. K. Kellogg was a reclusive and self-effacing man. Painfully shy, he peered out from under a green eye shade at the office and traveled under a pseudonym to avoid detection. He was extremely sensitive as well. Early cornflake package copy that read, "the original bears this signature" was changed to "the original has this signature" because W. K., long the butt of his brother's jokes, didn't want to be likened to a bear. In his later years, as he lost his eyesight, W. K. took to raising Arabian horses and touring the country in a chauffeured bus outfitted with beds, bath, and dining table. So grim was the cereal businessman that according to legend, the only time he smiled was when his seeing-eye dog, a direct descendant of Rin Tin Tin, suffered from flatulence in a small room packed with staff gathered for a sales meeting. Even then, W. K. didn't smile much.

---

territory. The case was settled out of court in W. K.'s favor a year later.

The hatred between the two brothers surfaced again in 1916 over the marketing of a relatively unknown food—bran. Dr. Kellogg asked the courts to restrain his brother from attaching the name Kellogg to a new product, Toasted Bran Flakes, as he himself sold 600,000 boxes a year of a cereal called Kellogg's Sterilized Bran. The case came to trial in 1917 and John Harvey Kellogg lost on every major point. Not only was W. K. allowed to market his new bran cereal, but Dr. Kellogg was forbidden to use the word "Kellogg" as any part of the name or title of any food product. This ruling was sustained by the Michigan Supreme Court in 1920 and a court order shut the case down in 1921. Testifying in court during the heat of the "Battle of the Bran," as the fight became known, W. K. knew what he wanted—control of a business, not a revolution in America's health. "I have never claimed any glory," he told the court. "The Doctor has claimed all that."

I Don't Like Applesauce

Though he did not collect glory, the younger Kellogg made vastly more money than his older brother. Unlike the older Kellogg, who felt comfortable spending money on travel, research, and grandiose projects, W. K. felt slightly uncomfortable with his riches. "I never had a taste for high living," he claimed accurately.

His years of endless work made him awkward in social situations. "I don't care greatly to be seen of men," he was fond of saying. The recreational activity he enjoyed most was sleep, a luxury that he could best enjoy while traveling on ocean cruises to Europe, the West Indies, Africa or Australia, or motoring with a chauffeur in his self-designed recreational vehicle, known as the Ark.

Kellogg did fulfill one boyhood fantasy. In memory of his old horse Spot, he created an Arabian horse ranch in Pomona, California. Kellogg's horses rode in films like *The Son of the Sheik, The Lives of a Bengal Lancer,* and *The Garden of Allah.* Though Rudolph Valentino, Tom Mix, Clara Bow, Will Rogers, the *Our Gang* kids, and other Hollywood celebrities frequented the ranch, Kellogg rarely mingled with them and never rode, preferring to watch his horses from afar.

W. K. had three children who grew to adulthood, but they brought him little comfort. His son John Leonard was the only one who joined in the business, but he resigned when W. K. interfered in his private life. For a time it seemed that W. K.'s grandson, John L. Jr., would become King Kellogg. But W. K. was disappointed once again when John L. Jr. left the company after conflicting with his grandfather over the ownership rights to a new type of corn-processing technique.

John set up his own company, Food Town Kitchens, and set out to market cheese-coated puffed corn. As his enterprise faltered in 1937, John made overtures to General Mills to see if they were interested in buying the corn-puffing technology. When W. K. Kellogg learned of this he promptly sued his grandson. The suit put John in a serious cash crunch. The twenty-six-year-old newlywed, with a baby on the way, saw no way out of his desperate situation. He committed suicide in his small Chicago office in the winter of 1938 by "swallowing a shotgun" according to his friend Jim McQuiston, assistant treasurer of the Kellogg Company. The corn-puffing process that indirectly caused the death of John L. Kellogg Jr. was adopted by the Kellogg Company some fifteen years later and used to create the cereal known as Corn Pops.

W. K. had much more luck with other people's children. On June 7, 1930, he established the W. K. Kellogg Foundation as a "child welfare foundation" and left it with an endowment of some $47 million. The foundation currently holds 35 percent of the stock of the Kellogg Company, worth some $2 billion, and has dispersed more than $1.5 billion to fund everything from improvements in California's middle schools to fish-pond building in Honduras to programming on the Public Broad-casting System. To the end, W. K. shunned the corporate and philan-thropic limelight. "I don't like applesauce," was how he verbalized his displeasure at people who made a scene.

Dr. Kellogg continued to make a scene for the rest of his life. Expelled from the Adventist Church for writing pantheistic statements like "God is not behind nature nor above nature; He is in nature" and for doubting the infallibility of Sister White, Dr. Kellogg nevertheless plunged ahead with his work at the Sanitarium. He continued to spew out healthy food creations—bags of gluten flour; Zo, the "Vitamin Breakfast Food"; Sanitarium Cooked Bran; Sanitarium Fig & Bran Flakes; Laxa, a combination wheat bran and agar; and Para-lax mineral oil, "a thick, creamy emulsion" to lubricate crippled bowels.

In 1929, Dr. Kellogg displayed his unique lack of business sense by plunging deep into debt to finance a massive expansion of the San. Reve-nues plunged with the Great Depression and changing lifestyles made health spas and dyspepsia old-fashioned. Dr. Kellogg and his dedicated staff struggled to keep the biologic dream alive. The Doctor established a more modest clinic in Florida, but in 1942, the San defaulted on its debt. The U.S. government purchased the health colossus and turned it into an amputee rehabilitation hospital. Today, Dr. Kellogg's dream is an office complex for the Civil Defense Administration.

Undaunted by his defeat, Dr. Kellogg vowed to take the $750,000 in liquid assets from the sale and rebuild. He moved across the street from the San to the fieldstone building formerly owned by C. W. Post and began promoting the Battle Creek Idea once again. W. K. couldn't resist the opportunity to annoy his fallen big brother. He helped the Adventist church file a claim for the funds from the sale of the Sanitar-ium. The two brothers, one eighty-eight the other eighty, found them-selves wrestling in the courts like two stubborn school kids.

The Doctor managed to hang on to a third of the money but the fight wore him out. Soon after the scrap, the two brothers who had fought, quarreled, and worked together for more than sixty years met for a long chat. W. K. encouraged J. H. to sell out and set something aside for his old employees. J. H. declared that he was ready to rebuild the San, that he was being rejuvenated by a mixture of malt, honey, vita-mins, and minerals and expressed concern that the use of tobacco by the army would cause the United States to lose World War II. The Doctor also confessed that he had wasted a great deal of time in his life by talk-ing unnecessarily.

Nearing the end of his life, the Doctor—who still enjoyed being photographed in his all-white suit with a cockatoo perched on his shoulder—heaved a contented sigh and admitted that he had "done pretty well for a grass eater." The Moses of the breakfast table, the man who led Americans from the apocalypse to calorie counting, died peacefully in his sleep in 1943, aged ninety-one years and ten months.

W. K. did not resign from the board of Kellogg until May, 1946, when he was eighty-five years old. Blinded by glaucoma, he liked nothing better than to be driven to a side street near the sprawling Kellogg plant, roll down his windows, and park for long periods of time "just to hear the noises from the factory."

While his older brother left his forty-two adopted children little more than a legacy of dietary principles, W. K. left one of America's best-managed corporations and a philanthropic legacy worth billions. The man who once bluntly summarized his career with the phrase "business built on advertising," died on October 6, 1951 at the age of ninety-one years and seven months. His body lay in state—in an open mahogany casket—in Kellogg's main office lobby from Monday afternoon until Tuesday morning so employees "from all shifts could pay their respects," according to Kellogg Company literature. In addition, more than three thousand Battle Creek townspeople shuffled by, while long-time Kellogg's employees acted as ushers. He was buried in the Kellogg family plot at Battle Creek's Oak Hill Cemetery, near his brother John Harvey Kellogg. Marking his grave is a modest bronze sundial, decorated with the sculpture of an early bird, a robin, pulling a worm out of the earth. The sculpture is a fitting memorial to the hard-working, early-rising, self-critical breakfast cereal millionaire who once said, "I was so overloaded with work that I am conscious that very little, if any of it, was performed satisfactorily."

II

The Dawn of the Grain Gods

6

Some Like It Hot and Mushy

While the twentieth century ushered in the age of the American cereal flake, one hot breakfast dish remained the favorite in the land. Oatmeal. Ever since colonial times, Americans have valued their oats. Court records show that a resident of colonial Virginia who stole three pints of oatmeal "had a bodkinge thrust through his tounge and was tyed with a chaine to a tree until he starved." In 1610, a native of Jamestown was accused of killing and eating his wife. Though the defendant admitted he had indeed killed his formerly beloved, he claimed that the action was motivated by hatred not hunger. The court ruled in his favor, noting that the alleged cannibal had in his home "a good quantitie of meale, oat-meale, beanes and pease," along with the severed body parts of the not-so-dearly departed.

Benjamin Franklin praised the therapeutic value of oatmeal gruel, as did the Philadelphia College of Pharmacy in their 1826 publication, *The Druggist's Manual*. In the eighteenth and early nineteenth centuries, druggists were the primary oatmeal merchants, dispensing the grain as a food for invalids. One popular book of the era, *The Cook's Oracle, Instituted in the Kitchen of a Physician*, recommended oatmeal "to the rational Epicure" as "the most comforting soother of an irritable stomach that we know—and particularly acceptable to it after a hard day's work of intemperate feasting."

The Oatmeal King

It was a German grocer named Ferdinand Schumacher who brought oatmeal from the American medicine closet to the kitchen pantry. In 1850, the twenty-eight-year-old Schumacher moved to the United States, settled with some relatives in Ohio, and married a German girl. The couple moved to Akron where Schumacher got into the grocery business, the only business he knew. He began the common practice of grinding oatmeal in the back of his store and selling it as an over-the-counter remedy. A man who knew his own place in history, Schumacher wrote in his book *Oatmeal: Its History,* "As late as 1856, the entire supply used by the American people . . . came from Scotland or Canada. It was then kept in drug stores as a remedial agent, and was hardly known as an article of dietetic value."

Schumacher's oatmeal proved so popular that he decided to increase his production and promote oats as a food, not just a remedy. He bought a water-powered woolen factory in Akron and converted it to an oatmeal mill. Grinding out 3,600 pounds of oatmeal a day, Schumacher renamed his operation the German American Oatmeal Factory.

The man who would be oatmeal king resembled a black-bearded C. Everett Koop. He was a short, wiry man with a large head and deep-set eyes who spoke in a thick German accent. He shunned the use of a stenographer or a typewriter and kept his books by hand. An ardent prohibitionist, he felt that alcohol "biteth like a serpent, and stingeth like an adder." Like the other cereal prophets, he was obsessed with his desire to conquer the American breakfast table; by the end of the Civil War he was the number one oatmeal producer in the land.

Though opposed to advertising in theory, Schumacher ran what is believed to be America's first cereal advertisement, which appeared in the *Akron Beacon* in 1870. The small printed announcement for "Rolled Avena" did not have as big an impact on Schumacher's oatmeal sales as did the huge influx of Scottish and Irish immigrants in the 1870s and 1880s. To meet the rapidly increasing demand for oatmeal, Schumacher opened a second oatmeal mill in Akron in 1883. Production increased to 360,000 pounds of oatmeal a day, which was shipped in 180-pound barrels to wholesalers in New England, New York, Pittsburgh, Chicago, Denver, and California. Two-pound export tins even made their way to Scotland, the land of oats. He was the largest employer and the biggest industrialist in Akron, truly the "Oatmeal King."

Three years after it opened, Schumacher's "Jumbo Mill" burned down. Unfortunately, the tight-fisted king was uninsured. "They wanted a fearful price for the premiums," he explained to a reporter after the fire. "I wouldn't pay." Worse yet, Schumacher quickly lost a huge bankroll speculating in water-power development and paper mills. His investments outside the oatmeal business were so bad that one of his colleagues joked that he needed only two bookkeeping entries, a debit for the initial speculation and a credit to "bad debt."

The man who was in a position to take advantage of Schumacher's misfortune was Henry Parsons Crowell. Born to an aristocratic New England family, Crowell suffered from tuberculosis, which killed his grandfather, his father, and his two brothers. He traveled west as a young man and made a pact with God that if his health improved, he would dedicate his talents to amassing money with which to finance Christian evangelism. Crowell's health did improve and he made himself a small fortune in western land speculation. For half a century thereafter he dedicated 65 percent of his earnings to Christian causes, most particularly the Moody Bible Institute headed up by Dwight L. Moody.

When he returned from the west, the blue-eyed Crowell settled in Cleveland where friends recommended that he purchase an oatmeal mill in Ravenna, Ohio. The mill was bankrupt but it did have one important asset—the brand name Quaker. The former mill owners Henry D. Seymour and William Heston both claimed to be the ones who had selected the Quaker name as a symbol of good quality and honest value. No matter which one had thought it up, America's first trademark for a breakfast cereal was filed as "the figure of a man in Quaker garb" with the U.S. patent office on August 17, 1877.

Crowell bought the Quaker Mill Company of Ravenna in November 1881. He immediately realized he had a problem—there was too much oatmeal on the market. Since it was all sold in bulk, price competition was ferocious. Like any good robber baron, Crowell contacted Schumacher and other millers and set up an oatmeal monopoly or trust under the corporate name the American Cereal Company in 1888. After a bitter proxy fight, Crowell, known as the "Godly Autocrat," ousted Schumacher, the "Oatmeal King," from the company and renamed it Quaker Oats in 1906.

Crowell eloquently explained the goals for the mighty oatmeal monopoly. "It was to scatter and diversify its business in all parts of the world and do educational and constructive work so as to awaken an interest in and create a demand for cereals where none existed. . . . Its policy . . . was to develop rapidly in all parts of the world, wherever oatmeal could be sold, an advertised brand." The advertised brand was, of course, Quaker Oats.

Autocrat of the Breakfast Table

If Post was the grandfather of American advertising, Crowell was the godfather of American merchandising. He realized that his package was the key to his success. Only with a package could Crowell hope to change oatmeal from a commodity to a valued consumer item. "This grocer dumps oats into a bin," the company magazine *The Daily Quaker* reported to its sales force, "Sets his rat traps on top of oats. Catches two

NOTHING IS BETTER FOR THEE THAN ME

A longstanding symbol of integrity, the "Man in Quaker garb" has been the Quaker Oats trademark since 1877. One of the best-known trademarks in the modern world, the Quaker man is still something of a controversial figure. Every year, a number of consumers contact the company, convinced that the Quaker is actually William Penn, founder of the Quaker colony which eventually became Pennsylvania. Quaker Oats maintains that the image is not based on William Penn, nor any other historical character.

Like Aunt Jemima, the Quaker Oats Quaker has changed with the times. Originally tall and dark, he became a robust Santa Claus–type in the 1940s. The fat Quaker was the creation of Harold Sunbloom, who illustrated the Coca Cola Santa and Rubenesque centerfold illustrations for *Playboy* magazine.

In 1990, the Quaker Oats Company launched a campaign dubbed Popeye the Quaker Man. The Religious Society of Friends objected to the use of the bellicose sailor in oatmeal ads, citing the church's centuries-old pacifism. "Quaker men do not go around resolving dispute and conflict by means of violence," said Elizabeth Foley, a spokesperson for members of the Quaker community. The Quaker Oats Company immediately ended the campaign and apologized, promising to be "sensitive to Friends' concerns" in the future.

rats the first night." The message was simple—bulk goods were "vile and dangerous to health."

Tin cans first appeared to feed the troops of Napoleon, glass bottles came to America in the 1820s, the first paper bag was patented in 1859, and the folding carton was developed in the 1870s, but Crowell chose a round carton emblazoned with a four-color Quaker to carry his oatmeal to the world. He realized that his box was his best sales pitch, and he worked tirelessly to get the Quaker everywhere. He handed out free samples and plastered the Quaker Oats trademark on the sides of buildings, on illuminated billboards, on streetcar cards, in grocery store windows, and on metal signs hung on rural fences. He even placed the words *Quaker Oats* on the White Cliffs of Dover, England, an act of marketing audacity that was condemned by the British Parliament.

He held cooking schools in grocery stores, set up exhibits at the Brooklyn Food Exhibition of 1891 and the 1893 Chicago World's Fair, stuffed his containers with the 24-page booklet *Quaker Nursery Rhymes,* the grasshopper circus comic book, and coupons good for the purchase of baby spoons and Turkish rockers. He flooded the mails with calendars, cookbooks, and blotters, and testified to the wonders of Quaker Oats on the backs of Sunday church bulletins. In 1891, Quaker Oats was introduced to Portland, Oregon, in a special Quaker Oats train that distributed free samples of Quaker Oats and garnered newspaper headlines from Ravenna, Ohio, to the West Coast.

Crowell launched educational programs in schools complete with charts, pictures, and booklets, quoting from noted men of science. "Non-flesh eaters have far greater endurance than those accustomed to the ordinary American diet," said Professor Fisher of Yale University, while Dr. Harvey W. Wiley, creator of the Pure Food and Drug Act, stated, "The cereal-eating nations of the world can endure more physical toil than the meat eaters."

Crowell advertised relentlessly in newspapers and periodicals such as the *Ladies Home Journal* and *Delineator,* in 1882 launching the first national magazine advertising campaign for a breakfast cereal. Advertisements pictured the Quaker bursting out from a shock of oats, cavorting with Little Lord Fauntleroy, emerging from a dark forest, floating on clouds, and standing as the central figure in a stained-glass window.

In 1898, he ran an illustration in several major periodicals showing a voluptuous, bare-breasted girl, sitting on a Quaker Oats box. "Ceres, fair goddess of the harvest fields, Now to the world her choicest treasure yields," read the caption, luring readers to the oatmeal toga party. "One pound of good beef costs as much as three pounds of Quaker Oats. One pound of Quaker Oats makes as much bone and muscle as three pounds of beef," stated more typical hard-selling Quaker copy. "Is that worth trying?"

In addition to conventional print advertising, Crowell distributed "blind" ads to the press—paid-for advertisements that looked like news stories. One of the most remarkable told the story of a "very charming young lady" who popped her head out of a train window to enjoy the passing scenery. Unfortunately, the train passed close by a telephone pole, with the result that the lady's neck was "completely telescoped between her shoulders." While her fellow passengers anxiously watched, a physician attended to her for nearly an hour. Finally, "there was a slight tremor of the limbs, a little flutter of the eyelids, and she opened her eyes . . . and a husky whisper escaped her lips, which the bystanders made out to be, 'Good morning, do you eat Quaker Rolled Oats?'"

Having conquered North America, Crowell went international. Quaker Oats fed the Boers and the English as they fought one another in South Africa. In Calcutta a brilliantly illuminated sign proclaimed Quaker Oats from the top of the Bristol Hotel. In Canton, China, billboards proclaimed "Old Man Brand Quaker Oats," while old-timers struggled to eat their oatmeal with chopsticks. From deep in the Congo a trader wrote, "In this land of malaria, black water fever and sleeping sickness, the sanitary watertight can of Quaker Oats has great appeal to the planter, missionary, hunter and pioneer."

The twenty-ounce Quaker Oats export tin traveled with Shackleton, Byrd, Perry, and Amundsen as they raced to the Poles. Scott didn't survive in his attempt, but his Quaker Oats did. Seventeen years after the failed expedition, a tin of Scott's Quaker Oats was opened, and the contents were found to be "altogether fresh and wholesome." In 1919, one Quaker executive told the company's stockholders, "We frequently hear that the sun never sets on the British flag. This saying can be applied even more literally to Quaker Oats."

There were those who attacked the Quaker. The Society of Friends, as the Quaker church is officially known, unsuccessfully petitioned Congress to restrain manufacturers from applying names of religious denominations to products intended for interstate commerce.

Others couldn't resist poking fun at the mushy foodstuff. In his dictionary, Samuel Johnson defined oats as "a grain which in England is generally given to horses, but in Scotland supports the people." Dr. Kellogg, an oatmeal hater, declared that one of his original reasons for creating the toasted cereal flake "was to displace the half-cooked, pasty, dyspepsia-producing breakfast mush."

A New York Times editorial, dated April 4, 1885, described oatmeal as "that execrable article of food." With oatmeal spoon securely in cheek, the editors warned that "the stomachs of our helpless little ones are ruined by oatmeal, and if the oatmeal craze continues the next generation of Americans will be as dyspeptic and Calvinistic as are the majority of Scotchmen."

The outraged management of Quaker Oats demanded a retraction, and the Times graciously agreed. "Oatmeal can no longer be held to be the cause of Scotch dyspepsia," the editors explained, "and there is good reason to believe that Carlyle owed his dyspepsia to his early exposure to bagpipes."

Despite such editorial jibes, Quaker Oats was the best selling breakfast cereal at the turn of the century, enjoying twelve million dollars in sales in 1899 alone. In a fitting tribute to the world's best-known cereal celebrity, Oliver Wendell Holmes dubbed the Quaker "The Autocrat of the Breakfast Table."

Rastus

Scottish thrift brought about the rise of another mushy cereal empire. During the financial panic of 1893 Thomson A. Amidon, the head miller at the Diamond Milling Company in Grand Forks, North Dakota, tried to save a little money by taking home "No. 1 purified middlins" for his wife to cook up as a porridge. It was nothing more than the coarse endosperm of the wheat kernel "purified" of all bran—wheat hijacked on the way to becoming flour. But it made such a tasty breakfast porridge that Amidon thought there would be a market for it.

The Scotsman pitched his idea to the owners of the mill. The three men—banker George Clifford, farmer George Bull, and newspaperman Emery Mapes—laughed at him. Why would anyone buy a box of wheat middlins from a mill in North Dakota, when each and every one of the thousands of flour mills across the country produced exactly the same product?

But Amidon persisted. He kept pestering his bosses. They, in turn, kept staring at their large, debt-ridden, underutilized mill. Finally they agreed to give Amidon's idea a try. The only thing they needed was a name. At a brainstorming session, George Clifford's brother Fred suggested that, since they were selling the best and whitest part of the wheat, they should call their product Cream of Wheat.

The partners agreed. Emery Mapes, who sported a walrus mustache and liked to be called "Colonel," dug around his printshop for a package design. He came up with an old woodcut of a black chef with a skillet slung over his shoulder. Amidon pasted together some packages with the woodcut on the cover, put them in ten crates he constructed from waste lumber, and loaded the crates into a train-car load of flour destined for the firm's New York brokers, Lamont, Corliss & Company. Three hours after the crudely designed packages hit the streets of the Big Apple, George Bull received a telegram from the brokers. According

THE CASE OF THE DISAPPEARING RASTUS

After first being introduced on packages of Cream of Wheat, Rastus became so popular that the cereal maker wished to hire him to model for more poses. Cream of Wheat executive Emery Mapes went in search of the cook he had first met traveling on the railroad. When Mapes couldn't find Rastus, artist David Brewer created a virtual Rastus by sculpting two clay busts of the chef. Brewer memorialized the birth of the clay figures in a painting entitled *A Proud Day for Rastus.* One of the busts sat in the office of Dan Bull, one of the company's co-founders. The other was used by artists to come up with new commercial renderings of the Cream of Wheat spokesman.

In the 1930s and 1940s, dozens of people claimed to be the original Rastus and sued Cream of Wheat. To counter the suits, the company hired a detective agency to track down the original model. The investigation continued for years, but Rastus was never found. The story told by Cream of Wheat executive Dave Bull was that Rastus, one of the most famous pitchmen in cereal history, "died in a knife fight somewhere in the slums of Chicago."

to breakfast lore, the telegram read, "Forget the flour. Send us a car of CREAM OF WHEAT."

The North Dakota boys abandoned their mill, formed the Cream of Wheat company, and moved to Minneapolis, the milling capital of the nothern plains. Soon after getting their first shipment out the door, "Colonel" Mapes was eating in a railroad dining car when he made the acquaintance of a black chef with a toothy grin. Mapes hired the chef to model for a picture used on boxes of Cream of Wheat. For his Cream of Wheat work, the chef, dubbed Rastus, was paid the sum of five dollars.

Under the advertising direction of "Colonel" Mapes, Rastus became one of the best-known images in American advertising. Rastus dolls, offered for only ten cents in stamps or coins and a box top, became one of the most popular premiums in American advertising history. In one ad, an old black man beamed over Rastus with the words "Dat's

Mah Boy!" During World War I, Rastus appeared in large posters "doing his bit" for the war effort.

Mapes balanced his Rastus campaign with full-page magazine ads featuring beautiful, full-color paintings by N. C. Wyeth, J. C. Leyendecker, Edward Brewer, and James Montgomery Flagg (who also created the famous Uncle Sam recruiting poster). Millions of Americans decorated their homes with these picture stories, the most famous of which pictured a cowhand delivering a letter to a frontier mailbox made from a Cream of Wheat crate. The ad bore the title, "Where the Mail Goes, Cream of Wheat goes."

I Dare You

One of the barons of hot cereal began his career feeding mush to horses, not people. In 1894, William H. Danforth teamed up with a friend to found the Robinson-Danforth Commission Company, peddling 175-pound sacks of feed with the slogan, "Cheaper Than Oats and Safer Than Corn."

After a tornado destroyed his feed plant in 1898, Danforth took a long, hard look at his business and decided that he would eventually make more money feeding people than livestock. He began to package and market a whole-wheat cereal, securing the endorsement of a prominent local health club president, Dr. Ralston. Ralston Wheat Cereal proved to be so popular that Danforth changed the name of his company to the Ralston Purina Company, taking the term *purina* from an earlier company slogan, "Where Purity is Paramount."

Danforth was convinced that eating Ralston was the key to a healthy lifestyle. He advertised that the tiny grains of Ralston were "full of the Vegetable Phosphorous that make children grow like magic and develop strong thinking." The cereal salesman kept himself in shape with a daily exercise routine that included touching the floor twenty times, twisting the liver fifty times, walking at least a mile, drinking a minimum of eight glasses of water, and eating Ralston to supply his brain with "all the phosphorous it can use in heavy thinking."

After his initial success with Ralston, Danforth put some heavy thinking into the search for a package. Reflecting on his childhood, he recalled the Browns, one of the most distinctive families in St. Louis. Everyone recognized the Browns, mainly because they all wore clothes made from the same material—red-and-white checkerboard cloth. If it worked for the Browns, Danforth thought, it will work for breakfast cereal. He put his products in checkerboard containers. He decorated walls, floors, and annual reports with checkerboards. He covered his headquarters building in the distinctive design. Even today, the site of the Ralston Purina Company headquarters in St. Louis is known as Checkerboard Square.

As his sales increased, Danforth added philosophy to his marketing mix. He wrote numerous self-help books, including *As a Man Thinketh*, *Power*, and *Random Ramblings in India*. He established self-betterment organizations including I Dare You Clubs, I Dare You Days, and I Dare You Programs, all designed to help people develop a "magnetic personality" by daring them to do their best. "Why not declare war?" Danforth lectured underachievers. "Why not put a bomb under your capabilities?"

Danforth knew each of his employees by name, refused to let them smoke on the job, and led them in morning and afternoon exercise sessions. After World War I, he began to call his animal feed products *chow*, borrowing a term for victuals popularized by the doughboys fighting in Europe. Once *chow* was introduced, any Ralston Purina employee who used the word *feed* was fined one dollar.

Danforth was always one to turn adversity into advantage. In 1904 he received a shipment of mis-sized checkerboard sacks. Instead of destroying the small sacks, he handed them out as free shopping bags during the St. Louis World's Fair, an exposition celebrating the Centennial of the Louisiana Purchase. Fair-goers clutched their checkerboard sacks as they sampled the world's newest junk foods—ice-cream cones and small sausages served on rolls, dubbed *hot dog*s. But they had to sit in bleachers to witness the Fair's premier exhibit of hi-tech food preparation.

A squadron of ordinance experts wheeled out eight red-hot brass cannons on a narrow-gauge railroad track. They halted the cannons in a huge cage, forty feet wide and two stories tall. At a given command, workmen knocked the covers from the artillery, sending forth a tremendous roar and filling the air with tiny, white, flavored nuggets. The attendants gathered up the edible bits, covered them with caramel, boxed them, and sold them to the amazed witnesses, including President Teddy Roosevelt. In all his days as a Rough Rider, the chief executive never dreamed that artillery could actually make puffed rice.

Shot from Guns

The man who unleashed the explosive puffing power of cereal was Dr. Alexander P. Anderson. A gaunt, thin-faced cereal enthusiast, Anderson devoted his life to uncovering the secrets of the grain cell. He began his quest while studying chemical biology at the University of Minnesota. Fascinated by starch, Anderson posed the question: Could the starch in grains be broken down to make it more digestible?

Thoughts like this filled Anderson's expansive cranium. Peering through his octagonal rimless spectacles, he read of research done at the University of Munich. He traveled to Bavaria in 1895 and watched in wonder as the foremost men of German science heated rice in test tubes and examined its changed composition. Anderson borrowed their laboratory to carry on his own experiments. His German colleagues warned him not to seal the ends of his test tubes or the steam released from the heated starch molecules in the grain might cause trouble.

The impetuous American ignored their advice. Closing the door, he put some rice in a test tube, sealed it tight, screened the apparatus with wire mesh, and slowly heated it with a Bunsen burner. After about an hour it happened. BOOM! The tube exploded. Anderson was amazed at the transformation that had taken place in the detonated rice grains. "That was as good a puffed rice as was ever puffed anywhere," he later declared.

Anderson returned to the United States, accepted a teaching position at Columbia University, and continued his explosive experiments at the New York Botanical Gardens. As he filled his work space with shattered test tubes and puffed grains, he learned more about the process; he was granted a patent in 1902. Looking for ways to bring the attention of the world to his creation, Anderson traveled to his native Minnesota and sought backing from the Quaker Oats Company.

The oatmen were intrigued. Crowell and his associates had made several attempts to branch out from mush to crunch. Quaker had actually purchased a plant in Battle Creek to produce cold cereals, including Zest, Brittle Bits, Toasted Corn Flakes, Toasted Wheat Flakes, and Apetizo, described as "the Great Hemoglobin Producer." None of these products proved to be a great success, but the possibilities of puffed cereal were attractive enough that the management of Quaker offered to fund Anderson's work if he would assign them his present and future patents.

Anderson agreed to the Quaker proposal. He built a secret laboratory in an old grain bin at the Empire Mill in Chicago. This was Quaker's first research laboratory—a space that was three stories high, yet had only ten square feet of floor space. Under strict security, Anderson continued his experiments using glass tubes, metal tubes, and an improvised cannon to blow up millet, barley, buckwheat, and any other grain he could lay his hands on. Mused one Quaker Oats executive, "It's a wonder he didn't blow himself up."

Though his experiments were successful, Anderson could not figure out how to explode enough grains to make large-scale production practical. An engineer for the company tried to develop a workable system in a machine shop in Akron. Several of his experiments tore out the building's floor, and eventually his workmen refused to go near the place. Myron T. Herrick, the governor of Ohio and a Quaker Oats board member, put the engineer in touch with a U. S. army artillery officer in Cleveland. The military expert successfully adapted a breach-loading recoiling cannon used during the Spanish American War. It was this army surplus weaponry that was displayed at the St. Louis World's Fair and has been used by the company in modified form ever since.

It took more than cannons to launch puffed cereals as a staple of the breakfast table. It took a marketing boom sparked by advertising man Albert D. Lasker. A native of Galveston, Texas, Lasker made his mark in journalism at the age of eighteen by getting an exclusive interview in 1893 with the controversial labor leader Eugene V. Debs. He moved into the world of advertising and took a position with the Chicago firm of Lord & Thomas, one of the ten to fourteen ad agencies that existed in the United States at that time. As a young ad man at the turn of the century, Lasker traveled through Battle Creek and saw the cereal boom in all its glory. Lasker, who later was to popularize the concept of orange juice and make Palmolive the leading toilet soap in the world, managed to land the Quaker Oats account in 1908.

Five years later Lasker took on the task of improving the sale of Puffed Rice, which the Quaker Company was then promoting as something of a novelty in ads featuring Japanese puffed rice eaters. "Advertising to the American people that you're going to 'Japanify' them is not an appeal," Lasker explained. He convinced the company to increase the price of the product from $.10 to $.12, to cover the cost of advertising.

To help create the campaign, Lasker relied on the talents of Claude C. Hopkins, a man he described as "the greatest copywriter who ever lived." Hopkins, a penny-pinching workaholic who used his copywriting magic to boost sales of everything from carpet sweepers to hearing aids, created his masterpiece in the 1913 campaign for Puffed Rice. After wandering through a few puffing factories, Hopkins advised, "They should advertise the process, because they have something unique there." The slogan Hopkins suggested was "The Grains That Are Shot From Guns."

The new ad campaign boosted sales tenfold and brought puffed cereal into the American pantry mainstream. It was probably the most effective campaign ever created by Lord & Thomas, a situation that led to a close bonding between the puffers and the pitchmen. At one point, Crowell, the chairman of the board of Quaker Oats and president of the Moody Bible Institute, invited Albert Lasker in for a surprise meeting. "I prayed to God all night to give me the courage to say what I am going to say to you," Crowell said. "One thing, and one thing only, separates us, the fact that you are a Jew. It is a great deal to ask, but would you consider renouncing your religion and joining ours?"

Lasker was astonished by the request. He refused. "But I can tell you this," Lasker offered diplomatically. "When it comes time for you to be taken from us here on earth, you will be welcome in *our* heaven."

7

Spoon in Tomorrow

As a post–World War I boom overtook the country, cereal makers wrung their hands and gazed heavenward for an answer to their marketing prayers. They didn't have far to look, for filling the sky was radio.

The mysterious whirrs, whines, and screeches of radio were first introduced to many American homes through boxes of Quaker Oats. In the early 1920s, the company gave away more than a million crystal radio sets designed to be mounted on top of empty Quaker Oats containers. In addition to providing hardware, Quaker Oats and the other cereal companies quickly became leading producers of radio programming, exerting a powerful influence over the American imagination and the media.

The First Jingle

At the dawn of the jazz age a radio frenzy gripped the United States. There was only one radio station in 1920. By 1923, 536 stations jammed the airwaves as newspapers, banks, pharmacies, creameries, chiropractic colleges, poultry farms, hardware stores, police departments, churches, goat gland specialists, and tractor mechanics jumped onto their own portion of the unregulated electromagnetic spectrum. So did Donald Davis, the athletic thirty-something secretary of the Minneapolis-based milling company that made Gold Medal Flour.

In 1924, Davis teamed up with the city of Minneapolis and a group of businessmen to buy a floundering local radio station, increase its power, and bring it back on the air. Davis dubbed the reborn station WCCO, letters that stood for his employer, the Washburn Crosby Company, which changed its name four years later to General Mills.

In the same year that Donald Davis introduced his company to the radio business, the flour-milling enterprise launched another experimental venture: the production and marketing of a ready-to-eat breakfast cereal. General Mills hagiographers maintain that their whole-wheat flake was developed by a Minneapolis health nut named

Mennen Minniberg, but it is much more likely that the cereal was the product of deliberate corporate planning. "Each cereal company invents its own mythology," explained John Long, long-time art buyer for the Leo Burnett advertising agency. "Every generation has done it all the way back to that Chinese emperor who destroyed everything of his predecessors to be sure China started with him. What General Mills did with Wheaties isn't particularly new to mankind."

Donald Davis's boss at General Mills was James Ford Bell, a man ever on the lookout for products that would appeal to what he described as "those sensitive little nerves that fringe the tongue . . . [and] . . . carry messages from the human tongue to the human pocketbook." A sophisticated executive whose father had run the business before him, Bell was undoubtedly aware of the inroads that the wheat flake had made into the American pocketbook. Edward Ellsworth had made a fortune with the wheat flake Force. When poor financial management forced Force to cut back its operations, both Post and Kellogg introduced their own wheat flakes to the market.

Bell's company did the same, going so far as to establish their wheat-flake production facility just a few hundred yards from the old Force plant in Buffalo, New York. With production under way, the company held a contest to see who could come up with a name for their new taste treat. Jane Bausman, the wife of a New York export manager, thought about appealing words for other things, like "movies" for moving pictures or "Post Toasties" for cornflakes. She won the contest with the simple diminutive epithet "Wheaties."

The initial marketing push for Wheaties in the winter of 1924 met with a resounding hush. It was then that Donald Davis decided to introduce breakfast cereal to the airwaves.

Late in 1926 Davis met with Earl Gammons, the manager of WCCO, and asked him to devise a special advertising campaign for Wheaties to "find out what that radio station of ours is good for." Gammons came up with an advertising breakthrough that forever changed the American media landscape: the first singing commercial.

On Christmas Eve, 1926, a quartet consisting of an undertaker, a bailiff, a printer and a businessman began singing a plaintive refrain to the tune of "She's a Jazz Baby":

> Have you tried Wheaties?
> They're whole wheat with all of the bran.
> Won't you try Wheaties?
> For wheat is the best food of man.

Skippy and the Lindbergh Baby

For the next six years, the group that became known as the Wheaties Quartet performed a half-hour program on WCCO of musical selections and advertising jingles for the fee of six dollars per week, a price that station management felt was "not too much if it worked." Unfortunately, it didn't work well enough for the management of General Mills. In 1929, the company was ready to drop the brand. Samuel Chester Gale of the advertising department came to the rescue of Wheaties. The man who was later to create Betty Crocker convinced the board that Wheaties would sell if advertised over the new coast-to-coast radio network, the Columbia Broadcasting System.

The Wheaties Quartet, redubbed the Gold Medal Fast Freight, went national with its tuneful broadcasts. Gale's instincts were proven right as sales of Wheaties tripled during the first year of national advertising and quadrupled during the second. Convinced that broadcast advertising could sell cereal, Gale, Davis, and the other managers at General Mills decided to aim directly at a huge and virtually untapped ocean of restless and gullible consumer power—kids.

The man they chose to deliver the kiddie market was Frank Hummert, the broadcasting guru at the Chicago ad agency of Blackett Sample Hummert. A mysterious, hard-nosed executive who told people that he had once served with the Texas Rangers, Hummert was the person responsible for creating continuing daytime radio dramas, purchasing airtime from the radio networks, and convincing soap companies to pay for the whole thing. As creator of the soap operas, Hummert was the most powerful man in broadcasting during the golden age of radio, the country's highest-paid advertising executive, and something of a jerk. "All clients are pigs," he once told a young David Ogilvy.

Hummert had worked with the "pigs" at General Mills to create *Betty and Bob,* a daytime drama sponsored by Gold Medal Flour. For Wheaties, Hummert looked to the Sunday funny papers, the same source he had used to create the immensely popular *Radio Orphan Annie* program for his client Ovaltine. The character Hummert picked for his cereal opera was Skippy, the Bart Simpson of his day, a naughty cartoon kid with a catlike ability to get in and out of trouble.

The Skippy radio program went airborne on station WMAQ-Chicago on August 3, 1931. With exciting adventures and numerous plugs for Wheaties, the fifteen-minute daily show was an instant hit. "The kiddies loved 'Skippy,' and Wheaties became a household word," wrote James Thurber. "You could get all the paraphernalia [a code book, instructions for a secret handshake] by sending in box tops, or facsimiles, and a signed statement from your mother that you ate Wheaties twice a day." In addition to the Skippy Secret Service Society, or S. S. S. S., which drew more than half a million responses, Thurber described another Skippy promotion—a contest for a trip to Chicago and a week of entertainment. Unfortunately, Thurber noted, the winner "turned out to be a difficult brat who hated Wheaties and whose many brothers and sisters had helped him send in more facsimiles of the Wheaties box top than any other contestant."

Skippy was not only the first cereal hero, he was the first one to be yanked off the air. On March 1, 1932, the producers aired an episode of Skippy in which one of his good friends was kidnapped. The next day, the nation was shocked to learn of the most famous real-life kidnapping in American history—that of Charles Augustus Lindbergh Jr., the Lindbergh baby.

Skippy's writers pounded out a new script that quickly brought the fictional kidnapping to a happy conclusion, but it was too late. Besieged by letters and calls from parents outraged at what they perceived as a crass attempt to profit from the Lindbergh's family misfortune, General Mills began to have second doubts about Skippy. When the kidnapping controversy was followed by a demand for more money by Skippy's creator, Percy Crosby, General Mills canceled the show. The company managed to maintain good relations with Lindy himself, who actually pitched Wheaties at one time as the way to "start the day right."

Other cereal companies had equally difficult early experiences with broadcasting. A radio campaign for Cream of Wheat featured the pampered offspring of the Rockefellers, the Astors, the Vanderbilts, and other American aristocrats. As the Great Depression put millions out of work, the campaign became a public relations disaster. "It was not selling Cream of Wheat," recalled Dave Bull, grandson of one of the company founders. "Studies found that people rightly said, 'Well, I don't care what the Vanderbilts are doing . . . I'm not driving a Rolls Royce like they are . . . I just gotta get by in life!'"

Another Cream of Wheat–sponsored program, *Jolly Bill and Jane,* was met by a storm of protest from mothers objecting to its content. Cream of Wheat pulled the show and replaced it with a talk show featuring Angelo Patrix, a respected but dull child expert. The mush merchants fired the educator and hired fictional space hero Buck Rogers until parents complained that his zapping death ray was too violent for kids. As *Fortune* magazine reported, "with little listeners demanding stronger and stronger meat and parent groups demanding the opposite, the company got off the air in 1936." A short time later the company got back into broadcasting with an appropriate advertising vehicle for its warm wheat cereal: weather reports.

Tom Mix

Another mush had better luck splattering itself across the airwaves. In 1932 the St. Louis–based Gardner Agency lost its lucrative Hot Ralston account to Batten, Barton, Durstine & Osborn, Inc. in New York. Gardner assigned twenty-something writers Charles Claggett and Margaret O'Reilly to come up with a scheme to lure the account back home. Claggett described Hot Ralston as "a hot cereal which kids hated" but decided to tear a page from Skippy and sell parents through their kids.

The two young writers interviewed school children and discovered that the most popular hero among seven- to twelve-year-olds was Tom Mix, "the King of the Silent Film Cowboys." Anyone who met Mix knew why *silent* was the operative word in his title. The cowboy hero spoke in a high, squeaky Oklahoma drawl, completely unsuitable for a he-man in talking pictures.

By the time Ralston ad man Claggett met him, the handsome stunt man with the great name ID was broke. While kids remembered his silent movie appearances, Mix, who was once the highest-paid man in Hollywood, had burned through his money and could get no work. The silent film star was thrilled to have a cereal endorsement deal land on his lap. He agreed to a five-year stint as the Hot Ralston pitchman and signed his name to a contract written on the back of an envelope.

In 1933, Tom Mix rode onto the breakfast table and stayed there for seventeen years. "First you had to get kid's attention, then you get his loyalty," recalled writer Claggett on the magic of the Mix program. "And once their hero tells them to do something, they do it. It's that simple." A full-page Tom Mix comic strip ad promoting the Ralston Straight-Shooters Club drew a quarter of a million responses to Checkerboard Square and "broke the record for returns from a single advertisement," recalled Claggett, who wrote the Straight-Shooters manual while nursing a bottle of brandy. "The more I sipped, the more I wrote," confessed the author of the slogan, "Straight shooters always win, law breakers always lose. It pays to shoot straight."

The Straight-Shooter's Club print campaign was a hit with everyone but William H. Danforth, the president of Ralston Purina. The founder of the "I Dare You!" program railed against spending so much money on advertising until "we literally buried him in box tops,"

HOT MUSH MARTYR

When Tom Mix signed on to pitch Hot Ralston cereal in 1933, America's first action hero submitted a personal fact sheet that casually listed he'd been "blown up once, shot 12 times and injured 47 times in movie stunting." To underscore the flesh-and-blood reality of their breakfast hero, Ralston Purina illustrated Tom Mix's injuries in a manual that was distributed to each of the millions of kids who joined the Ralston Straight-Shooters Club. Each booklet featured a ghostly outline of the cereal hero marked with all twenty-six letters of the alphabet, one letter per wound, plus Xs and Os—Xs for major trauma and Os for minor injuries like "shot through the jaw by sniper in Spanish American War" and "nose injured when artillery cart blew up in China." A postscript apologized for the illustrations' shortcomings, explaining that "scars from 22 knife wounds are not indicated, nor is it possible to show in the diagram the hole 4 inches square that was blown in Tom's back from a dynamite explosion."

Nor was mention made in the booklet of another serious wound—a bullet lodged near the Hot Ralston spokesman's spine. That wound was inflicted by one of Tom Mix's five ex-wives in retaliation for his compulsive skirt chasing.

remembered Claggett. "We took a picture of him with his head sticking out of a pile of box tops and then he was all for it."

Once Danforth found Straight-Shooter religion, he became convinced that Tom Mix and Hot Ralston could save the health of America's children. By the end of 1933, Danforth agreed to spread the word by radio. Claggett was dispatched to meet with Mix and have him sign an agreement for the new radio program. Claggett found the hero who was worshipped by millions of young Straight Shooters "drinking very heavily" in a trailer behind a small-time circus road show. "We couldn't have used him because his voice was so bad," sighed Claggett, who felt sorry for him. "Besides, I don't think the guy could read too well."

In exchange for regular checks, Tom happily agreed to sign away all control over the content of radio show that bore his name. The fifteen-minute *Tom Mix Ralston Straight Shooters* show won a huge and loyal following with tales of Tom's exploits in the Boxer Rebellion, the Boer War, and the Spanish American War—some of which were even true.

Millions of kids found only one drawback to collecting Hot Ralston box tops for rodeo ropes, comic books, decoder badges, branding irons, face masks, spurs, cowboy hats, and other Tom Mix paraphernalia. Once mom had shelled out a quarter to buy the steaming paste, "the little monsters had to eat it," laughed Claggett. Some not-so-little monsters discovered a unique use for the Tom Mix full-sized wooden .38 caliber revolver premium. According to Claggett, "It was so realistic that a couple of guys used it to break out of prison."

The death of Tom Mix in a 1940 car accident did nothing to check the popularity of the Tom Mix radio show. "Even though Tom Mix has gone to the Great Beyond," wrote Claggett for the program, the day after the accident, "the spirit of Tom Mix rides on."

Shazam!

Dozens of other cereal-pitching heroes rode across the American airwaves during the 1930s and 1940s, following in the hoofprints of Tom Mix and his horse Tony.

Bobby Benson of the H-Bar-O pitched cereals for H-O Oats, dispatching 1,200 cowboys with stagecoaches and chuckwagons to appear at schools and playgrounds in 1932 to sign up H-Bar-O Rangers. Rancher Steve Adams disappeared in times of trouble to reemerge as the Comanche warrior Straight Arrow, screaming his war cry "Kennah," to promote sales of Nabisco Shredded Wheat. The original singing cowboy, Gene Autry, crooned for Quaker on his CBS radio series *Melody Ranch,* and Buck Jones, a retired rodeo champion turned B western star, appeared in the series *Hoof Beats* for Grape-Nuts Flakes. "When it comes to grub for breakfast," announced the cowboy, who died a hero's death trying to rescue victims of a Boston nightclub fire, "nothing hits the spot with me like a heapin' bowl of Grape-Nuts Flakes!"

Listeners who tired of the western plains could tune into other cereal-created environments, like the African jungle inhabited by Tarzan, who pounded his chest for Heinz Rice Flakes—"The Cereal That Is Different!" Clyde Beatty, "King of the Animal Trainers," whipped the savage cereal aisle into shape on behalf of Quaker Wheat Crackels, while Major Tom, a rugged explorer and big-game hunter traveled around the globe with a pet monkey on his shoulder and a longing in his heart for Post Toasties. "It's great to be back in this country where you can get THIS FOUR-STAR BREAKFAST," the radio hero proclaimed.

From the steamy jungles, cereal took Americans to the icy reaches of the Poles. During the winter of 1933, radio audiences thrilled to the real-life adventures of Admiral Byrd as he made radio reports of his journey to the South Pole. The noted explorer claimed that Post's Grape-Nuts Flakes was breakfast food his men should eat "to fortify themselves against the punishing cold and hardships of the Antarctic."

In the early 1930s, superheroes began to zoom across the electromagnetic spectrum destroying evil and pitching cereal. Buck Rogers led the charge, enthralling kids with "25th century thrills and adventures" and commercials for Pep!, "the peppy cereal." A post–World War II campaign for Post Toasties featured Buck standing next to a mushroom cloud, with the words "Buck Rogers—Beyond the Atom Bomb." Batman and Robin made special appearances on the *Superman* show sponsored by Kellogg. Newsboy Billy Batson uttered the magic word "Shazam!" to transform himself into the "world's mightiest mortal" Captain Marvel, who joined Ibis the Invincible, Crime Smasher, and Golden Arrow in pitching Wheaties. The Green Hornet, the Lone Ranger's great nephew, and his loyal manservant Kato came to the aid of General Mills by offering a glow-in-the-dark Secret Seal ring that drew over half a million responses.

Cereal-pitching wise guys were as popular as adventurers and superheroes. Inspector Post was a hard-bitten gumshoe, who presided over the Junior Detective Corps and fought crime over the air for Post. Quaker sponsored two dicks, Dick Daring and Dick Tracy. In order to join the "Dick Tracy Secret Service Patrol," kids had to eat their way through thirty-nine boxes of Puffed Wheat or Puffed Rice.

Real-life G-man Melvin Purvis, who helped bring Pretty Boy Floyd and other depression-era crooks to justice, was hired by Post to be the "Chief Special-Agent-in-Charge of the Junior G-Man Corps." Though popular on cereal boxes and comic strips, Purvis didn't find the same satisfaction pitching cereal as he had pinching crooks. In 1960, he took his own life with a .45 caliber pistol, the same one he allegedly used to kill John Dillinger.

After Pearl Harbor was attacked, cereal radio joined in the war effort. Hop Harrigan fueled up on Grape-Nuts Flakes before piloting his B-29 Superfortress in radio-simulated "bombing" missions over Japan, while Don Winslow of the Navy cruised the seas for Kellogg's Wheat Krispies and later for Post Toasties as he battled the Scorpion, a

Nazi villain with global ambitions. Premiums included a rubber-band-powered cardboard gun battery inscribed with the words, "Try Post Toasties and Grape-Nuts Flakes—THEY HIT THE SPOT!"

An even more direct hit on the Nazis was offered by Quaker Oats, sponsors of *Terry and the Pirates,* the radio version of the popular comic strip. The young pilot and his gang of misfits, villains, and beauties pitched Sparkies cereal and offered listeners the chance to participate in an actual bombing mission. For the price of one box top, bloodthirsty kids could have their names added to a microfilmed list that was turned over to an actual B-25 bomber crew along with the message, "Drop one on the Japs and Nazis for me!"

The All-American Boy

The greatest of all the radio heroes ate the same cereal that brought the first jingle to the radio. After the Skippy debacle in 1933, Frank Hummert came up with a new hero he was sure would become the next American byword. His name was Red Jones. General Mills ad manager Samuel Gale felt that the name *Red* might cause trouble: it could identify anyone from an eccentric to a communist. Gale decided instead to name the new Wheaties hero after one of his Minneapolis neighbors, Jack Armstrong.

Premiering in 1933, *Jack Armstrong* became one of the most popular radio shows of all time, a staple of the airwaves for the next eighteen years. A perennial student, the "All-American Boy" took thirteen years to graduate from Hudson High—not surprising given the staggering range of his adventures. Jack played football, baseball, and swam. He flew planes, foiled spies, and outfoxed saboteurs. He captained submarines, skied the Himalayas, rode horseback through blazing deserts, chatted in Zulu, debated with the Dalai Lama, scouted buried treasure, and even collected stamps. And all the while he ate Wheaties.

Of all his varied activities, it was only the stamp collecting that truly threatened the survival of America's favorite radio star. In 1935, Jack's mother fell sick and desperately needed an expensive operation. The only way Jack could get the money to save his mother's life was by recovering a rare stamp, valued at some $20,000. As the hero struggled to find the fictional stamp on the radio, he encouraged his listeners to send in a nickel and a Wheaties box top to receive their own Jack Armstrong premium stamp. The Federal Trade Commission did not look kindly on the promotion, claiming that the 300,000 kids who responded to the offer believed that they were helping to raise money for Jack's dying mother. General Mills stopped the promotion, and Jack Armstrong gave up his hobby.

Other premiums associated with Jack Armstrong plots proved to be more successful. In one 1938 episode, a gang of thugs captured Jack's friend Betty and took her to a secret hideout in the South American jungle. Jack and his pals Billy and Uncle Jim set out to rescue Betty, relying on their trusty compass and something called a Hike-o-Meter to guide them through an impenetrable labyrinth. After finally rescuing Betty, Jack announced that listeners at home could get their own Hike-o-Meters. Three weeks later, more than 1,200,000 Hike-o-Meter–hungry listeners flooded the Minneapolis post office with orders and box tops.

The man behind the Hike-o-Meter, the Egyptian Whistle Ring, the Magic Answer Box, and many other Jack Armstrong premiums was a Montana farm boy, log-cabin builder, paint supplier, and self-taught ad man named Gage Davis. On his third day at work for General Mills, Davis was assigned to conduct a door-to-door survey of Minneapolis households to determine whether or not the company should offer a Daisy water pistol for two box tops from Wheaties. Packing the black metal Colt .45 watergun in his hip pocket, Davis hopped a street car, jumped off at Forty-ninth Street and France, and marched up to a modest home. When he rang the doorbell, a plump blonde woman answered. The market-testing greenhorn stammered an introduction and pulled out the pistol. "Her eyes protruded and she slammed the door," Davis laughed years later. "I didn't wait for the body to hit the floor. I was more scared than she was—I headed for a bench at the park across the way."

The Jack Armstrong scripts were so well researched that they anticipated many scientific advances—so many in fact that the U.S. government took notice of the program during World War II. By 1942, it was common knowledge that the Norden bombsight was being developed by General Electric under the strictest secrecy. Premium man Gage Davis decided to build a Jack Armstrong Secret Bombsight for Wheaties eaters and presented his creation to the management at General Mills. "When I returned home, there were two men—from the FBI—who wanted to know, 'What's all this about bombsights?'" recalled Davis, who eventually left the cereal trade to design one of the world's first humidifiers and market a long-handled sponge mop.

On several occasions, Jack Armstrong had an impact on real-world

Even America's favorite child star, Shirley Temple, whose face appeared at the bottom of five million Wheaties cereal bowls, couldn't resist the magical allure of premiums offered on the Jack Armstrong program. In 1939, one of the eighty female workers in the coupons service at General Mills was amazed to read through a letter requesting a Jack Armstrong Pedometer. Written in a childish scrawl and addressed to "Dear Jack Armstrong," the letter was signed "Shirley Temple."

General Mills turned the starlet's innocent request into a major marketing coup, reproducing the letter again and again in press releases, articles, and company histories down through the decades. As recently as 1991, a retired General Mills executive once again brought up the Jack Armstrong incident during a meeting with Shirley Temple Black, who was then serving as the U.S. ambassador to Czechoslovakia. The executive had an audience with the publicity-shy public servant—"a very sharp lady who looks like a million bucks"—in Prague and presented her with the document yet again—"for a smile." Ambassador Black replied by letter, thanking the executive diplomatically for his remembrance of days long past and of his interest "in a strong, resurgent Czechoslovakia. May we both be as successful now, as then."

events. In the fall of 1935, two Minneapolis kids tuned in to the Jack Armstrong program while their parents went shopping. In the middle of the program, the kids heard a gunshot from the alley immediately beneath their window. Looking down, they saw their father lying dead on the ground. The next day, the Minneapolis police department requested a copy of the Jack Armstrong script in order to determine the actual time of the murder, since the kids remembered what was happening during the program when they heard the shot. According to the official General Mills account of the incident, a company representative who testified at the subsequent trial gave the grieving children "a thrill by presenting them with a copy of the Jack Armstrong script, auto-graphed by Jim Ameche, Sara Jane Wells, and John Gannon—Jack, Betty and Billy."

Breakfast of Champions

Cereal makers didn't forget adults in their rush to reach kiddies' ears. In the 1930s Post sponsored the popular *Burns and Allen* radio show. Low-key George Burns praised Grape-Nuts. "So crisp, so crunchy, so nut-like," he commented, to which his wife Gracie Allen responded, "Yes, Georgie, and I'm pretty too!" Kate Smith spent a decade singing for Post over the air, and Phil Baker played his accordion for Shredded Ralston on the *Take It or Leave It* show, which brought the phrase "sixty-four dollar question" into the American lexicon. Jack Benny became the Nero of the breakfast table, scratching away on the fiddle to promote Grape-Nuts Flakes. "Take it from Benny," the boxes read, "they're bet-ter than *any!*" General Mills sponsored *The Grouch Club*, whose listen-ers formed their own Grouch Clubs in solidarity with the program's Rush Limbaugh-like host, Jack "Grouchmaster" Lescoulie.

Morning was a natural time to promote breakfast cereal, and nobody did it better than Tom Breneman, host of the early forties hit pro-gram *Breakfast in Hollywood.* Described by *Life* magazine as "a dumpy, middle-aged ex-vaudeville baritone," Breneman attracted a huge num-ber of female listeners with live-action radio hijinks. Over half of Amer-ica's radio audience listened one morning as Breneman turned a plump housewife over his knee, paddled her with a pancake turner and later invited everyone to "join the regulars with Kellogg's All Bran."

In the early 1930s General Mills made a play to attract grown-ups to the Wheaties table by sponsoring broadcasts of the Minneapolis Millers minor league baseball games. In April of 1933, ad man Knox Reeves came to Nicollet Park to watch the Millers play. The park man-ager told him that Wheaties had the right to put an advertisement on the billboard in center field. The manager asked the ad man what he should put on the sign. Reeves thought for a moment, wrote down a few words and handed them to the park manager. The following week the billboard read, "Wheaties—Breakfast of Champions."

Two years later, General Mills was spending $100,000 a year on its Wheaties baseball broadcasts. "Breakfast of Champions" was well on its way to becoming a national byword, backed up by an all-star roster. Babe Ruth was the first to hit the box. "There's nothing like them to give you energy and pep," said the Sultan of Swat, who demonstrated his slugging ability in the flip book *How to Hit a Home Run* available for one Wheaties box top.

With a decided preference for liquified over flaked-grain products, the Babe was as popular and unpredictable in the broadcast booth as he was in the batter's box. Rehearsing a live pitch for a Wheaties cookie on the Jack Armstrong show, Babe kept saying "cooookies" instead of "cookies." On the air, the Babe got through the entire pitch before delivering the last line, "And so, boys and girls, don't forget to tell your mother to buy Wheaties, so she can make these cooookies." There was silence for a moment, before listeners across the country heard Babe blurt out, "I'm a son-of-a-bitch if I didn't say cooookies again." No one complained—a testament to the power of the Babe.

Unlike today, the endorsements of sports stars came cheap in the 1930s. Philadelphia Athletics pitcher Howard Ehmke signed up his teammates Jimmy Fox, Al Simmons, Mickey Cochrane, Lefty Grove, and George Earnshaw to pitch Wheaties. Total cost to General Mills: one hundred dollars. The "Breakfast of Champions" compensated some star performers with flakes rather than cash. Joe Hauser of the Minnesota Millers collected 792 boxes of Wheaties. A player for the Atlanta Crackers donated his Wheaties to sportscaster Ernie Harwell, who claimed "my cocker spaniel loved them."

From the mid-thirties until the early fifties Joe DiMaggio, Billy Herman, Charlie Gehringer, Bob Feller, Mel Ott, Harold Trotsky, Ralph Kiner, Johnny Mize, Jackie Robinson, Luke Appling, Roy Campanella, Yogi Berra, Al Rosen, Pee Wee Reese, Phil Rizzuto, George Kell, Stan Musial, and many others cheered for Wheaties. In the 1939 All Star Game, forty-six of the fifty-one players had contracts with Wheaties. Other more exotic athletes were also lured to the flakes. Maria Rasputin, billed as "Europe's sensational wild animal trainer—fearless daughter of Russia's Mad Monk," appeared on the orange-and-blue Wheaties box sitting next to a lion. "To start the day right," she was quoted as saying, "I always recommend Wheaties."

Some athletes had little choice about whether or not to promote the cereal. Local radio announcers like Dutch Reagan, who later became better known as President Ronald Reagan, were always sure to mention the players who endorsed Wheaties. The other players they could afford to ignore. "We were able to sell these people by saying, 'If you don't do it, we won't mention you in our broadcasts,'" said Robert Stafford, who at one point was president of the agency founded by Knox Reeves.

In 1937, Post decided to throw General Mills a curve ball and introduced its own whole-wheat flake cereal, Huskies. "Start your day the Huskies way," urged a massive sports-oriented advertising campaign, "and make your breakfast table a training table." Huskies enlisted Johnny "No Hit" Vander Meer, Fred Perry, and Slingin' Sammy Baugh to endorse the cereal with a good deal of success. "I remember at one time, Huskies was going to drive us from the market," mused Stafford.

Huskies' biggest advertising coup was signing up Lou Gehrig, the pride of the Yankees, to pose for huge store displays uttering the slogan, "You'll sure go for Huskies." Gehrig's most important endorsement was scheduled for *Believe It or Not,* a popular radio show hosted by Robert Ripley and sponsored by Post Huskies. When Ripley asked the Iron Man how he started his day, Gehrig answered live over the air, "I usually start with a big bowl of Wheaties." "There was a long pause, believe me!" recalled Stafford.

By 1941, Wheaties, the "Breakfast of Champions" promoted by the first advertising jingle, was America's number one cereal in terms of dollar volume of sales. This great success had nothing to do with the taste or the actual energy value of the humble wheat flake. According to Stafford, General Mills opened sales meetings in the 1940s with a blind taste test. Unmarked bowls of Wheaties and other rival whole-wheat cereals such as Pep, Huskies, and Force were placed in front of every salesman, who promptly munched down. "And time after time, year after year, they couldn't tell the difference in the taste," recalled Stafford. "Wheaties was a child of advertising."

Jim Fish, a former vice president for advertising at General Mills, agreed. "The product is no different from anybody else's," he confessed after retiring from the company. "It's just a product of unique and consistent advertising."

8

Building a Better Mouth Trap

The originators of the ready-to-eat breakfast cereal industry were crusading eccentrics, men who mixed philosophy with food technology to create a breakfast revolution. By the end of World War I, their campaign was complete—America's stomach was conquered. "Probably no other meal has been so completely revolutionized by modern inventions as breakfast," wrote one author at the time. "Modern breakfast food has brought about wholesome change in the diet of practically all civilized people."

One of the last of the breakfast visionaries was a man who dropped out of elementary school and went on to live, breathe, and eat cereal. His name was Eugene "Gene" McKay.

Snap, Crackle, Pop

The Tom Edison of the twentieth-century cereal industry was born and raised in Battle Creek. In 1901, the seventeen-year-old McKay was swept up in the turn-of-the-century cereal boom and went to work for the Malta Vita Pure Food Company, makers of the "perfect food for brain and muscle." It was there that Gene McKay discovered his true genius: the ability to create good tasting, unique breakfast cereals.

When Malta Vita folded in 1916, McKay joined his brother George at W. K. Kellogg's cereal company. W. K. paid Gene thirty dollars a week with instructions to "just look around." The local boy with a sixth-grade education and a knack for creative cookery grew close to the taciturn W. K. and quickly rose to the job of chief manufacturing executive for the company.

For Gene McKay, cereal research and development was a certifiable passion. Not content with his day job at the Kellogg plant, McKay built a forty-by-twenty-foot cereal laboratory behind his Battle Creek home. He packed his puttering space with an assortment of cereal working tools, including a toasting oven, a miniature flaking roller, a steam cooker, extruders, grinders, pellet-making machines, a puffing gun, and several dryers, not to mention "a girl who worked for him to keep the notes," according to his son, Eugene McKay Jr.

McKay threw himself into his lab during his spare time, burning the midnight oil to boil, strain, extrude, puff, pop, toast, and mash all sorts of grains, grits, and doughs in search of the next lip-smackin' bowl-buster. Self-taught, Gene McKay had odd work habits. His main organizational tool wasn't a desk or a file cabinet, but a kind of compost heap of ideas—a foot-thick scrapbook filled with pictures cut from magazines and newspapers, marketing insights, and notes to himself.

One of McKay's earliest efforts was to clone shredded wheat for Kellogg. When his creation, Kellogg's Wheat Biscuit, crumbled in its package, McKay suggested crumbling it still further and selling the shreds as Krumbles, which the public ate up. "The first thing we knew," recalled Roy Eastman, Kellogg's second advertising manager, "we were breaking up perfectly good biscuits to meet the demand."

McKay's laboratories created All Bran in 1916, followed by Rice Flakes, Bran Flakes, and Pep, "The Vital Food," in 1923. In 1927 the cereal artist cooked up his masterpiece and brought a sample of it to the ultimate arbiter of breakfast taste, W. K. Kellogg. W. K. inspected the amber colored cereal bubbles, added sugar and milk, and took a bite. With an air of final judgement he pronounced, "You've got something here!" McKay called his new cereal creation Rice Krispies.

McKay's food-engineering skills paid off in a salary of $50,000 per year, a staggering sum for the late 1920s. When the Great Depression hit, McKay proved that he was as generous as he was hard working. The rail yards out behind the Kellogg plant in Battle Creek were thick with hungry hobos, some of whom broke open the boxcars with crowbars and ate the dry Corn Flakes and Krumbles packed inside. McKay not only bought groceries for the hobos, he distributed vouchers good for meals at local restaurants, and hired as many as he could to work in the Kellogg plant. In turn, the Battle Creek homeless expressed their affection for McKay by crowning him "King of the Tramps."

McKay's creative spirit inspired some who lived far away from Battle Creek. In 1931, Vernon Grant was painting in his low-rent Greenwich Village studio when he tuned his radio to *The Singing Lady,* a children's program hosted by Ireene Wicker. Grant was amused by the Mother Goose stories and nursery rhymes featured on the program, but what really fired the imagination of the twenty-nine-year-old commercial artist were the program's advertisements.

"She [Ireene Wicker] kept talking about the sponsor, this new cereal called Rice Krispies, that was so crisp that when you put milk on it, it would snap, crackle and pop," recalled Grant, who did not realize that an eleven-year-old girl from Seattle had actually coined the phrase "snap, crackle, pop."

"'Snap, Crackle and Pop. Snap, Crackle and Pop,' they kept saying," he said. "So I thought, 'Well, why not have a Mr. Snap, Mr. Crackle and Mr. Pop? What would they look like? What would the little characters look like?'"

Grant began to sketch. As he worked, he remembered the hand-me-down clothes he had worn as a child in South Dakota: overalls cut from a pair of English riding breeches, a stovepipe hat made from a fur hand warmer, and a pair of women's button-up shoes, with the heels knocked off and the upturned toes packed with rags. He recalled the fantasy worlds he had once created, the gnomes he had molded from clay in the cool dark washes beneath the South Dakota prairie wind and sun, the characters he had drawn as a quick-sketch vaudevillian, and the dancing brownies he had painted as a student at the Art Institute of Chicago. Over the course of a few weeks, an elfin trio came to life on Grant's easel. Finally, the artist was ready to introduce Snap, Crackle, and Pop to the rest of the world.

Grant opened the Manhattan telephone directory, found a listing for Kellogg, and dialed the number—"Just cold turkey." He managed to reach Clarence Jordan, the executive vice president of Kellogg's ad agency, N. W. Ayer and Son. Grant arranged a meeting. "Young fellow," Ayer ad man Algonquin Collins said after examining Grant's artwork, "if you'll put yourself in my hands for about a week, you've got a fortune in your hands."

"For about two weeks a parade of guys came into my studio," laughed Grant years later. "The best art directors in the city. . . . It was unbelievable." After a few weeks of polishing his images, Grant sold his characters to one of the most powerful men in American advertising.

"I don't think that either of us knew that Snap, Crackle, and Pop would last for over fifty years," Grant mused.

By 1933, Rice Krispies had rocketed from the bottom of Kellogg's brand heap to the top, second only to Corn Flakes. Snap, Crackle, and Pop appeared in magazine advertisements, in promotional pamphlets, and in illustrations Grant painted for the back of the Rice Krispies box. "I knew I had arrived," laughed Grant, "when I saw that Snap, Crackle, and Pop were in Peking with Chinese captions."

The trio made history in 1937 when they jumped from the grocery aisle to the silver screen and appeared in the first animated cereal advertisement, a ninety-second short film that was played in movie theaters throughout the country. Entitled "Breakfast Pals," the cartoon told the tale of a young boy named Bobby, whose breakfast was saved from a gang of mush producing bad guys by the heroic efforts of Snap, Crackle, and Pop.

The value of Kellogg Company stock soared, as did Grant's income. By 1942, his three little creations had earned him more than a quarter of a million dollars, and a certain amount of hubris. When Kellogg's shifted its ad account from N. W. Ayer to the Chicago-based J. Walter Thompson, Grant took offense, complaining that the new agency was "one headache." Kellogg thought that Grant was an even bigger headache, and fired him. Grant, who by this time smoked a pipe and looked like a cross between Norman Rockwell and Fred Flintstone, sued Kellogg in federal court for control of his characters.

While the judge deliberated, the commercial art and advertising worlds that bought characters from artists on a daily basis froze. In October 1944, the court ruled in Kellogg's favor. "Snap, Crackle, and Pop," wrote Judge Bright, "never had any personality or characteristic except as Rice Krispie [sic] salesmen. They lived no life like Mutt & Jeff, Buster Brown and dog, Jiggs, Superman, Betty Boop, Sparkplug and other inhabitants of the comic strip world. . . . they had no significance except as decoys to beguile the public into reading about Rice Krispies."

"I guess there came a time when Vernon Grant became unmanageable," reflected Grant, who went on to illustrate 228 magazine covers for *Colliers, Saturday Evening Post, Ladies Home Journal,* and many other publications before his death in 1990. "They wanted to get rid of me and hire imitators. It really knocked the pins out from under me. I got too big for my britches is what happened."

The Mouse that Scored

Snap, Crackle, and Pop's ability to sell cereal brought other creatures to the box. While Force's Sunny Jim, the Quaker man, and Rastus had given cereal boxes adult appeal for many years, Post took a kid's eye view of the grocery aisle and in 1935 slapped a licensed rodent on the front of the Post Toasties box. The rodent's name was Mickey Mouse, star of the 1928 cartoon "Steamboat Willie."

The man who brought Mickey to breakfast was Herman "Kay" Kamen, a well-known ad man from Kansas City who looked like a well-dressed rutabaga. Kamen followed the progress of the Disney empire and noticed Disney souvenirs in store windows. When he inquired about how much the manufacturers paid for using the images of Pluto,

---

CANNON FODDER

In 1941, the War Department signed a contract with Quaker Oats to package bombs instead of oatmeal. The multi-million-dollar deal to manufacture 100- to 2,000-pound aerial bombs and 105-MM artillery shells was inked with Quaker not because of its slogan "shot from guns," but because of its flawless record controlling dust explosions in its nitrogen-rich grain silos. The patriotic company spent $30 million to build the Cornhusker Ordnance plant in Grand Island, Nebraska, and turned out more than fourteen million shells and bombs during the war years. The only accident at the plant occurred when lightning struck one of the buildings, detonating a stockpile of explosives and killing nine workers. After the war, Quaker found that it could not stay away from weaponry.

In the 1950s, Gabby Hayes pointed a cannon to the camera at the end of each episode of his television series, *The Gabby Hayes Show*. Urging viewers to "stand back away from your sets now," the cowboy blasted his audience at home with a shower of puffed cereal and the words "Yesssirrreee. It's Deeelicious!" The Quaker exhibit at the 1965 New York World's Fair drew huge crowds four times a day when it fired off a giant cannon loaded with a member of the Zacchini Troupe. The human cannon balls soared high above a mammoth Quaker puffed cereal package before landing in a safety net.

Goofy, and Minnie, he was intrigued to learn that they were taking them for free.

Kamen called Walt Disney. Disney agreed to meet with the promo man—as long as he paid his own way to California. Kamen took the train to Los Angeles and handed Walt Disney $50,000 cash. Kamen said that he would guarantee the cartoon producer a minimum of $50,000 a year if he was given the exclusive rights to license the Disney characters.

Disney looked at the cash and at the big nose, thick glasses, and six-foot frame of the bulky Kamen. How could he refuse? In 1933, for 66 percent of the revenue, Kamen secured exclusive licensing rights to Mickey Mouse, Pluto the pup, the Three Little Pigs, and other Disney creations. In their first year together during the depths of the depression, the Disney/Kamen operation sold thirty-five million dollars' worth of Mickey Mouse merchandise licenses. The dapper mouse appeared on hundreds of different items, including cookie cutters, lunch pails, watches, and packages of Post Toasties.

Post paid $1.5 million to get Mickey on their box, but it proved to be well worth it. For the price of a box of cornflakes, impoverished parents could provide their children with nourishment *and* Disney character cut-out toys. "If Post Toasties are good enough for their friend 'Mickey,'" *Modern Packaging* wrote of the attitude of the depression-era kids, "then Post Toasties are good enough for them."

Virtually overnight, Kellogg and Quaker Oats copied Post and turned their packages into colorful toys. Boxes of Corn Flakes, Pep, and Puffed Wheat were adorned with western scenes, historical vignettes, and masks of Moon Mullins, Lord Plushbottom, and other popular comic-strip characters. The wildly successful Kamen branched out, cutting big-money Disney licensing deals with a host of different companies, including rival cereal companies. One of his typical deals was with General Mills. Kamen took no advance, just a 5 percent royalty on each box of cereal *printed* with the Disney characters, an arrangement that netted Kamen and Disney millions of dollars, regardless of actual sales.

Kamen's merchandising was so lucrative and his deal with Disney so tight that he became a powerful and feared man within the Burbank organization. When he died in a plane crash on October 28, 1949, the Disney organization took back total control over the licensing rights to all their characters. Wrote one Disney historian, "Without Kay Kamen, there would be no Disney studios today."

The Mental Kid

It wasn't just the outside of the cereal box that changed during the 1930s. The power of premiums changed as well, due to the popularity of the radio heroes promoting cereal and the energy of marketing maven Samuel H. Gold, a close friend of Kay Kamen. Heralded by *Life* magazine as "the top idea man of the premium business," Gold was an enthusiastic salesman who could transform bits of metal, paper, and plastic into the sculptured dreams of American youth—all for pennies apiece. "This business was an obsession with my father," said Gordon K. Gold, Sam's son. Gold himself, who looked like Don Ameche with black, slicked-back hair and a pencil-thin mustache, explained his success with the words "Mentally, I'm a kid."

Gold may have been a kid mentally, but economically he was a shark. He started selling premiums in 1919, but his business didn't really take off until the depression, when cash-strapped consumers were desperate to get something for nothing. The premium offered for a box top-and-a-coin, known in the trade as a "self-liquidator," served to boost public interest in a cereal product. Since the cost of the premium was covered by its purchase price, the cereal companies also got something for nothing: free advertising. "Imagine," rhapsodized Gold. "For the cost of pennies each, you could get that child to work for you."

Gold routinely made the rounds by train from Chicago to Minneapolis to Battle Creek to St. Louis and back to Chicago, pitching his ideas to the cereal giants. "People who knew Gold say he was a bit of an actor who could dramatize an infant idea in great detail, get the order and then figure out how to do what he said he could," wrote premium historian Tom Tumbusch. "He was instrumental in coming up with the prizes that made kids tug on their mom's skirts and say, 'Mommy, I want that.'"

In creating the rings, decoders, badges, and beanies that attracted millions of box tops and small coins, Gold employed some of the most talented designers and artists in the business. He obtained many of his paper premiums from Fred Voges, described by an advertising historian as one of the best paper engineers "since the oriental origami masters." Among Voges' cereal designs were the Buck Rogers and Dick Tracy rubber-band guns, and Captain Sparks' Aviation Training Cockpit.

Gold's other paper artist was Wally Weist. Weist was able to copy the style of any artist—from Van Gogh to Milt Caniff. In the early 1940s, Sam Gold lured both Voges and Weist to his company offices on the upper floors of a building in downtown Chicago. There the premium artists created hundreds of premiums, including a series of paper airplanes for Kellogg's Pep cereal. The mischievous pair test flew each of the forty different airplane models out the office window high above the el train on Wacker Drive. During the war, the designers supplemented their meager twenty-five-dollars-per-week salaries by trading armfuls of the planes at local grocery stores for rationed meat.

In 1949, *Life* said that the premium business was the "fastest growing, most secretive and most melodramatic brand of advertising." The methods used to order and manufacture premiums accounted for some of their mystique. Cereal companies usually approved premium ideas only after several newspaper ads and radio spots had run. The initial response from kids was used by management to gauge the number of

---

PREMIUM GOLD RUSH

Shouting "On, King! On, you huskies!" over the stirring Donna Diana overture, Sergeant Preston and his dog Yukon King sledded across the airwaves loaded with Quaker Puffed Wheat and Puffed Rice from 1947 until 1957. A creation of Lone Ranger originator George W. Trendle, *The Challenge of the Yukon* starring the stalwart mountie was a popular program on both radio and television, and was responsible for the greatest premium rush in cereal history. In 1955, the Canadian lawman offered fans "the deed to one square inch of Yukon land." To acquire the real estate for the scheme, Chicago ad man Bruce Baker and a Quaker attorney traveled to the Yukon, where they suffered frostbite and nearly drowned when their motor boat hit a rock. The actual promotion was much more successful than the scouting mission. Consumers snapped up twenty-one million packages of Quaker Puffed Wheat and Puffed Rice, each one containing a deed for one square inch of Yukon territory. A decade later, several of the deed holders, one of whom had amassed 10,800 deeds, contacted Quaker about claiming title to their land. The company informed the cereal land barons that the nineteen-acre plot it had originally acquired had reverted back to the Canadian government for failure to pay $37.20 in taxes.

---

premiums to be produced, if any. Once manufactured, the premiums were shipped to Battle Creek, Chicago, or St. Louis for "fulfillment" or mailing out to kids. The famous phrase, "allow six to eight weeks for delivery," should more accurately have read, "allow six to eight weeks for market survey, manufacture, distribution, and delivery."

Cheerioats

Don Davis, who brought General Mills into the radio business and eventually rose to become president of the company, displayed a sign on his office wall that read "Facts, Not Opinions." Convinced of the fact that he could improve his company's share of the ready-to-eat cereal market, Davis assigned his researchers the job of finding a chink in his rival's cereal armor. The investigators came up with two choice bits of information: consumers hated soggy cereals and loved the idea of the newly popularized nutritional substances known as vitamins.

The year 1929 presented a tremendous opportunity to those in search of a nonsoggy cereal, as the patents on the puffing process, developed and owned by Quaker, expired. Davis sent his research team to the lab to come up with a me-too puff. The scientists mixed corn meal, malted barley, vegetable oil, salt, and sugar into a dough, and added vitamin B, vitamin D, phosphorus, and calcium. The dough was extruded through a die that shaped it into pellets. These pellets were dried on a belt blown by hot air until the desired moisture level was achieved. Then the pellets were blasted out of a puffing gun—the same sort of puffing gun used to make Puffed Wheat and Puffed Rice. The finished product landed in a large bin, which was then sprayed with more vitamins.

The rough little half-inch clumps of what looked like crystallized sponge were ready to test market in 1937, under the brand name Kix. Pitched as a sog-resistant cereal more nutritious than Corn Flakes or Toasties, corn Kix was an instant hit. A year or two later, a *Life* magazine ad pictured the vitamin pellets bouncing around the breakfast table with the question "How would you like to have something new for breakfast—something that will give you a genuine lift?"

In a defensive maneuver, Quaker showered its puffs with a misty spray of thiamin, niacin, and iron, and called the new cereal concoction Vitamin Rain. The cereal flopped as General Mills launched a new volley from its puffing guns. Using the extrusion techniques developed for Kix, General Mills created an oat-based dough and pushed it through a die to produce little donut-shaped puffs the color of sand.

By this time, the creation of a cereal was a corporate affair. Scientists, laboratory technicians, market analysts, statisticians, psychologists, and radio performers all worked to bring General Mills' new puffed cereal to market. The introduction was delayed for a few months, when the General Mills plant in Buffalo burned to the ground in a fire that was believed to have started in a storage room full of airplane premiums. Finally, in May 1941, the new product, dubbed Cheerioats, hit the shelves.

Two years later General Mills coined the slogan "He's Feeling His Cheerioats" to promote special 1-ounce Yank Packs of the floating donuts sold to military personnel only. When Quaker objected to the use of the term "oats" as a commercial name in 1945, General Mills edited the offending word to create the much more appealing title Cheerios.

At first the technology was too primitive to create an actual hole in each Cheerio, but eventually the hole did appear consistently, as Cheerios rode into the hearts of America, carried in the saddle bags of the Lone Ranger.

Premiering on January 30, 1933, with the sound of thundering hoofbeats, the William Tell Overture, and an invitation to "those thrilling days of yesteryear," the Lone Ranger began to pitch Cheerios in 1941, and continued to do so until his final "Hi Yo Silver" on May 27, 1955.

Created by George W. Trendle, owner of radio station WXYZ in Detroit, *The Lone Ranger* show was so popular that other stations clamoring to carry the western grew into the Mutual Radio Network. The popularity of the radio program created a premium boom for Cheerios cereal. Eleven million kids purchased Cheerios boxes printed with Lone Ranger masks, as well as pedometers, badges, signed photos, a flashlight pistol, posters, and a six-shooter ring that drew 934,000 responses from kids who didn't mind too much when the ring's rich gold finish wore away in a few days. Two million kids sent away for the paper base on which to build the Lone Ranger Frontier Town, a western layout consisting of seventy-nine buildings cut from Cheerios box backs.

As the corporate machine in Minneapolis pushed Cheerios down America's throat, Gene McKay, who had brought Rice Krispies to the breakfast table, continued to putter around his backyard cereal shop. He was instrumental in designing the single-serving box for Kellogg and was even offered the job of president, but quit the company in disgust when management decided to axe their generous pension plan. Instead, the last of the great cereal tinkerers bought Dr. Kellogg's old Sanitarium Equipment Company building in downtown Battle Creek and established his own business, McKay Laboratories.

When World War II broke out, McKay turned his talents to feeding the Allies. The War Department hired McKay to create individual serving boxes for GIs. McKay designed a military food packet stuffed with cigarettes, chocolate, and chewing gum and arranged to have them manufactured at the plant of his long-time employer. Millions of American fighting men became all too well acquainted with the convenient food package McKay helped to create, the K-ration. After the war, Gene McKay and his brother George returned to the health-food roots of the cereal business. They purchased the struggling Battle Creek Food Company, the health-food business originally established by Dr.

Kellogg, and set out once again to make a better mouth trap. Unfortunately, Eugene McKay, the last wizard of the breakfast table, passed away in 1957, just after *Business Week* magazine heralded the introduction of his last creation, the world's first brown-rice flake cereal, Surprize!.

III

Presweet Stampede

9

Dynamite in a Dish

The birth of the atomic age created a revolution in American tastes and preoccupations. In Detroit, automakers were faced with a more affluent, more sophisticated public that rejected the old, square designs and demanded swoopy fins and wide-grin grills. A hundred miles away in Battle Creek, cereal makers found that plain cornflakes, oatmeal, puffed rice, and shredded wheat just didn't cut it anymore.

The fuel that jet-age cereal makers discovered to propel sales was sugar. The introduction of factory presweetened cereal ushered in a new breakfast-food era, one described by the company publication the *Kellogg News* as "young but lusty."

Ranger Joe Breaks Trail

The cereal that introduced Americans to the young but lusty presweetened world was the brainchild of a Philadelphia heating-equipment salesman. In 1939 Jim Rex sat at the breakfast table in disgust as he watched his children bury their puffed-wheat cereal in spoonful after spoonful of sugar. Sickened by the sugary excess, Rex began to think of ways he could get his kids to eat their cereal without plunging into the sugar bowl. The solution came to him in a flash of inspiration. Why not create a cereal "already sugar'd?"

Putting his heating-equipment expertise to use, Rex devised a process whereby airy granules of puffed cereal were dipped in a diluted mixture of honey and corn syrup, then flash-baked at high temperatures to give the coating a hard, varnishlike seal. When he found that his kids liked the new breakfast concoction, Rex hit up his friends, scraped together a few thousand dollars, and launched his own cereal empire under the name Ranger Joe.

Inspired by the popularity of the Lone Ranger, Rex hired an artist to draw the company logo: a portrait of Ranger Joe wearing a white cowboy hat and standing next to his white horse. Soon little cellophane bags full of Ranger Joe Popped Wheat Honnies began appearing in Philadelphia area stores shipped out from the Ranger Joe Cereal Company headquarters in Chester, Pennsylvania.

"The Original Coated Popped Wheat Honnies" ran into serious problems from the get go. Poor air conditioning at the plant and leaky cellophane bags caused the product to solidify into sticky bricks, which were impossible to eat and impossible to sell. Rex struggled to solve his production snags, but he couldn't raise the money he needed for essential new equipment. Within nine months of opening its doors, the fledgling Ranger Joe Breakfast Food Company, in the words of one observer, "just flopped."

Believing that he could make more money heating houses than cereal puffs, Rex sold his company to a forty-five-year-old Philadelphia civil-engineer-turned-stockbroker named Moses Berger. Berger had designed bridges for the Navy before getting into the marketing game. He was intrigued by the Ranger Joe ethos and felt that he could build a business on it. "He could sell anything," his widow recalled. "The name caught his imagination. He decided it was something he could promote and he did."

Moses Berger expanded the Chester, Philadelphia, plant, improved the manufacturing process, and created an edible product. Year after year he drove around to supermarkets throughout the Northeast, setting up giant Ranger Joe aisle displays, handing out Ranger Joe cereal bowls and "ranch" mugs, and serving up free Ranger Joe samples in cold milk for hungry shoppers. The factory dropped toy airplanes and sheriff badges into packages. Orders poured in.

"My dad always talked about what a big financial risk it was for him at that stage of his life," remembers Elliott Berger, Moses Berger's son. "There were so many sleepless nights early on. If there was ever a problem with Ranger Joe, he'd buy it back from the store, no questions asked. And he did that on more than one occasion."

Despite the financial stress, being the son of a cereal boss had its definite upside for Elliot. Like little Charlie Bucket in *Charlie and the Chocolate Factory*, the coated-puff prince had paradise on a string . . . or maybe a spoon. "I loved to go to my dad's factory," recalled Berger decades later. "They treated me real nice 'cause I was the boss's kid and it was an exciting place to go. Those booming puffing guns looked huge."

Every evening, Pop brought home a factory-fresh box of Ranger Joe for his son, along with the latest toy prizes for him to play with. "This is what I lived on when I was a kid," laughed Elliott, remembering his cereal habit. "Look at the ingredients: puffed-wheat coated with sugar, honey, and corn syrup. It was my standard breakfast, afternoon snack, after-dinner dessert, and late-at-night fare. I had a major sweet tooth. And if that wasn't sweet enough, I ate it with whole milk, heavy whipping cream, and more sugar spread on top of it! It blows me away that I used to eat like that because I'm a very health-oriented person today!"

Back in Philadelphia, Moses Berger was "kind of annoyed," remembered his wife, when he opened the *Inquirer* one day in 1949 to a full-page ad for "A honey of a cereal! New! Post's Sugar Crisp." Berger knew that he didn't have the money to go national with his breakfast food, but that didn't make it any easier when a competitor appeared with deeper pockets. "The major cereal companies were going to start copying his product so he had to sell out while he still could," said Elliott.

Both General Mills and the National Biscuit Company sent reps to the Chester plant to kick the puffing guns and look over the books. The biscuit company wound up buying Ranger Joe in 1954 for a sizeable sum and immediately made changes to their new franchise. Though Moses Berger stayed on as general manager of the plant until he retired in 1960, Wheat and Rice Honnies were renamed Wheat and Rice Honeys, an animated insect named Buffalo Bee replaced Ranger Joe, and Jim Rex's grainchild finally went coast to coast.

Elliott Berger remembered that his father didn't stop in his pursuit of presweets. "After he'd sold Joe to Nabisco, he invented a cereal called MiLoMaise, a little round coated puff, and it was processed in a similar way to the Wheat Honnies . . . but better. He made up a bunch of cases and I got to eat it for about a year. I loved it to death . . . but Nabisco never wanted to introduce the product so it never went anywhere."

Cuts Up Your Mouth Like Glass

Sniffing the air in Battle Creek, the folks at Post soon caught wind of Ranger Joe's sweet idea. As early as 1948, Post began to develop their own sugar-coated wheat puff. When the former psycho-nutritional health-food company began to explore presweets in earnest, researchers, technicians, and marketers debated whether or not sugar was the right thing to add to a breakfast cereal.

The investigators at Post agreed with the observations Ranger Joe creator Jim Rex had made at his breakfast table. Kids really liked to pile on the sugar. Presweet proponents argued that adding sugar to cereal in the plant was preferable to adding it at the breakfast table. They made the point that factory presweets would contain a lot less sugar than self-sweets.

Other presweet promoters put forward an equally convincing argument. "You're trading off sugar carbohydrates for grain carbohydrates—*and sugar and starch are metabolized in exactly the same way*—you really don't change the nutritional value of the product," explained Post executive Kent Mitchell. "It's six of one, half a dozen of the other."

The most convincing argument came from the marketing men, who believed strongly that presweetened cereals would sell. Swayed by this argument, Post developed a product that they believed could double as a breakfast food and a snack. The company called the stuff Happy Jax, which drew the ire of the Cracker Jack Company.

Redubbed Sugar Crisp, and packaged like Ranger Joe in see-through cellophane bags, the presweet was rolled out from coast to coast in 1949. Kellogg, the industry leader, was blindsided by the sugar-coated marketing push. "I remember going to a small department store and finding twenty to thirty cases [of Sugar Crisp], which was a lot of cereal," recalled a Kellogg salesman. "And believe you me, it made the Kellogg people shudder."

Fortunately for Kellogg, Post's first presweet suffered from the same stubborn caking problem that sunk Jim Rex's original Ranger Joe venture. "The stuff used to turn into bricks," laughed one old Post hand. "They solidified so you couldn't pound them apart. You'd just rip the bag off and gnaw on a piece!"

Post abandoned the leaky cellophane in 1951 in favor of "triple wrap boxes," a fancy name for a foil liner, a cardboard carton, and a waxed-paper outer wrap. The packaging improved the caking problem somewhat, and itself became the focus of an advertising push. "We put on a big 'wrapped for freshness' advertising campaign in *Life* and other consumer magazines," recalled a Post ad man. "It had some impact but like all other advertising gimmicks, it gave out."

Sugar Crisp was a spectacular success, increasing Post's overall share of the breakfast cereal market from 19 to 25 percent. Post looked around for other products to sugar coat. Six months after Sugar Crisp appeared, Post introduced another presweet, Krinkles, the "candy-kissed rice" cereal. The product was essentially a caramel-coated rice krispie, designed to gnaw away at the strong market for Kellogg's Rice Krispies. Instead of the crystalline coating of Sugar Crisp, the puffs were jacketed with a new clump-resistant glassy coating. Once again,

---

RAPE-NUTS

In the early fifties the Grape-Nuts package came with a waxed-paper overwrap. The overwrap included a V-shaped fold in which the words *Grape-Nuts* appeared. According to a Post art director, a packaging engineer at the company made a small but significant error in designing the blueprint that told the artists where they could print and where they could not print. "They put the overwraps on the packaging machine and they were folding when all of a sudden, they had the product manager in my office saying, 'My God! My God! We've got a million packages that say Rape-Nuts on the side!'" The art director had a good laugh, but the packaging engineer responsible for the error failed to see the humor in the situation. "It was his product," the art director recalled, "and they had to recall all the packages and tear off the overwraps and put new ones on."

---

the product caught Kellogg flat-footed. "I had packages of it," laughed one Kellogg's salesman. "I sold one to somebody."

At this time, Post Toasties was second only to Kellogg's Corn Flakes in overall sales and way ahead of Corn Flakes in the central section of the country and Texas. Why not come out with a candy-coated Toastie? Late in 1951, Post launched Corn Fetti, a coated flake designed to stay crispy and sweet in milk. "We were a little bit shook up with Corn Fetti," recalled a Kellogg salesman. "This wholesaler told me, 'Boy, Post's got Corn Fetti, they're really going to take you guys to the cleaners now!'"

But it wasn't long before Kellogg realized that Corn Fetti wasn't selling. "It was a disaster," recalled Bob Traverse, the artist who drew the package. "The flakes hardened with this really beautiful, clear-candy coating. But it was so insoluble, it would cut your mouth all up like glass."

Technical problems combined with bureaucratic sluggishness to hamper Post's effort to capitalize on the presweetened cornflake breakthrough. Instead of fixing the Corn Fetti formula fast and re-introducing it to the market, General Foods, the corporate entity that owned Post, began an exhaustive, time-consuming product-testing process. "We were all so frustrated with this situation," remembered Bill Betts, Post's art director at the time. "While we had our sales force standing in line to introduce again, they continued to test market and test market . . . to the point where the competition stole the idea."

Frosting on the Flakes

Inside Kellogg's Food Research Department, the debate raged for years about presweets and their impact on children's health. The issue ran deep into the heart of Kellogg corporate culture. At the turn of the century, Dr. John Harvey Kellogg had argued strongly with Will Keith Kellogg about adding sugar to cornflakes. Because sugar-flavored corn-flakes sold better, W. K. had won the argument.

By the mid-fifties the battling Kellogg brothers had passed away, but a large percentage of Kellogg stock was owned by the W. K. Kellogg Foundation, a charitable organization established to promote children's health and education. Was it right for a company owned by a children's health organization to manufacture presweetened cereals? As had happened half a century earlier, the decision was based on marketing concerns. Presweets sold well, so Kellogg decided to make them.

Spurred by Post's lucrative launch of Sugar Crisp and Krinkles, Kellogg rushed to get a competitive presweetened product on the store shelves. The company turned to Corn Pops, a nonsweetened puffed corn grit developed back in the 1930s by cereal wizard Gene McKay. While the basic gun-puffing process for making the product was familiar to all the major cereal makers, the exact flavor, texture, and appearance of its candy coating presented the crucial challenge.

The Kellogg Company developed several sugar coatings—laced with vitamins B_1 and D—and left the final decision up to the consumer. One thousand families in the Battle Creek area were selected for the taste tests. These guinea pigs included members of what the company called the "Junior Jury," the under-twelve-year-old consumers who were recognized as the product's target market.

Everyone agreed that the presweetened Corn Pops, renamed Sugar Corn Pops, tasted good—but like Post's Sugar Crisp, caking was a problem. In addition, "I remember the Sugar Corn Pops package as very plain," recalled a Kellogg salesman. "The only thing going for them was the wrap-around deal—two packages for the price of one [49 cents]."

After slightly adjusting the sugar-coating formula, Kellogg launched Sugar Corn Pops in 1950. The public gobbled up so much of the cereal that the company had to import high-caliber European puffing guns from Europe and run their Omaha, Nebraska, plant twenty-four hours a day to meet demand.

After the success of Sugar Corn Pops, Kellogg raced to capture the sugar-coated cornflake market like "it was their salvation," observed one Post man. Initially there was some concern within Kellogg that tampering with the cornflake was the wrong thing to do. "Their worry was that [Corn Flakes] was one of the cornerstones of the company's prosperity. Adding sugar might split the market," recalled Art Linkletter, Kellogg pitchman and consultant. "I said I thought the sugar would give them a new story to augment the campaign, rather than divide it. Thank goodness I was right on that one."

Introduced in 1952, Kellogg's presweetened cornflake trounced the inedible Corn Fetti and went on to become America's most popular candy-coated cereal for many years. Instead of Post's crystalline coating, the Kellogg sugar-coating process resulted in "the bright appearance of frost," according to the *Kellogg News*. More importantly, instead of a confusing name like Corn Fetti, Kellogg gave their product the simple yet elegant title Sugar Frosted Flakes. Still, all was not right at first. "When the Frosted Flakes came out," said a Kellogg salesman, "they got lumpy."

Kellogg got the lumps out in a hurry. Within weeks Sugar Frosted Flakes reappeared on the grocery store aisle. "They just took the Corn Fetti market away from us," sighed Betts. "It was just another case of Post pioneering but loosing its advantage to Kellogg."

Having consumed Post's Corn Fetti market, in 1953 Kellogg went after Post's Sugar Crisp with Sugar Smacks. The "scientifically presweetened" breakfast food was manufactured at Kellogg's Omaha plant, twelve pounds at a time. Once puffed, the stuff moved down a belt where workers removed the imperfect pieces, called "old maids," before dumping the puffs in a vitamin-enriched corn-syrup bath, drying them and packing them in "weather foil" inner bags, which the company claimed kept "Sugar Smacks fresh up to ten times longer than standard-type liners." Smacks, noted *Kellogg News*, "has the additional advantage of leaving no after-taste."

Post saw the challenge and dug in its heels. Under the headline "Product Imitation" in the company newsletter *Post Box*, Louis Parker, the general manager, ignored his own company's debt to Ranger Joe and complained that "Sugar Smacks is the closest possible copy cat of our own Sugar Crisp product. . . . when you add to that the fact that their packaging imitates very closely our Sugar Krinkles packaging . . . consumers are going to be confused."

In 1959, Kellogg decided to confuse consumers even more by taking a swipe at Cheerios with their own ready-to-eat presweetened oat

PROPHYLACTIC FLAKES

In the early 1950s Post secretly explored the idea of creating a fluoridated cereal that would actually fight cavities. The plot was uncovered by an alert Kellogg salesman when one of his customers, an Indiana institution for the mentally retarded, suddenly stopped ordering the Kellogg cereal Pep. Naturally, the Kellogg salesman looked into the loss of business and found that Post had donated "cases and cases" of Toasties and Krinkles marked "X" or "Y" to the home for a survey they were undertaking. Intrigued, he sent samples of the cereal up to the Kellogg lab in Battle Creek, which reported that "fluoride was present in one but not in the other." Post operatives gave flakes marked "X" to residents of one cottage, while giving flakes marked "Y" to another cottage. "Each month," recalled the salesman, "they would check the children's teeth and see if there were less cavities on the kids." The results of the tests were never made public, perhaps because many Americans during the Cold War era believed that fluoride was a communist tool that dissolved the freedom-loving part of the brain. Post later went public with a new anticavity crusade. In 1967 the company announced that it had hired Indiana University's Dr. Joseph C. Muhler, developer of the stannous fluoride formula used in Crest toothpaste, to create a cavity-fighting cereal. The prophylactic flakes never hit the market.

cereal OKs. Inexplicably, Kellogg had a hard time with oats, the strong suit of arch rival General Mills. The individual OKs tasted great, tested great, and looked great until they were shipped to stores. Upon arrival, the little puffs collapsed like so many failed soufflés, victims of heat and vibration. "When people bought the boxes, it looked like it was half full," recalled a Kellogg ad man. "They had a helluva time with that." A Kellogg salesman agreed. "The product didn't cut it against Cheerios. . . . It powdered in the bottom of the package."

As interest in OKs deflated, Kellogg shifted its focus to chocolate, which was as controversial among employees in the Kellogg research department as sugar had been. In 1958 a compromise was reached.

"Our dieticians said that all this sweetness is not the best for children," recalled a Kellogg salesman, but "they said that bittersweet chocolate was good and healthy and it wouldn't be harmful to them."

The problem was that kids didn't like the taste of the bittersweet-chocolate-flavored cereal dubbed Cocoa Krispies. "They did not reorder," said the salesman, "so we changed the formula." The new cereal was a dietary flop, and a sales bonanza.

Edible Alphabet

General Mills jumped into the candy-coated fray in 1953. Wringing its hands over the possible dietary effects of presweets on children, the Minneapolis company slapped together a bizarre mixture of plain Wheaties and sugar-frosted Kix and shipped them out as Sugar Smiles—"You can't help smiling the minute you taste it"—to its test market in Cincinnati, Ohio. To make sure mom took the bait, the company threw a "Cheerios Free" coupon into the deal.

General Mills executives had been held in check for years by a staff nutritionist who "really fought against us getting in to any presweetened cereal," recalled Jim Fish, vice president for advertising at the time. "It was a nutritional thing. . . . he felt we just shouldn't be doing it. [But] it was overcome by marketing people who said, 'We've got to be able to move into this area to survive!'"

Within months, General Mills took the Wheaties out of Smiles and repackaged the coated Kix as Sugar Jets, a new cereal "as crunchy as ice-cream cones." Packaged in Toledo, tens of thousands of little green-and-orange sample boxes were mailed to every address in the test market of Buffalo. "It tasted like a dead Sugar Pop," recalled one observer.

Perhaps because it was late to the presweet party, General Mills adopted a strategy known as "product proliferation," whereby it attempted to increase its market share not by cutting the cost to the consumer of individual products, but by introducing ever more products. To accomplish this, General Mills essentially made new cereals out of old, altering the look, taste, color, and packaging of existing brands just enough to make them seem different.

To proliferate the presweet product, the cereal alchemists at General Mills started with the basic, standard-issue extruded corn puff, covered it with sugar, fruit flavoring, and chocolate, and introduced Sugar Jets, Trix, and Cocoa Puffs in the three-year period between 1954 and 1956.

Stung by the marketing sophistication of Kellogg and the shelf-grabbing strategy of General Mills, General Foods' brass canned the general manager of Post cereals and brought in a real fire-breather. The new executive, who hailed from General Food's financial department, was George M. Laimbeer. "He was a brilliant, brilliant man . . . and a real bastard," whispered Bill Betts, who worked under him as art director. "His gift was getting on people's ass and making 'em perform. I can remember people *running* down to his office."

Laimbeer hungered for new ideas to restore the company's cereal fortunes and found a real winner in the imagination of Al Clausi, the new head of product development dispatched to Battle Creek from the General Foods research laboratories in New Jersey. The Italian-American didn't know anything about the cereal business, but he did know his pasta. "The thought crossed my mind," remembered Clausi, "why not take pasta, which comes in a multitudinous number of forms and shapes, and subject it to this gun-puffing process?"

So Clausi puffed up a bunch of alphabet pasta and showed it to his boss Laimbeer. The tough guy exclaimed, "Oh, my God! This is terrific! This is tremendous! This is what we're looking for."

The first Alpha Bits were made from a mixture of oat flour and corn starch extruded through macaroni equipment trucked to Battle Creek for the purpose. The twenty-six different dies had to be modified to compensate for the distortion from the puffing process. "It was easier to expand some letters than others so we never had an equal number of each," continues Clausi, who went on to become a General Foods vice president. "The worst letters were the ones that had open sides—like *C*s or *W*s—their members would go off in all directions." These flaws did not keep Alpha Bits from eating up an incredible 2 percent of the ready-to-eat cereal market when it was launched in 1957.

The Big Red K

Though nutritionists at all the major cereal companies lost out to the sugary visions of the marketing departments in the 1950s, some of the innovations in food technologies proved that there was still a strong market for health. Legend has it that W. K. Kellogg long nurtured the dream of combining essential nutrients from different grains to create a concentrated, high-protein all-purpose food. As early as 1948, Kellogg's food research department was reportedly working "with the research departments of two great universities" to develop a cereal that provided 100 percent of the daily minimum requirements of protein, vitamins, and minerals. In 1955, four years after his death, Kellogg's dream was introduced to America as the modern miracle food—Special K.

Marketed in a white box emblazoned with a big red *K*, the puffy flaked cereal combined rice with wheat gluten, wheat germ, dry skim milk, and brewer's yeast, and claimed to offer more protein than "any other leading cereal, hot or cold." In addition, the package noted that a dose of Special K provided "substantial percentages of daily requirements" of vitamin C, vitamin D, vitamin B_{12}, niacin, folacin, copper, iron, phosphorus, and other nutrients. Chirped the *Kellogg News*, "Get set to try Special K!"

Four years later Kellogg followed Special K with an even more potent pill called Concentrate. Advertising for the product bragged that one third of a cup of the tiny flakes contained as much protein as an egg and two strips of bacon, as much iron as two ounces of beef liver, as much folacin as three ounces of broccoli, and as much vitamin B_1 as three ounces of pork. "You'd only want to pour three big tablespoons into a bowl and you had a meal," recalled a Kellogg salesman. "It looked like seeds from some plant or what you'd feed goldfish."

To signal the consumer that they had finally arrived at their perfect all-purpose edible, Kellogg sold the "new kind of food" in a gold foil box, equipped with a pour spout like dishwasher detergent to "insure no waste." "Once more," reported *Kellogg News*, "'The Best to You Each Morning' has real punch behind it."

To market the super stuff, Kellogg signed up football coach Woody Hayes. Reclusive movie actress Claudette Colbert praised the product in an unsolicited letter dispatched from her Hawaiian hideaway: she confessed that she practically lived on the tiny flakes. An even more potent endorsement of the power of Concentrate came from within the Kellogg company. "There was an older Kellogg manager who married a younger woman and his wife did get pregnant by him," laughed a Kellogg salesman. "They all made the joke that he was eating Concentrate."

10

Leo the Lion

In 1949 Watson Vanderploeg, the chairman of the Kellogg Company, was riding on a train to Chicago when he struck up a conversation with a fellow in his fifties seated across the aisle. In a rumpled suit dusted with cigarette ashes, this paunchy, round-shouldered individual with black-rimmed bifocals claimed to be in the advertising business.

Vanderploeg had listened to hundreds of ad men before, but the guy next to him on the train was different—sincere, plain-spoken, and kind of a slob. The ruler of the Kellogg empire removed his wire-rimmed spectacles, stroked his thinning white hair, and started explaining his problems. The advertising issue that most concerned him was the emergence of the media behemoth known as television. Video had enormous potential and enormous costs. How should Kellogg handle it?

The balding ad man not only listened to Vanderploeg, but offered fresh insights into the new medium and the mind of the American consumer. As the train neared Union Station, he gave Vanderploeg a smudged card, waved goodbye, and shouted, "Just give me one of your products and I'll show you what I can do." Vanderploeg looked down at the card and read the name Leo Burnett.

Black-and-White Breakfast

"Television has the impact of an atomic bomb," wrote advertising executive William Morris in June 1949. As the television bomb exploded over the United States, Vanderploeg and other cereal executives scrambled to take advantage of the awesome sales power unleashed by the new medium. "If, as many believe, television assumes a powerful cultural role, the program can do more than sell," wrote the *Kellogg News* in the days of early video, "it can make millions of close friends for Kellogg's."

Kellogg and other advertisers realized that they would have to spend millions to make television friends. Total television ad revenues jumped from $12.5 million in 1949 to $128 million just two years later. "Television, as a medium for sales demonstrations right in the customer's living room," observed the *Kellogg News*, "is a gold mine for manufacturers of quality products."

Although many of the programming and marketing techniques developed for radio were applicable to the new medium, television was in many ways a whole new ball game for advertising agencies, sponsors, and networks. "Nobody knew what the hell they were doing!" laughed Max Bryer, a commercial director for the ad agency Benton & Bowles. "Most of the fellas were flying blind because there was nobody you could go to and say, 'Well, how did *you* do it?'"

Kellogg's ad agency, the New York–based Kenyon & Eckhardt, launched *The Singing Lady,* the first television show sponsored by the cereal maker, in the early months of 1949. The program was a television translation of the long-running Kellogg radio program hosted by Ireene Wicker that had first inspired Vernon Grant to create the characters Snap, Crackle, and Pop.

In keeping with the system developed during the radio years, Kellogg was the owner and sole sponsor of the program. The company paid for all the costs of production, and simply purchased time from the television network—in this case ABC. The cereal maker's first video venture was anything but sophisticated. Assisted by a little boy and girl, Wicker provided the voices of puppets who "acted out her lovable stories," according to the *Kellogg News*. Between skits, Wicker pitched Kellogg's Shredded Wheat and Corn Soya, two bad apples in Kellogg's product barrel that, a company spokesman noted, "are particularly suited to television advertising at this time."

Kenyon & Eckhardt soon expanded Kellogg's television grubstake to include a selling platform for Rice Krispies. Kellogg joined Wonder Bread, Poll-Parrot Shoes, Mars Candy, and Welch's Grape Juice in sponsoring a daily fifteen-minute show starring a freckled marionette— his strings in full view and his feet clumping with each step—and his flesh-and-blood friend, Buffalo Bob Smith. A fast-moving mixture of live action, cartoons, old movie clips, and commercial pitches, *Howdy Doody* was so popular that bars across the country stopped serving alcohol during the program so that kids could come in and enjoy the show. "In a middle class home, there is perhaps nothing as welcome to the mother as something that will keep the small fry intently absorbed and out of possible mischief," raved *Variety*. "This program can almost be guaranteed to pin down the squirmiest of the brood."

"We presented scripts to Bob and worked out routines with the characters and Kellogg," recalled an ad man. "Buffalo Bob did a lot of work holding up the packages. He was more cooperative than most." If Howdy made a mess pouring Rice Krispies during live spots, Buffalo Bob stepped in to add the milk with graceful ease. Snap, Crackle, and Pop hand puppets occasionally joined in the hijinks. In time, Kellogg offered a variety of Howdy Doody premiums including cut-out masks, hand puppets —"Put on your own TV show!"—and a two-foot inflatable doll for a dollar and a box top, which *Kellogg News* described as the "perfect playmate." Though extremely popular, the Kellogg material amounted to just a fraction of the sales of Howdy-licensed merchandise, which came to $25 million a year in the late 1950s. Howdy-licensed ads in *Life* magazine showed the carved cowboy holding up a platter of sticky Rice Krispies Marshmallow Crispy Squares, while a word balloon declared "It's Howdy's Favorite Treat!"

In the summer of 1950, executives from Kenyon & Eckhardt traveled to Battle Creek with an idea for a new program. The pitch was for a show about space, just the thing, the ad men argued, to move a vast payload of Kellogg's standards like Pep, Corn Flakes, and Raisin Bran into the giddy weightlessness of high-volume sales.

Kellogg bit on the idea and paid for television production costs as well as airtime on the CBS network. In October 1950, "the greatest name in cereals" rolled out *Tom Corbett: Space Cadet*. Based on a Robert Heinlein novel, the series was set in the year 2350 A.D. at the Space Academy, U.S.A. Here young men and women trained hard to become Solar Guards, an elite group of space police who patrolled the solar system wearing the Space Cadet uniform with its massive, patented, head-through-a-giant-studded-beef-tongue collar.

By the second week on the air Kellogg knew it had a huge hit on its hands. "Disc jockeys were picking up our phrases like 'Go blow your jets,' 'Don't fuse your tubes' and 'Spacemen's luck,'" recalled Frankie Thomas, who played the lead cadet.

Like many other programs of the prehistoric video era, *Tom Corbett* was produced live, creating ample opportunity for flubbed lines, missed cues, and mix ups. "I'd be walking on one of the moons of Jupiter in a storm with the fog machine working like mad and confetti flying around me, and a camera would go out," remembered Thomas. "The floor manager would be waving and pointing to the other camera . . . '*Turn and head into that!*'" At breaks in the action, Tom would splash some milk in a bowl, wipe the sweat from his brow, and tell his audience that "Pep, the build-up wheat cereal" was "a welcome change from food capsules."

Kellogg was intrigued by research that showed that the program, though aimed at kids, had a large adult audience as well. "I guess they're all working in the space program now," laughed Thomas. "I've had letters from people down in Florida and Texas saying 'This is how I got into this, I used to watch Tom Corbett.'"

The Gold Dust Twins

A few weeks after his chance meeting with Kellogg president Vander-ploeg in 1949, Leo Burnett got a call from the Kellogg Company. It seemed that the boys in Battle Creek were having problems with one of their products: Corn Soya. The shredded product born from Dr. Kellogg's belief in soy beans and World War II shortages was not moving, and *The Singing Lady* television program created by Kenyon & Eckhardt wasn't doing that much to help. Did Burnett think he could do something better?

Leo sure did. A poorly educated Chicago man in an advertising world dominated by Madison Avenue Ivy Leaguers, Burnett stood out like a loud belch. He began his career as a boy in Iron Mountain, Michigan, helping his father lay out ads for his store on the family dining-room table. When he started his own agency in 1935, the people who had worked with Burnett in New York said "Leo's too unkempt to ever be a successful advertising man. How's he going to go talk to clients?"

"The story is that when Leo Burnett was working for another agency and he decided to go off and start his own agency, the other agency he was with predicted that he would be out on the corner selling apples within a year," recalled Joe Barbera, whose cartoon production studio did a great deal of work for Burnett. "So he kept that as a symbol. Every year he sent out a package of beautifully wrapped, exquisite apples."

Burnett beat the odds. He worked 364 days a year, bragging that he and his associates were "working stiffs" who spat on their hands before getting down to work with big, black pencils. Burnett described the key to good advertising as the ability to capture the "inherent drama" in any product. The man who was to coin the phrases "You're in Good Hands with All State" and "Fly the Friendly Skies of United" kept a folder in his desk marked "Corny Language," which he described as containing "words, phrases and apt analogies which convey a feeling of sodbuster honesty and drive home a point." Characters created by Burnett's agency, including the Jolly Green Giant, the Pillsbury Doughboy, and Star-Kist's Charlie the Tuna, added personality to the selling points. Wrote Ken Jones, a Burnett creative director, "Leo was the great representative of the American public."

NOSE PICKER

Leo Burnett prided himself on being a crass Midwesterner whose advertising instincts were in touch with the
average American consumer. He despised the "Ivy
League sophisticates" who populated the East Coast
agencies, and he refused to maintain an office on Madison Avenue, long touted as the heart of the industry. Leo
was fond of telling a story that defined the difference
between himself and his New York counterparts. After
giving a speech on advertising to members of Harvard's
M.B.A. class in Boston, Leo had dinner at "one of these
goddamn Harvard clubs" in New York City, during
which he got into a conversation with a snob across the
table. "You must be a Harvard man," Leo said, sick of his
dinner companion's attitude.

"Why yes, how did you know that?" his companion
responded.

Leo answered sarcastically, "Well, I could tell by the
way you carried yourself . . . your deportment . . . your
demeanor . . . there's a certain polish . . . there's a certain
poise."

The Harvard man, insulted, struck back. "Well that's
very interesting Leo, thank you. You went to the University of Michigan, didn't you?"

Leo answered, "Why, that's true. How did you know
that?"

"I saw your ring when you were picking your nose,"
the Harvard man sneered. After the incident, Leo
Burnett never missed a chance to refer to himself as "a
nose picker."

Though a print man to the bitter end, Leo realized that television
was destined to become America's favorite medium. With his eye for
creative talent and his midwestern sensibility, Burnett had more to do
with the shaping of cereal advertising, and America's breakfast habits,
than any other person in the last half of the twentieth century.

The man known as "Leo the Lion" established television production offices in New York and Los Angeles and recruited the best television writers, art directors, commercial directors, and producers he could
get his nicotine-stained hands on. "He just allowed us to grow even

though he grumbled a lot," said a Burnett television writer. "Leo struggled with his own prejudices against this nutty new medium."

One of the TV creatives Leo hired to handle his burgeoning television operation was Don Tennant, a short, soft-spoken radio writer who cut his video teeth on *Hold'r Newt*, a puppet show about a country store he created for WENR-TV in Chicago. Leo recognized Tennant's keen sense of visual drama and his ability to tell a story, talents that were to serve Kellogg extremely well. "Leo taught me advertising, and I taught Leo what I knew about television," remembered Tennant, who went on to develop the most successful icon in advertising history, the Marlboro Man.

Another recruit to the Burnett video stable was a sandy-haired young writer named Kensinger Jones. So prolific was Ken Jones that when Burnett's recruiter met him in St. Louis, he asked, "Are you a syndicate?" "Leo's idea of employing special guys to be television writers was just smart as hell because everybody else was trying to get print writers to write television," declared Jones. "They didn't recognize the dynamics . . . they didn't understand comedy."

Tennant and Jones became famous in Battle Creek as the Gold Dust Twins. They didn't just pitch their ideas for commercials to the Kellogg brass, they performed them, one singing and dancing while the other pointed to the appropriate storyboard panel set up along the conference room. "Burnett was a wonderful place. We had a lot of fun doing this stuff," laughed Jones. "Hell, we had a ball."

The Jones-Tennant team amused everyone except Mark Leaver, Kellogg's top sales director, who had a bad habit of nodding out during their presentations. "We could hardly keep from breaking up because the most important guy was fast asleep," laughed Don Tennant. "What used to kill us was, we'd finish and everybody would applaud and Mark would wake up and say, 'Terrific, terrific!'" A Kellogg district manager was equally mysterious in his enthusiasm for the Burnett agency's work. "What I liked specifically," the Kellogg salesman commented after a presentation, "was the whole thing in general."

Sugar Pops are Tops

Burnett knew how to handle television. His only problem was that he was saddled with a soggy product, Corn Soya. He sent his troops out to search for a vehicle to bring the cereal close to the American heart. In the spring of 1950, Gordon Minter, a freelance commercial director new to the Burnett family, saw a Wild West show at the Graumann's Chinese Theater in Hollywood. The show starred Colonel Tim

McCoy, a Wyoming-born army officer, Indian sign-language expert, silent-screen legend, and former aide to General George Patton.

Minter signed Tim McCoy to pitch Corn Soya in a "rootin' tootin'" low-budget Saturday-evening program for kids. Debuting in the spring of 1950 on KTLA in Los Angeles, the first cereal TV show created by the Leo Burnett agency opened to the beat of tom-toms as the colonel stepped up to the camera and dramatically exclaimed "WAS TAY!"—the Nez Percé version of "Yo, Dude!"—while waving his hand in front of his body according to an ancient and arcane formula. The introduction was followed by the meat of the program, the rerun of an old Hopalong Cassidy western and Tim McCoy's live-action plugs for Corn Soya.

In 1950, Kellogg was impressed enough with Leo Burnett's work on Corn Soya to throw the new Sugar Corn Pops account to the Chicago agency instead of Kenyon & Eckhardt. As boxcars of the new presweet made their way to California markets, Burnett tore the Corn Soya box from Colonel Tim McCoy's talking hands and replaced it with Sugar Corn Pops. His mouth full of the half-chewed corn pops, the cowboy grinned at the camera and sputtered at kids at home to "Eat 'em for breakfast, or munch on 'em during the rest of the day!"

With Sugar Corn Pops, Leo Burnett finally had a Kellogg product he could sink his teeth into. Late in 1950 he found a new advertising vehicle for Sugar Corn Pops, one cut from the same thematic rawhide as Tim McCoy. A couple of Los Angeles–based freelance producers had made a pilot for a western TV series and a companion radio show starring Andy Devine and Guy Madison called *Wild Bill Hickok*. Burnett persuaded Kellogg to buy the show, finance production of it, and purchase air time. Sugar Corn Pops owned the program, lock, stock, and sugar barrel.

Leo sent Don Tennant to Los Angeles to supervise the first few weeks of production for *Wild Bill Hickok*. Instead of an exciting launch pad for Sugar Corn Pops, what Tennant found was a potential video disaster. "The scripts launching *Wild Bill Hickok* were terrible," he groaned. "They opened with a scene of a homesteader's burned house after an Indian raid. . . . Out in the front yard was the mother and a couple of kids with arrows stuck in their backs!" Tennant called up Chicago and cried, "My God, Kellogg can't sponsor anything like this."

Leo agreed that dramatizing bloody massacres wasn't the way to sell breakfast food. Tennant penned an official Kellogg "blue book" of *do*s and *don't*s for the show's writers, and stayed for thirteen weeks on the *Hickok* set. His successful doctoring of the program so impressed Leo that he asked the former puppeteer to head up the agency's newly formed Television Commercial Group, which was devoted exclusively to writing and producing TV commercials for clients like Kellogg. No other advertising agency in the world had such a group at that time.

Tennant's wild west adventure hit the airwaves in April of 1951, during the late afternoon when kids got home from school. Guy Madison, the show's star, was a pleasant, hardworking, and handsome actor—a good punch thrower and an even better horseman. But his television presence was overshadowed by his robust and hilarious co-star, Andy Devine.

Dressing in floppy fringed buckskins, Andy was more than just comic relief, he was the 300-pound soul of the show. He was one of the funniest, best-loved characters Hollywood has ever produced; and from 1951 to 1958, Kellogg owned him. His inimitable whine resulted from a childhood accident in which he fell down with a stick in his mouth. Andy got laughs at nearly every turn in the TV plot line simply by holding his hat on his head and wheedling, "Wait fer me, Wild Bill!" as his boss galloped off down the trail. Repeating the slogan "Sugar Pops are Tops," Wild Bill and his sidekick drew as much as 80 percent of America's television-viewing audience in 1954, who eagerly waited to hear the Kellogg cowboys holler, "Yip-EE, a rip-snortin' cereal, a rootin'-tootin' snack!"

"We did a hell of a job selling that stuff," remembered Guy Madison. "We made personal appearances all over the U.S. Our record was 20,000 people in nine hours in Louisiana. We gave them each a box of Sugar Pops and a picture of Andy Devine and myself." For his efforts at merchandising the Wild Bill Hickok character, Madison received a total of $250. "I wasn't bitter, no," Madison explained. "Just disappointed."

Superman

In 1952, due largely to the cereal-selling bellow of Andy Devine, Burnett won the entire Kellogg account away from Kenyon & Eckhardt. According to the savage laws of Madison Avenue, Burnett set about creating an entirely new identity for Kellogg by killing most Kenyon & Eckhardt productions, including the successful *Tom Corbett: Space Cadet*. "The fact that Leo got this account frosted the heck out of a lot of New York agencies," said Ken Jones.

In 1952, under the watchful eye of Burnett, Kellogg sponsored the first half hour of *Super Circus*. The Sunday afternoon extravaganza was broadcast live from the Civic Theater in Chicago. A huge crowd puller,

---

KELLOGG: NOT FONDA HENRY

During the 1950s the price actors often had to pay for a starring role in a television series was the obligatory cast commercial. Most stars agreed to participate, but not Henry Fonda, an actor who prized his artistic integrity more than his sponsor's sales. Signed in 1959 to star in a Kellogg-sponsored western series entitled *The Deputy*, Fonda balked at pitching the cereal-maker's product. When asked to look directly at the camera and say, "I like Kellogg's Corn Flakes," Fonda refused. "I've never talked to the camera in my life," the actor declared. "I can't do that." After a flurry of phone calls between Chicago, Battle Creek, and Hollywood, Fonda rewrote the spot to suit his artistic sensibility. Walking into the set's general store, the actor pointed to merchandise on the shelves and commented, "There are buggy whips and licorice whips and then there's Kellogg's Corn Flakes . . . and Kellogg's Corn Flakes are a favorite of mine." More than twenty-five years later, Henry Fonda's granddaughter, Bridget Fonda, starred in the movie *The Road to Wellville*, a highly critical account of Dr. John Harvey Kellogg's Battle Creek Sanitarium.

Super Circus was one of the nation's top ten shows with an estimated weekly audience of more than ten million.

While kids delighted in the antics of ringmaster Claude Kirchner and the clowns Nicky, Cliffy, and Scampy, the true secret of the show's success was the gorgeous screen-lighting smile, short skirts, and long legs of platinum blonde Mary Hartline. "She was a symbol for everybody," said Claude Kirchner. "For the kids she was a fairy godmother. She was a sex symbol for men, and the women hated her because they knew what men thought. . . . she was wonderful, brassy, outgoing and superb. She was a phenomenon!"

While Mary Hartline attracted adult male viewers to *Super Circus*, other Burnett creations for Kellogg were pitched directly at the older set. For the golden years crowd, cereal wasn't a sweet treat. It was a trusted friend who kept the body regular. To promote All-Bran and Pep, Burnett employed some of the most trusted names in American entertainment, creating a seamless blur between programming and pitch.

Burnett found one of television's most persuasive personalities in Art Linkletter. Born in Moose Jaw, Canada, Linkletter turned an insatiable curiosity about people into a media fortune. He started as a radio announcer but quickly moved into hosting special events. At one time he traveled up the front of a skyscraper in a bosun's chair interviewing people through open windows. By 1952, his regular program, *Art Linkletter's House Party,* had moved from radio to television and was aired live from Los Angeles every afternoon on CBS. Burnett bought Tuesdays and Thursdays for Kellogg.

The program was an easygoing blend of talk and audience participation—the perfect set-up for Linkletter's cereal pitch, which began with the simple words "Here's Art Linkletter for All-Bran."

"I was always looking for an interesting lead-in involving regularity that would get Art gracefully into the product," recalled Burnett writer Ken Jones, who supplied Linkletter with commercial copy aimed at constipated seniors. "You know . . [stories like] the old clock maker in Cologne who became famous because his clocks were always regular."

"I wasn't enthusiastic about being the voice of their All-Bran" the peristaltic persuader admitted forty years later. The future author of *Kids Say the Darndest Things* admitted that regularity was "a delicate subject" and discussion of the topic was skirted "with careful verbiage" in the 1950s. Instead of a box of constipation relief, Linkletter described All-Bran as a "healthy boost" to a balanced life style. Recalled the television host, "I thought we were doing a good job until we received a letter from an elderly woman who said she had watched me so often she did not need to buy the product any longer as she had a secured a photo of me which hung in her bathroom!"

While Linkletter was the undisputed king of West Coast talk TV, Arthur Godfrey ruled the New York video roost with three different television shows and a radio program. A self-educated hard worker who began his broadcasting career in 1930, Godfrey parlayed his common-touch, third-rate ukelele strumming and soft-spoken "Howa'ya, howa'ya, howa'ya" into an unassailable position at the top of the American media pantheon. Hailed as the second most influential man in America after Eisenhower, the slow-drawling demagogue drew a weekly audience of eighty-two million viewers. "Leo was the biggest believer in Arthur Godfrey," recalled Burnett man Dick Esmail. "He felt that Godfrey could take a brand new cereal and pitch it on the air one day and the shelves would be empty the next day. . . . Leo thought Godfrey was the master."

Billed in the *Kellogg News* as "the Greatest Salesman in the history of radio and television," Godfrey became Kellogg's favorite shill in the fall of 1953 as the cereal giant sponsored the first half hour of *Arthur Godfrey Time* on Tuesdays and Thursdays. The one-two punch of Linkletter and Godfrey on those two days each week gave Kellogg "the strongest daytime combination ever put behind a line of food products in the history of American selling."

Arthur Godfrey may have been a great salesman, but behind the "Old Red Head's" easy-going delivery lurked a monstrous off-camera ego, a dictatorial will, and a mercurial temper, perhaps due in part to his poor health. "You'd talk to his people about what he liked to do so you'd write something for him," said Don Tennant. "And you'd go over it with him and he'd throw it off and say, 'That's shit. I'm not going to do that. I'm not going to do that . . . I'm going to do this.'"

The Burnett agency learned to give Godfrey a simple fact sheet every week about each cereal, which was put on his desk or taped to the back of the cereal box for his on-air pitch. "Godfrey was a prick. He was an absolute son of a bitch," spat Don Tennant. "He was one of the nastiest guys I've ever met and treated everybody like they were dirt."

A more relaxed personality, Garry Moore, joined Kellogg's television sales force in 1953 when the cereal giant sponsored Moore's Friday afternoon show. A multi-faceted man and a favorite with housewives, Moore once collaborated with F. Scott Fitzgerald on an unpublished play and pitched Kellogg's brand of dry dog food along with the company's human products. His salesmanship earned him the praise of the *Kellogg News* as "an expert at interviewing dogs for testimonials on Kellogg's Gro-Pup."

The greatest of Burnett's cereal pitchmen wasn't even human. It was Superman. Born in Jerry Siegel and Joe Shuster's June 1938 issue of *Action Comics,* America's Man of Steel moved onto Mutual radio in the early 1940s, a show co-sponsored by Kellogg. After dropping its sponsorship of the *Superman* radio show in the late 1940s, Kellogg continued its "never-ending fight for Truth, Justice and the American Way" on television in 1953.

Starring George Reeves, once the light heavyweight wrestling champion at Pasadena Junior College, *The Adventures of Superman* actually began production in late 1951. Explaining the character's appeal, Jack Larson, who grew out of the role of Jimmy Olson to become a successful writer and opera libretticist, said, "He is the alien that embodies our goodness."

Kellogg paid for production of the series with a bite-sized budget. To create the famous flying sequence, Burnett director Gordon Minter put Reeves in a harness, hoisted him up in the air on invisible wires, and turned on a wind machine. Footage of the windswept superhero was used as much as possible to fill time. Wrote one observer, "In one episode Superman changed direction while flying, which was accomplished by simply turning the film around—making the 'S' on his uniform backward!"

In spite of the low budget, Superman became an extremely popular character and a powerful flake salesman. Some of his most memorable spots were created for the "Better get a spare" Corn Flakes campaign in 1955. In one, Clark and Jimmy sat down to breakfast to find the Corn Flakes box empty. Clark suggested that Jimmy run down to the store and pick up a new box. Glancing at his watch, Jimmy announced there wasn't time. "Who do you think I am, Superman?" he whined. Clark shook his head knowingly, removed his glasses, and disappeared down the hall pulling at his tie while Jimmy groused, "Out of Kellogg's Corn Flakes, fine host he is!" After a brief scene of Superman flying through clouds, the whistling wind, fluttering curtain, and sudden appearance of a new Corn Flakes box signaled the Man of Tomorrow's miraculous intervention. The announcer intoned, "Even if Superman did deliver Kellogg's Corn Flakes, he'd have a tough time keeping everybody happy."

"The funny thing about it," said Jack Larson, "is that when they asked me to do the commercials I happened to eat Kellogg's Corn Flakes. So it wasn't a lie to do the commercials." What made Larson even happier was that he made much more money doing the commercials than he made doing the Superman shows. Noelle Neil, the actress who played Lois Lane, never had the opportunity to get a piece of the cereal commercial work. "They did not ask her to do commercials, on the basis that they were all early morning things and it would look unseemly for her to be at Clark's house in the morning," remembered Larson. "But they didn't mind if Jimmy and Perry spent the night."

In 1957 Kellogg dropped out of the show, a move that had a shattering impact on George Reeves. On June 16, 1959, two weeks after an automobile crash for which he was prescribed pain killers, the actor was found dead from a gunshot to the head. Some suspected foul play, but the coroner called it a suicide. "Most people would look at him and say, 'George, we can't cast you because you're Superman,'" recalled Burnett director Gordon Minter. "I think that really bugged him." Reeves's death also bothered the producers of the program, who invited Jack Larson to star in a thirteen-part series pieced together from Superman rescue scenes, entitled *Superman's Pal Jimmy Olson.* Larson turned down the offer.

11

Galloping Goodness

The video victories of Leo Burnett and Kellogg inspired Post, General Mills, and Quaker to stampede into television. In 1954 General Mills spent over $7.3 million on network television advertising, a 37 percent increase over the previous year, while Quaker and General Mills boosted their television advertising outlays by 44 percent and 50 percent respectively. By 1958, the four cereal makers were pumping more than $47 million a year into network television.

By virtue of its advertising expenditures, the cereal industry exerted a strong influence over the television images that flickered across the nation in the Eisenhower era. For better or worse, a powerful force behind the American media began to emerge from the bottom of the cereal bowl.

Wizards of the Breakfast Table

Though critics have vilified the influence of television on American youth, in the early days of video, cereal manufacturers maintained surprisingly high standards for sponsorship. "Violence, horror and psychiatric conflict programs may attract audiences, but they are not suitable for viewing by the entire family," wrote *Inside Battle Creek*, a guide to the Cereal City published in 1958. "They are incompatible with the pleasure found in eating and, hence, not good background for commercials."

In 1951, the Cereal Institute, a trade organization representing the interests of the industry, sponsored one of the most successful educational programs ever produced for television: *Watch Mr. Wizard*. The half-hour program, originating in Chicago, starred science teacher Don Herbert, who explained the basic principles underlying the universe. "Eat a good breakfast of fruit and cereal, one with bread and butter or other foods for variety, eggs or breakfast meats," America's Merlin intoned during pauses between experiments with hot-air balloons, disappearing ink, and small rockets. Herbert never pushed any particular

126

brand of flakes but quoted from "a University of Iowa study on nutrition as the director switched to a shot of a bowl of cereal or the Cereal Institute logo," recalled one observer.

General Mills sponsored one of the first educational shows aimed at preschoolers, *Ding Dong School*. Hitting the airwaves in 1953, this forerunner of *Sesame Street* starred Dr. Frances Horwich—known to millions of kids as "Miss Frances." What most children didn't realize was that Dr. Horwich was a child education specialist and chairwoman of the Children's Program Review Committee, a TV watchdog group. Each day's show began as she rang the school bell, ding dong, and instructed two- to five-year-olds in modeling clay, making finger puppets, singing songs, and, of course, eating Wheaties.

A few years after the show began, the Breakfast of Champions offered a special Ding Dong School blackboard package back, which Miss Frances demonstrated on her well-padded lap. "Now boys and girls," said the video schoolteacher. "When it's breakfast time or lunch time or supper time, what are you going to do? You're going to fill the cereal bowl with Wheeeeeaaties. Say it, Wheeeeeaaties. Breakfast of Champions."

By 1955, Ralston parodied these flaky educators with Professor Checkerboard, a bizarre character in checkered tails and top hat who used reverse psychology to sell kids on Ralston's line of shredded wheat and rice cereals called Chex. "Children," he bullied in television commercials, "Wheat Chex are *only* for adults. *Don't eat Chex.*"

In 1955, Post signed another kind of wizard to pitch Sugar Crisp and Toasties in a series of TV commercials. With his craggy features and shock of white hair, eighty-year-old Blackstone the Magician should have been a memorable video presence, except for the fact that his own memory was not so good. "He was already at the point where he couldn't remember the tricks," recalled Benton & Bowles commercial director Max Bryer. "It was so sad because he would be in the middle of a trick . . . and he would just go blank."

Blast Off

Blackstone was no spacier than any of the astral travelers who cruised the airwaves in the 1950s trying to sell cereal. Late in 1949, the New York-based Benton & Bowles agency sold Post on a science-fiction TV series called *Captain Video*. The series followed the adventures of a brainy inventor and his Video Rangers, a squad of young do-gooders who battled galactic evil in the twenty-second century. The purchase of air time for the program on the now-defunct DuMont network was heralded in *Advertising Age* as "the biggest piece of business garnered by DuMont to date."

The program blasted off every week night at the dinner hour, as Wagner's overture to *The Flying Dutchman* blared in the background, and Morse code beeps spelled letters out across the screen. As the suspense deepened, the announcer intoned "P . . . O . . . S . . . T . . . . P . . . O . . . S . . . T. . . . The cereals you like the most! The cereals made by Post . . . take you to the secret mountain retreat of Captain Video!"

The program was classic cheese—so underfunded by Post that it was considered camp even in the early 1950s. Hailed by the *New York Times* as "a triumph of carpentry and wiring rather than of writing," the program chronicled the victories of Captain Video over Nargola, Mook the Man, Dr. Clysmok, Heng Foo Seeng, and various space outlaws, played by Ernest Borgnine, Tony Randall, Jack Klugman, and other young actors. "The Guardian of the Safety of the World" defended the universe with a dazzling array of gadgets, including the remote tele-carrier, the radio scillograph, and the cosmic ray vibrator—all created with a special-effects budget of twenty-five dollars a week—for five shows. One recidivist was sent screaming to his fiery reward with a blast from the trusty opticon scillometer, a device one observer described as "a length of pipe with some spare parts bolted on."

Before fading to black, Captain Video spawned a flying saucer ring and millions of inch-high "Space men" who inhabited specially marked boxes of Post Raisin Bran. Eclectically costumed in Robin Hood tights, ear muffs, and beaked welders' helmets, the little mottled plastic figures looked like refugees from an *Animal House* party. After the invasion of the "space men . . . all the [in-pack] premiums were put in separate bags in with the cereal because someone broke a tooth," recalled a cereal salesman.

Meanwhile, out in Los Angeles, Mike Mosser was peddling an idea for a different sci-fi show to local TV stations. Mosser told *Time* magazine that the idea for a kiddie space opera came to him while he was flying across the Pacific. "It started me wondering and thinking about the universe," mused the World War II Air Force veteran.

Space Patrol blasted off in September 1950 over footage of a model rocket bubbling exhaust as it followed its pull string out of an Art deco bathtub. The program was sponsored by Ralston Purina and produced on a schedule so tight it was dangerous. In one episode, the lead space patrolman Buzz Corey was tied to a tree, facing an Amazon's crossbow, when the stage weapon accidentally fired. "It missed my head," laughed

Ed Kemmer, who played Corey. "It landed about three feet directly below!"

Space Patrol's announcer Captain Jack was performed with cheerful precision by Jack Narz, who went on to host *Beat the Clock* and *Concentration*. Narz also pitched cereal on occasion. "The thing I remember most about the commercials was the importance attached to doing them exactly word for word," the actor recalled years later. "For instance, the copy would read, 'A great breakfast with Rice Chex will give you 'Go Power' to last all day.' Or words to that effect. The key word was 'with.' You could not say, 'A great breakfast *of* . . .' In other words, we were not saying that the cereal gave you the 'go power' but rather that a great breakfast of eggs, bacon, toast, milk *and* cereal gave you the 'go power'. . . . There is always one word buried somewhere in the copy that changes the whole meaning."

Space Patrol took the cereal cast commercial to new heights. The Gardner agency wove pitches for Chex and Hot Ralston right into the story line. In the "Case of the Giant Marine Clam," for example, Prince Baccarratti, alias the Black Falcon, handcuffed Commander Corey and tied two of his crew members, Carol and Happy, in a tank filling fast with water. "Do you talk, or do Carol and Happy try to breath water?" the Prince threatened Buzz. Before he could answer, the Commander broke for a commercial with crew member Happy. Seated under a "Space Patrol Galley" sign, the two gulped down brimming bowls of Rice and Wheat Chex and speculated that their chances of escape were excellent, thanks to their regular Ralston habit. Before slipping back into the water tank for the exciting conclusion of the program, Happy urged his audience of more than six million viewers to "Charge up with Chex for Fun Power. You'll agree they're superific."

"Superific" space patrol premiums offered for box tops and small change included an outer-space helmet, a glow-in-the-dark decoder belt buckle, a space-o-phone, and the Space Patrol Lunar Fleet Base—a cardboard punchout layout that transformed an Eisenhower-era living-room rug into a thirtieth-century space port. The premium was so popular that Ralston Purina could not meet the demand and had to send consolation letters out to disappointed fans. "Hope you'll accept my apology, and keep this photo of the Space Patrol gang as a souvenir," read the correspondence, signed Buzz Corey.

General Mills entered the video space race in 1954, co-sponsoring the popular program, *Captain Midnight*. The descendant of radio hero Captain Albright, a World War I flying ace, Captain Midnight was a

THE RALSTON ROCKETS

In 1952 Ralston Purina Company commissioned the Standard Carriage Company of Los Angeles to build a full-sized rocket ship to promote its daily sci-fi TV show *Space Patrol*. The thirty-five-foot "Ralston Rocket" was constructed from twenty-gauge steel sheets riveted to oak ribbing and mounted on a flat bed, for a total cost of more than $40,000. For two years the rocket toured the United States, parking in front of supermarkets to the delight of millions of young space patrollers, who waited hours to wiggle through the cockpit packed with a repeller ray, astro-radar, and two-way space-o-phones.

The next year, Ralston ordered a second rocket to be given away as the first prize in the "Name Planet X" contest. Instead of a warship, the second rocket was the ultimate clubhouse, complete with eight fold-down beds, a kitchen, and dining room. Out of millions of entrants, ten-year-old Ricky Walker of Washington, Illinois, won the contest with the name "Caesaria." The five-ton rocket was delivered to his doorstep on January 14, 1954. Ricky enjoyed his dream-come-true for only two years before his family sold it to a traveling carnival. Twenty-five years later, the rusted hulk turned up on a weedy lot outside of Albany, New York, only to be demolished in 1990. "It was unbelievable," said *Space Patrol* memorabilia collector Dale Ames. "If there are seven wonders of the world, this was ninth or tenth."

hardened, steel-eyed, cold warrior dedicated to ferreting out communist leeches sucking the life blood from the Free World's young arteries. *TV Guide* described it as "a violent series with gallons of gore."

The role was played to polished-pine perfection by Richard Webb, a hard-fighting World War II veteran who was the lead in the Cold War classic *I Was a Communist for the FBI*. Outfitted in a suede bomber jacket, silk scarf, and crash helmet, the ultra-American headed up the Secret Squadron, a hush-hush platoon of McCarthyite vigilantes dedicated to routing out spies, harnessing volcanic energy, and making the world a better place to enjoy "Kix, the crispy corn cereal that's 83 percent energy food."

That same year General Mills chose another para-military hero to boost sales of Sugar Jets, a presweetened cereal introduced during the Korean War. Major Jet was a fictional test pilot, presented in both live action and animated form, who linked the cereal's sugary taste with the exhilaration of fighter jet afterburners, urging his young recruits to "Jet up and go with Sugar Jets."

The Major Jet shtick was so successful that over six million young Americans bought Major Jet magic goggles from toy stores, and General Mills acquired its own air force, an F-94 fighter photographed for Major Jet promo shots with General Mills, not U.S. Air Force, markings.

The National Biscuit Company sponsored its own air-borne show, *Sky King.* Set in the contemporary West, the program tracked the adventures of a rancher who solved crimes from the cockpit of his small airplane, the Sky Bird, a twin-engine Cessna 310-B. Grant Kirby, the real-life pilot who portrayed Skylar King for a salary comparable to the industry standard of $300 per week, was eager to emulate the marketing success of his predecessor, Major Jet. The high flyer submitted sketches and prototypes of model planes, geiger counters, shirts, pistols, and other toys to the sponsor, which turned down every one of his plans to make money off his television persona. "I don't know why," sighed the actor years later. "I wanted to desperately."

Oaters

On the ground, a herd of cowpokes thundered onto the television set to pitch cereal. The cereal posse was led by *Ranger Joe,* a modest fifteen-minute cowboy series, carried out of Philadelphia to eighteen other East Coast cities on the fledgling ABC network in 1949. The program starred Will Rogers' nephew Jesse Rogers, who perched on a corral fence, demonstrated how to use a lariat, and narrated silent cowboy films. Wrote *Variety,* "Ranger Joe, newest hero for living room wranglers, feeds his horse Topaz and his cowpokes Ranger Joe Breakfast Food. Commercials are easily tied in with the camera doings, since the hero and the product have the same label. Cereal plugs . . . make it a must on mamma's shopping list."

In that same year, General Mills decided to move *The Lone Ranger* radio show to television as a vehicle for selling Cheerios. The first television episodes rode into a storm of controversy. Appalled by the fact that the story line continued from one episode to the next, Jack Gould of the *New York Times* attacked General Mills and George W. Trendle, the show's producer, for keeping young rangers "emotionally hopped up" and attempting to "capitalize on the normal anxiety and sensitiveness of youngsters." "The use of the old cliff-hanging technique should be abandoned promptly," wrote the curmudgeon. "Everyone concerned with the TV version of *The Lone Ranger* should stop and think what they are doing."

General Mills thought Gould was all soggy, and TV audiences agreed. By 1950, *The Lone Ranger* was America's seventh most popular show. Clayton Moore never tired of his role as the masked man, which he played for seven years. "I just never wanted to do anything else after I started *The Lone Ranger*," confessed the former pilot and stunt man who wore the Ranger's costume like a body tatoo. "I fell in love with the character."

So did others. Lone Ranger merchandise became so popular that the video lawman became known as a "Corporation on Horseback." On specially marked boxes of Kix, the Lone Ranger, icon of cold cereal, became the ultimate cold warrior. The mysterious rider kept the West safe for democracy with the deterrent power of his "seething, scientific sensation," the Kix atom bomb ring. Over six million of the shiny, gold-plated rings shaped like a miniature warhead were mailed out by General Mills in what many consider to be the most popular premium of all time. The ring was so popular that the Massachusetts-based Robbins Premium Company required three separate manufacturing runs to meet the demand.

Kids who weren't satisfied with cardboard or atom bomb rings could walk in their idol's footsteps. Tourists were welcome at the *Lone Ranger* set, located in Chatsworth, California, which featured such highlights as the pile of boulders that marked the Lone Ranger's campground and a snack bar stocked with General Mills cereals and plenty of cold milk.

Those who couldn't make it to the shrine of the Lone Ranger sought to get up close and personal with the lawman through fan mail. Out of millions of epistles sent to the Lone Ranger in care of General Mills, a few of the most memorable survived. In 1956, a person identified only as "a christian" was driven by guilt to write the masked lawman. "I made a false statement sometime ago and thereby cheated your department out of two dollars. The Lord has been speaking to me about that sin and I want to make things right so I am enclosing that amount. Am sorry I stooped so low for in God's sight, a small sin is just as hideous as a large sin. Please forgive me."

In similar vein, Mr. Kurt Biedermann of Dearborn, Michigan, sought salvation for his wife who had used phony names to acquire a large collection of Lone Ranger silverware. "If you can . . . scare her without bringing my name into it, you might save a soul," the anxious husband counseled the company.

In 1950, Quaker Oats thought they had the perfect video cereal wrangler to compete with the Lone Ranger in the form of Roy Rogers. The "King of the Cowboys" was the star of numerous B western films and the *Roy Rogers* radio series, in which he sung the praises of Quaker Oats with lines like "Delicious, nutritious, makes you feel ambitious."

Quaker pressed Roy to follow the Lone Ranger's trail from radio to television. But there was a hitch. Rogers was signed to Republic Pictures and the studio would not release its buckaroo from a binding contract. Lamented Art Rush, Roy's manager at the time who was forced to scout around for other sponsors, "When I couldn't deliver Roy to Quaker Oats for TV, they canceled our radio show."

Quaker looked around Hollywood for another western actor without Roy's contractual saddlebags. They found just the right showman in George "Gabby" Hayes, a grizzled old character actor who had roamed the range with Gene Autry, Roy Rogers, William Boyd, John Wayne, and other riders of the B western purple sage.

The Gabby Hayes Show debuted September 30, 1950, on NBC in the fifteen-minute slot immediately before the popular *Howdy Doody*. Screeching "Yessirree, Bob! It's Dee-licious!," in his inimitable style, the scruffy old coot wiped milk from his beard as he munched on Puffed Rice and Puffed Wheat, told tall tales, and screened serialized clips from his old movies, which he despised.

"I hate 'em," he admitted later. "Simply can't stand them. I made all those movies and hardly knew I was acting in them."

Meanwhile, Roy Rogers was in the middle of a high-stakes syndication poker game. Republic threatened to serialize Roy's old movies to TV—a move that would have ruined the actor's chances of getting his own TV show. Roy filed an injunction against the studio.

While Roy's attorneys were busy in court, Roy's manager, Art Rush, hopped a train to New York in hopes of selling Roy's proposed TV series to an advertising agency. Rush got off the train in Grand Central Station to find nothing but closed doors on Madison Avenue. He sat in his New York hotel room, his hopes crushed, until he got a call from Foote, Cone & Belding, the agency that managed the Postum, Krinkles, and Toasties accounts for Post. The number-two cereal company wanted their own television cowboy show to run neck and neck against Kellogg's popular *Wild Bill Hickok*. Post was willing to sponsor the controversial cowboy's TV show on one condition. The company reserved the right to cancel Roy's show if Republic ever brought his films to television. Rogers agreed to the Post contract, out-bluffing Republic, which never acted on its threat to block the cowboy's video career.

Produced by Roy's own production company, *The Roy Rogers Show* premiered on NBC in December, 1951, and beat *Hickok* out in the ratings race. Roy and his wife, Dale Evans, ended each show by slurping down some "Delicious candy-kissed Krinkles," then throwing themselves into a stirring rendition of "Happy Trails to You."

Dale and Roy's trails turned out to be happy indeed. Though their troubles with Republic kept them from acting in the movies, by 1956 Roy's merchandising corporation employed 2,000 people and grossed $50 million a year from more than 350 licensed products. Post turned the cereal aisle into a franchised shrine to the King of the Cowboys. "We saturated the market with Roy Rogers," recalled Bill Betts, Post's art director at the time. "Every package in the line—it was called a line promotion—had a picture of Roy Rogers on it and some sort of Roy Rogers premium packed inside it."

Some of the earliest Roy Rogers giveaways were pop-out trading cards, one dropped in each specially marked package. The series of "action-packed" dioramas of "authentic" Double R Bar ranch life caused a sensation. "By adding dimension, they blew the other cereal trading cards right off the toilet," gushed one collector.

Selling Roy Rogers to the public extended well beyond television and the cereal aisle. Post sponsored award-winning appearances by Roy and Dale in the Rose Bowl's "Tournament of Roses" parade, a televised spectacle watched by over seventy million potential Post customers across America. The King of the Cowboys rode atop horses, waterfalls, wagons, and television sets with pictures of thundering stage coaches created from millions of freshly cut flowers. Wrote the company publication *The Post Box*, "Even the wheels of the coach turned as a typical 'family,' sitting on a floral replica of a hooked rug, watched the drama unfold."

During the mid-1950s, cereal sponsors helped create a new genre of television, the adult western drama. Post co-sponsored *Gunsmoke,* gathering Matt Dillon, Festus, Doc, and others around Miss Kitty's table for a breakfast of Toasties or Grape-Nuts. General Mills launched *The Life and Times of Wyatt Earp*. "In an adult western," recalled leading man Hugh O'Brian, who reprised his role in a 1994 TV movie, "the cowboy still kissed his horse, but he worried about it!"

O'Brian thoroughly enjoyed his days as Wyatt Earp. "We had two

HOPPY AND THE FLOOZY

Both Post and Kellogg used their leverage as big spending sponsors to attract celebrities to Battle Creek. These
appearances served as morale boosters for the workers
who actually ground out the cereals. Arthur Godfrey
toured the Kellogg plant in 1953. "Amazing," he mused
as he watched a railway freight car being loaded with
cases of cereal. "And to think it is all eaten by the spoonful!" Roy Rogers and Dale Evans paraded their
entourage through the city, performing a wild west show
for all the Post workers at the W. K. Kellogg Auditorium.
Although Dale's tendency to praise the Lord caused fits
among her Post handlers, the Rogers appearance was a
smash hit. William Boyd, star of the Post-sponsored
Hopalong Cassidy radio show, was less popular. When he
came to town in 1950, the folks in Battle Creek expected
a gentle knight of the old West. Instead they got an abrasive celebrity dressed in black who waved off autograph
seekers with the words, "Get away from me! I am the
star! I don't have to do this sort of thing!" The company
Hoppy kept was even more shocking than his attitude.
"He showed up with his very hard-looking babe,"
remembered one former Post employee. "We wanted the
Sweetheart of the Corn! We weren't ready for this
floozy!"

sponsors, Gleem toothpaste and Cheerios," he laughed decades after
the fact. "I used to tell all the kids to eat Gleem and brush their teeth
with Cheerios."

By the late 1950s, the westerns that had dominated the infancy of
American television were growing a bit stale. When Post brought out -
Alpha Bits ("Sugar-sparkled ABC's") in 1957, it decided to drop its
sponsorship of *The Roy Rogers Show* and advertise its product on a different type of oater, *Fury*, the story of "a horse and the boy who loved him."

Starring a black stallion whose real name was Beauty, *Fury* enjoyed
great ratings and industry-wide admiration. "This horse was the most
talented horse I've ever encountered," pronounced Max Bryer, who
directed the cereal commercials for the program. While the human
members of the cast chowed down around the ranch-house breakfast

table, Fury waited patiently for his cue before he "stuck his head in through the open window and nuzzled the box of Alpha Bits or Sugar Crisp," recalled Bryer. Even more amazing to Bryer was the fact that the equine star could "actually play left field," chasing grounders, shagging flies, and running the bases in cast-and-crew games of softball.

Less cooperative were the Marquis Chimps, a group of trained chimpanzees who once pitched Post cereals on *The Jack Benny Show*. "The monkeys were extraordinary performers," recalled Max Bryer, who directed the television commercial. "But we had to do really quick food shots because they'd spill the stuff all over. . . . Boy, what a difficult chore!"

The most popular pitch-animal of the 1950s was Rin Tin Tin IV, star of *The Adventures of Rin Tin Tin*, sponsored by the National Biscuit Company. In addition to attracting a large audience, Private Rin Tin Tin of the 101st Cavalry spawned a vast assortment of premiums, including canteens, pennants, plastic mugs, bugles, belts, cavalry hats, mess kits, cut-out masks, T-shirts, plastic rings, televiewers, and toy rifles. Arguably, the pick of the litter was the foot-high stuffed Rinty dog. "It seemed to have more balls than my Lassie doll," observed one Rinty fan.

Rin Tin Tin IV was a direct descendant of Rin Tin Tin I, who starred in several silent films in the 1920s. Alongside his best buddy, Corporal Rusty, the four-footed soldier helped Sergeant Biff and Lieutenant Rip tame the West. Unfortunately for Frank Martello, the young director in charge of filming the shredded wheat ads for the series, Rin Tin Tin IV proved to be "absolutely inbred," so dumb that as many as four different dogs were used to film a single scene.

"The dog couldn't take any directions," complained Martello of the animal that collected $2,300 per week, eight times the salary of his human co-stars. "He just sat there . . . like a favorite pet."

12

The Carton Club

While Captain Video, Tom Corbett, Rin Tin Tin, Fury, and Mr. Wizard fought the on-air war for the American stomach, the cereal GIs, the salesmen, hammered away on the ground. These foot soldiers for market share saw their in-store trenches undergo a dramatic change in the 1950s. Gone were the mom-and-pop grocery stores and the grab stick used to pull cereal boxes from the top shelf. These were replaced by the magic of self-service and the suburban food-shopping wonder known as the supermarket.

As a result of the food-retailing revolution, the battle between breakfast-food makers shifted from the floor, where the sales force once fought tooth and nail for point-of-purchase displays and product pyramids, to the shelf, where they struggled for "facings" (numbers of packages facing out from the shelf) and eye-catching product design. According to W. H. Vanderploeg, the president of Kellogg, the idea was "to make every package a display piece."

The Colorful Subconscious

Ad man Leo Burnett was a believer in packaging. In 1951, Burnett pitched Vanderploeg on a new concept: creating cereal boxes with as much visual appeal as magazines. Vanderploeg liked the idea. "If you count each Kellogg package that goes through grocery store shelves," said the president of the Kellogg Company, "that's a circulation of upwards of half a billion a year—better than *Life*."

Kellogg used the April 14, 1952, issue of *Life* to announce its new line of boxes, produced with a state-of-the-art five-color rotogravure printing press. Under the headline "New Faces," the company proclaimed that "seeing a new Kellogg package for the first time . . . was like suddenly discovering that the freckle-faced girl next door had blossomed into a raving beauty!"

Burnett transformed the freckle-faced cereal box into a raving beauty by relegating the Kellogg name to a square in the upper left corner of every package, while freeing up the rest of the space for TV star head shots, cartoon character appearances, premium advertisements, or special announcements that might beckon the consumer—or her kids— as she hiked down the aisle. In so doing, Burnett loosened up the whole concept of package design and turned the stodgy cereal aisle into a noisy magazine rack stocked with the crunchy equivalents of *True Detective*, *Sports Illustrated,* and *Confidential.* "There is something very unique about Burnett and Kellogg. That's the fact that the advertising agency did most of the packaging," said Dick Weiner, a Burnett art director. "That's not usual."

Burnett was heavily influenced in his packaging ideas by motivational research. A theoretical cross between psychology, sociology, philosophy, and statistical market analysis, "MR," as it was called, achieved tremendous popularity in the ad world of the 1950s. Ernest Dichter, president of the Institute for Motivational Research, Inc., was one of the prophets of the movement, the man who said that Chrysler sold fewer convertibles than sedans because men regarded the former as mistresses, the latter as wives. Dichter provided Burnett's creative team with valued insights, convincing them that advertising must appeal to feelings "deep in the psychological recesses of the mind."

Motivational enthusiast E. L. Bernays asserted in 1954 that the crunch in the most successful breakfast cereals gave consumers an outlet for their hostile and aggressive feelings. Other MR enthusiasts studied the eye-blink rate of shoppers and found that women went into a light trance in the cereal aisle. "You have to have a carton that attracts and hypnotizes this woman," said Gerald Stahl, executive vice president of the Package Designers Council, "like waving a flashlight in front of her eyes."

Motivational research had its most direct impact on the cereal box in regard to color. Leo Burnett was a devotee of motivational researcher Louis Cheskin, director of the Color Research Institute of America. Burnett hired Cheskin to design the masculine red-and-white package that helped shift Marlboro cigarettes from a ladies' brand to the all-male smoke. He worked with Cheskin to create cereal boxes with the delicate emotional underpinnings of the rainbow.

"Certain colors can be aimed at particular consumer groups," declared a Cheskin-influenced Burnett memo. "A product that will be bought by children may be packaged in bright vibrant colors, but if it's a product to be used by children, but bought by mothers, a subdued, pastel shade is more desirable."

Kellogg used the book *Color Psychology* by Faber Birren as its color bible. Jungle green, described in the book as "peaceful, quieting, refreshing—a strong appetite color," was the hue chosen for Sugar Frosted Flakes packages in 1952. Sugar Corn Pops positively oozed "cheerful, inspiring, vital" yellow, while packages of Rice Krispies and Corn Flakes remained white—and therefore "pure, clean and youthful." Pep stumbled into the danger zone of deep blue—"subduing, sober"—before paying the price by disappearing from shelves forever. This approach, however ingenious, ran into problems for the agency. "We had so many products we ran out of colors," recalled Dick Weiner.

In keeping with his strategy to create magazine-like cereal packaging, Burnett hired some of America's greatest commercial artists to illustrate the Kellogg's boxes. Norman Rockwell, Carl Timmons, Dale Maxey, and Tom Hoyne were just some of the illustrators who created eye-catching renderings of Wild Bill Hickok, Tom Corbett, and freckle-faced, cornflake munching, all-American kids that graced America's cereal aisles in the mid-1950s.

To grab the attention of children coming down the cereal aisle, the eyes on cereal box characters got bigger, wider, and, in some cases, more demented. "If you'll examine the early forms of Snap, Crackle, and Pop on Kellogg's Rice Krispies packages, you'll see that their eyes changed and got larger," declared Ted Carr, a freelance illustrator in the Burnett orbit. "I even have stuff where the characters' eyes on the back of the package are small and ones on the front are large, which is sort of nutty."

Mix-ups between artists and production people were rare but costly. One Special K package featured a recipe for Special K cookies. The cookies were drawn in a delicious rich brown, but when they were printed on the package the baked goods turned blue. According to John Long, Burnett's sharp-eyed ad men caught the mistake, after printing only "a couple hundred thousand of the damned things."

Leo Burnett's obsession with color extended from the cereal aisle to the electromagnetic spectrum. "Color TV will be the greatest of all great media in the greatest of all advertising countries," gushed Burnett's TV czar DeWitt O'Kieffe in May 1954. "We should cut color TV into our long-range thinking beginning right now if this agency is going to break out in front of color TV—and stay there."

There were risks in entering the wonderful world of color. Some experts warned of the "fatigue quotient," sensory overload from too much of a good thing. Burnett estimated that adding color to TV programs increased production expenses by 40 percent or more. "Will the first color TV account in its field simply massacre competition," mused an internal Burnett memo, "or get massacred?"

In 1954, Kellogg's colorful advertising agenda was further enhanced when the Leo Burnett agency picked up the color television advertising account for Motorola Incorporated, which was having trouble selling its color sets. Leo implemented a bold new advertising approach for the company. Instead of just creating TV and print commercials to sell hardware, Burnett decided to create color television programming for all his clients, including Kellogg. His thinking was that consumers would want to watch stars like Mary Hartline on Kellogg's *Super Circus* so much that they'd run out and buy a new Motorola color set. Reasoned a Burnett memo, "We eat with our eyes just about as much as we eat with our digestive organs, and now the eyes will really have an 'eating' job."

In 1954, the laboratory for Kellogg color video was *Kukla, Fran and Ollie*. The popular puppet show originated from a studio in Chicago. During one commercial break, the hosts replaced Kukla, Fran, and Ollie with Snap, Crackle, and Pop hand puppets and scurried over to a bowl of Rice Krispies. "The result was really terrible," remembered Burnett color correction expert Dick Esmail, who watched the monitor as the red strawberries pictured on the front of the Rice Krispies box spread out to saturate the whole image with a pinkish hue. "We were a little disappointed."

Despite the blurred visions, later that year, with only 70,000 color sets coast to coast, Burnett began to broadcast all of Kellogg's child-oriented programming in color. It was a first for the cereal industry and the results were dramatic. By 1956, Kellogg had captured 45 percent of the total cereal market, more than the market shares of Post and General Mills combined.

Post Tries Harder

Kellogg's overwhelming success infuriated the folks at Post. By the 1950s, General Foods management in White Plains, New York, looked at the Post division as a very minor concern, almost an industrial museum piece, which made a very small contribution to the company's total revenue stream. Management really wanted to get out of the cereal business "but they were stuck with it because Old Man Post started General Foods corporation and his daughter was still the big shot stockholder at that time," observed Post artist Bob Traverse. "Kellogg was different.

Cereal was their meat and potatoes. Everything they had was important."

"We were out for the top spot, but of course, we didn't have a chance of achieving this. General Foods execs at the New York office knew this—but the troops in the field didn't—we were out to win!" explained Post executive Bill Betts. "Our ignorance was, in part, the driving force that made the cereal business so exciting at the time."

Betts, a Midwesterner with a fondness for practical jokes, became the man in charge of Post's internal art department in the late 1940s. Betts' positive outlook was enhanced in the early 1950s when, the only relative to attend the funeral of an uncle, he inherited a substantial hunk of money from his late uncle's estate. His inheritance was the subject of much kidding within the Post marketing department.

Under Betts' direction, Post made the first push into brightly colored cereal packaging. In 1949, the company installed rotogravure presses, capable of high-speed color printing. "We were making Kellogg look crumby from the package standpoint," said Betts, who acknowledged the fact that the faces on some of the Post packages took on a peculiar purple tinge. "Ultimately they [Kellogg] had to scrap their presses and go to rotogravure, too—a tremendous expense."

When Burnett inspired Kellogg to adopt the magazine package in 1952 and design a new line of eye-catching box fronts, Betts hired the Bahlman Studios in Kalamazoo, Michigan, to help reinvigorate Post's packaging. Bahlman's top illustrator was Bob Traverse, a tall, laconic man from rural Michigan who enjoyed occasionally working portraits of his kids into his illustrations. He put his son Kim on the package of Alpha Bits. A box of Sugar Coated Corn Flakes was a veritable gallery of more distant Traverse relations. "That's my brother-in-law," laughed the artist, pointing to a smiling boy with short cropped hair, "and that's my niece, Paula Kemp."

While Traverse and Betts worked together for years, other cereal-artist collaborations weren't as mutually satisfying. In 1957, Post joined with Al Capp, creator of the extremely popular comic strip *Li'l Abner,* to promote Grape-Nuts, Grape-Nuts Flakes, and 40% Bran Flakes. Not only did Capp demand an exorbitant royalty fee, he forced Post to hire his own team of artists, who knew nothing about package design. A "very difficult, abrasive man," was how Betts described Capp. "A pain in the ass" was how artist Bob Traverse characterized the creator of Hairless Joe and the Schmoos.

DESIGN FLAWS

Some of the designs created in the cereal-packaging revolution of the 1950s scored a direct miss. In 1953, a new Quaker Puffed Wheat box was described in *Advertising Age* as "a new luminous package printed with fluorescent ink, which glows when illuminated by black light." Hailed as a "merchandising first," the black-light package proved to be ahead of its time, and quickly disappeared.

In 1955, at the height of the motivational research fad, General Mills introduced a new Wheaties package design called "The Face." The Face was a Pac Man-like silhouette, portrayed on the Wheaties box in four different colors, each of which was supposed to lure a different member of the family according to their primal color needs. "Brother Face" came in red, "Sister Face" in yellow, "Mother Face" in blue, and "Father Face" in brown. "It was a mistake," admitted Robert Stafford of the Knox Reeves agency." The Face boxes had a certain stopping power just as design, but Wheaties is much more than design."

There were problems with the design of cereal box prizes as well. Burnett writer Kensinger Jones had the chance to try out the prototype for a baking powder propelled atomic submarine to be given away in boxes of Kellogg's cereal. "My son was about five years old at the time and was taking a bath," recalled Jones. "I came bursting into the bathroom with this thing in my hand. We put baking powder in it, put it in the tub. It promptly capsized and kept capsizing." After Jones complained to Kellogg, the faulty sub was redesigned. "It was absolutely beautiful," laughed Jones. "It just went up and down like a real submarine."

By Nook or By Crook

With vastly greater budgets at its command, Kellogg was the undisputed master of cereal advertising in the 1950s. The fight for the in-store impulse buy remained a brawl between number-one Kellogg and number-two Post. Kellogg concentrated on the high-volume supermarkets, Post on the individually owned stores. Burnett gave Kellogg class. Poverty made Post crass.

Betts' design team churned out an astonishing array of displays and other promotional material for Post's street-level merchandizing onslaught. Huge motorized supermarket displays featured Ted Williams swatting a Sugar Crisp box thirty times a minute, a pennant-waving Bugs Bunny standing atop a replica of the Mayflower urging kids to "Sail into Post," vinyl blow-up "Injun" canoes floating serenely across the top of the aisles loaded with Toasties, and full-scale two-dimensional standees of Danny Thomas, Hopalong Cassidy, and Li'l Abner, pitching, lassoing, and stomping down the aisles for Toasties, Grape-Nuts Flakes, and Sugar Crisp. "I was always under the gun with promotions," said Betts. "The relentless change kept us on our toes all the time."

Sometimes biology got in the way of production. At one point, Betts designed a life-sized display of Roy Rogers leaning against a red corral fence post to pitch a toy pistol premium. Hounded by a production deadline, Betts needed a photo of Rogers and needed it fast. Unfortunately, the King of the Cowboys was recuperating from an operation in a California hospital. Post's photographer had to pull Rogers out of his sickbed, dress him in tight riding pants, and drag him to a Hollywood set for the shoot. "He looked terrible—washed out, no color, no suntan," remembered Betts. "We had to do a lot of retouching in order to get some color into him because he was so sick."

The Post sales force was ever on the lookout for new gimmicks to move product. Pony rides, magic demonstrations, clowns, a live goldfish give-away, even the appearance of salesmen dressed as Grandma Moses helped spread the Post cereal message. In 1956, the cereal salesmen held a news conference inside the monkey house at the zoo in Oklahoma City to announce a circus premium inside Toasties. "Noses pressed against glass, a vast audience of mothers with children watched the procedure with interest," wrote a reporter for the company publication *The Post Box*. "Salesmen left . . . with the vivid awareness . . . any wild beast can bring."

Grocery-store owners didn't give away their retail real estate for free. Some managers settled for "trade premiums," promotional toys like Trigger Junior, a corrugated cardboard hobby horse, that made great gifts for the kids. Others demanded cash. "A salesman could go in and for five dollars buy the use of the space," recalled a Post point-of-purchase supplier. "Now that was big money then . . . an end aisle today costs hundreds of dollars."

Post's merchandising operation was highly effective in the Southeast, the Southwest, and Texas—areas of the country in which supermarkets had not yet displaced mom-and-pop grocery stores. "Post was the leader in that market," said Stan Austin, a veteran Quaker Oats salesman who covered West Texas, driving 250 miles a day to stock twenty stores. "They had Toasties and Grape-Nuts Flakes. Kellogg, with only Sugar Frosted Flakes, Krumbles, and Corn Flakes, was not the big gun."

While Post relied on one-on-one selling and aisle showmanship, Kellogg began an all-out effort to groom the cereal aisle as its own backyard. Kellogg theoreticians developed an equation: proper shelf longitude plus proper shelf latitude plus positioning next to other Kellogg's products equals increased sales. Recalled Burnett's John Long, "I remember making books called *Shelf Management* which really meant kicking the hell out of the other guys."

In public, the instrument of Kellogg's shelf management was the "fair share" plan for shelf allocation. Each member of the Kellogg sales force was outfitted with a long, narrow attaché case. The case opened to reveal rows of postage-stamp-sized cereal box magnets, showing each cereal-maker's products in a different color. The salesman stuck these magnets on the inside lid of the case to create a "Plan-O-Gram"—a representation of the amount of space for each brand on the basis of its percentage of sales. The salesman developed a program for each particular store and argued that if a product fell below a certain sales level, it should be discontinued.

In practice, the Plan-O-Gram worked more like "Grease-the-Palm"; rank-and-file Kellogg salesmen were supplied with baseball and football tickets and other bribes, which they spread around to the managers of big chain stores in order to gain advantageous cereal placement. "If the Kellogg guy was in good with the head merchandiser at one of these companies, why, he was able to get things accomplished . . . let's put it that way," admitted a Kellogg salesman.

By the mid-1950s, thanks to Kellogg's ubiquitous Plan-O-Gram, the cereal aisles in all of America's largest supermarkets looked pretty much alike. Brands were grouped by manufacturer, with the big-volume items such as Kellogg's Corn Flakes in the "bin" or bottom shelf; the kiddie favorites, including the Sugar Corn Pops, in the middle shelf; and the adult cereals like All-Bran and Grape-Nuts on the top shelf. Low-volume items like Wheat Honeys and Rice Honeys, referred to by Kellogg's salesmen as "dogs," were stuck in the "hole," the upper shelves at the ends of the cereal aisle, where they were often overlooked by shoppers pushing their carts around the corner.

A favorite trick to maximize "facings" was to take the label strips off the spots where rival brands were supposed to go in the hopes that busy restocking clerks would leave the competition in the back room. After sales of the forgotten rival dropped off, "We would show them figures on how they sold and try to get the grocer to discontinue them so he could put in our new brand," explained a Kellogg salesman.

Wheaties was a favorite target of the Kellogg sales crew. In the 1950s, the company issued its sales force four-shelf aluminum cereal racks for use in restaurants. "It was supposed to be exclusive for Kellogg's," laughed a Kellogg salesman, "but I was smart enough to tell the restaurant owner that he could put Wheaties on the top shelf. Of course, restaurants had a little grease in the air, and that's where the grease settled—on the top Wheaties boxes."

One of the other major responsibilities of the sales staff was to take care of customer complaints, most of which turned out to be bogus. Salesmen were instructed to be polite but firm with those who claimed to find glass, rocks, or other foreign items in their cereal.

"It seems silly but there are a lot of people looking for a fast buck," explained a Kellogg salesman who got several complaints from people claiming that they found steel chips mixed in with their breakfast flakes. "I explained to people that there were ninety-two check points in the processing of cereal with magnets that got within a half an inch of the flakes and would pick it up."

This particular salesman had a chance to witness firsthand the effectiveness of the cereal safety system. While on a tour of the Kellogg plant in Battle Creek, the salesman stopped at the point where liquid vitamins were sprayed onto Pep and threw a penny onto the conveyor belt. "Red lights came on," laughed the penny pitcher, who watched in awe as a blast of compressed air blew a four-foot-long section of cereal off the conveyor belt and into a container. "That was a good experience," the salesman later admitted. "It just showed they don't waste any cereal. What was blown off the belt was sold for animal food after they checked it."

The process for selecting cereal premiums was so painstaking that unforeseen problems rarely occurred. When they did, it was the salesmen who had to clean up the mess. In the 1950s, Kellogg stuffed boxes of Pep with a premium called a Whirl-A-Rang. The device was a plastic stick with a rubber band to propel it into the air. Unfortunately, if kids launched the Whirl-A-Rang the wrong way, it shot up into their faces.

As reports of Whirl-A-Rang mishaps trickled back into Battle Creek, Kellogg instructed its sales force to go from store to store to pick up Pep packages carrying the Whirl-A-Rang and destroy them. Kellogg salesman Frank Staley had completely filled up his car with recalled Pep packages when he noticed a house with a chicken pen behind it. "I talked to the owner," Staley recalled, "and offered him a loaded station-wagon of Pep if he would feed it to the chickens and burn the boxes."

The Burnett agency worked closely with Kellogg to maintain its stranglehold on the cereal aisle. "We would go into the supermarket and take pictures," recalled Dick Weiner, one of the many ad men who prowled the linoleum, scoping out the latest competition. John Long recalled the agency placing dummy Kellogg boxes on store shelves and recording consumer habits with clandestine surveillance. "Burnett had stores with secret cameras in them," he remembered.

Kellogg Culture

In Battle Creek itself, the headquarters for both Post and Kellogg, daily life and work took on the drama of a cold cereal war. Battle Creek, Michigan, was a city divided. "It was a dog fight, " said former Kellogg assistant treasurer Jim McQuiston. "You didn't speak to those folks."

Post people lived in what was known as Postumville, near the site of the Post Plant and the original La Vita Inn. Kellogg people lived all over town, as did the folks from Ralston Purina, which also operated a major cereal-manufacturing plant in Battle Creek.

Even in relaxation, the Post and Kellogg clans stuck to their own. Post executives loosened their ties in the bar of the Post Tavern, known as the "Wee Nippy." The Kellogg crowd hung out a few blocks away at the Tac Room, located in the Hart Hotel, a modest three-story structure built in the 1920s by W. K. Kellogg.

The Hart Hotel was more than a company meeting place. It was the navel of the Kellogg social universe, the place where employees were expected to celebrate important moments of their lives. One salesman who joined Kellogg in February, 1941, got married in April and went up to Battle Creek for his honeymoon. "I remember paying six dollars a night for a double at the Hart Hotel," said Elmer Klett. "I still have the receipts and they took our picture and I have the insert from the *Kellogg News* with our picture."

Kellogg people were even supposed to sin at the Hart Hotel. "The Beauty Parlor was the whore house," remembered one Burnett ad man fondly. "When I say 'whore house,' I mean the assignations were all arranged there. There was the assumption that if you visited Battle Creek on behalf of Leo Burnett, you would be treated right."

SPOONTANEOUS COMBUSTION

Cereal can be dangerous stuff. Starch dust generated in the manufacture of cereal can be highly explosive. The danger does not end at the factory door. In the 1950s a Kellogg salesman was called into the Mason City, Iowa, fire-chief's office to explain why the breakfast treat he was peddling had suddenly turned into a public health threat. It seemed that a local housewife, described in the press as being "of moral character" accidentally knocked an unopened Kellogg Variety Pac onto the floor as she walked through the kitchen with a load of laundry. Without seeing the package, she stepped on it and left the room. A few minutes later, she returned to the kitchen, and was shocked to find the package on fire. After conferring with the local fire officials, the Kellogg salesman visited the woman and tried to make amends by offering to replace her Variety Pac. The inflamed consumer refused the offer, declaring instead that she was "switching to the General Mills' Fun Pac."

Johnny Carson's long-time sidekick Ed McMahon also discovered that cereal was hot stuff. In the early 1950s McMahon designed a cereal spoof for the Saturday morning TV show *The Big Top*. The skit featured a hot cereal that was really on fire, a cold cereal freezing with dry ice, and the "World's Largest Cereal Box," packed with a real horse and rider. "What I didn't know," recalled McMahon, "was that the hot cereal we used could ignite and explode once it was ground into fine form." Broadcast live across the country, the skit went amok when the set caught fire and the horse panicked inside its box. "It all worked out," said McMahon. "But for a moment, not only did I think my career was ended, I thought my life was over."

The managers at Kellogg and Post lived in fear and suspicion of everyone. "If you have two businesses like Kellogg and General Foods in one small town of 50,000 people, you can't keep secrets," explained Post man Howard Slutz. "You might have a man working at Kellogg and his wife working at Post—they talk."

Post art director Bill Betts insisted that freelance studios maintain strictly controlled access to all sketches and designs created for Post. Some suspected that even the most loyal Post artists had their price. When a Post brand manager accused Bob Traverse of passing along trade secrets to Kellogg, Betts was appalled. "You've got to be out of your mind," said Betts to the manager. "There is no way that Bob Traverse would leak—he'd just be cutting his own throat!"

"I always felt that the ad agencies leaked," said Al Clausi, Alpha Bits inventor and one-time vice president of General Foods. "As a result, I was very reluctant to tell them a great deal about what was going on. It became a need-to-know sort of thing."

Kellogg was even more uptight than Post, perhaps because it did not share Post's affiliation with a larger corporate world. "I tried to talk to a guy over at Kellogg and even to *this day*, he won't talk to me," recalled Bill Betts recently, who retired from Post thirty years ago.

The structure of the Kellogg corporate hierarchy was most clearly reflected in the parking lot. At Kellogg, you were what you drove. Only Kellogg president Watson Vanderploeg drove a Cadillac. Vice presidents drove Oldsmobiles. Managers drove Buicks, their assistants drove Pontiacs, and the vast rank and file of Kellogg workers all drove Chevrolets—or walked to work. Said a Burnett insider long familiar with Kellogg culture, "Woe unto the guy below the manager level if he bought a Buick—he'd be out just like that." One observer recalled that the arrival of a well-paid Burnett advertising man in a Cadillac caused "a sensation" at the Kellogg plant. After that, the ad men from Burnett were careful to drive Buicks.

"If you stop to consider the isolation of some those people," said the Burnett insider, "everything became a symbol." Privately, Burnett ad men complained that Battle Creek was a throwback, a cereal fiefdom. "I could not believe this was going on in 1950," sighed one Burnett man. "I could believe it in 1760."

The visiting Chicago city slickers were amazed to see Kellogg managers "discussing who'd get to sit next to whom in the company dining room . . . just like little kids talking about car seats on a trip with mom and dad." One Burnett ad man summed up the situation: "You're dealing with something peculiar there, you're dealing with a monastery."

13

Disney Diaspora

A fierce tension gripped Mickey Mouse, Donald Duck, and the 1,000 humans who staffed the Disney operation in the spring of 1940. The company had narrowly escaped crumbling beneath a $4.5 million debt. Creative artists who had once enjoyed the freewheeling camaraderie of an open studio and close contact with Walt Disney were now confined to work units with a "control desk" supervising their actions.

Rumors began to circulate about massive layoffs and the massive profits Disney himself was making. On May 19, 1941, the animators who created *Pinocchio, Fantasia,* and other Disney classics struck the studio. "You can't stand this strike," union organizer Herbert K. Sorrell threatened Walt Disney. "I will smear you and I will make a dust bowl out of your plant." The bitter standoff came to an end in the fall of 1941.

The confrontation turned Walt Disney into a passionate anti-Communist. Testifying in front of the House Committee on Un-American Activities in 1947, the creator of Mickey Mouse told Washington that the Communists in the movie industry "really ought to be smoked out and shown up for what they are." As he said this, some of the "reds" who had left his studio were experimenting with the most American of media art forms: the animated television cereal commercial.

He's GR-R-REAT!

Bill Tytla was one of the animators who was forced out of Disney after the strike. By the end of World War II, the artistic perfectionist responsible for the terrifying "Black God" of *Fantasia*'s "Night on Bald Mountain" sequence was on the streets of New York, hustling for work.

Tytla arrived in the Big Apple at the right time. Television was just appearing on the American media horizon. Network executives, independent producers, and advertising agencies were working furiously to fill the twenty-four-hour-a-day video vacuum, at a profit. While many believed that the future of television lay in *Wild Bill Hickok, Captain Video,* and other programs produced and owned by sponsors, others, including those working for the networks, believed that the newspaper model had more potential—selling single announcements to advertisers at a set price. According to this model, sponsors could get their messages out to the public with none of the headaches involved in program creation and production. The idea of spot advertising intrigued cereal companies and their ad agencies, who looked around for ways to pack a powerful advertising punch into sixty seconds.

For animators, television represented big budgets and big challenges. "Outside of Disney there was no full animation," remembered George Bakes, who went on to animate the Trix rabbit. "Commercials had the biggest budget per foot for animation work. And Bill Tytla was the name of the game."

In 1949, the advertising agency of Benton & Bowles approached Tytla to produce an animated TV commercial for Sugar Crisp featuring three identical bears named Candy, Dandy, and Handy. The furry trio scampered through commercial misadventures while an announcer declared, "For breakfast it's Dandy. For snacks it's so Handy. Or eat it like Candy."

Though crude by Tytla's standards, the ads for Sugar Crisp were historic. For the first time, animated characters appeared on the television screen to sell cereal to children. Tytla was not able to capitalize fully on his breakthrough, both because of artistry and politics. "His main drive was in the art form itself," said Jack Zander, a rival animator. "You had to be a politician to get along with the agency bullshit."

On June 22, 1950, the blacklisting group American Business Consultants published *Red Channels: The Report of Communist Influence in Radio and Television,* which fingered Bill Tytla and 150 other people as a threat to national security. Tytla was an easy mark. Not only had he been involved with the Disney strike, but his parents had immigrated from Russia. His real first name was Vladimir. As paranoia increased across the country, clients yanked their business from the alleged Communist. "Friday, things were going fine," recalled Dan Hunn, who worked with Tytla in New York, "and Monday his studio was up for sale."

The three Sugar Crisp bears were moved to Pelican Films, a "clean" New York-based studio run by Jack Zander, a former MGM animator. Zander admitted that his attempts at making animated advertisements for Post cereal were crude at best. "Fumbling" was how he described them. "When we needed to create new cereal characters," Zander recalled, "we lined up all the existing ones and . . . went to work trying to come up with something new."

Nonetheless, the Sugar Crisp bears caused immediate concern within the industry. In 1951 Kellogg informed Leo Burnett that a new presweet called Sugar Frosted Flakes was on the way. "Sugar Crisp had the sugar bears so Kellogg said, 'We want animals too,'" recalled Don Tennant, the leader of Burnett's television production group.

Tennant and his colleagues at the Leo Burnett Agency had to come up with an animal that would overcome the parental bias against a sugar-coated cereal while still attracting children. As these ad men looked through motivational research and other theoretical works, behaviorist Konrad Lorenz published *Studies in Animal and Human Behavior*. In this book, Lorenz discussed the fact that the physical features of juvenility triggered "innate releasing mechanisms" for affection in adults. Big eyes, broad foreheads, and small chins made parents sigh. Perhaps, thought Burnett executives, they also made them buy.

"Animals were obviously children's friends," said Burnett's John Long, in a more pragmatic vein. "And children do play with their food. So the animals were a natural."

Leo Burnett assigned Jack Baxter, the creative director in charge of the Kellogg account; Jack Tolzein, an art director; and John Matthews, a copywriter, to come up with some animals for Sugar Frosted Flakes. The three brainstormed until they narrowed the zoological field to four: a kangaroo, an elephant, a gnu, and a tiger. "The tiger was put in at that time because it was a symbol of energy," recalled Dick Weiner, a Burnett art director.

With rough sketches in hand, Jack Tolzein first approached Martin and Alice Provensen, a pair of well-known children's book illustrators in New York, to craft a look for each of the four presweet pets. The Provensens were too busy illustrating Golden Books to accept the job, so Tolzein hired freelance Chicago artist Phoebe Moore to paint the cereal wildlife in the Provensens' feathery, almost Oriental style.

Once fleshed out, Baxter brought in TV smith Don Tennant to start writing the actual commercials. "I named them all," said Tennant. "I named them Tony the Tiger and Katy the Kangaroo and Newt the Gnu and Elmo the Elephant." Jack Baxter and John Matthews then wrote a newspaper comic strip jingle for each critter. Tony's four-lined poem ended with one of the most memorable lines in advertising history, "Sugar Frosted Flakes are GR-R-REAT!"

"It's been claimed by everybody under the sun," said Matthews, "but I was there, and it was Jack Baxter who came up with Tony's GR-R-REAT." Baxter, known at Burnett as a "creative nut" with a penchant for late-night celebrating, disappeared from the agency soon after coining one of the most popular slogans in advertising history.

Elmo the Elephant and Newt the Gnu quickly disappeared from view, but Tony the Tiger and Katy the Kangaroo appeared on store

shelves touting Sugar Frosted Flakes in 1952. Some in the advertising
world couldn't see Tony's potential. "I am very fond of dry breakfast
cereals, but this tiger concept completely fails to give me a hankering,"
wrote advertising critic James D. Woolf in *Advertising Age*.

Consumers knew better. Tony's packages flew off the shelves while
Katy's just sat there. Ignoring the critics, the ad men at Kellogg decided
to retire the kangaroo and focus their energies exclusively on the tiger.

Don Tennant took Tony out to L.A. to animate. His first efforts
flopped, as the style of the character did not translate at all well to the
screen. Tennant changed studios and headed for a shop run by Howard
Swift. Like Tytla, Swift was a Disney refugee; he had worked as the principal animator for *Dumbo* before being forced out of the Disney organization after the strike. A gifted character designer, Swift transformed the
storybook Tony into the character who has roamed the American cereal
aisles and airwaves for the past forty years.

Tennant cast a basso profundo named Thurl Ravenscroft as the
voice of the tiger. Ravenscroft had a singing quartet called the Mello-
men, which had belted out the Sugar Pops jingle—"Bang-bang, Sugar
Pops are tops"—in the original *Wild Bill Hickok* commercials. Man and
animal were a good match. "He's been the voice ever since," laughed
Tennant. "Thurl would come in and just work his tail off for you,"
remembered Burnett director Gordon Minter. "He worked on 'They're
G R-R-REAT!' till it was just perfect."

Sometimes a bit too perfect. During his more than forty years with
Kellogg, Ravenscroft had many other voice gigs, including innumerable
beer commercials. "When I did a commercial for another company, and
it had the word 'great' in it, they would change it," roared the voice of
Tony. "Because even if I said 'great' straight, it would be identifiable."

Tennant and Burnett worked out a format for the early Tony the
Tiger spots that became not only the Frosted Flakes standard, but the
commercial formula for the industry. Instead of using sixty seconds of
animation as in the Sugar Crisp spots, "One of Leo's original ideas was
to have an introduction, followed by the first thirty seconds of animation
and then dissolve to live action," recalled Dick Esmail, Burnett's TV
graphic director in the 1950s. "For the live-action segment you would
either come in with a principal of a show, say Captain Kangaroo or
Superman, then a final shot of the package and cereal. It was almost a
formula with Leo and it was pursued almost across the board on Kellogg's shows—and we bought into a lot of shows."

As Burnett's mastery of TV increased, Tony was tuned to selling
perfection. In 1955 the process known as rotoscoping allowed Tony's

trainers to combine animation and live action, giving Tony the chance to co-star with the human video stars of the 1950s. To rehearse these cereal spots, Burnett producers used a life-sized plywood cut-out of Tony on the set. The human actors rehearsed the scene with the cut-out, then performed to the empty space when filming the action. Tony jumped

TONY AND HIS TART

In the early sixties a crew from the Leo Burnett Agency shot a series of live-tiger commercials for Frosted Flakes at a Chicago zoo. The crew wanted to capture the jaw movements of the tiger on film and later refine them through animation to simulate Tony praising his bowl of cereal. One morning, the film crew set up in front of the tiger pen ready to shoot the male tiger. But there was a hitch. A female tiger was in heat. "You are not going to get him to do anything until he is sexually satisfied," the zookeeper told the director of the crew.

Trying to keep his production time to a minimum, the director told the zookeeper, "Fine, have him satisfied and let's get the production rolling." With the cameras running, the zoo keeper brought in the female and the two tigers had sexual intercourse. After sex, the male tiger gobbled down his breakfast, and the ad men captured just the jaw action they were looking for.

After producing the ad for Kellogg, the Burnett crew decided to have a little fun with their extra tiger footage. They took the fornication scene, stripped in the animated jaw footage, and dubbed in a new audio track. At the climax of the newly edited X-rated commercial, Tony dropped his jaw and howled, "It's GR-R-REAT!"

into the frame later. "Kids, particularly kids at a table who are supposed to be talking to Tony, were very good at that," recalled cereal animator Gus Jekel. "Better than adults. Adults couldn't get into the make believe as well."

Americans watched in awe as Tony mugged in commercials with Kellogg stars such as Andy Devine, Garry Moore, and Groucho Marx, star of the Kellogg-sponsored *You Bet Your Life*. Groucho did not think much of co-starring with an animated tiger. "Today the sponsors pull the strings and we are the puppets," he said. "Radio and television announcers have to be liars."

Big Oafish

Other cereal makers recognized that Leo Burnett had worked something wonderful with Tony the Tiger. The image of a cuddly, loveable animal who roared a clever, deep-throated slogan bounced a child's mind back and forth between pictures and words until he was captured by its charms. Simply put, Tony was magic. "Leo Burnett was real watershed stuff," confessed Dancer Fitzgerald Sample writer Gene Cleaves, who later crafted the "I'm cuckoo for Cocoa Puffs" tag line for General Mills. "Tony the Tiger with his 'They're GR-R-REAT' . . . it's perfect."

Other cereal makers set out to replicate the Tony mystique. In late 1951 Captain Jolly, the first cartoon pirate of crunch, sailed the video seas to sell the unappetizing presweetened Post cereal Corn Fetti with the jolly bluster, "Ho-Ho-Ho! No one can stay away from Corn Fetti . . . It never gets sticky, even in the box!"

General Mills introduced the Cheerios Kid in 1954, a suburban superhero who saved his paramour Sue from jungle, wild west, and outer space cliff-hangers with the cry, "I call on my Cheerios!" A hyper honeybee in a cowboy hat buzzed onto the screen in that same year to sell Rice and Wheat Honeys for the National Biscuit Company. With a high-pitched Texas twang, provided by Mae Questel, the voice of Betty Boop, Buffalo Bee rapped "Knock, knock, knock" on America's TV screens and became one of the most memorable cartoon characters of the 1950s, while the Nabisco Spoonmen, a trio of lovable aliens created by premium designer John "Wally" Walworth, pitched cereal with a space-age twist.

After relying solely on Tony the Tiger to carry the cartoon weight for a number of years, Burnett introduced a new line of cartoon cereal creations. An animated sun promoted the vitamin C content of Corn Flakes with the line "I come each sunny day, from 93 million miles away. Sun for Kellogg's Corn Flakes." Burnett art director Don Keller brought Vernon Grant's Snap, Crackle, and Pop to the boob tube. "They were a little stringy and not suitable for television," scowled Keller who worked with character designer Chuck Mackelmurry to make the threesome more video friendly. At one point in the mid-1950s, Burnett even added a fourth character named "Pow" to drive home the cereal's nutritional punch.

Smaxey the Seal briefly flapped for Kellogg's Sugar Smacks in the late 1950s, waving his cap and barking "Smackin' good for breakfast . . . Smackin' good for snacks." When his staff was having difficulty coming up with a cereal critter to promote the new cereal Cocoa Krispies, Leo Burnett sent a telegram to creative director John Matthews. "John," the telegram read, "of course we must consider the monkey."

Leo Burnett liked monkeys so much he kept them as pets. John Matthews shared his boss's prejudice for primates. "Like a chocolate milkshake, only crunchy," was the slogan Matthews coined for a Cocoa Krispie-pitching monkey.

Former Disney animator Ross Wetzel was hired by Burnett art director Gene Kolkey to draw the animated creature. To prove that he was going all out for Cocoa Krispies, Wetzel hired a pet trainer to come into his studio with a real-live monkey. "Of course, I wanted to impress Gene with the fact that I was really going into depth on this thing, so the goddamn monkey was sitting up on the edge of the drawing board and I'm drawing him," laughed Wetzel. "Just as Gene came walking in the door, the damn little bugger peed all over my drawing. Gene loved it . . . he just loved it." As soon as Wetzel cleaned his drawing board, he went back to work, and a monkey has pitched Cocoa Krispies on and off ever since.

Burnett artist Don Keller had to dispense with reality altogether to come up with the design for a critter to pitch Kellogg's Sugar Pops. When writer Alan Kent invented a prairie dog pup named Sugar Pops Pete to sell the cereal, all the artists at Burnett ran to the library to check out books on southwestern wildlife. Keller took another approach. "Leo doesn't care if it looks like a real prairie dog," Keller concluded. "He's hearing prairie pup."

Keller drew a rendering of a prairie pup and gave it to Alan Kent. "I went to lunch and they had a meeting," recalled Keller. "When I came back, the drawing was on my desk with a heart around it, and the words 'Leo loves Sugar Pops Pete!'"

In commercials, Sugar Pops Pete became the spunky sheriff of a Tombstone-like Western town where he kept the local riff raff in line with his "sugar popper," a candy-striped six shooter that sent out a beam of sparkly sugar dust which "sweetened up" bad guys. "We never condescended to kids," recalled Rudy Perz who wrote many of the Sugar Pops ads. "In fact, we had to sell the stories to clients; they were written to make adults laugh."

Other characters created by Burnett were not so well loved. "Big Oafish," was how one Burnett writer referred to Big Otis, a Scottish warrior in a tartan kilt created to pitch Kellogg's OKs by driving home the connection between Scotland, oats, and strength. One live-action commercial featured stuntman Hal Baylor plying a one-man rowboat across a lake. "After a couple of takes suddenly the darn thing just cracked in half and the front end went up and the back end went up and it ate him like a giant bird beak," laughed a Burnett writer who was on location at the time. Back in Battle Creek, Big Otis was not missed. John Matthews overheard Kellogg's president Lyle Roll once growl, "I hate that big, red-bearded son of a bitch."

Marky Maypo Steals the Show

While creatives at Burnett and the other big shops struggled with company politics, motivational research, sophisticated market analyses, and rigorous strategic formulas to develop successful cereal cartoon creations, John Hubley listened to his heart.

The man who created one of the most successful television animation campaigns of all time decided early in his life to be a painter. The Wisconsin native traveled to the West Coast to study at the Art Center of Los Angeles, but was detoured by an offer from the Disney organization in 1935.

Hubley worked as an apprentice on *Snow White* and was promoted to associate art director on classics such as *Pinocchio, Fantasia, Bambi,* and *Dumbo.* He was personally responsible for the "Rite of Spring" segment of *Fantasia,* in which life evolved to the music of Stravinsky. After leaving Disney and serving in the Air Force, where he animated training films, Hubley joined a host of other former-Disney artists to create United Productions of America, an avant garde animation house in L.A.

Hubley was instrumental in shaping the flat, minimalistic UPA style that revolutionized the animation industry. *Mister Magoo,* patterned after Hubley's bull-headed uncle, brought the studio its first commercial success. The 1951 short *Gerald McBoing Boing* won an Academy Award. "John was absolutely a giant in the business," said animator Gus Jekel. "Everything he did was ground breaking." Bill Melendez, who today animates the *Peanuts* television specials, agreed. "John was one of the great inventive designers in the business."

By the early 1950s Hubley and other UPA founders were fingered by Walt Disney. Hubley appeared before a subcommittee chaired by a young congressman from California named Richard Nixon. When the red-baiting Republican hauled Hubley into a closed-session hearing and accused him of being a Communist, the cartoon maker stood up. "I am an artist," Hubley said. "I have a right to say what I want. And I have a right to say what I don't want."

For his display of courage, Hubley was blacklisted and fired from his job by UPA studio chief Steve Bosustow, who wasted no time in pasting his own name over all of Hubley's animation credits. While UPA went on to create ads for Spoon Sized Shredded Wheat and Pink Panther cartoons, Hubley moved to New York and joined the production shop of another alleged fellow traveler, Bill Tytla. Hubley was involved in producing a couple of Kellogg commercials before Tytla's studio was destroyed by Cold War politics.

Though Hubley was blacklisted, "agencies didn't seem to be reluctant to do business with him," said Jack Zander. "He was so good." He went into business for himself, in order to keep bread on the table and raise funds for production of the independent art films he made with his wife Faith. One of his first animated commercials, in which a man spelled out "F-O-R-D" with his mouth, attracted the attention of the advertising world. "Just yesterday we saw a sample reel from Storyboard, Incorporated," wrote Burnett's Ken Jones in an internal memo praising Hubley's company. "It included some of the freshest, most delightful commercials that we have seen in some time. It would be worthwhile for the entire Plans Board to view the work this outfit has done."

While Burnett lauded Hubley, a little-known cereal maker signed him up. Heublein Inc., which sold distilled liquors, A-1 Steak Sauce, Grey-Poupon Mustard, and Sizzl-Spray, an aerosol barbeque sauce, had recently purchased the Vermont-based Maltex Company, creators of Maypo—a maple-syrup-flavored hot cereal. In an effort to create tax-deductible expenses, Heublein decided to launch an expensive TV campaign for the poorly selling Maltex product.

"They came to us because we were notoriously independent and they said, 'Make a commercial that's not a commercial, just do a slice of life, a dramatic piece,'" recalled Faith Hubley. "They didn't want the cereal company to make a profit so they gave us total creative freedom to do whatever we wanted to do. It was a really absurd contract; we had all the things that you *never* got from an agency."

Since making *Gerald McBoing Boing*, Hubley had been fascinated by the natural sounds of children. In 1956 the Hubleys had made a short film for the Guggenheim Museum, "tracing the development of the child and the loss of the child's [creative] vision," recalled Faith, "so we just loved the idea of doing something natural and truthful with a non-professional actor—our boy, Mark."

In keeping with his credo that a good commercial "plays humor around a human situation related to the product," John picked a situation familiar to every home, a scene in which a child refuses to eat his food. "It had to appeal to kids, so it was done from their point of view,"

Hubley told *Sponsor* magazine. "Marky couldn't be a 'brat'—Marky had to be a child as children see themselves."

For days, John Hubley followed his four-year-old son around with a microphone and "just recorded his jabber and then just constructed a story around it," explained family friend Bill Melendez. "In a way, Marky Maypo was co-created by young Marky," recalled Faith Hubley. "We did not use a script. We culled the improvisation for the best lines and adapted the storyboard from the improvisation." When Marky mispronounced "energy" as "enjerny" during the recording, they kept it. As far as the central scene was concerned, Marky didn't have to act very much. He really and truly hated Maypo. "Marky didn't like it because it tasted like oatmeal," recalled his mother.

Marky Maypo debuted on New York and New England television stations in September 1956. The spot started with stubborn Marky, a rough 'n' ready little cartoon cowboy, sitting on a stool at the breakfast table while his dad cajoled him into eating his hot mush. "Cowboys don't eat cereal," Marky mumbled, crossing his arms and pouting as his oversized cowboy hat slipped down over his mouth. His dad offered him a spoonful of hot mush, which he ignored. In exasperation, his dad grabbed the hat off Marky's head and offered another spoonful. Marky screamed, "I want my hat," but refused another spoonful with clamped jaws. Wearing the hat, Dad tried the cereal himself. "It tastes like maple sugar candy," he said, beaming with conspicuous delight as he gobbled the cereal down. Seeing a happy father, a jealous little Marky screamed "I want my Maypo!"

Much to the shock of the Heublein management, the sixty-second spot was a smash hit. Instead of hurting revenues as planned, the ad increased sales of Maypo "an average of 78 percent . . . and as high as 186 percent in some markets," reported *Sponsor* magazine. New York *Herald Tribune* TV critic John Crosby, who normally reviewed new programs, devoted a third of his column to telling readers, "The plug is full of deliciously funny and true child psychology that will appeal to everyone who has children . . . and kids howl at it, too." Millions of kids across America began yelling, "I want my Maypo!" The line even turned up at a Boston football game, according to one ad man who reported that "an entire band section yelled it from the grandstand."

Seeing that they could profit from the hot cereal, Heublein changed their strategy and started to put money into Maypo. By the second year of the campaign, the "I want my Maypo" spot ran on forty-two stations in nineteen markets—mainly during popular weekday afternoon and Saturday morning programming. The company set up huge store dis-

plays, distributed Marky balloons and buttons, and redesigned their original package in favor of a king-sized drawing of Marky in his ten-gallon
hat on the fronts of Maypo packages. "This, as far as I know, is the first
time a TV commercial bred a character that became the logotype in
product packaging," crowed one of the Maltex ad men, Bob Philpott.

In 1960, the Hubleys produced a second Maypo spot, inspired by
the abstract painter Gregorio Prestopino, who stayed over at the Hubley
house once a week. "Marky adored him," said Faith. "He used to wake
up at six o'clock, go to the couch and jump on Presto and say, 'Well, look
you old rattlesnake,'" a line heard in the commercials. The voice of
Prestopino, renamed Uncle Ralphie for the commercial, was provided
by Faith's old acting-school chum, Academy Award-winning actor
Martin Balsam. "In a sense, our contribution [to commercials] was to
bring wonderful actors who were accustomed to Stanislavsky improvisation and let them act instead of screaming at the audience to buy this
and buy that," said Faith.

The Hubleys produced advertising for other Heublein cereal products, but eventually fell out with the company. The inevitable break
came over the question of merchandising their animated son. In addition to plastering Marky on the package, a step the Hubleys resisted as
vulgar, Heublein tried to merchandise Marky in other ways only to be
blocked by the Hubleys' unusual contract. "The client had a love/hate
relationship with us," laughed Faith. "They loved the work but they
hated that we had all this power. They came to the studio and said they
wanted to put a little bust of Marky in the boxes," recalled Faith.
"Johnny and I took a look at them and teasingly said, 'Why don't you
put a bust of Beethoven in?' We vetoed a lot of things and eventually,
they stopped coming to us. I can't stand those advertising people!"

In the 1960s, Heublein bought the troublesome Hubleys out of
their contract—"we were very, very well paid"—and promptly produced
a nine-inch vinyl Marky bank available for box tops. Without the Hubleys behind the creative controls, however, Maypo's market share
slipped away. In the mid-1960s, Heublein sold the Maltex Company to
American Home Products, a huge conglomerate that added Maypo and
Maltex to Wheatena and its other hot breakfast foods.

The Hubleys went on to produce independent films like *Moonbird*,
which won an Academy Award, and numerous shorts for the *Sesame
Street* series. Perhaps the biggest compliment to the Hubleys' work came
with the birth of music television. There is no doubt that the writers who
coined the slogan "I want my MTV!" were echoing the words of a
finicky four-year-old in a cowboy hat.

PINK ELEPHANTS

As cereal companies rushed to design cartoon animals
for their packages, ad men and artists discovered how
surprisingly difficult it was to come up with just the right
critter. In the late fifties Kellogg briefly replaced Little
Jose, the monkey on the Cocoa Krispies box, with a pink
elephant named Coco. The creature created a furor at
Kellogg Company headquarters and was quickly pulled
from the cereal aisle because "you see pink elephants if
you drink too much," explained Orrin Bowers, an ad
man who did work for Kellogg. "It sounds crazy but
advertisers, Kellogg especially, take that very seriously."

In 1967 Post launched Corn Crackos. The box featured the Waker Upper Bird perched on a bowl of candy-
coated twists. An internal company memo noted that "It
looks like a bird eating worms; who wants worms for
breakfast?"

Quaker ran into trouble in 1975 with Punch
Crunch. The screaming pink box featured Harry S., an
exuberant hippo in a sailor suit making goo-goo eyes at
Cap'n Crunch. Many chain stores perceived the hippo as
gay and refused to carry the cereal. Marveled one
Quaker salesman, "How that one ever got through, I'll
never understand."

"The only commercials that I ever enjoyed were the Maypos," confessed Faith Hubley, whose husband died in 1977. "They were tasteful
and they were warm, loving and all the rest. They said something about
parent/child relationships, and they kept a certain balance and decency.
They didn't hurt anybody. And actually the character supported the
child's right to eat what he wanted."

Today Mark Hubley is happily married with two boys of his own
and lives in upstate New York working as a horse breeder and trainer. He
still hates the taste of Maypo.

IV

Tummy Vision

A combination of healer, hotelier, and promoter, **Dr. John Harvey Kellogg** was one of the best known figures of nineteenth-century American medicine. After announcing that white clothing was medically beneficial, the good doctor sported nothing but white apparel. The influence of the publicity loving physician continues to hold sway over the world's breakfast table. (Courtesy of the Willard Memorial Library, Battle Creek, Michigan)

The **Battle Creek Sanitarium** in the 1890s. The Italian Rennaissance edifice sported a solarium, a large gymnasium, and an Acidophilus milk bar. The stream of wealthy international guests included Thomas Edison, Harvey Firestone, and Henry Ford. (Courtesy of the Adventist Historic Properties, Battle Creek)

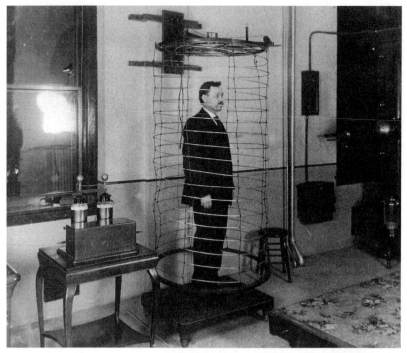

Under Dr. Kellogg's guidance, the San was transformed into a Disneyland of medical marvels. Innovative treatments included **electric baths** and a high-powered enema machine that pumped sixteen gallons of water through the bowel in a matter of minutes. (Courtesy of the Adventist Historic Properties, Battle Creek)

As a precursor to group aerobics, patients at the San were encouraged to join in the rooftop **"Grand March"** at the end of the day. (Courtesy of the Adventist Historic Properties, Battle Creek)

Before stumbling onto a fortune in health foods, **Charles Wilson Post** marketed (and modeled) "miracle scientific suspenders" of his own design. Another failed scheme involved hoisting dynamite into the air on kites to induce rain. (Courtesy of the Willard Memorial Library, Battle Creek)

In 1905, Post followed Postum and Grape-Nuts with a third product, a cornflake called **Elijah's Manna.** Religionists screamed that Post was enlisting Old Testament prophets to sell his cornflakes and demanded that he stop using Elijah's name in vain. By 1908, the controversy cut into sales and Post dropped the biblical name in favor of Post Toasties. (Courtesy of Willard Memorial Library, Battle Creek)

Hailed as the **"White City,"** C. W. Post's Postum Cereal Company plant was a utopian industrial complex and a major tourist destination by 1902, just seven years after he introduced Postum to the market. The outdoor conveyer belt that carried Grape-Nuts from the bakery (foreground building) to the grinding room was called the "Road to Wellville." (Courtesy of the Willard Memorial Library, Battle Creek)

The only known photograph that includes both **Dr. John Harvey Kellogg,** dressed in white, and **C. W. Post,** dressed in black, was shot during a campaign visit to Battle Creek by **President William Howard Taft** in September 1911. Many believed that Post stole his recipes from Kellogg. Kellogg called Post the "original imitator" of his ideas. (Courtesy of the Willard Memorial Library, Battle Creek)

In 1927, Dr. Kellogg added a **fifteen-story addition** to his sanitarium, which made the tower the tallest building between Detroit and Chicago. The doctor lost control of the building during the great Depression. Today it's the national headquarters for the Civil Defense Administration. (Courtesy of the Adventist Historic Properties, Battle Creek)

An elderly **W. K. Kellogg** and his faithful Rinette, a German shepherd who descended from the original Rin Tin Tin. At the age of forty-five in 1906, W. K. got out from under the shadow of his tyrannical older brother and founded the Kellogg Company. The cornflake king ruled his empire until his death in 1951. (Courtesy of the Willard Memorial Library, Battle Creek)

A man of imposing Victorian demeanor and percolative imagination, **Eugene McKay Sr.** was the last great cereal wizard. He ran the research and development for the Kellogg Company and invented All-Bran, Rice Krispies, and a product that would later be marketed as Sugar Corn Pops. During the Depression, McKay's generosity to the homeless earned him the title "King of the Hoboes." (Courtesy of Eugene McKay Jr.)

On Christmas Eve 1926, a barbershop quartet consisting of a bailiff, a printer, a businessman, and an undertaker broadcast the first singing radio commercial to the tune of "She's a Jazz Baby." The melodious **Wheaties Quartet** made Wheaties a household word. (Used with permisssion of General Mills, Inc.)

In 1934, cowboy hero **Tom Mix** and Donald Danforth Sr. posed with thousands of box-tops mailed in to Checker-board Square by kids eager for Ralston's Straight Shooter Club premiums. Offered in newspaper ads and on the ra-dio, the merchandising scheme revolutionized cereal market-ing. (Courtesy of Ralston Purina)

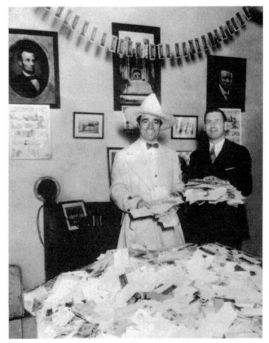

After years of hi-tech research, Kix burst from **puffing guns** in 1937. It was followed in 1941 by Cheerioats. After a legal challenge by Quaker Oats, General Mills changed the name of the little donuts to Cheerios. (Used with permission of General Mills, Inc.)

Illustrator **Vernon Grant** was an artist struggling in Greenwich Village when a radio ad for "talking cereal" fired up his imagination. In 1933 Kellogg introduced the world to Grant's cereal-pitching characters: Snap, Crackle, and Pop. Grant is pictured here with two of his lesser gnomic creations. (Courtesy of York County Museum, Rockhill, South Carolina)

A civil engineer turned cereal visionary, **Moses Berger** was the godfather of pre-sweetened cereal. Launched in 1939, Ranger Joe Wheat Honnies were copied by Post and Kellogg. Nabisco bought the Ranger Joe company in 1954 and changed the name Honnies to Honeys. (Photo by Scott Bruce)

The ultimate cold-cereal warrior, **the Lone Ranger** rode onto television in 1949 on behalf of General Mills's Cheerios, Kix, and Wheaties. Billed as a "seething, scientific sensation," his atom bomb ring was the probably the most popular cereal premium of all time. (Used with permisssion of General Mills, Inc.)

Leo Burnett Alumni
August 8, 1986

An unrepentant slob with a genius for advertising, **Leo Burnett** had the most influence on the breakfast table of any man since C. W. Post. Beginning in 1951, the Leo Burnett Agency seized the Kellogg cereal account and never let go. (Cartoon by Don Keller and used with permission)

One of the most popular cereal promotions of all time, the deed to a **square inch of the Klondike** caused thirty-five million boxes of Puffed Wheat and Puffed Rice to disappear off store shelves in 1955. (Photo by Scott Bruce)

Tony the Tiger has evolved during his long career. In 1953 Kellogg's most valuable feline crept across the pages of *Life* magazine on all fours. His latest incarnation resembles a man more than a jungle cat. (Photo by Scott Bruce)

During the Korean war, **Major Jet** roared, "Jet up with Sugar Jets . . . they make you feel jet-powered." The major was played in TV commercials by Roger Pace, an actor who had a bit part in the movie *The Bridges at Toko-Ri*. (Used with permission of General Mills, Inc.)

The most expensive cereal promotion of all time, the **Ralston Rocket** cost $40,000 to build in 1952. For two years Checkerboard Square booked the spacecraft into supermarket parking lots across the country where eager young Space Patrolers waited in line for hours for their chance to crawl through the cockpit packed with a repeller ray, astro radar, and two-way space phones. (Courtesy of Ralston Purina)

In 1956 kiss-and-tell *Confidential* magazine exposed the secret link between **Frank Sinatra**'s legendary sexual prowess and Wheaties. Though the flap tickled General Mills, the company never exploited the free publicity, choosing Olympian Bob Richards to champion the cereal instead. (Photo by Stephen Govoni Jr.)

In 1956 Post art director Bill Betts entertained the troops at an all-male sales conference with **Sugar Nipples,** his quick-sketch fantasy of the perfect breakfast food. (Courtesy of Bill Betts)

In a remarkable example of a cereal character plugging one of his own kind, **Bullwinkle Moose** introduced the Trix rabbit in 1960. The "silly rabbit" appeared first as a hand puppet on *Rocky and His Friends*, produced by Jay Ward. (Photo by Scott Bruce)

Jay Ward, the extremely shy co-creator of Rocky and Bullwinkle, was fond of dressing up for public appearances in a Napoleonic uniform. In this caricature, Ward bears a strong resemblance to another of his cartoon creations, Cap'n Crunch. (Courtesy of Ramona Ward)

Kalamazoo-based **Bob Traverse** illustrated boxes of Alpha Bits, Sugar Crisp, and other Post cereals. When assigned to redesign Pink Panther Flakes in the early 1970s, Traverse said, "I don't even want to bother with it." (Courtesy of Robert Traverse)

Animator John Hubley modeled **Markey Maypo** on his own four-year-old son, Mark. The fussy buckaroo's war cry, "I want my Maypo," became a generation's anthem. (Photo by Scott Bruce)

Working on the General Mills account, art director Bill Tollis gave **Sonny the Cuckoo Bird** his wings in 1962. Sonny's immortal "Wuuuck!" was supplied for fourteen years by actor **Chuck McCann**. The award-winning McCann also voiced other cereal characters including Sugar Bear, Colodny, Twinkles the elephant, and occasionally Bullwinkle Moose. (Courtesy of Chuck McCann)

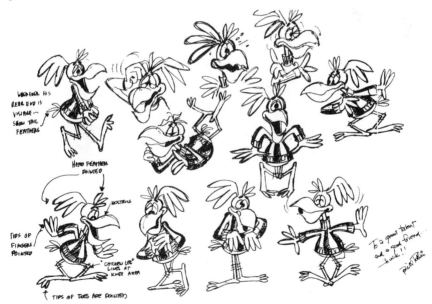

Quaker Oats launched **Cap'n Crunch** cereal in 1963. Many animation studios competed for the chance to create the character. Jay Ward got the job mainly because Quaker brass loved Bullwinkle. (Used with permission of the Quaker Oats Company)

14

From Hillbillies to Bubblegum

In 1958 Kellogg announced that it was moving out of the production of network television shows, and was instead spending as much as $7 million to purchase one-minute or thirty-second video billboards known as spots. Kellogg's move to spot advertising reflected the general trend in the television industry. By 1960 sponsors and advertising agencies no longer produced and owned the majority of shows on TV. Instead, advertisers bought television spots according to the ratings—numbers generated by the A. C. Nielsen Company that indicated how many people watched a particular program at a particular time.

The ratings system gave the television networks control over programming production and ownership, and forced advertisers into the tight sales format of a thirty- or sixty-second product pitch. The pitchmen who succeeded in selling cereal according to the ratings numbers included a small town sheriff, a bumbling marine, and a mountain man who loaded up his truck and moved to Beverly—Hills that is.

Mornings in Mayberry

By the late 1950s, the Madison Avenue agency Benton & Bowles, which handled several Post cereals, had finally created a television production team equal to the video crew at Leo Burnett. The knock 'em dead television department was headed up by three future media giants: Lee Rich, who later produced *The Godfather* and other Lorimar blockbusters; Grant Tinker, who became President of NBC; and Phil Capice, who rose high in the CBS system before stepping out on his own.

The first television program this trio bought for Post was *The Danny Thomas Show*, a sit-com about the family life of a New York nightclub entertainer. Rated as the second most popular show in 1957, *The Danny Thomas Show* was Post's first really successful foray onto the small screen. The television commercials were produced at the Sands Hotel in Las Vegas, during breaks in Thomas' popular stage act.

Thomas and his television family pitched the full line of Post cereal brands on a living room set just out of sight of the slot machines, driving home their campaign with a jingle penned by Lem McKenzie: "All Post cereals happen to be . . . just a little bit better, a little bit better, Post happens to be."

The sales-tracking Nielsen Food Index, operated by the same company that tracked television ratings, revealed that Danny Thomas' slick big-city image turned off much of rural America. The team at Benton & Bowles began to believe that a series geared to America's real country tastes was in order. "In those days," recalled Benton & Bowles writer Joe Bacal, "agencies were incredibly involved in the shows."

Benton & Bowles set out to get Grape-Nuts back to the country. They voiced their concerns to Sheldon Leonard, Thomas' manager and producer of *The Danny Thomas Show*. Leonard obligingly produced an episode of the program that brought the New York nightclub singer into rural North Carolina. In the episode, Thomas traveled to the small town of Mayberry, where he was put under arrest by a slow-moving but fair-minded sheriff named Andy Taylor. Audiences loved the homespun characters so much that Leonard, Post, and the Benton & Bowles ad men decided to spin off a Mayberry-based program, entitled *The Andy Griffith Show*.

The program premiered on October 3, 1960, featuring a cast of small-town eccentrics that have delighted audiences, and inspired cereal sales, for thirty-five years. Straight from his starring role in Broadway's *No Time for Sergeants*, Andy Griffith played Sheriff Andy Taylor, a sensible widower devoted to his six-year-old son, Opie, played by future Hollywood mogul Ron Howard, and his spinster relative Aunt Bee, a gentle-hearted busybody who took tremendous pride in mothering Andy, Opie, and everyone else in town. Whatever the problems faced by the cast, Sheriff Andy saw to it that the virtues of small-town living won out.

The same went for small-town eating. "In those days," recalled Max Bryer who directed the Mayberry cast commercials for Post, "most of the people who were in the shows felt completely relaxed doing the commercials."

This comfort level made for effective selling. Sheriff Andy's sincere plugs for Grape-Nuts from his jail-house desk brought a gentle voice of authority to the breakfast table, while Aunt Bee's pitch for "frozen lemon pie" from the cozy Taylor kitchen sent millions of mothers racing to the supermarket for Grape-Nuts Flakes. Deputy Barney Fife employed extra ingenuity to con his boss Andy out of bowls of Grape-Nuts. "At the end of every spot," recalled Max Bryer, "he [Deputy Fife] would always freeze on that scene and come off with some sort of a gag like peering around the box or holding it upside down or putting it on his head."

Early in the life of the series, Benton & Bowles sent music director Roy Eaton out to Hollywood to record *The Andy Griffith Show* cast singing the Post cereal theme song, so that the show's familiar opening whistle would flow seamlessly into the Post jingle. "We had them record the tag 'Start your day, a little bit better, a little better cereal, fresh from Post,'" recalled Eaton. While Andy Griffith was a well-known singer, it was the Mayberry gas-monkey who stole the microphone. "You'd look at him," recalled Bryer of actor Jim Nabors, "and you'd see this boob of a character from the back woods. And all of a sudden, you hear this voice come out of this weird, weird lookin' guy!"

The man behind the operatic voice played the goofiest character in Mayberry, Gomer Pyle. Gomer was the wise fool, the man who was too dumb to dupe and greeted the wonders of the world with a magnificent "Goooolllleeeeyyy. Shazam!" Played by Jim Nabors, who began his career as a singing waiter at a Santa Monica restaurant, Gomer became so popular that he got his very own Post-sponsored spin-off series in 1964, *Gomer Pyle U.S.M.C.*

Private Pyle was so good at selling cereal that Post whipped up a series of army-chow type recipes, including corned-beef hash made from Post Toasties. "I did a bunch of commercials for Gomer Pyle," recalls Ed Hannibal, a Benton & Bowles writer. "I remember one where Jim Nabors had his uniform on and went into a mess hall kitchen on the set and gave a funny stand-up spiel about some Post cereal. He was a lovely guy."

The Jethro Bowl

As Mayberry became part of America's mythological rural landscape, another television series germinated in the mind of Paul Henning. Gassing up in Kentucky during a 15,000-mile car trip, the seasoned television producer heard about a few Ozark mountain men who blocked the construction of a new highway because they didn't want no "furriners" passing through their hills. Even though he was on vacation, Henning could recognize a good idea. Back in Hollywood he penned a pilot about a white-trash brood who moved to Tinseltown after striking oil. The characters were hicks but their bumbling naivete masked a definite shrewdness. Henning called his creation *The Hillbillies of Beverly Hills.*

After shooting the pilot with Buddy Ebson as Jed Clampett, Irene Ryan as Granny, Donna Douglas as Elly May, and Max Baer Jr., son of the former heavyweight boxing champion, as Jethro, Henning and executive producer Al Simon sold sponsorship of the show to Kellogg and Winston cigarettes.

The show, renamed *The Beverly Hillbillies,* premiered on September 26, 1962, on CBS. Savaged by the critics—"We're liable to be Beverly Hillbillied to death," fumed TV drama producer David Susskind, "write your Congressmen"—the series rocketed to first place in the Nielsen ratings by January and stayed there through 1964. Of the national media, only the *Dallas Morning News* dared to give voice to the multitude by proclaiming, "It's corn, all right, but crisp, crunchy, and rather refreshing."

Kellogg's claim on TV's first family lay in its ability to use the Beverly Hillbillies in its cereal commercials. For the Kellogg's "Food is a Bargain" campaign, the writers at Burnett crafted the message to fit each cast member's personality. Granny barked, "Today your vittle-money fetches more than ever before," as she wheeled in a shopping cart loaded with Kellogg's Corn Flakes, while Jethro brayed, "I sure growed up big on today's vittles!" as he carried his own overflowing cart into the house. Bad grammar aside, America seemed to agree with Kellogg that "Eatin's gettin' easier and much more fun!"

Actress Donna Douglas was the show's hot dish. The twenty-something former Miss Baton Rouge had the same effect on the Burnett staff as she had on the men who were watching at home. "Boy, she turned me on," recalled Burnett writer Bill Stratton. "I was on the Hillbillies set on the telephone talking to Chicago and I said something like, 'I'm not sure how good my idea is . . . but it's the only idea I've got right now,' and Donna was there right by the wall phone smiling at me. She was rather voluptuous. I don't know where she put her hand the first time but when I hung up the phone, she was saying, 'I think you have *real* good ideas. . . . Got any ideas right now?'"

Max Baer Jr., who went on to a successful career as a film producer, had the most trouble with the cast commercial shtick. The instrument of Baer's displeasure was the famous "Jethro bowl," a salad bowl–sized cereal dish that has reentered the American pop lexicon as a Jerry Seinfeld reference. As scripted in the Kellogg's cereal ads, Jethro didn't merely eat his breakfast, he had to wolf it down.

"It drove me nuts! Absolutely crazy!" Baer yelled in a recent interview. "Buddy [Ebsen] knew it would get to me so he would sometimes intentionally screw up the commercial during the time I was eating so I'd have to do the eating sequence over again. And then he'd screw it up again. Then Irene would screw it up. Then Donna would screw it up, and I'd say, 'Come on you guys. I can't keep eating all this.'"

"I would do this from seven in the morning until about noon. I would eat about fifteen boxes of Corn Flakes, then they'd call lunch . . . lunch? Christ, I was ready to explode!"

"The weird thing about it is," Baer confessed, "I like Corn Flakes. Even now I eat 'em."

Oh, That's Corny

In the spring of 1962 Kellogg's world headquarters in Battle Creek was rocked by the first salvo in a brand war that threatened the company's sacred fifty-year-old cash cow, Kellogg's Corn Flakes. The threat came from the number three player in the cereal sweepstakes, General Mills. Since the mid-1950s, scientists deep inside General Mills' laboratories in Minneapolis had labored to develop a new improved corn flake, one that would taste better and crunch more explosively than any other corn- flake ever made. By 1961, they had stumbled upon it: a puff made from degerminated corn meal, rice, sugar, salt, and malt syrup. They called their new creation Country Corn Flakes and prepared for a coast-to-coast roll out.

Ad executive John E. Matthews told the Kellogg brass that the introduction of Country Corn Flakes was a "kick in the groin." Taste tests revealed that the rival flake was indeed "lighter" and "sweeter" than Kellogg's war horse; moreover, it was "much crisper" and didn't get "soggy so fast," reported a Kellogg memo. Kellogg knew it couldn't beat the flavor of the General Mills cornflake. Instead the company chose to crush Country Corn Flakes with an overpowering ad campaign.

At the Leo Burnett Agency, writers Hal Weinstein and Elaine Goldstein were assigned to drive a stake through Country Corn Flakes' heart. "I came up with the idea of 'the corniest flakes that anybody makes are Kellogg's,'" laughed Weinstein. "The idea was to do puns, corny puns such as 'What's the corniest school in the U.S., why it's Cornell!,' or 'What's the corniest state in the union, why it's Corn-tucky!'"

To deliver the corny lines, Weinstein chose Henry Doyle Haynes and Kenneth C. Burns, better known as Homer and Jethro, a fixture of the country humor pantheon since the 1940s. After getting grudging clearance from his bosses, Weinstein took Homer and Jethro into a Chicago studio to record the *Corny Radio* campaign, a series of corn-ball gags:

> JETHRO: Hey Homer, what are you taking for your cold?
> HOMER: Well, Jethro, the doctor told me to drink carrot juice after a hot bath.
> JETHRO: Well, how do you like carrot juice?
> HOMER: I don't know yet, I'm still drinking the hot bath.
> BOTH: Ooooooh . . . that's corny!

As "ooooh, that's corny!" became an American catchphrase, Homer and Jethro moved from radio to television commercials and succeeded in killing General Mill's superior cornflake. "Incredible as it may seem, this routine did the job," reported *Fortune* in 1967. "General Mills Country Corn Flakes today has less than 1 percent of the market."

Bob Richards for President

The success of Homer and Jethro in promoting Kellogg's inferior corn-flakes was overshadowed by the performance of the 1960s most ubiqui-tous cereal pitchman, the Pole-Vaulting Preacher Bob Richards. Like Sylvester Graham, Sister Ellen White, Dr. John Harvey Kellogg, and other cereal prophets, Richards led a personal crusade that sparked national interest in health and breakfast food.

The brand of cereal that Richards promoted was Wheaties. Wheaties was the cereal that radio built, the first product to be adver-tised with a singing jingle, and the sponsor of the most popular radio hero of all time—Jack Armstrong, the All-American boy. The breakfast of champions also had the distinction of appearing in the first television cereal advertisement.

The historic cereal pitch took place in 1939, during a baseball game between the Cincinnati Reds and the Brooklyn Dodgers—the first base-ball game ever to be televised. Between breaks in the action, announcer Red Barber hawked products from the catbird seat. "First I put on a ser-vice-station cap and talked about Mobil Oil. Then I picked up a bar of soap that was about 44/100ths percent pure," recalled Barber in *Sports Illustrated*. "But the big extravaganza was for Wheaties. I poured out an individual serving, added bananas, sugar, and cream and said, 'This is the breakfast of champions.'"

But as television eclipsed radio as America's dramatic medium of choice, the video generation considered Wheaties to be old-fashioned. Even the flashiest sports stars couldn't seem to improve the sluggish sales.

WHEATIES, BREAKFAST OF LOVERS

"He's had the nation's front-rank playboys dizzy for years trying to discover his secret," proclaimed the gossip magazine *Confidential* discussing the sexual power of Frank Sinatra in 1956. "Ava Gardner, Lana Turner, Gloria Vanderbilt, Anita Ekberg—how does that skinny little guy do it? Vitamin pills? No. Goat-gland extract? Nope. *Wheaties!* That's the magic, gentlemen. Where other Casanovas wilt under the pressure of a torrid romance, Frankie boy just pours himself a big bowl of crispy, crackly Wheaties and comes back rarin' to go."

According to the article, the "Tarzan of the Boudoir," as Sinatra was called, spent two sleepless loved-filled days in Palm Springs "on Wheaties." *Confidential* ended its investigative report with the question, "What's in that stuff, anyway?"

"Sinatra gave Wheaties more promotion than anyone that has ever lived," declared long-time Wheaties spokesperson Bob Richards, "because he claimed that before every one of his sexual exploits—and he slept with everyone in Hollywood—he had a bowl of Wheaties."

General Mills never publicly acknowledged Sinatra's endorsement, preferring to keep Wheaties in the locker room rather than the bedroom.

Dissatisfied with the television endorsements of Bob Feller, Sam Snead, and Ted Williams, Wheaties left the sports arena for the video playgrounds of *Champy the Lion, Ding Dong School, The Lone Ranger,* and *The Mickey Mouse Club.* By 1956 General Mills knew its switch to kiddie fare was a disaster; sales dropped as much as 10 percent in one year alone. "We recognized our mistake and turned back unashamedly to 'Breakfast of Champions,'" recalled Robert Stafford, an ad man who worked for Knox Reeves Advertising Inc., the agency founded by the man who originally coined the powerful Wheaties slogan.

Stafford was given the job of finding a new breakthrough Wheaties spokesperson. But he was stuck. If Mickey Mantle couldn't sell Wheaties, who could? A friend at a rival ad agency gave the young man a few words of advice. "There's two things to look for. Somebody who can sell insurance or somebody who can sell religion. Because they are both intangible and they're very hard to sell. Anybody who can sell religion can sell Wheaties."

Stafford's first choice was Bud Wilkinson, the great football coach at the University of Oklahoma. The University would not allow Wilkinson to take on the commercial project, but the coach recommended a guy he thought could do the job, an Olympic track-and-field gold-medal winner named Bob Richards. The most interesting thing about Richards from Stafford's perspective was that he was also a Christian minister, known to his evangelical congregation as the "Pole-Vaulting Preacher."

Stafford tracked Richards down in Los Angeles. He found that Richards had given up the pulpit for the podium and become a full-time motivational speaker. In addition, Richards had gained television experience as the host of a weekly Los Angeles sports show sponsored by Union Oil. "We checked him out, and, of course, he turned out to be pure white," recalled Stafford.

Richards had grown up on Jack Armstrong and Wheaties and was absolutely thrilled with the job. In 1958, the Reverend Bob Richards put his clean-cut missionary zeal to work for Wheaties, opening every sales meeting and grocer's convention with a prayer and closing with handstand pushups to demonstrate his prodigious upper-body strength. "We announced him as a Reverend," recalled Jim Fish, a former General Mills vice president of advertising. "He was the kind of guy who, after thirty minutes of public speaking, you'd walk off a cliff after him if he told you to."

Richards and Wheaties launched the most powerful campaign for fitness and health America had ever seen. The cereal zealot starred in *Life's Higher Goals* and numerous other motivational films. He traveled to gyms, ballrooms, and meeting halls around the country, delivering some 17,000 motivational talks. He wrote dozens of self-help books with great champions like Fran Tarkinton, Tim Carver, and Warren Spahn. He traveled to Russia to film a Soviet-American track meet in 1958, and sold the clips to stations around the country, a programming breakthrough that later evolved into *ABC's Wide World of Sports.* He used cereal box back panels and television spots to get people to do push ups, dance, or start jogging. He formed the Junior Champs with the Junior

Chamber of Commerce and the U.S. Olympic Committee, which actually developed a number of Olympic champions. In 1969, O. J. Simpson and Art Linkletter saw him off on a cross-country promotional jogging and bicycle tour. "But Lord, we had a heavy program," sighed Richards years later. "I was in the air 70 percent of the time going all over the country. And every thing I'd go to they'd serve up a great big bowl of Wheaties instead of a steak."

The entire annual budget for the Wheaties Sports Federation was only $56,000 a year—including Richards' modest salary—yet, over his thirteen-year reign, from 1957 to 1970, he exerted an enormous amount of influence. "It was a crusade," sighed Richards. "I didn't think about money. To me it was always the cause, the cause, the cause."

Richards' marketing efforts paid off handsomely for both General Mills and its ad agency Knox Reeves. Not only was the Wheaties ad campaign among the most cost effective in the industry, but Knox Reeves charged $500 rental fees for each Bob Richards inspirational film, which were seen by more than sixty-five million people over a twenty-year period.

In 1958, Richards made cereal history by becoming the first athlete to appear on the front of a Wheaties box. From then on, his toothy smile was a fixture on scores of different Wheaties packages. "It wasn't until after I had left the whole program that I began to realize the tremendous respect the public had for people on the Wheaties box," admitted Richards. "You would never think that something that was a commercial pitch could be such a real symbol and to the athlete, a high honor. It's quite a Hall of Honor to be on the Wheaties package."

Richards tried to receive an even higher honor, when he launched a bid for the presidency in 1984. Backed by the ultra right-wing Populist Party, which later supported former Ku Klux Klan Grand Dragon David Duke, Richards garnered only 62,000 votes, losing the election to another former Wheaties pitchman Ronald Reagan. "I truly believe you are what you eat," said Richards to a reporter prior to his electoral debacle. "Why, last night I ate Wheaties for dinner."

Rock 'n' Bowl

The cereal aisle reflected all the cultural elements of the 1960s. Even Elvis Presley couldn't resist the occasional salad bowl–sized serving of shredded wheat, as rock-and-roll music found a welcome home on boxes of America's most beloved breakfast food.

The Mouseketeers broke the cereal sound barrier in 1956 when General Mills served up 78-RPM singles stamped on the fronts of Wheaties packages that allowed kids to "Hear Mickey Mouse, Donald Duck, Chip 'n' Dale, Goofy and the Mouseketeers sing!" This innovative gimmick was followed up by the offer of more Disney records—thick orange pizza-like seven-inch 78s—available for box tops and change from Wheaties box backs. Though General Mills sponsored *The Mickey Mouse Club* program on television, Disney maintained such tight marketing control over its characters that Annette and the other Mouseketeers were forbidden to pitch cereal during the broadcast.

General Mills really got into the groove when it co-sponsored Dick Clark's *American Bandstand* in 1957. Cheerios offered an American Bandstand 45-RPM record comprised of "hits of the past five years" like "Rock Around the Clock," "Honky Tonk," and "Green Door." The cereal maker avoided hefty licensing fees by hiring studio musicians to perform cover versions of the big bandstand hits.

Kellogg was the first to bring the driving tom-tom beat of the Southern California beach party to the breakfast table. In the early 1960s, Bill Stratton, a burly, fun-in-the-sun Burnett writer sold Kellogg on a series of thirty-second radio send-ups of Beach Boy–type songs for Corn Flakes, mixed by the Beach Boys' engineer Bones Howell, and voiced by future F-Trooper Larry Storch.

Totally stoked from experiencing the now sounds of the sixties, Kellogg sponsored *The Monkees* from 1966 to 1968. The first made-for-TV rock quartet was an effort to bring the inspired ad lib sophistication of the Beatles' *A Hard Day's Night* to TV. "Obviously Dick Lester [director of the Beatles film] was the real father of the Monkees. Bobby Rafaelson, who produced *The Monkees,* stole all Lester's ideas and turned them into a half-hour sit-com," said veteran commercial director Peter Israelson.

Burnett put many of its best writers, art directors, and producers to work devising cast commercials for the hot new show. Producer Bert Schneider was nervous that the Burnett-Kellogg aesthetic would prove to be a square peg in the hip round hole of the Monkees program. Burnett writer Bill Stratton reassured Schneider. "These are thirty-second commercials. We're going to have to keep it tight, whatever the hell it is."

In the first Monkee cereal ad, Peter Tork oozed out of his chair and fainted only to be whisked to a hospital emergency room and fed Rice Krispies by Doctor Mickey Dolenz. When Tork revived, Mike Nesmith exclaimed, "It's a miracle! Do you think he'll be able to play the bass

---

DOIN' THE FLAKE

The breakfast table's first real rock hit was "Doin' the Flake." The 1965 Kellogg's Corn Flakes promotion was recorded by Gary Lewis and the Playboys, a Beverly Hills garage band founded in 1964 by Gary Lewis, the son of actor-comedian Jerry Lewis. A surfer type song co-written by Leon Russell, who also provided the deep-throated "flake-flake-flake" background vocals, "Doin' the Flake" was a bargain for only thirty-five cents and a box top. The flip side of the record featured the Playboys hits "This Diamond Ring" and "Little Miss Go-Go."

Crazy new dance, it's the talk of the town,
It's the Flake

"'Doin' the Flake' . . . was within the promotional thing of 'Hey, your career *needs* this!'" Gary Lewis explained nearly thirty years later, "but all it got me was about 43,000 cases of Corn Flakes!"

---

again?" Dr. Dolenz replied, "Why yes, with enough Rice Krispies regularly every morning, I don't see any reason why he can't." Davy Jones ended the ad with the observation, "That's funny, he couldn't play the bass before."

"I love it," Schneider told Stratton, who had borrowed the idea for the spot from the very unhip Danny Kaye movie, *Up in Arms.*

After the Monkees split the television scene in 1969, Post hired an ape to promote their cereals. Fresh from the popular TV series *Lancelot Link/Secret Chimp,* Timmy the chimp mugged it up as a disc jockey in a series of thirty-second spots produced by Benton & Bowles that tried to boost cereal sales by offering a series of records on the backs of Krinkles and Honeycomb boxes.

"That was as bizarre as it gets," marveled Peter Israelson, a veteran commercial director who was in his early twenties when he directed the spots for Post. "He did only a couple of things: he went 'Ark, Ark, Ark' and he put his hand on the queuing needle and got the turntable going. He was really cooperative. Naturally, he trashed the studio, all chimps do that."

Kellogg co-sponsored *The Partridge Family* from 1970 to 1974.

Starring Shirley Jones and her stepson David Cassidy, the sit-com chronicled the adventures of a widow and her musical brood, who traveled from their comfortable ranch house to gigs on an old school bus, a suburban version of Ken Kesey's Merry Pranksters.

Though ad men found her "a terrific person," Shirley Jones put so little value in her cereal advertising experience that it has slipped her memory completely. "My connection . . . or 'exposure' to *ANY* commercial Partridge tie-in, was *SO NON-EXISTENT*," she wrote later. "But for Oldsmobile (we got a free car every year), I had absolutely *NO KNOWLEDGE* of who our sponsors were, nor did I participate in any commercials or promotions, nor, I'm sorry to say, did I ingest *ANY* Post [sic] cereals."

"She's a neighbor of mine now," laughs Joel Hochberg, a Burnett writer in the days of the Partridge family. "Next time I run into her I'm going to say, 'Remember me?'"

With monster bubblegum rock hits like "Sugar, Sugar," the cartoon group the Archies was the ideal band to promote presweetened cereal. They sung the praises of Post cereals on *The Archie Show,* a Saturday morning cartoon rocker. Kellogg countered with a cartoon band of its own, *Josie and the Pussycats,* a Saturday morning series about an all-girl rock band produced by Hanna-Barbera.

Rock cerealebrity reached new heights in 1972 when Post launched the Sugar Bears, an electric quartet exploiting the huge popularity of Sugar Bear, the cool mascot of Post's Sugar Crisp. Decked out in fringe vests, bell bottoms, and platform shoes, the Sugar Bears wailed in a series of thirty-second commercials and on five sound-sheet records stamped onto the boxes of Sugar Crisp cereal.

Post signed heartthrob Bobby Sherman to pitch its short-lived Cinnamon Raisin Bran to teenyboppers. To make his commercial Sherman traveled to a studio in New York City, where he was to appear as a tiny pitchman on the edge of a huge cereal bowl. In the days before sophisticated video effects, this was quite a trick. The production crew constructed a giant cereal bowl thirty feet across and fifteen feet high from lumber, chicken wire and papier-mâché. "I was quite dwarfed by it," recalled the singer, who clambered up a ladder to take his position. "I had to perch there with a bowl of cereal in one hand and a spoon in the other and deliver lines to the camera."

Post printed up millions of Cinnamon Raisin Bran boxes adorned with Bobby's toothy smile and stamped with his hits including "Easy Come, Easy Go" and "Seattle." When the promotion took off, Bobby was hassled at concerts and personal appearances by angry moms and dads, who complained that their kids ripped the records off the box without eating the cereal. "They would come up to me and say, 'I've got cereal all over the kitchen from your damn cereal boxes.'"

The greatest pop music icon to grace the cereal box was Michael Jackson, who shared the breakfast spotlight with his brothers as part of the chart-topping group the Jackson Five. Motown Records burned five of their songs —"I Want You Back," "I'll Bet You," "Darling Dear," "Maybe Tomorrow," and their mega hit "ABC"—into the backs of approximately 100 million specially-marked boxes of Frosted Rice Krinkles and Alpha Bits. In addition, Michael and his brothers appeared in five television spots.

Writer Frank Corre went to work crafting the scripts. Music director Roy Eaton worked out the arrangements and Peter Israelson directed thirteen-year-old Michael and his brothers Tito, Marlon, Jackie, and Jermaine. The first spot, filmed in the pop-fashion style of jump cutting, reworked one of their hits to pitch a popular breakfast food. While singing " ABC, talking about ABC . . . you and me . . . Post Alpha Bits . . . is history," the kids danced around tossing up imaginary Alpha Bits, which, thanks to the magic of animation, became the letters in POST ALPHA BITS on screen. "For once, brand association with a real hot little group was appropriate," commented Israelson. "There was some sort of a link connecting their music with something they were selling."

Russ Mayberry, Peter Israelson, and other directors doing rock 'n' roll television commercial spots in the 1960s and early 1970s established a unique production style that was to become the basis for a new cultural phenomenon in the 1980s: Music Television. The freewheeling camera work, the bright vivid colors, the high-spirited energy, the sped-up action, the slow motion, the jump cuts that have become staples of music videos, "all started . . . in the early 1970s when cereal commercials were the only game in town," observed Peter Israelson.

The reason was simple. While other products like Buicks, Tide, and Green Giant peas could rely on traditional commercial styles, cereal spots lived or died by their ability to express high energy directly to kids, the same market segment that later tuned into MTV. "We had to go one step further to glamorize and to energize," said Israelson, "so kids would pay attention to them." Not only the style, but also the substance of the cereal commercial world traveled to Music Television. Former cereal commercial director Peter Israelson went on to do, in his words, "a million things for MTV," including music videos for Whitney Houston and Anita Baker.

15

Yogi and the Fun Hogs

As the television ratings system became increasingly sophisticated in the 1960s, advertisers began to learn not only just how many people were watching their spots, but exactly who those people were. This was especially helpful for the cereal companies, which were interested in reaching a particular segment of the television-viewing audience—children.

The ratings proved what everyone had assumed to be true. Children, home from school on the weekends, watched a lot of television on Saturday mornings. Realizing this, the cereal companies led an all-out advertising assault for the eyes and stomachs of the American child. Ad agencies created cereal spots featuring child-pleasing animated characters, while the cereal companies spent 90 percent of their total advertising budget to purchase kid-friendly television time. By the mid-sixties, one out of every three Saturday morning commercials pitched ready-to-eat breakfast cereal. The overpowering presence of the cereal companies in children's prime time prompted one network executive to observe, "You might say they invented Saturday morning."

Smarter than the Average Bear

The first cartoon program made for Saturday morning television portrayed the adventures of a slow-witted pooch and a feisty cat fighting off the forces of evil. The *Ruff and Reddy Show*, which debuted in December 1957, was co-sponsored by Post cereals and created by Bill Hanna and Joe Barbera.

The Hanna-Barbera team had formed in the late thirties at the MGM animation studios in Hollywood. Joe Barbera was a former banker from New York who was brought to MGM by animator Jack Zander. Bill Hanna was an aspiring MGM cartoonist who gave up a career as a structural engineer "to run for coffee, to wipe cells, to sweep up, and to drown my bosses with story ideas," as he later put it. Never a great artist himself, Hanna had an eye for talented individuals like

Barbera. Said Hanna, "He had the ability to capture mood and expression in a quick sketch better than anyone I've ever known."

Once brought together as a team, Hanna and Barbera bonded into the McCartney and Lennon of the animation world; Hanna brought organizational skills and a razor-sharp sense of comic timing, and Barbera had the artistic and gag-writing abilities. The two spent twenty years at MGM producing cartoons for theatrical release featuring a cat named Tom, a mouse named Jerry, and other characters.

Bill and Joe worked on *Tom and Jerry*—spending as much as a year and a half from initial story to finished film—until the animation department at MGM folded in 1957 under pressure of budget cuts. As they wondered what to do next, they were approached by George Sidney, a Hollywood director and *Tom and Jerry* fan, who had an idea. Sidney offered to bankroll the pair to produce cheap color cartoons for TV. Bill and Joe agreed. They offered the idea first to MGM, but were refused.

The two men opened their own studio, Hanna-Barbera Productions, and perfected a stream-lined form of cartooning based on the UPA style developed by John Hubley and the other artists at United Productions of America. Hanna-Barbera relied on sparsely drawn figures and static backgrounds to create their "limited animation." "What Hanna-Barbera did was recognize that there was a market if you could make it cheap enough," said animator Gus Jekel. "When what the rest of us were doing cost a hundred dollars a minute, they were doing it for twenty dollars a minute."

Their first television series, *Ruff and Reddy*, was really rough-and-ready stuff, produced on a wafer-thin budget. "We received about $2,700 instead of $40,000 [for *Tom and Jerry*], and that was after great negotiating and pleading," recalled Barbera. Announcer Jimmy Blane provided live continuity between the *Ruff and Reddy* cartoons, and pitched Post cereals with songs and puppet routines. One hand puppet created for a Post Toasties spot was a corn cob. "You opened it up and Toasties was spelled out on the inside," recalled Benton & Bowles writer Joe Bacal. "That's how we stayed alive," laughed Barbera.

In 1958 Hanna-Barbera approached Post with the pilot for another television series, *The Huckleberry Hound Show*, starring a slow-moving blue dog created by Barbera and character designer Ed Benedict. Supporting characters included a pistol-packing horse named Quick Draw McGraw, a mouse-hating cat named Jinx, a cowardly lion named Snagglepuss, and a bear with a penchant for pilfering "pic-a-nic" baskets named Yogi.

After Post turned down an opportunity to sponsor the series, Joe

Barbera made a presentation to Kellogg. As he began to screen one of two samples of the new cartoon show, his heart stopped. The sound tracks had been switched, and Yogi talked with the voice of Jinx. "We are dead," thought a sweating Barbera as he rearranged the tracks and proceeded to run the shorts. "The people fell off their chairs laughing," said Barbera, remembering his tremendous relief. "It was unbelievable."

The Huckleberry Hound Show debuted in 1958 to critical and popular acclaim. Kids across America sat glued to their TV screens to hear the opening song—"The biggest show in town, is Huckleberry Hound, for all you guys and gals / The biggest clown in town is Huckleberry Hound, with all his cartoon pals"—and watch the Kellogg rooster crow and fly off the box of Corn Flakes. "Even though it was 'The Huckleberry Hound Show,' the entire opening was the Kellogg rooster running around the circus . . . Huck Hound isn't even in the thing," observed animation expert Jerry Beck. "You'd think it was 'The Kellogg Rooster Show.'"

Huck and his co-stars were everything a sponsor could want. They were cheap and funny and familiar. Huck himself, voiced by animation veteran Daws Butler, was loosely based on Arthur Godfrey, the most popular television personality in the 1950s and a particular favorite of Burnett's. "In a way, yes," acknowledged Barbera when asked if Huck was inspired by the ukulele-strumming pitchman. "He had that drawl—'Howdy, everybody . . . *yes sir!*'"

"That's a recurring motif in the animation business," explained animator Gus Jekel. "You try to design your characters so that as soon as people hear the voices, they have an idea of what they are about."

While Huck Hound fan clubs sprouted up around the country, the blue dog's popularity was soon eclipsed by his co-stars. Jinx, the cat who hated "meeses to pieces," loved Kellogg's Raisin Bran. Quick Draw McGraw, who debuted in his own show in 1959, slurped down Sugar Smacks. "And dooon' you fergit it," he told his sidekick, a burro named Baba Looey. Snagglepuss introduced the phrase "Heavens to Mergatroid, exit stage right" into the lexicon of popular culture as he chomped on Cocoa Krispies.

The animated feline helped boost cereal sales as well as the career of Burnett writer Bill Stratton. "I think I was the only guy who could get by imitating Bert Lahr for Snagglepuss," laughed the burly Stratton. "Snagglepuss could sound kind of swishy . . . and Kellogg definitely likes their guys to be all male." Stratton did his best sputtering Snagglepuss imitation as he pitched a commercial concept to Lyle Roll, the president of Kellogg. "The presentation started on his hotel bed, putting up storyboards, but he had to catch a plane so I continued in the taxi cab . . . holding storyboards . . . doing imitations . . . can you imagine that?" laughed the ad man. "Later Lyle took Leo aside and said, 'He's your best writer, give him a raise!'"

Yogi Bear—"Smarter than the average bear . . . always in the Ranger's hair"—started his career as a bit player in Huckleberry Hound's gang, but his irresistible charm—"Hey, hey, hey"—quickly catapulted him into a series of his own.

WET AND SLOPPY

For some reason, Kellogg's Sugar Smacks proved to be a fiendishly difficult product to tie in with a cartoon character. First pitched by Smaxey the Seal, the product fell into the hands of the Hanna-Barbera creation Quick Draw McGraw, "the slowest gun in the West." When Quick Draw's endorsement failed to increase sales, Burnett writer Bill Stratton devised another creature who had an equally brief tenure pitching Sugar Smacks. The Smackin' Bandit was an awkward-looking half kangaroo/half mule with gigantic wet lips. Everyone feared the slobberous smooch of the Bandit, including Bill Hanna. To record the audio for the Smackin' Bandit television spots, Stratton went to the Hanna-Barbera studios. As scripted, all the cartoon characters circled their wagons and brandished their weapons in self-defense, fearing the kiss of the Smackin' Bandit. For this key crowd-reaction scene Stratton needed lungs, so he went up and down the studio hallways pressing into service anybody and everybody he could find. "There were about ten or twelve of us in the little room including Bill Hanna and Daws Butler," laughed Stratton. "All of us were standing there around these microphones screaming out in terror. I can still see white-haired Bill Hanna giving it his full melodious expression! 'Oh no! . . . Don't do it to me! . . . Don't do that to me!'"

The Yogi Bear Show, wrote *Variety*, is "the funniest and most inspired of all the charming, contagious Bill Hanna-Joe Barbera cartoon characters. . . . The beauty of Yogi Bear . . . as well as most of the other Hanna-Barbera creations, is that he can be appreciated wholeheartedly by adults as well as children. In the world of animated animals, he has no peer."

Besides working out clever—or not so clever—ways to pilfer "pic-a-nic" baskets, Yogi and his sidekick Boo-Boo, pitched Kellogg's Corn Flakes. Yogi was like Huckleberry Hound in that his character was also voiced by Daws Butler and based on a real-live video legend, Art Carney's Norton from the series *The Honeymooners*.

"We had people do a take-off on him but not an out-and-out imitation," explained Barbera. "When we laid the track and listened to 'em side by side, Carney had a thinner voice." Yogi's name was also a take-off. When the bear first appeared, Barbera remembered people saying, "Hey, Yogi Berra isn't going to like this." Despite the derivative nature of their cereal superstars, Bill and Joe claim no one ever sued the studio on that point. "We never ran into any trouble with it at all," said Barbera. "We were very careful."

By 1963, Hanna-Barbera's menagerie had migrated from tube to package, as five million boxes of cereal a day streamed out of the Kellogg plant adorned with pictures of Huck, Jinx, Snagglepuss, Quick Draw, Yogi, and Boo-Boo. Kellogg merchandising provided a steady cash flow into the Hanna-Barbera bank account.

"I can tell you that the reason the sponsorship continued was that the arrangement was reasonable and not a burden," explained Hanna-Barbera licensing czar Ed Justin. "We didn't get rich over night but it was a nice arrangement where the income was steady, and they didn't feel pressure."

Asked years later if Yogi Bear pulled the Hanna-Barbera studios into fame and fortune on the back of Kellogg's Corn Flakes, Joe Barbera replied, "Well, there's a lot of truth there. Frankly, I remember one time they said they had taken a picture of Yogi Bear out as a test and showed it to various housewives, children, and people and asked, 'What does this say to you?' . . . and they all said, 'Kellogg's Corn Flakes' . . . I love that bear."

The Banana Splits

Hanna-Barbera was more than just a Saturday morning powerhouse. The producers controlled a big block of prime time with their animated creations. "They had a Kellogg-sponsored show on Monday, one on Wednesday, and one on Friday," remembered Joe Barbera. "Three shows which I called 'The Kellogg Network.'"

Thanks to the steady volume of work from Battle Creek, Hanna-Barbera moved out of their old Hollywood quarters into a brand-new building adorned with statues of Yogi and Huck. "We brought back the entire MGM studio, which was the best one in the business at that time, and hired people from other studios," said Barbera. "We were booming along."

The boom didn't last long. By 1965, Yogi and the gang were on the way out, as adventure-type cartoon shows became the Saturday morning rage. Hanna and Barbera rolled with the punches, selling their studio to Taft Broadcasting in 1966 for $12 million. By that time, Saturday morning had come of age, transformed into a strict ratings game like other television time slots. "So great was the demand for time and so central in the networks' thinking are the ratings that sponsors have nowhere near the programming power they once had to influence program content," wrote *Fortune*.

Kellogg was worried by this trend and sought creative solutions. In 1967 Lee Rich, who had migrated from Benton & Bowles, was head of the Kellogg account at Burnett. He convinced his cereal-making client to produce an hour-long Saturday morning kiddie show. Rich went around to all the producers in Hollywood, including Hanna-Barbera, looking for the best show idea. "We ought to try something different," mused Joe Barbera in considering the project. "The hosts of this show should not be animated . . . they should be characters in costumes . . . we should develop something new."

Something new turned out to be giant puppets. Joe Barbera developed the idea and went to Chicago to present it to the ad men from Burnett, as well as Grant Tinker and the other NBC network brass. When Barbera ushered in an actor dressed in a Yogi costume who had been hiding in the men's room all morning, Tinker leaned over to the chairman of the network and passed him a note, which said, "Barbera just sold the show."

Debuting in 1968, *The Banana Splits* was a take-off of *The Monkees*, which in turn had been a take-off of the Beatles film *A Hard Day's Night*. The three-dimensional Barbera cartoon starred Drooper the lion, Snorky the elephant, Fleegle the dog, and Bingo the monkey who pounded out rock 'n' roll tunes, showed cartoons, and sold Kellogg's cereals. "We got an incredible sixty-five share the first year," blurted Barbera.

The next year was a disaster. "We learned the hard way," explained

Barbera. "We did all new segments but we didn't change the background [of the set]. When a kid turned on to see, it seemed to be the same old show. They didn't wait to hear the new material." The Bananas danced their last in 1970, and Kellogg split from Hanna-Barbera.

Little Leos

The men who put the cereal into the hands and mouths of Yogi, Huck, Snagglepuss, and the Banana Splits were the creatives at Leo Burnett, Inc., some of the best and highest paid individuals in the advertising industry. Faced with bruising deadlines, the fickle tastes of children, and a tough market in which one or two share points could make or break a career, the men at Burnett still managed to keep perspective on the fact that they made their money acting like kids. "If there was one word to describe a business that you ordinarily think of as cutthroat, it would be *fun*," laughed Burnett writer Bill Stratton. "I thought of us as being the fun hogs. We could have all the fun we wanted and still get paid."

One of the lead fun hogs was Nelson B. Winkless III, creative director of Burnett's television group. Wink, as he was called, combined a flare for clever copy with a musical ear and great skill at pitching ideas. "He was short, sort of Fred Astaire-like," recalled writer Carl Hixon, "and he had these marvelous moves."

In 1967, Wink created the immortal "Snap, Crackle, and Pop Fugue" ("Snap, what a happy sound, Snap is the happiest sound I've found . . . ") modeled on the fugue for tin horns in *Guys and Dolls*. To make his presentation to Kellogg, Wink traveled to Battle Creek. Kellogg had just remodeled its advertising conference room with a "big, beautiful mahogany table about twenty feet long," said Burnett writer Carl Hixon. At the end of his pitch, Wink backed up and slid about ten feet down the conference table on his belly while mouthing his punch line. "You could hear this terrible scriiiiiIITCH! noise and when he rolled over, he had a big belt bucket on him which had grooved the whole conference table. Very embarrassing," laughed Hixon. "We never let him forget it."

After coming up with the "Doin' the Flake" music promotion, which was choreographed for the animated Kellogg's character Cornelius rooster, Wink devised a singing blue giraffe to sell Triple Snack, and the Wizard of Oats to make boxes of Kellogg's All★Stars disappear from store shelves. To boost sales of All★Stars, Kellogg briefly sponsored *The Magic Land of AllaKazaam*, a Saturday morning program starring illusionist Mark Wilson. "At the start of each show I would ask the children in our audience, 'What's the magic word?'" recalled Wilson. "They would reply in unison, 'KELLOGG'S!'" Wink himself disappeared from Burnett some time after *AllaKazaam* and became an expert on crap shooting, an occupation almost as risky as advertising.

Burnett writer Carl Hixon and art director Gene Kolkey created several species of cereal critter that still survive today. In 1963, Kolkey and Hixon traveled from Chicago to Battle Creek to discuss Kellogg's new fruit-flavored corn-based presweet, Froot Loops.

On the return trip, as they tossed out ideas over whiskeys in a train club car, Kolkey began doodling on a cocktail napkin. The doodle developed into a colorful bird, a toucan, to represent the colorful new cereal. "I positioned it as the secret cereal," remembered Hixon. "I wrote a song with Dick Marx which was in pig latin with the chorus 'Crispy and elicious-day for breakfast or for acking-snay, made with real fruit avorflay, oot-fray oops-lay.' That was the secret name." Toucan Sam's television call became a standard of breakfast Americana. "I got tickled about a year later when a whole bunch of Boy Scouts marched over a hill about a quarter of a mile away all singing 'oot-fray oops-lay.'"

Another fruitful Hixon-Kolkey collaboration was Apple Jack, for the oat cereal called Apple Jacks. "It was an oat cereal, with added nourishment," recalled Hixon. "We were looking for some way to dramatize the added nourishment . . . and Kolkey said, 'You know, when I was a kid, bullies were always a big deal. They were always beating me up. If I had some kind of cereal that would keep the bullies away, I would have thought it was terrific and eaten it every day.' . . . So I burst out with what became the campaign slogan, 'How about a bowl a day keeps the bullies away?'"

"All of us were students of pop culture," reflected Hixon, "Sometimes, something would pop a button in our heads." A few years later, Polynesian pop culture gave rise to the campaign for a brown-sugar glazed rice product. "It was twice puffed in the manufacturing process. So I was thinking, 'Twice puffed, twice puffed, twice puffed,'" recalled Hixon. "I'd just been to Hawaii where I'd been amused by Hawaiian singing with the 'A-ah, a-ah' sound in it so I thought, 'Well, Puff . . . Puffa . . . what if there were Puffa-Puffa Rice?' Then it began to sound Polynesian and out of that simply came the concept of a cereal with a kind of Hawaiian flavor called Puffa-Puffa Rice and a song, which we wrote about, "A-newa, A-nowa, a Kellogg's a bring a you—ah!"

One of Gene Kolkey's most enduring critters was Dig 'Em, the frog who croaked for Sugar Smacks. In 1971, Kolkey blended the finished frog from a composite of imported images. "They took the facial features from California, trunk and legs from New York, and the hands, baseball cap, and spoon from Pete Eaton in Chicago," recalled Eaton's agent, Tom Gentile. "Then Kolkey had him jump around from bowl to bowl."

"Dig 'Em was one of Leo's favorite characters," recalled Burnett graphics manager Dick Esmail. One of Kolkey's last campaigns was for a series of "real people" cornflakes boxes, featuring pictures of average Americans to dramatize the "healthy, sunlit energy you get from eating corn." The ad man had a personal interest in good health, as he was stricken with cancer just as the campaign got under way.

For eight years, from 1959 to 1967, a six-foot-two-inch-tall, 225-pound former football player named Bill Stratton wrote the words for Tony the Tiger. "I took Tony the Tiger to all the places I wanted to go: skiing at Vail, surfing in Hawaii, skydiving, tennis, you name it," laughed the writer who once rode a skateboard into a conference room to make a pitch. "I said, 'Hey, we're talking to kids . . . let's get Tony into some sports where he gets his ass kicked and have fun with it.'"

Stratton made sure every Tony spot ended with a pun. At Marineland, the proud tiger fell into the pool and wound up riding on the back of a Flipper look-alike. "Gee Pop," asked Tony's cub, Tony Jr., "did you do that on purpose?" "Son," roared Tony, "I did that on porpoise!"

After a couple of big-budget live-action wild west commercials for Rice Krispies involving bar-room brawlers, a steam train, and hundreds of war-whooping extras in Indian costumes, Stratton was assigned to pitch an orange-, chocolate-, and strawberry-flavored cereal dubbed Kombos. Stratton thought back to the English music-hall team of Flanders and Swann. "They had a song where a guy walked through a zoo and came across an animal he didn't recognize," said Stratton. "And he said, 'I have no idea what you might be' . . . and the animal replied, 'How do you do. I am a Gnu, the gnicest work of gnature in the gzoo.'" From the gnice gnu evolved the Blue Gnu, a buck-toothed, Kombo-chomping creature in a Navy pea jacket designed by Don Keller.

Stratton, who left advertising to write for *The Rockford Files* and *Hawaii Five 0*, was a firm believer in the Burnett gospel of advertising. "When you think you've used up all the ideas about Raisin Bran, you go and sit and look at the reels of commercials that have been done on this product. And you look at the reels the competition has done—what the hell can you say anymore about raisins and bran? And it's late and you're tired . . . but then you remember some of these truths about Leo, the sweated-out imagination, he called it, and you remember the second effort."

In the late 1960s, a thirty-something Burnett writer named Danny Nichols was sweating it out to come up with a new campaign for Kellogg's Raisin Bran. He had done all his research and had spent many long hours analyzing the product, trying to come up with a new commercial angle.

Following the advice of a colleague, Danny took the box of Raisin Bran home. He stared at it. He smelled it. He ate it. He fiddled with it. Finally he dumped the entire box out on his kitchen table and began to play with it. He picked up a little scoop he had for coffee and filled it with raisins. He emptied the scoop and filled it again. The next day, he rushed into the office of his friend Jim Gillmore. "I've got a great idea!" Nichols said excitedly. "There are two scoops of raisins in every box of Raisin Bran!"

Nichols, who later helped create the "You deserve a break today" campaign for McDonald's, died of a heart attack in his early forties. Before he passed away, he worked with Joel Hochberg to create what Hochberg dubbed "the Jewish phase" of Kellogg advertising. For the Raisin Bran spot that launched Danny Nichols's "Two scoops" slogan, "we needed a character shtick to make it come off so we cast a very well known character actor who was bald headed and mustachioed—like me a little bit . . . a little Jewish oriented," laughed Hochberg. "And when Tom Tinsley, who was the Kellogg client at the time, saw the rough cut, he said, 'Don't you think it's a little Jewish, Joel?' . . . I laughed and said, 'Tom, it's a lot Jewish!'"

In another Hochberg creation, an astronaut waited tensely in his capsule as he listened to the countdown for blast off. Suddenly, the door opened and his mother popped in. The astronaut turned his head in surprise, "Ma?" "Look, Mr. Big Shot Astronaut," his mother replied, "You're going to the moon and you haven't even eaten your breakfast . . . have some Kellogg's Corn Flakes."

Hochberg's "Jewish mother" commercials were almost as memorable as his classic bel canto cereal spoofs. In a sixty-second take-off of *Vesta La Giubba*, an Italian family sat around an empty box. "No more Rice Krispies," sang the operatic father. "I brought thee Rice Krispies . . . " came the response from the mother.

"In the case of *Madame Butterfly*, we went to a lot of very elaborate trouble," recalled Burnett television man Rudy Behlmer, who directed the Cleo award-winning spot. "To have a butterfly wistfully circling above the shot where this woman in traditional Japanese garb is preparing Rice Krispies with chop sticks, we hired this butterfly wrangler who used wires and threads to actually wrangle the live insect."

The campaign almost didn't get off the ground. Hochberg entered the Kellogg conference room to make his initial pitch just as another group was finishing up their presentation. Trying to be inconspicuous, Hochberg bent down "with my rear end facing the table," and began to pull a slide tray out of its box "when that slide tray box made a funny raspberry sound like a fart," laughed Hochberg. "Of course, it was loud enough that everybody turned around and they saw me in that position so I knew immediately what they're thinking and I said, 'It wasn't me . . . it wasn't me . . . it was the box!' . . . it broke everybody up!" Hochberg, who wrote more than 300 Kellogg ads for Bob Keeshan, aka Captain Kangaroo, and had the good fortune to recruit Farrah Fawcett to appear as Miss Tony the Tiger, later went on to become the head of marketing for 20th Century Fox.

In the 1960s, a typical Burnett print campaign for Kellogg involved writers, art directors, and creative directors working together to perfect the words and images that would move the most product. The focal point in the creation of a print campaign, the guy in charge of dealing with freelance artists, in-house creatives, and nervous sponsors was Burnett's art buyer, John Long.

Long was an acerbic manager who understood the needs of his talented and idiosyncratic constituency. As the center of a creative cyclone, he saw his job as not unlike that of a ringmaster: everybody had to be stroked, prodded, berated, coddled, or scolded according to their individual needs. He had a unique perspective on the operation. "No matter how ridiculous the deadlines were, we met them," said Long. "My job was to make certain that we didn't look like assholes."

To come up with really fresh and original ideas at Burnett, Long understood that the people he worked with had to be able to regress in service of product. "When you have somebody forty-five or fifty arguing with another guy forty-five or fifty as to what a singing cereal bowl sounds like—and serious as hell—'He sings like this! [falsetto]' . . . 'No, he sings like this! [bass]' . . . you're dealing with somebody whose fantasy life is a lot stronger than his normal life. He's peculiarly able to become a child."

Long oversaw the execution of at least 5,000 Kellogg packages—fronts, backs, sides, and so forth—while at Burnett and also pulled together the print advertising for Kellogg. "When CBS went color in 1962, it just about canceled out the whole print budget," recalled Long.

TWENTY-SEVEN MILLION MISTAKES

Sometimes production mistakes in the Burnett advertising shop had unintended results. In 1965 writer Curt Jones penned the copy for a series of Kellogg's cereal box backs devoted to "American Folk Heroes." One of the boxes told the story of Huck Finn and his Aunt Sally. Huck's Aunt Sally? Wasn't it Tom Sawyer's Aunt Sally? Indeed it was. A Mark Twain fan in Grand Rapids, Michigan, was the first to catch the error. He called the Associated Press, which soon had the media barking at Kellogg's door. "By the time anyone in the firm caught the mistake, a sixty-day supply of four products—Sugar Smacks, Sugar Stars, Sugar Pops, and Cocoa Krispies— had already been shipped," *Consumer Advertising* told its readers. Instead of lying scorned on the shelves as Kellogg feared, the twenty-seven million boxes with the twisted tale were sold in record time. "We couldn't have bought this publicity," read a Burnett memo dated March 16, 1965. Despite the success of the mistake, copywriters were warned against making copycat errors. "That's fine," said Kellogg President Lyle Roll after reading about the incident in the *Wall Street Journal*. "But don't let it happen again."

"I know because I had worked my buns off and a whole year's work was in the toilet. Because television sold faster than print. It gave you more thousand customers per buck than print did. So the dominance of television started in the late fifties, certainly in the early sixties, and more and more and more—with no end in sight."

The strongest believer in print at Burnett was John E. Matthews, one of the copywriters responsible for the creation of Tony the Tiger. Matthews believed to the bottom of his ink well soul that all advertising ideas and creativity originated with print. "Don't say *just* a copywriter because copywriters are first and foremost," he admonished. "Ideas originate with the copywriters."

Many good ideas did indeed originate with Matthews. His "Tall up with Kellogg's Corn Flakes" campaign created with Carl Hixon gave a much-needed boost to the cereal standard. When Kellogg created a fortified cereal to compete with General Mills' Total in 1966, they looked to Matthews to come up with a name. "I was going through one of those awful searches," recalled Matthews, "when I happened to notice that it was the nineteenth product that Kellogg had been working on that year. That was just a coincidence but I was desperately looking for some fresh name, so I named it Product 19."

In addition to talent, Matthews had connections. In the mid-1950s, he attended a Kellogg district meeting at a hotel in St. Louis. "I wound up sitting at the bar next to this guy I didn't know and it was Lyle Roll," recalled Matthews, referring to the man who took over the leadership of Kellogg in the late 1950s. "Lyle was a heavy Scotch drinker."

The two men struck up a friendship that was so close that Matthews sponsored Roll's membership in the Chicago Playboy Club in 1961. Wrote Matthews in the application letter, "The key statement and any mailings should be sent to him at the Inn, Battle Creek, Michigan."

Matthews hated the tube and its minions at Burnett. "Television-land was inhabited by a bunch of refugees from Little Theater groups, whose chief stock in trade was a new disease—Termitis. ECU, Pan, Wipe, Dissolve, Zoom, Dolly, Swishpanalley!" raved Matthews in *The Copywriter*, a book that he self-published in 1964. He claimed that his television enemies eventually forced him out of the agency. "He was more than a curmugdeon," said Carl Hixon. "He was rabid."

Still bitter, Matthews had nothing but contempt for television when asked recently about the highly successful "Taste 'em again for the first time" television campaign for Kellogg's Corn Flakes. "Some of the stuff I see today makes me puke," he commented. "'Taste them again for the first time' . . . is the biggest bunch of crap I ever saw."

16

Post Mortem

In the late 1950s Post sponsored *The Mighty Mouse Playhouse,* an animated Superman parody starring a caped rodent who was prone to operatic outbursts—"Here I come to save the day!" A thin stand-offish actor named Tommy Morrison provided the Mighty voice. "He was an unusual, weird character," said Max Bryer, a commercial director who worked with Morrison. "I'd come in and record his voices and then get out quick because he was so wrapped up in the character, he was the character. It carried over into his everyday living . . . it was very difficult to talk to him without his reverting to the character . . . he'd become Mighty Mouse."

Even Mighty Mouse couldn't save the day for Post. As breakfast entered the era of spot advertising and animated cartoons, the first company to make a fortune on ready-to-eat breakfast cereal saw its market share shrink to a mere echo of its former crunch.

The Advertising Beat

Mighty Mouse defended Post on Saturday mornings, while a cast of well-known characters, led by a "skwoowee wabbit," advertised its products in prime time. *The Bugs Bunny Show* debuted in the fall of 1960. Once he hit the small screen, the wise–guy fur ball created by Warner Brothers in 1938 attracted an audience of more than thirty million viewers per week.

During the show, Bugs, Daffy Duck, Elmer Fudd, and other cartoon characters from the Warner stable clutched Post cereal packages in ads written by Post's agency, Benton & Bowles. The most memorable portion of the Bugs cereal shtick was the hip, upbeat music that captured the irreverent spirit of the Warner menagerie. The man behind the jingle "Start your day a little bit better . . . start your day with a cereal fresh from Post" was Roy Eaton.

A classically trained composer, Eaton first came to Madison Avenue as a composer for Young and Rubicam, where he created the

"We're having Beefaroni" jingle and the "You can trust your car" tune for Texaco. He moved to Benton & Bowles in 1959, and became the music director, the first black man to reach a high-management level in the advertising business.

Eaton brought a unique sensibility to the ad world, a planet once described by Nat King Cole as being "afraid of the dark." Eaton's music for the Post account set the ads apart from those of the competition, which Eaton described as sounding like "white bread."

"The listener should always come away feeling better about himself," said Eaton, who practiced meditation. "The Post jingle was aimed primarily at the parents but it had to appeal to the children. . . . So the idea of 'Starting your day a little bit better' is a care concept—you know, parents taking care of their children—but the attitude of the tune, which was a syncopated, fast, bright and cheery rag, had a wake-up quality to it." Eaton recalled that his recording sessions were as upbeat as his compositions. Laughed the composer, "I didn't give a damn if there was one wrong note if the spirit was right."

Eaton managed to capture the right spirit even under the most stressful conditions. In 1960, Eaton and the rest of the Benton & Bowles team were up against a drop-dead deadline. They had to record a version of the Post jingle with the entire menagerie of Warner characters. Unfortunately, Mel Blanc, the man who provided the voice for Bugs, Daffy, Elmer, and other key characters, had just been in a car accident and was in traction in his Beverly Hills home. Blanc agreed to do the recording if he could stay in his bed. Eaton and the other ad men drove over in a sound truck to cut the jingle. "Mel was able to give us the voices but since it's impossible to speak without moving your body, he'd twitch inside his cast," recalled commercial director Max Bryer, who accompanied Eaton. "We'd wince every time he did a character."

Linus the Lionhearted

Before launching the Bugs campaign, Dick Bloede, the creative director of the Post account at Benton & Bowles, realized he needed to beef up his writing staff. Composer Roy Eaton told Bloede about Gene Schinto, a twenty-three-year-old writer at Young and Rubicam, "who had real crazy ideas." A few years earlier, Schinto had created the cartoon characters of Bert and Harry Piel to advertise the New York–based Piel brewery. Voiced by comedians Bob and Ray, the two characters "were so popular that the *New York Times* used to publish the times you could tune in to see the commercials," recalled animator Ed Graham.

Schinto's first assignment on the Post account was to create a character to pitch Sugar Coated Corn Flakes, Post's answer to Sugar Frosted Flakes. "Kellogg's had Tony the Tiger and we had a very little budget compared to Tony the Tiger," recalled Schinto. Schinto's low-budget breakthrough was a talking corn-cob puppet, Cornelius C. Sugarcoat, who appeared on Hanna-Barbera's first television cartoon, *Ruff and Reddy.*

Schinto followed Cornelius with a gentle Asian character named So-Hi. Personifying the culinary preferences of the Far East in his pitch for sugar-coated Rice Krinkles, the cartoon kid was named So-Hi "because he was only so high," laughed package artist Traverse.

The talking corn cob and the rice-munching Asian were preludes to Schinto's most memorable cereal creations. Taking a tip from animal crackers, Post decided to create an animal-shaped version of Alpha Bits to extend its presweet line. Thus was born Crispy Critters, a sugar-coated zoo of hippopotami, lions, horses, rhinoceri, elephants, goats, donkeys, and camels.

The product needed a champion. "It was a wonderful opportunity to create a character and if you're going to have a series of animals . . . you might has well have a king of the animals be the leader," recalled Schinto, who christened the cereal lion king "Linus the Lionhearted."

To provide the roar for Linus, Schinto turned to one of his childhood heroes, Sheldon Leonard. An actor with a powerful New York mobster accent who made his name portraying leg breakers in a series of 1940s gangster films, Leonard had long ago quit the acting game to become the powerhouse producer of three of television's most successful sit-coms: *The Danny Thomas Show, The Dick Van Dyke Show* and *The Andy Griffith Show,* all sponsored by General Foods.

Though no one thought that Leonard would be interested, Schinto contacted him and asked him to reprise his tough-guy role in a series of cereal commercials. "He got the biggest kick out of somebody remembering that character and he said he'd be happy to do it for laughs to amuse his grandchildren," recalled Schinto. "In fact, he was so damn rich he didn't even want any money . . . he did it for a new suit!"

Leonard's generosity saved Post a lot of money. "If you went for any personality, you had to offer at least $50,000 at that time, which would be like a quarter of a million dollars today," said Bryer. "He did it as a lark."

Schinto wrote and recorded a series of Crispy Critters commercials with Leonard purring "It's fer-ro-ciously delicious." In the spring of 1962, "The *one* and *only* cereal that comes in the shape of animals" charged into the cereal aisle to the music of Roy Eaton, great reviews, and a market share that briefly equaled that of Alpha Bits.

After the successful debut of Linus, Gene Schinto turned his attention to Alpha Bits. The writer came up with an animated mailman "because the postman delivers all the letters of the alphabet," recalled Schinto. To voice the letter carrier, Schinto signed up the acerbic comic Jack E. Leonard. Reduced to a two-dimensional cartoon postal worker, Leonard traipsed through Alpha Bits commercials showering abuse on kids while running a gauntlet of snapping dogs. "It just amused me to have an aggressive and insulting character for kids," remembered Schinto. "Somehow they let me get away with it."

Not for long. In less than a year, Leonard was pulled from the Alpha Bits campaign by the management of General Foods. "Some executive at General Foods didn't want his cereal connected with a Jewish comedian," recalled Schinto. "General Foods kept saying about Jack E. Leonard, 'This character is too harsh . . . he's too aggressive, we want somebody lovable,' so I just got pissed off and I said, They want somebody lovable? I'll give them somebody so lovable that your ass will fall off!" In revenge, Schinto created Lovable Truly, a postman "so lovable he was an idiot," laughed Schinto.

Bob Traverse was given the new, improved postman to illustrate for Alpha Bits packages. The artist hated him on sight. "Lovable Truly was a wimp," said Traverse. "In fact, after a year or so, they were embarrassed because he was so wimpy that they asked me to *masculinize* him. So I made his chest bigger, I bowed his belly in, put more masculine shoulders on him to look more like Arthur Godfrey."

By 1963, Schinto realized that Post lacked any long-term thinking about their cereal characters. On the one hand, the company sponsored programs like *The Bugs Bunny Show* and *Alvin and the Chipmunks,* while on the other hand they paid to create cartoon characters like Linus and Lovable for spot advertisements. Schinto went to the president of Benton & Bowles and presented him with a suggestion: why not give Linus the Lionhearted his own television show?

"Nothing so obvious had ever been done before," remembered Schinto. "Now they'll jump on your toes if you have a half-hour commercial but in those days it was unheard of to have characters created for commercials brought into life on the show. That was really something new."

After Benton & Bowles gave him the okay, Schinto approached his old buddy, animator Ed Graham, to produce the program. Post gave Schinto and Graham the go-ahead, with the proviso that the program had to be good quality. Most of the Saturday morning cartoons at the time were limited animation productions that cost $20,000 per half hour. General Foods wanted the same degree of movement found in the cereal commercials, which were budgeted at between $12,000 to $15,000 a minute. "The cost for Linus, about $75,000 per half hour, was the most that had ever been put into a Saturday morning show," said Graham. "It was a real quality show. The money went to full animation and the talent performing it."

Linus the Lionhearted starred the good-natured king of the beasts who presided over his jungle domain from the comfort and sanctity of an old barber's chair. Joining Linus were So-Hi, Lovable Truly, and other cereal brand mascots, whose individual episodes were strung together into a half-hour show. The talent lineup was a Who's Who of early 1960s television. Carl Reiner, creator of *The Dick Van Dyke Show*, played Billy Bird and Dinny Kangaroo. Ruth Buzzi voiced Granny Goodwitch, the only human in the jungle. Jonathan Winters portrayed the Giant, So-Hi's mother, and other characters, providing ad lib lines like "Jumping Buddha" and "Twisted sneaker." Sheldon Leonard continued to provide the voice of Linus, though his notoriety caused some headaches. "Outside the studio, Sheldon Leonard has a problem," reported *TV Guide*. "Children keep asking him to 'say something like Linus.' He says he can never think of anything except 'I just had an argument with Abe Lastfogel at the William Morris office.'" "It's true," agreed *Linus* producer Ed Graham, who also provided the voice for the Mockingbird. "He used to come to me and say, 'Could you write me some stuff that Linus might say, 'cause I don't know what to say to them.'"

In addition, Post ran separate commercials for their cereals featuring the same characters. "In those days, you could drift from a story to a commercial presentation and back without annoying the people who govern TV," said Graham. "We didn't see anything wrong with it," said Dick Bloede, Benton & Bowles' creative director. "It was a good show—kids liked it." Kids liked it so much that Macy's insisted on a Linus balloon in its 1964 Thanksgiving Day Parade down Manhattan's Fifth Avenue. "It was one of the biggest balloons in the parade," marveled Schinto, who took his family downtown to see it. "I was really thrilled . . . and so were my children."

After the first season, Schinto and Graham decided to beef up *Linus the Lionhearted* with another star. They considered including the Honeycomb Kid, a wiry, squinty-eyed cartoon wrangler designed to pitch the wagonwheel-shaped cereal Honeycombs, but decided against him. A cool jiving bear seemed a much more reasonable choice.

"Since I had already established Linus and several other characters, General Foods was getting hip to the idea that Sugar Crisp needed
someone stronger than three bears imitated by squeaky little old
ladies," recalled Schinto, referring to some of the earliest cereal cartoon
creations. Schinto took the persona of a jive-talking disc jockey, teamed
it up with some sketches, and created Sugar Bear. With a tip of the hat
to Bing Crosby, nightclub comic Gerry Mathews supplied the voice.
"Gerry Mathews used to do a voice like that at parties—'A little walkin'
space never hurt anyone.' You know, sort of an attitude kind of thing,"
said writer Joe Bacal, who was instrumental in developing the voice.
"So he really nailed it when he said, 'Hi there, this is your old pal Sugar
Bear. . . .'"

Sugar Bear joined the cast of the *Linus* show in 1965. "Right away
we knew he was a very strong character; in fact, he was a stronger character than Linus," recalled Schinto. "I recommended to General Foods
in the second year of the show that they change the program to 'Sugar
Bear and his Friends.' They should have because they're still running
Sugar Bear today while Linus is long gone."

Linus attracted an ever-larger audience, but Crispy Critters sales
lagged. Post tried adding pink elephants to the cereal mix, then orange
moose, grape apes, and finally white pushme-pullyous in a promotional
tie-in to the movie *Dr. Dolittle*. The company even produced a Linus the
Lionhearted album, with music written by Roy Eaton and performed by
Ruth Buzzi, Carl Reiner, Sheldon Leonard, and the rest of the cast.
"They sold like a million of 'em," laughed Bacal, who wrote the lyrics for
the discs that sold for eighty-five cents and two Crispy Critter box tops.
"It was great fun."

The fun was not enough to satisfy General Foods, which canceled
production of Linus in 1966 "because it didn't get high enough ratings,"
said Schinto. "I was terribly irritated they didn't know the potential of
what they had." The program lived on in Saturday morning syndication
until the Federal Communications Commission ruled in 1969 that children's television shows could not feature characters associated with specific products. "They said children couldn't tell the difference between
what was entertainment and what was pitch," recalled Graham. "So the
show was taken off the air—rather abruptly."

Breakfast in Bedrock

Just as Huckleberry Hound was taking off in the service of Kellogg, Bill
Hanna and Joe Barbera came up with another cartoon creation that

would provide Post with one of cereal land's longest-lasting animated tie-ins. Expanding the Yogi Bear concept, the animators decided to create a whole cartoon program with characters derived from the hit television series, *The Honeymooners*. Premiering in 1960, *The Flintstones* was originally an adult program aired in prime time and sponsored by Winston cigarettes.

"It had absolutely no licensing interest the first year," recalled Ed Justin, Hanna-Barbera's merchandising maven. "So I got Bill and Joe to put kids into the show—Pebbles was my godchild and Bamm-Bamm was my second godchild—then I had licensing potential. The minute they put Pebbles and Bamm-Bamm in, we got a kid audience."

In 1969, just as Hanna-Barbera was ending its long relationship with Kellogg, Justin sent out a mailing to potential licensees around the world announcing the availability of the Bedrock characters to hawk product. Meanwhile Post was pulling Rice Krinkles from the market and exploring a fruit-flavored version of the puffed rice, which could pass as little rocks. "General Foods had a good product, but they didn't have any characters so they used the Flintstones characters and put them on the package," recalled Max Lomont, who was head of package design at General Foods before moving over to Quaker as a vice president in 1966. Recalled Justin, "Some guy at the agency got my mailing piece and called me and that's it . . . a very simple negotiation." Joe Barbera was pleased with the license: "The name fit the cereal perfectly," he said.

"Pebbles, the Cereal of the Flintstones," came in a Pepto-Bismol pink package that featured Fred yabba-dabba-dooing across the front—an attractive come-on in the cereal aisle. "My idea was a fiesta cereal," recalled Stan Reesman, a long-time Post research and development man who created the cheery rice concoction, "something that looked good and tasted good." In 1970, Post redubbed the cereal Fruity Pebbles and introduced a second flavor, Cocoa Pebbles. Reesman slaved for months to create a Cocoa Pebble that did not come out green. "That," Reesman remembered, "was a blinger," his word for a tough problem. Fruity and Cocoa Pebbles proved to be strong sellers for decades, and received an added marketing push from the movie *The Flintstones* released in 1994. "That's probably the longest license in existence that I can ever remember," said Bill Hanna, considering twenty-five years of Pebbles. "That was a long one . . . still is."

After their success with the prehistoric cartoon world, the management at Post decided to think pink. In 1972, Post co-sponsored *The Pink Panther Show* on Saturday mornings. Post developed a product to go along with its new star, pink-dyed sugar-coated flakes named Pink Pan-

SHAW! ON PEBBLES

The Flintstones hit Scott Shaw! like a ton of rocks. "I was nine when I saw the very first episode on its premier night," recalled Shaw!, who was offered a job at Jay Ward Productions at age fifteen and insists on using an exclamation point as part of his name. "I loved dinosaurs and cartoons and it inspired me to be a cartoonist." Since the mid-1980s, Shaw! has been the art director in charge of Pebbles TV commercials for the advertising agency Ogilvy & Mather. According to Shaw!, some of his best work has never hit the small screen.

Spots featuring Barney as a female bowler, an aerobics instructor, and a fairy godmother, have all been vetoed by Post brass. "There was one [Post] executive who has since retired who absolutely did not want to see Barney in drag," recalled Shaw!, who is quick to point out that Barney cross-dressed in the original cartoon series to fool Betty and Wilma.

In the early 1990s Post introduced Dinos, the cereal namesake of Fred Flintstone's pet dinosaur. "A question that came up constantly was 'We've got Cocoa Pebbles and we've got Fruity Pebbles . . . so what flavor is Dino?'" laughed Shaw!. "Unfortunately, it sounds like something Fred would be getting off his lawn instead of something you'd want to be eating. . . . I know they lost money on it."

ther Flakes. To launch the new breakfast creation, an enterprising Post salesman in North Carolina named Don Parham donned a Pink Panther costume made by his long-suffering wife and personally pitched the stuff in his area's stores. "Although he's been seen regularly in and around telephone booths, Don is quick to say he's just phoning in the many new orders," chuckled the company publication *The Post Box.*

Although Parham's antics were appealing, the bubblegum-colored flakes were not. "After it had been on the market for a while, they got complaints," package illustrator Bob Traverse recalled. Friz Freleng, the veteran Warner Brothers animator who co-created the character for producer Blake Edwards in 1964, agreed. "They tested the cereal up in Oregon and it ran into problems because the color came off in the milk and kids didn't like that," recalled Freleng. "There were no repeat sales. The box was the most attractive thing they ever had."

Before Post killed the brand in 1974 and released the panther to pitch home insulation, the company asked artist Bob Traverse for fresh ideas. "They were looking for any kind of a device to make this a positive thing," laughed Traverse. "I looked at them and said, 'I don't even want to mess with it. I can't even force myself to think about this product in a positive way.'"

Freeze-Dried Flop

As Pebbles, Bamm-Bamm, Linus the Lionhearted, Sugar Bear, and the other Post characters fought a valiant television campaign to defend the Post market share, Post's managerial eye wandered toward freeze-dried fruits. Freeze-drying, a technology developed during World War II to preserve blood plasma in the field, came to the cereal industry in the early 1960s when General Foods developed the orange drink Tang for the Mercury space program. In 1963, the Post division spent millions perfecting a vacuum process that allowed bits of cork-like strawberries, peaches, or blueberries—laced with cyclamates—to be packed with corn flakes in foil-lined boxes. Post called its innovation Corn Flakes & Strawberries. "We said Corn Flakes instead of Toasties because there were people who didn't know Post Toasties were cornflakes," said Kent Mitchell, a Post manager at the time.

To satisfy production demands for the space-age cereal, which sold for twice the price of a regular box of cornflakes, Post built a state-of-the-art freeze-drying plant in Battle Creek and began to suck up every serviceable strawberry on the continent. "We outstripped the supply of strawberries from the West Coast and most of Mexico," recalled GF vice president Al Clausi. "The demand to satisfy the pipeline was incredible. In fact, there was a real question as to whether we would out-strip the world's supply [of denser, non-fresh market strawberries]." Kent Mitchell agreed. "We had to have something like a third of the world's strawberry crop . . . an enormous amount."

"Kellogg was very worried about our [fruit in the box] products because Corn Flakes is their bread-and-butter business—their solid cash cow," recalled Al Clausi. "Post had never been really able to make a dent in that business until this line of products came out—we really had 'em worried."

Kellogg tried to play freeze-dried catch-up by introducing Kream Krunch—frosted-oat loops mixed with cubes of freeze-dried vanilla, orange, or strawberry ice cream. Kellogg salesman Frank Staley serviced the Ohio markets where Kream Krunch was tested. "The product kind of melted into gooey ice cream in milk," recalled Staley, who sold one chain store forty-five cases only to pick them up a short time later. "It just wasn't appetizing."

A year later, Kellogg signed Jimmy Durante to launch Corn Flakes and Instant Bananas with an update of one of his standard songs. Seated at the piano, the old vaudevillian belted out, "Yes, we now have bananas . . . " Sales were brisk for a few months, then dropped like a rock, as store owners like I. J. Salkin complained that the product tasted like "cardboard discs in a box." Burnett commercial director Rudy Behlmer agreed. "Those little banana wafers looked like holy communion wafers. When you put milk on them, they started to look dark and mushy."

In 1966, Kellogg pulled the plug on Corn Flakes and Instant Bananas. "We tested the market carefully, we tried, we failed, and we're getting out of the market," Kellogg's Ken Englert told *Consumer Advertising* magazine. Without informing the star of their decision, Kellogg decided to move Durante over from Instant Bananas to Kellogg's main line, Corn Flakes. "Everything was kept quiet until Carl Hixon [a Burnett writer] and myself went to New York to shoot him in a couple of commercials for Kellogg's Corn Flakes," recalled commercial director Rudy Behlmer. "Suddenly he looks at the [story] boards and he says, 'Where are da bananas?' and we said, 'Well, Jimmy . . . this is without bananas,' and he said, 'No bananas, no Durante.'"

Time was running out for Post, too. Despite press releases promising a cereal revolution, the company's space-age miracle had two fatal flaws: the flakes got soggy and the strawberries stuck to the roof of the mouth. Said Tom Hollingsworth, a General Foods art director, "Everybody tried those new cereals—once."

Heads rolled at General Foods. "Chairman Tex Cook took Victor Bonomo, thirty-eight, out of the Kool-Aid division and put him in charge of the Post division," reported *Fortune* in 1967. "Estimates place Post's loss to date in freeze-dried fruit-in-cereal at anywhere from $7 million to $12 million." Post recouped some of its losses by supplying instant meat and potatoes to the troops in Vietnam. "I don't know if we ever got our money back," said former General Foods vice president Al Clausi.

Little Boxes—Big Problems

Post not only had problems with the stuff they put in the packages, they had problems with the packages themselves. By the mid-1960s, the ready-to-eat cereal industry was getting heat from food retailers and the

---

SPITTING PRETTY

Post's fruit-in-the-box cereals were heavily promoted by the stars of *The Andy Griffith Show* in a series of network and spot commercials. *Printer's Ink* told its readers, "It is considered by company officials to be the most intensive adult-oriented campaign that Post has ever scheduled." In 1965 Carol Channing, the platinum-topped, blue-eyed star of Broadway's *Hello Dolly!* appeared in an episode of *The Andy Griffith Show*. As part of her appearance, Channing was scheduled to participate in a cast commercial. The Post advertising staff planned to have the Broadway star join Sheriff Andy in enjoying a bowl of Corn Flakes & Strawberries. The trouble was that Channing couldn't enjoy the cereal because of allergies. "If she ate one of those strawberries, she'd break out into hives," recalled Max Bryer, who directed the commercial. "We would be up on a tight shot of her. . . . She would fake swallowing then spit the strawberry out into a bucket off screen. There were several times when with just the strawberries in her mouth, she'd break out. We had to have make-up standing by constantly. But it was just a temporary condition . . . nothing permanent. And she was still willing. They were all willing in those days."

U.S. Congress. In an effort to increase their market share, the big four cereal makers were pouring out products faster than retailers could sell them. Lucky Charms, Cap'n Crunch, Triple Treat, Crispy Critters, Country Corn Flakes, Bran Buds, Oat Flakes, Wheat Stax, Sugar Stars, Count-Off!, Twinkles, Froot Loops, Good News, Puffed Corn Flakes, TEAM Flakes, Life, and Total were just some of the new brands, each in at least two sizes, that manufacturers tried to squeeze onto retail shelves between the years 1960 and 1963.

"We like new items," complained a cereal buyer in the Detroit area, "but the cereal people get a little ridiculous. They never discontinue anything. We're at the point, both at the warehouse and store level, where there is just no more room for cereals. When a new one comes along, we have to take it because of the way they advertise it. . . . We have the same twenty or twenty-four feet of shelf space we've always had for cereals and something's got to give."

The space squeeze was made worse by the fact that cereal makers were packaging their new brands in "billboard" or "envelope boxes," so called because they were very wide and thin, designed to grab consumer attention in the increasingly crowded cereal aisle. Many of these boxes were too tall to fit on pantry shelves, a point not missed by annoyed shoppers, who complained that the packaging was deceptive.

Michigan Senator Philip A. Hart heard the vox populi echoing from the cereal aisle and launched a congressional crusade for truth in packaging. Hart accused the cereal makers of using billboard boxes to promise more product than was actually delivered. "He was talking about slack fill," explained Jim Fish, a former advertising vice president for General Mills. "'Slack fill' being when you start out with a flaked cereal and with shipping and transport it kind of breaks up and by the time you open the package it looks half full. We addressed it by saying on the package 'Contents measured by weight, not volume.'"

Hart held a series of congressional hearings to discuss the national threat posed by oversized cereal boxes, warning manufacturers that they had better look into the matter as well. Trying hard to cooperate, General Foods hired the consulting firm of McKinsey & Co. to study the issue. The consultant's report drew some intriguing conclusions: "If cereal-package size could be cut by one third without reducing its weight and volume or retail price, its direct product profit per cubic foot [of shelf space] would more than double."

In a radical move, Post decided to do something drastic about its packaging. Some engineers at the Post Package Research Laboratory recommended plastic cereal containers in the shape of tugboats, sailboats, delivery trucks, drums, Sugar Bear masks, and hand puppets. Others recommended the compact.

"A lot of things at the time were going compact," explained Tom Hollingsworth, a Post art director at the time. "There were compact cars coming along and 'compact' was a good word." Post thought it was such a good word that it decided to test a line of compact cereal boxes.

"The activists thought it was a great idea, the supermarkets thought it was a great idea, packaging people thought it was a great idea, management thought it was a great idea," said Al Clausi, then a General Foods vice president, who recalled the success of the compact box test marketing operation. After much soul searching, Post took the plunge and introduced an entire line of compact cereal boxes in 1964.

The government-supported action proved to be one of the greatest marketing blunders in American retail history. "Kellogg never moved their sizes and nobody else did and General Foods [which owned Post] got killed because everybody thought there was less product," said Max

Lomont, head of package design at the time. "What was intended to be a user-friendly, environmental, and economically wise thing to do turned out to be a bomb," chuckled Clausi years later. "That was a fiasco."

The move to compacts quickly sliced four points off Post's share of the market, worth about $4 million in pretax profits. Almost immediately, Post began reinflating their boxes and, in 1969, the company reintroduced the big envelope box with a vengeance. "General Foods at one time had more package sizes than anybody else in the industry because as a comeback from this disaster, they decided to get the biggest damn face panel they could," said Lomont. "They went right back to what everybody else had before."

As the 1970s rolled on and its market share did not improve, Post got desperate. For the slow-selling brand Rice Krinkles, Post designers were told to take inspiration from the top-selling Kellogg's Rice Krispies package. "They said we want a box so close to what Kellogg has that it's going to confuse people," recalled artist Bob Traverse. "So I made one up, and when you looked at the two side by side, you couldn't tell them apart. It wasn't on the shelf long before they got a call from the president of Kellogg, who said, 'Oh, come on, you guys . . . get that package off there!' So they realized that they'd been caught. It was kind of embarrassing."

As a result of meager advertising budgets, compact packages, and corporate neglect, Post's position in the market continued to erode. "It kept going down, down, down," sighed Hollingsworth. "When I was there, Post Toasties had a five or six point share of the market, and now it probably has half of one percent or less. It's just incredible that they let the thing slip away. . . . No matter what they did, it didn't help them."

17

Psychedelic Cereal

In the late 1950s General Mills ran a distant third in the cereal race, behind Kellogg and Post. This fact bothered General Mills' marketing manager Lowry Crites. Crites realized that General Mills cereals like Cheerios, Trix, and Kix had forceful but distinct identities. He also realized that there was strength in numbers. For half a century, the leading cereal maker had displayed the Kellogg name on each of the various Kellogg brands.

After conferring with his boss, Cyril W. Plattes (who had once considered the possibility of making cereal out of seaweed), Crites came up with a plan: a unified company design to tie the disparate brands together.

In 1958 Crites placed all the General Mills cereals except Wheaties in the hands of the New York–based advertising agency Dancer Fitzgerald Sample. From the agency emerged a logotype for the entire General Mills cereal line—a large *G* inside a white triangle placed the upper-left-hand corner of each and every box. To verbalize the new corporate solidarity, Dancer ad man Stanley Baum came up with a slogan, "The Big G stands for Goodness." Reported *Fortune* magazine, "That elusive thing called corporate identity was born." During the next decade, the corporate entity known as Big G would flood America's grocery stores with the wildest assortment of breakfast creations the world had ever known.

Rocky and Bullwinkle

On a pleasant afternoon in 1949 a young businessman sat in his real-estate office at the bottom of a steep hill in Berkeley, California. His future looked good. The postwar housing market was strong, and his Harvard M.B.A. promised to attract a high-class kind of clientele. As he was considering his prospects, the young man heard a loud screech coming from the street outside. He looked up just in time to watch as a truck crashed directly into his office. In an instant, he was pinned against a wall by the vehicle. His knee was smashed, and his life, as well as the future of American breakfast food, was changed forever.

As Jay Ward lay in his hospital bed recovering from the accident, he decided to leave behind the world of mortgages and interest rates. Ward and his boyhood friend Alex Anderson, a nephew of Terrytoons animator Paul Terry, went to work producing cartoons in Anderson's garage and came up with the idea for cartoon characters named Rocket J. Squirrel and Bullwinkle Moose, a moose named after a Berkeley used-car dealership.

While Anderson decided to take a job with an advertising firm, Jay Ward headed south with Bullwinkle on the brain. In Los Angeles he met Bill Scott, a talented animation writer at UPA, the studio co-founded by Marky Maypo creator John Hubley. "Scott was a writer . . . a writer who because he was writing for cartoon factories became a great cartoonist, too," said animator Bill Melendez. Writer, gag man, cartoonist, and simplified UPA-style animation designer, "Bill Scott was probably the most all-around gifted story man that animation has ever produced," said Bill Hurtz, who worked with Scott for many years as his animation director.

Bill Scott and Jay Ward formed Jay Ward Productions in 1958. Their first creation was the pilot for *Rocky and His Friends*. Scott provided the voice for Bullwinkle, while June Foray gave voice to Rocky. Jay Ward provided the creative spark and was supposed to come up with the money.

"As the story goes, Jay Ward was in big financial trouble and was going around knocking on doors saying, 'Hey, I've got this great program, it's called *Rocky and His Friends* . . . anybody want to buy it?'" recalled Leo Stuchkus, an art director at Dancer Fitzgerald Sample. Ward hit pay dirt when he made his pitch to Big G. The company had a huge advertising war chest and was looking for a vehicle to sell Cheerios. The men at Big G liked Rocky and Bullwinkle so much they demanded to own the whole show, including the characters. Ward was reluctant to sign away his animated offspring to a cereal company, but he felt he had little choice. "Evidentally they gave him a ton of money but they owned that whole package of *Rocky and His Friends*" said Stuchkus. "General Mills really ripped off Jay Ward and all those characters."

Debuting in 1959 at four o'clock in the afternoon on a New York TV station, *Rocky and His Friends* opened with a low-tech Rocky and Bullwinkle hand-puppet sequence. The cartoon portion of the program whizzed over the heads of most of the young audience. Ward and Scott had a penchant for literary and historical puns revealed in such episode titles as "The Whale: Maybe Dick," "The Guns of Abalone," and "On the Shores of Veronica Lake There Sails the Ruby Yacht of Omar

Khayyam." "It was the first time that I can recall my parents watching a cartoon show over my shoulder and laughing in places I couldn't comprehend," film director Steven Spielberg told the *New York Times*.

When Rocky's ratings proved to be disappointing, Big G's ad firm changed its broadcast time so that it aired immediately before *The Wonderful World of Disney*. Although Rocky appeared on a different channel than the popular Disney production, the Bullwinkle gang figured out a foolproof way to keep kids from switching channels. "Kiddies," animator Bill Hurtz recalled the goofy moose saying one night during the opening hand-puppet segment. "I hear that you like this show. Here's what you do so you can see it next week. Go to your television set and pull off the knob. It will stay where it is and next week it will be all there for you to see the Bullwinkle show." Hurtz said more than 10,000 kids took Scott's suggestion and pulled the knobs off their TV sets. "Disney was very unhappy," laughed Hurtz. "After that, Walt always referred to anything from our studio as that 'Jay Ward shit.'"

Plugs for Big G cereals were worked into the hand puppet opening, as was a ten-second shot of an animated Big G outdoor billboard. Moose and squirrel also pulled their weight as animated pitch critters. "Cheerios helps build moosles. Or, if you are not a moose, muscles," chirped Bullwinkle. In time, the 'toons pitched Cocoa Puffs, Trix, and Wheat Hearts as well. In spots written by Dancer ad man Tony Jaffe for Jets, "the sugar-coated oat and wheat goodness" cereal, Bullwinkle borrowed the Wheaties shtick and became a winded jock, until his squirrely little buddy helped him "Win with Jets."

Bill Conrad of *Cannon* and *Jake and the Fatman* fame narrated both the series and the commercials. Sitting in the director's booth during production, Ward drove Conrad to read faster and faster. "I can't read this any faster," Conrad once complained. "Yes you can, Bill . . . you can do it,'" Ward encouraged him. Eventually, the hyperventilating Conrad achieved the breathless driving style that Ward wanted. "He had the uncanny knack of knowing what is right," remembered Foray. "Jay often said, 'Well, I didn't like that. Let's do it again.' And he was always right."

To keep production costs down, the storyboards were completed in the States, then shipped to Mexico to be animated. The move "saved a half a million bucks a year over Hollywood costs," said Bill Hurtz. However, "they didn't have good animators down there," recalled Leo Stuchkus, a Dancer art director. "Their mixing facilities for sound were horrible and to make the cels, they were using acrylic house paint."

Big G also saved money by paying Jay Ward and his friends a lot less than Hanna-Barbera and other animation firms received for their work.

Ward and Scott took revenge on their tight-fisted cereal patrons by creating a nine-part Bullwinkle story entitled "Boxtop Robbery." In the series, the world's economy was based on cereal box tops and was threatened by box top counterfeiter Boris Badenov. "Some lower echelon guy [at Dancer] read the script and approved it," said Hurtz. "They really didn't know what they had approved until it got on the air . . . then they were really put out . . . they went crazy trying to kill it!" But it was too late. Half the episodes had already aired. Rather than face millions of irate viewers demanding to know the outcome, Big G and its ad agency had no choice but to let the story run its course. "Bill and Jay enjoyed the situation," laughed Bill Hurtz. "No doubt about that."

Fearless in the studio, Jay Ward was painfully shy in the office. He suffered from an extreme form of paranoia caused by the truck accident that turned him to animation. "When he hired me," said Bill Hurtz, "I had to go in and see him and he apologized for not being able to come out of his office. He had therapy and eventually cured himself of this extreme fear to the point where he'd go out to lunch."

Compensating in part for his private disability, Ward embarked on a series of outrageous publicity stunts, paid for by General Mills. The most lavish stunt was the Great Moosylvania Statehood caper. In 1962 Ward bought an island on the Canadian-U.S. border and launched a campaign to turn it into the great state of Moosylvania. To achieve statehood, Ward promoted Moosylvania on the *Rocky and Bullwinkle* television series, then donned a Napoleon outfit, boarded a van with a public address system, and set out across America to drum up grassroots support.

First stop was Las Vegas, where advance men placed ads inviting "all the freaks and exhibitionists to come out and be in this parade," recalled Hurtz. "They did that anti-parade parade in town after town as a sort of a joke on the Rose Bowl." When Ward got to New York City, he hired a marching band. "They pulled up in front of Dancer Fitzgerald Sample," laughed Hurtz, "walked straight past the receptionist with the band playing, marched through the agency, turned around and came out again without stopping . . . and left."

In Washington, D.C., Ward picked up an NBC cameraman and Senator Hubert Humphrey's young daughter and headed for the White House to turn a fistful of signed Moosylvania petitions over to President Kennedy, who was busy dealing with the Cuban Missile Crisis. "They were stopped at the White House gate by a red-faced cop," recalled Hurtz. The guard ordered Ward to leave, and to turn off his sound system, which was blaring the Moosylvania fight song. "We have a constitutional right to petition," Ward shouted over the music. After a few moments, Ward and his entourage marched off. "This stunt made all the papers," said Hurtz. "It was called 'The most ingenious idea since the midget sat on J. P. Morgan's knee in a Congressional hearing.'"

In 1961 General Mills halted production of *Rocky and His Friends* and repackaged the episodes for syndication as *The Bullwinkle Show.* Two years later, the company sponsored Jay Ward's *The Adventures of Hoppity Hooper* for a short time. By 1967 Big G was rerunning 350 half hours of *Bullwinkle,* and had roared ahead of Post to become the second biggest cereal seller in America. *Fortune* magazine noted that General Mills had achieved its success "largely through the televised efforts of an awesomely stupid moose named Bullwinkle."

Over the last thirty years, Rocky and Bullwinkle have gained in popularity, as aging baby boomers look back fondly on the critters who inhabited "Ifanyonecan, Yukon," and other video locations. Even Ward's competitors compliment the quality of his weird and wonderful work, which was as much a product of General Mills as Cheerios. "Nobody else could touch it," admits Joe Barbera, half of the Hanna-Barbera animation team. "Brilliant stuff."

Silly Rabbit

While Rocky and Bullwinkle took the cereal spotlight, the Cheerios Kid and his pal Sue continued to push Big G's little Os. Like Alice in Wonderland, the advertising creatures had a disturbing tendency to grow and shrink in size. "There was always a battle with the Cheerios Kid depending on who the account person was," recalled Leo Stuchkus, an art director at Dancer. "One year they said, 'Let's make the kid look older,' and the next year, 'Let's make him look younger.' They were always going back and forth." The Kid's warcry, "Big G, little O, go with Cheerios," was penned by copywriter Tony Jaffe, who spent six years in the service of a difficult yet silly taskmaster, the Trix rabbit.

The original Trix rabbit was a hand puppet who appeared on the introduction to *Rocky and His Friends, Captain Kangaroo,* and other programs sponsored by Big G. This rag-doll rabbit first adorned the single-serving Trix box in 1959. In that same year, the rabbit appeared in animated form spouting the pitchline "I'm a rabbit and rabbits are supposed to like carrots. But I hate carrots. I like Trix." With his long ears telegraphing his mood swings, his resourcefulness, and his wheedling need for his favorite cereal, even the first crude Trix rabbit was lovably human.

"Joe Harris came up with that concept, 'Silly rabbit, Trix are for kids,'" recalled Bill Tollis, the art director for Dancer Fitzgerald Sample who storyboarded the first Trix rabbit commercials. "That was a tremendous success and still ongoing today." Joe Harris left the agency and was replaced by Tony Jaffe. "Joe had invented him," said Jaffe. "I got him to those plots where he tried to get the Trix and disguised himself and had to be uncovered. Actually, I'd give Joe credit for the basic scenario. I sophisticated it."

"Tony's executions were very ingenious," recalled co-worker Gene Cleaves. "I always remember one. . . . The rabbit disguised himself as an Indian, then he did a rain dance, which brought the rain and the rain came down and revealed him to the kids as the rabbit." The kids took back their cereal with the words, "Silly rabbit, Trix are for kids."

"Those stories were extremely difficult to write, you know, to have him revealed in a clever way," Jaffe sighed years later. "In the thirty-second time frame, you can't develop the character . . . you just have him do his thing."

To test the effectiveness of his rabbit creations, Jaffe watched the cereal sales charts. "I cared about that . . . damn right I did. Because if it didn't move, it was back to the drawing board . . . if you saw a bump in sales, you knew it was working."

Some cereal critters were a lot easier to work for than the Trix rabbit. In 1962, Gene Cleaves got the assignment to come up with an alternative to the animated kids who were pitching Cocoa Puffs by imitating choo-choo sounds. "All of a sudden I had this thought," Cleaves recalled, "'You're cuckoo for Cocoa Puffs, You're cuckoo for Cocoa Puffs, You're cuckoo for Cocoa Puffs,' . . . and I thought, Hey, that's a bird! A cuckoo bird who says, 'I'm cuckoo for Cocoa Puffs.'"

With a design for Sonny the Cuckoo and a storyboard for the first commercial in hand, Cleaves auditioned New York's best voice talent. "They came to me and they showed me this crazy bird that Bill Tollis designed and they said, 'What can you do for its voice?'" recalled Chuck McCann, who went on to perform the cuckoo voice for twelve years. "I took one look at that screaming bird, I mean the attitude of the bird and thought, 'Geez . . . wouldn't it be a . . . let's try this, and I did this squawk at the beginning . . . 'Wuuwk . . . I'M CUCKOO FOR COCOA PUFFS.'"

"The bird went on the air in 1963," recalled Jack Keil, "and in six to eight months, the share went up half a point, which is the equivalent of something like four to five million dollars increase in sales—just from that campaign."

CEREAL SALUTATIONS

Consumers contact cereal makers to express a variety of important and not-so-important concerns. During a typical month in 1972, documents from General Mills recorded several interesting letters concerning the company's cereal commercials. "You are discriminating against the rabbit," wrote one activist. "We at the Rabbit Foundation have had enough of this action. You have a great product but we fail to see why you won't give the rabbit Trix. Your cereal should be enjoyed by all, regardless of race, color, creed, or species."

Another correspondent was concerned about a commercial for Wheaties that pictured a small boy sitting at a table explaining how "gutsy" his cereal tasted. "I can't picture him sitting there eating guts," wrote the offended viewer. "Please remove the commercial from TV before sales of your product are reduced to those who enjoy eating intestines for breakfast."

In 1978, Mr. B. N. Balsleg mailed back his official Wheaties athletic wear to spokesperson Bruce Jenner with a note. "I received my running shorts but they are female," complained the jogger. "There is no hole for my penis."

In 1964 Big G turned its attention to Kix. At Dancer, Tony Jaffe was given the task of invigorating the product. Jaffe, who wrote jazz songs in addition to Trix rabbit story lines, looked for inspiration outside the cereal establishment.

"Just about every character on kids' cereals was a very well defined character," said Jaffe. "Rather than come up and invent the same kind of thing—an alligator or some kind of a talking animal—I wanted something more amorphous, something like Al Capp's Schmoos." Working with the New York animation house Stars and Stripes Forever, Jaffe came up with not one, but six two-legged blobs—Colodny, Gzorpe, Swerdlog, Glyk, Zilch, and Schtickdooper. "A bit of his Jewish background in there," laughed art director Leo Stuchkus.

Before Colodny and company performed for the masses, Jaffe flew out to Minneapolis to get approval from the brass at Big G. Jaffe was scheduled to make his pitch at the tail end of a sober meeting during which Dancer Fitzgerald chairman Gordon Johnson presented a media plan designed to save his client millions. "I followed him with my presentation," Jaffe recalled. "I got up there and I said, 'I don't know how I'm going to top ten million dollars' . . . and I brought out this big orange fuzzy thing I bought in a dime store which had two eyes and feet attached to the head and I said, 'This is a Gzorpe.' So they looked at this thing and totally cracked up."

Jaffe's favorite cereal advertising campaign was a sixties period piece. Inspired by the Simon and Garfunkle hit "The 59th Street Bridge Song," Jaffe dubbed his mid-sixties campaign for Cheerios "Feelin' Groovy." "It was the first commercial with a white kid and a black kid playing basketball. . . . That might seem trite right now but to my knowledge, it was the first time a black person was ever used as a principal in a commercial," Jaffe said proudly, recalling the campaign that won a Clio award. "I remember presenting it to the Cheerios brand manager at the time, Bruce Atwater, who later became chairman of the board of General Mills, and he congratulated the agency, the brand group—they were absolutely thrilled with it."

Marbits and Monstrosities

For the management of General Mills, each newly perfected cereal production technique was a marketing opportunity. For the creative staff, the extruders and puffing guns were nightmares. "They would call and say, 'We now have capacity for a puffed cereal,' or 'a coated something,' and 'can you come up with concepts?'" recalled Jack Keil.

As the technology improved, General Mills launched a product proliferation binge resulting in the creation of sugary cereals and psychedelic ad campaigns. "It was better than *Upstairs Downstairs*," said General Mills marketing manager Lowery Crites, "the best show in town."

In 1960, an orange, rotor-tailed elephant pitched the first cereal ever to share a name with its animated character, the star-shaped Twinkles. Even after being coated in multicolored jimmies by a cartoon fireman dubbed the Twinkles Sprinkler, the product eventually disappeared from the shelves.

Jimmies didn't light a fire of consumer interest, but multicolored marshmallow candy bits—"marbits" in industry jargon—did. In a move that brought the cereal bowl even closer to the candy dish, Post began experimenting with a marbit breakfast called Huckle Flakes around 1960. The cereal combined cornflakes with "little marshmallow balls dyed dark blue like huckleberries," recalled Bob Traverse, the illustrator who drew the experimental package. "The agency came up with the concept of an Italian mustachioed organ grinder character for it," Traverse continued. "I never figured out the association between huckleberries and Italians but, anyway, they asked me to do the package." The nation at large was spared the sight of the organ grinding huckleberry hawker, as Huckle Flakes died in test markets.

Big G decided to experiment with marbits even after Post's Huckle Flakes flop. "We asked, 'Can you put them into shapes?' and they said, 'Yes, we can,'" recalled Jack Keil, a Dancer creative director. "So somebody came up with the idea of the Irish cereal—'Iddly diddly dee.'" Other Big G creatives suggested marbits shaped like shamrocks, half moons, stars, and diamonds. Lucky the Leprechaun was created to promote the product, which was given the name Lucky Charms. In minute-long ads first created by Bill Melendez, Lucky danced a jig to the jingle, "'Tis lucky to catch a leprechaun/But of course, nobody can/Catch me and you catch me Lucky Charms."

"He tied into the product perfectly and he was easy to use because he was magical," recalled Trix rabbit writer Tony Jaffe, wistfully. "He wasn't in this boxed format which was tough to write for. Obviously, a lot of people liked him. It was a wonderful product-character fit."

Using new extrusion dies, General Mills cut a variety of new cereal shapes. In 1965, Tony Jaffe was presented with a pile of strangely shaped cereal puffs. "Seeing that they were oddball, I thought Wackies was kind of a good name for 'em. Then they added a banana marbit to it, like the Lucky Charms, so it became Banana Wackies. . . . 'New from General Mills, the wack, wack, wackiest cereal.'"

Though Jaffe created an animated elf and a singing gorilla to pitch Wackies, the cereal flopped. "It had nothing to do with the advertising," recalled Jaffe. "It had to do with the fact that not that many people liked bananas. If they had put in another kind of a marbit, it probably would have flown."

Other Big G cereals also flopped. Jack Keil pitched a concept for Stan and Ollie Flakes in 1966 using the Laurel and Hardy shtick. He was frustrated in his efforts by the bozo who owned the rights to the characters, Larry Harmon, who actually played the television clown Bozo at one point. Stan and Ollie Flakes were followed in 1968 by Louis Flakes, pitched by Lou the Kangaroo. "We even had a cereal called Smith, Brian, Cohen and Fernske Flakes, named for the men who developed it," laughed Keil. "You can see we went wild."

In 1966, Hattie the Alligator appeared briefly to sell Corn Bursts as a "mouthful of flavor." A sugar-frosted oats-and-raisins product

> ### QUICK STEP COCOA PUFFS
>
> In the mid-sixties Jack Keil, a gangly six-footer, became a legend at General Mills for his Cocoa Puffs routine. "I worked out something called the Cocoa Puffs quick step and the idea was to teach kids, watching television, 'OK, learn the Cocoa Puffs Quick Step, kids!'" remembered Keil. To sell his promotion to Big G, Keil flew to Minneapolis and scheduled a formal presentation to the company's top marketing brass. The presentation was planned for a conference room packed with eight or ten people around a huge table. "I looked at this and I said, 'I'm dead!' . . . It was going to be tough enough anyway to demonstrate this quick step . . . but how was I ever going to demonstrate this," remembered Keil. The ad man decided there was only one space left in the conference room to show off his commercial idea. "So I quickly took my shoes off, jumped up on the conference table, and slid across going 'Huff, huff Cocoa Puffs, yum, yum, yum.' . . . I nearly slid into president Don Swanson's lap . . . It was a hit!"

emerged as El-Cruncho, pitched by a Zorro-esque character intent on stealing the cereal "blended for heroes." "Ees also del—eecious, amigo," assured the caped cereal crusader. Sighed El-Cruncho's creator Bill Tollis, "It never got off the ground."

Tollis created a herd of pixies dubbed Floops to sell another stillborn Big G cereal, Sugaroos. "It had a song," said Tollis: "'Of course little Floops might eat one or two / and they're so sugary sweet, you know what to do. [and they flipped] Floppity, flippity, floppity, floop . . . and you'll flip—floppity floop for new Sugaroos, too.' I don't remember what the product was like. I just remember we worked our butts off on that one but it didn't go very far." Day-o, the world's first calypso-inspired presweetened cereal, was equally short lived.

Clackers, launched in 1968 with the biggest promotion campaign in General Mills history, featured live action versions of historical vignettes. "You'd have Patrick Henry saying, 'Give me liberty or give me . . .' and then a voice would come in . . . 'CLACKERS!'" recalled Jaffe. Similar things happened to nursery-rhyme characters. "Little Miss Muffet, who sat on her . . . CLACKERS!" Much to Big G's delight, the gagline entered the nation's short-term vocabulary alongside *Laugh In*'s "Sock it to me!" and "Here comes the judge!"

"We used to go around the agency yelling 'Clackers!'" laughed Gene Cleaves. "In fact, I used to play golf with some guy who had gotten that on his brain and every time he putted he yelled 'Clackers!'" Despite the funny campaign and fabulous word of mouth, the cereal failed. "The rigidity of Clackers was such that it bruised and even cut people's gums," sighed Jaffe. "Ten years later the stuff was perfected as Golden Grahams."

After the failure of Clackers, Big G began experimenting with soft puffs impregnated with various sweet fillings. In 1972, the company launched Mr. Wonderfull's Surprize, pitched by Mr. Wonderfull, a lanky dynamo with a periscope perched on the top of his head. The puff filled with a sweet center came in both vanilla and chocolate flavors but suffered from lack of quality control; some balls burst while others remained hollow. Inside Scoop was another cereal puff filled with a sweet center. The rococo puffs were promoted by cartoon reporter Phil Flash, a newshound always on the lookout for "the inside scoop."

An animated top hat pitched Big G's Magic Hats, a candy-coated cream-filled puff that mercifully died in its test market, while Crazy Cow, in both strawberry and chocolate flavors, managed to trot a bit further. Advertisements for the cereal, which ran for several years, promised that the colored balls made "strawberry milk." "How now, Crazy Cow," the announcer intoned.

Big G made so many new cereals, and had so many marketing disappointments, that at one point it tried to market Ooops, a cereal based on a mistake. Animated commercials for the cereal were based on the premise that someone went "ooops" during the manufacturing process, creating a mound of randomly shaped breakfast food. "We wrote a song for it," Keil recalled. "Ooops, it's a crazy mistake, hey ooops, it's a cereal that's great!" Ooops did indeed turn out to be a mistake, as it disappeared quickly from the market.

In 1971, Big G introduced its most enduring breakfast monstrosities. Inspired by the popular television shows *The Addams Family* and *The Munsters,* copywriter Laura Levine, who later wrote for several television series including *Laverne and Shirley* and *Love Boat* suggested a line of horribly memorable breakfast monsters: Franken Berry and Count Chocula. After clearing the Count Chocula advertising campaign with the estate of Bela Lugosi, on whose portrayal of Dracula the character was based, Big G ran into a major public relations problem with Franken Berry. "Within weeks they recalled and pulled the lot of it off the shelves," laughed Bill Tollis, the artist who designed the scary breakfast characters, "because when kids went to the bathroom, their stools were pink from the food coloring." Tollis surmised that the problem probably happened with both cereals, "But with Count Chocola being brown, who would know?" Reformulated and reintroduced to the market, Franken Berry and Count Chocula were a tremendous success, although the ghostly Boo Berry and the werewolf cereal Fruit Brute proved to be not as popular.

As the cereal monsters ate up market share, General Mills decided to create two new cereals in the kid-pleasing flavors of raspberry and grape. "They put an agency competition out for people to come up with ideas for these two flavors," recalled art director Leo Stuchkus. "In the back of my head was a George Peppard movie called *The Blue Max* about a World War I flying ace that came out about the time of the Snoopy in his Sopwith Camel battling the Red Baron. It all coincided . . . raspberry . . . grape flavor . . . grape flavor . . . raspberry . . . so somehow the visual idea came into my head of two aviators, one English, one German, and I called them Baron Von Raspberry and Sir Grapefellow."

The cereal aces achieved notable success, but not at the Stuchkus home. "My kids never ate them at my house," recalled Stuchkus. "The sugar content alone was—you need an insulin shot if you eat of bowl of that."

While cereal animation was funny to audiences, to the animators responsible for the commercials it was often another matter. "There was nothing funny about them. . . . Deadlines, deadlines," groaned animator George Bakes. "They kept you busy until five o'clock on the phone with meetings, and then from there, you had to do the thing, so you were up all night, night after night. For years. They didn't care if you slept or not. That's the nature of the business."

"You can't imagine what it was like working in this agency at that time," recalled Jack Keil. "You'd walk down a hall, and you'd go by each office and somebody would be in there [falsetto] 'Hi, how are ya doing?' [deep voice] 'Hi ro-ho-ro-ho,' [bouncy tenor voice] 'Hi, I'm Lou the kangaroo,' all these voices coming out, and all the writers were working on different characters, it was like Disney, it was like a funny farm."

"When you work on those things, you get a little nuts," confessed Tony Jaffe. "I used to dream about the characters—Bullwinkle, Rocky, the Rabbit . . . even Lucky the Leprechaun. . . . They took over an aspect of . . . people I knew." Eventually, the cereal strain proved to be too much for Jaffe. "I actually asked to work on some adult stuff," recalled the writer. "It was a bit disturbing."

18

The Kingdom of Crunch

The frenzied activity among the top three cereal makers during the 1960s was contagious. Quaker and the National Biscuit Company, which changed its name to Nabisco in 1971, were caught up in the marketing tornado, stretching the limits of taste in their efforts to find their place at the breakfast table.

Cap'n Crunch

In 1944 the executive who would lead Quaker Oats into the world of presweets was on a mission of another sort. Twenty-one-year-old Ken Mason traveled behind the German lines in France to organize resistance prior to the Allied invasion on D-Day. Mason's ability to adapt to the local language and customs not only assured his survival during months of delicate espionage work, it enabled him to advance rapidly when he entered the corporate world after the war. "If there is a father of the postwar Quaker Oats Company," said Mike Barna, Quaker package designer, "It's Mason."

The prewar Quaker Oats Company had delighted consumers with candy-coated cereal puffs at the St. Louis World's Fair in 1904, but since that time, the company had shied away from presweets, assuming that America's sweet tooth was a passing fad. "It was a very big mistake," declared a Quaker Oats salesman, who saw Puffed Wheat's market share dwindle year by year because of Sugar Crisp. "A very big mistake, because they let General Foods take the market away from Puffed Wheat."

Finally, late in the 1950s, Quaker decided to enter the presweet market, but it failed in a half-hearted attempt to market a concoction called Sugar Puffs. In the early 1960s, as vice president in charge of the U.S. grocery division of Quaker Oats, Mason scanned the American supermarket aisle with the same exacting precision he had once used to scan the French countryside. He found an area of opportunity in a little sliver of shelf space between extruded brands like Alpha Bits and coated puffs like Krinkles.

Ordinarily breakfast cereals were developed in the lab, then turned over to ad agencies for naming, packaging, promotion, and marketing. Mason broke that mold. He first studied market research, which revealed that American kids under ten—a market of some forty million mouths—preferred crunch to mush or flakes. Mason decided that crunch would be the key to Quaker's new cereal.

To develop the ideal flavor, Mason turned to Arthur D. Little, Inc., a consulting firm based in Cambridge, Massachusetts, that was known for its state-of-the-art food lab. Working with Quaker's technical team in Barrington, Illinois, Little's chemical engineers formulated the ultimate taste, a corn-oats extruded, pillow-shaped kernel with a butterscotch-flavored sugar coating. "They believed at the time that it was a short term kind of product," said David Kendell, an Arthur D. Little chemist, "that it would really be a seller for three, four, five, maybe ten years at the outside."

Flavor, texture, and shape in hand, Ken Mason turned to Chicago-based Compton Advertising for a red-hot marketing concept. Instructed as to the importance of crunch, ad man Bruce Baker came up with the idea of giving both product and pitchman the same alliterative name, Cap'n Crunch. In 1962, Compton began to shop around for an animation producer to bring the Cap'n to life.

"Originally they wanted to have a Cap'n Crunch Saturday morning TV show, but the FCC wouldn't sit still for that," recalled Bill Hurtz of Jay Ward Productions, whose studio had just finished production of *Rocky and His Friends* for General Mills. "A whole show whose central characters had the same name as a product? A network would get killed."

For Jay Ward's presentation to Quaker management, Bill Scott wrote the scripts with Al Burns. To put words in the mouth of the Cap'n, Jay Ward chose Daws Butler, the cartoon veteran who had provided the voices for Yogi Bear, Snagglepuss, and other popular Hanna-Barbera characters.

After presentations by various producers, including Hanna-Barbera, Jay Ward's Cap'n Crunch got the nod, in no small part because "Ken Mason was a great lover of Bullwinkle," recalled Max Lomont, a Quaker vice president. It was a natural fit in more ways than one. "Jay Ward resembled Cap'n Crunch," said Charles Ulrich, a Ward expert. "There is a caricature of him in his admiral's uniform which people always mistake for Cap'n Crunch."

Regardless of the coincidence, Bill Hurtz stared at the bottom line.

"This thing just came in the nick of time and saved the studio," he recalled. "We didn't have any work."

Once the commercial production got under way, Mason turned to educating his national cereal sales force in advance of the Cap'n Crunch launch. One morning in the summer of 1963, members of the nationwide Quaker sales team boarded cruise ships staffed with local actors impersonating Cap'n Horatio Crunch and his nemesis Jean LaFoote. "They gave us little plastic Cap'n Crunch bowls and we had a big breakfast of Cap'n Crunch on the boat," recalled Stan Austin, one of the salesmen. "It was not very sweet at that time—in fact some guys didn't know it was presweetened and put sugar on it." Once the crews' reaction to the new stuff had been duly recorded, the real voyage began. "They gave us a Cap'n Crunch mug and we drank all the tap beer we wanted," said Austin.

While the Quaker crew nursed their hangovers, Ken Mason's cartoon ship set sail. In September 1963, the Cap'n's ship *Guppy* appeared on American television screens, with a crew of kids named Alfie, Brunhilde, Dave, and Carlyle, and a barking first mate named Seadog. The bristly, barefoot pirate LaFoote, voiced by Bill Scott with a French accent, lusted after their sweet cargo. "It's got corn for crunch, oats for punch, and it stays crunchy even in milk," bragged the bumbling old skipper Cap'n Crunch.

Cap'n Crunch was a sea-monster hit. Stores couldn't keep the stuff in stock, forcing Quaker to build a plant specifically for Cap'n Crunch production. Within two years of its launch, Cap'n Crunch was the ninth best selling cereal in the country, beating out standbys like Alpha Bits, Grape-Nuts and Total. Cap'n Crunch commanded an incredible 3 percent of the ready-to-eat cereal market, a number that translated into something on the order of $3 million in pretax profits for Quaker. To buy that ranking, Quaker spent almost $3 million a year on advertising—a full 30 percent of its total advertising budget—most of it on television.

By 1966, Quaker Oats was test marketing an entire Cap'n Crunch line of products including cookies, "munch box" snacks, and Ship Shakes, a powdered breakfast drink made from oat flour. The product originally came with its own shaker mug emblazoned with the Cap'n's picture. "The lids wouldn't stay on," laughed Austin. "People added the stuff to the milk, shook it up and the lids came off. . . . It was a real dog, a real dud!"

Quaker also unleashed a sea of prizes. Comic books stated the Cap'n's age at 576 (he had discovered the Fountain of Youth). A treasure chest was crammed with a cereal bowl, a spoon, phony doubloons, and a secret compartment. There were figure banks, plush dolls, and membership clubs. One premium changed the course of American telecommunications. In 1965, "phone freak" John Draper used a bo'sun whistle premium to hack into the phone system and make free long-distance calls. Draper is still known today in cyberspace as the legendary "Cap'n Crunch."

The Cap'n Crunch premiums annoyed other cereal makers as much as they did the phone company. The crunchy give-aways appeared just as the industry was going through one of its periodic premium moratoria. "It almost became sort of an industry agreement. I don't want to make this sound antitrust or anything, but we'd say, 'For God's sake, this is stupid, let's knock it off!' and everybody would stop," recalled Bob Schaeberle of Nabisco, head of the Special Products Division at the time and future CEO.

"We never told each other what we were doing," protested Al Clausi, a General Foods vice president, who once testified in front of a Senate subcommittee to explain the phenomenon. "There was a lot of following. . . . From time to time we would say, 'You know, this premium stuff is getting out of control. Why don't we use coupons for a while.' So we would stop premiums. . . . And yes, when we stopped, very often the others stopped as well." Once Quaker broke the cease-fire with Cap'n Crunch, Kellogg, General Mills, and Post were forced to reenter the premium game.

The big three didn't follow Quaker when the company tried to put Cap'n Crunch in a flip-top box, however. Designed by the 3M Company, the container was similar to an oversized hard-pack cigarette box—unique, striking, innovative, and totally impractical. "If you had that flip-top box open and you tried to pour . . . the damn box lid would close and you'd have cereal all over the table," commented former Quaker art director Max Lomont. "It was screwed, and we were paying a royalty to 3M besides."

After experimenting with premiums and packages to boost the power of Cap'n Crunch, Quaker decided to increase its 7 percent share of the ready-to-eat cereal market in the late 1960s by creating "flavor flankers." Similar to the General Mills strategy of product proliferation, flavor flanking expanded Cap'n Crunch's cereal flotilla with a variety of spin-offs. The Crunchberry Beast pitched Crunchberries. Smedley the elephant promoted Cap'n Crunch's Peanut Butter Cereal. Harry S. Hippo made goo-goo eyes at Horatio Crunch for Punch Crunch. Jean LaFoote's Cinnamon Crunch seemed like a sure winner, but tasted "like Lavoris," according to Max Lomont.

In 1971 Cap'n Crunch's first mate Seadog was assigned to the cereal Vanilly Crunch, only to be replaced by a white whale named Wilma, decked out in heavy mascara and lipstick. Six years later a chameleon-like blob named the Choco Beast gurgled "Chockle! Chockle!" as it metamorphosed into a variety of forms to aquire the last of Cap'n Crunch's flavor flankers, Choco Crunch.

"What basically happened after Harry the Hippo, Wilma the Whale and Chockle, [was that] we realized that there are only three products the Cap'n can carry—the original product, Crunchberries, and Peanut Butter Crunch," said Max Lomont. "We realized that you cannot extend things beyond a certain point."

Quisp and Quake

Beyond the flavor flankers, Quaker enlisted the team of Ward and Scott to come up with characters for new brands of ready-to-eat cereals. In 1965, Bill Scott gave birth to two dueling cerealebrities. One half of the team was Quisp, a propeller-headed pink alien voiced by Daws Butler, who championed "the biggest selling cereal from Saturn to Alpha Centauri." Quisp's rival was Quake (not related to the company name), a spelunking superhero in a hard hat and logging boots whose brawny arms and chest enabled him to swim at terrific speed through bedrock. Voiced by Bill Conrad, who narrated *Rocky and His Friends,* Quake came from the center of the earth, where he made his breakfast food "with deep-down sweetness and vitamins to give you the power of an earthquake."

While Quake brought brute strength to the table—he once broke open a granite cliff with his head—Quisp was agile and brainy. He once defeated a giant ball of yarn by knitting it into a necktie eighty-seven miles long. The focus of their "quazy" conflict was deciding who represented the better cereal. An "earthquake-powered cereal," the hard hat belched, "Quake is best!" Quisp flitted into the scene and chirped, "For quazy energy . . . Quisp is best!" The announcer, usually Paul Frees, invited viewers to decide: "Take sides with either—two new cereals from Quaker, sort of a breakfast feud."

To launch the stuff in supermarkets, Quaker pulled out all the stops. "When we first came out with them, we had these little pink helmets with a spinner on top like an airplane and you put a couple of batteries in it," recalled Stan Austin. "We had those as premiums to the grocer. In other words, if he'd buy five cases, we'd give him one of those hats. . . . And, of course, they'd want to buy ten because they had two kids." A Quake battery-operated miner's helmet was also offered.

Though the two cereals tasted virtually the same, Quake sales lagged far behind Quisp. "Quisp had a lot of better things going for him. He was light and happy and joyful and such. Kids liked him better than Quake," said Mike Barna, then Quaker package designer. Speculating on Quake's unpopularity, Max Lomont observed, "It's fairly difficult to make somebody who comes out of the earth appealing."

Jay Ward and Bill Scott tried to lighten Quake's heavy image, but to no avail. He was eased off the shelves by a new product, Quake's Orange Quangaroos, promoted by Simon the Quangeroo, a bush-hatted, spotted 'roo that jumped out of the Jay Ward-Bill Scott studios.

Heralded in television ads as "sweet and crunchy, with a bright orange color, bright orange flavor, and every bowlful with a whole day's supply of vitamin C," Quangaroos competed with other orange cereals—Nabisco's Orange Norman's and Post's Super Orange Crisp. The only problem with the Quaker product was that it didn't taste good. "It tasted brittle, metallic," recalled Lomont. "Some of those artificial flavors are not the best in the world."

With the final demise of his arch-rival Quake, Quisp continued to fly high. "A lot of people have tried to kill Quisp but he survives," said Lomont. "He refuses to die."

While Cap'n Crunch was clearly targeted at the kiddie market, Ward and Scott also created animated characters designed to sell cereals to adults. After successfully launching Life cereal in 1962, and failing to interest weight-watching adults with cyclamate-coated Diet Frosted Puffed Wheat and Diet Frosted Puffed Rice in 1966, Quaker developed a super-enriched vitamin presweetened cereal. "It started out as King Vitamin," recalled Quaker salesman Stan Austin. "But the government wouldn't let us call it King Vitamin because it was not a vitamin."

Quaker redubbed the cereal King Vitaman, after buying the copyright to the Vitaman name from Ralston Purina for "something like ten cents a case for fifteen years," said Austin. Even with an expensive name, the cereal ran into problems. "The vitamins used in it spoiled on the shelf," recalled Bill Hurtz. "The taste of the thing would fizzle out and turn sour in a few weeks."

Reformulated as "tasty, sugary little crowns with a full day's supply of vitamins and iron," King Vitaman was reintroduced in 1970 with an animated king created by Jay Ward's gang. After a year, Quaker switched over to a real-life king. "There was a big promotion and then it died down until the WIC [Women, Infants and Children] coupon program started in the late seventies," recalled Quaker man Harold Gottlieb, referring to a government program that subsidized the purchase of the cereal for low-income families. "If it wasn't for that, King Vitaman would have disappeared."

Although King Vitaman survived, the Jay Ward studio did not. The unusually close creative collaboration between Quaker Oats and Jay

---

LIQUID BREAKFAST

After a year of promoting King Vitaman cereal with a Jay Ward cartoon character, Quaker switched over to real-live cereal king George Mann. Dressed in a red-and-white-checked tablecloth robe and a crown of golden spoons, the tall, white-haired veteran thespian urged kids "to have breakfast with me!" During the peak of the campaign in 1971, Quaker paraded Mann—in full regalia—at employee picnics in the Chicago area where he sat enthroned on the grass.

Children were thrilled by the reigning actor. Quaker management was not. "He was a hell of a lush," recalled vice president Max Lomont. "You wouldn't want to trust your little girl to his lap. You had to watch him." Even getting the red-nosed Mann to look like a king for photography sessions took some doing. "I got one of the best makeup men in Chicago working on it," recalled studio photographer Dick Jones. "He looked like a lush." Though he died in 1977, Mann's alcoholic grin continues to beam forth from packages of Quaker's King Vitaman to this day.

Ward lasted twenty-two years, during which time Bill Scott estimated that he wrote 700 commercials. Quaker apparently paid Ward well "because I never had a budget," said animation director Bill Hurtz. "We just did what we did . . . I never knew what they cost . . . or anything about that." Ken Mason and Jay Ward grew to be extremely close friends. "Ken was really dazzled by Jay and they were very good friends," recalled Quaker's Max Lomont. "Jay and [Jay's wife] Billie would go to Ken's island up in Wisconsin and later visited him in Maine."

But friction developed over the years as Ward became protective of the Cap'n Crunch character. "There's no question that the Cap'n has always been a very engaging character, but he had to sell harder because it was getting to be a tough business," remembered Lomont. "It had always been a tough business." By the early eighties, Ward's long-standing relationship with Quaker was strained. "Jay didn't want to be told what to do," recalled Hurtz. "He got along famously with Ken Mason, Quaker's CEO, but when Ken retired, things started to go downhill."

When Quaker refused to renew Ward's annual contract, Ward decided to get out of the animation business altogether, and closed his studio for good in 1984. The following year both animator Bill Scott and Daws Butler, the voice of Cap'n Crunch for twenty-two years, passed away. A few years later Jay Ward also died, leaving for posterity a rats' nest of lawsuits and a pantheon of squirrels, spies, and crunchy characters that continue to entertain and sell to a new generation of Americans.

Team Players

The staid National Biscuit Company, which had dominated the American cookie and cracker business for a century with brands like Oreos, Fig Newtons, Cheese Nips, and Triscuits, felt a bit uncomfortable with the sixties cereal revolution. "We weren't big character people. We were product people," explained former Nabisco executive Craig Carragan. "To me characters are a frill."

Despite the corporate discomfort, the company made good money from its line of cereals—Shredded Wheat, Wheat Honeys, and Rice Honeys. In the late 1950s, Minneapolis-based Cream of Wheat caught Nabisco's acquisitive eye. "Cream of Wheat [before it was acquired by National Biscuit] was making ten percent after taxes on sales—a respectable profit by any measure," *Printer's Ink* told its readers.

Nabisco was not the first to look at Rastus and smell money. In the mid-1950s, Kellogg had approached the mush maker with a mind to a friendly merger but then backed off. "They had 40 percent of the RTE [ready-to-eat cereal] business at the time and we had 15 to 20 percent of the total hot cereal business," recalled Dave Bull, president of Cream of Wheat at the time. "It was felt by Kellogg lawyers that the merger wouldn't fly—the problem was antitrust."

Antitrust was not a concern for Nabisco, which controlled only around 5 percent of the breakfast cereal market. In 1961 the company purchased Cream of Wheat and placed the blond-colored mush alongside Shredded Wheat, Milk-Bone brand doggie treats, and other items in the Special Products Division, where Bull also found a home.

Under Dave Bull and Robert Schaeberle, the Special Products Division went ahead with an ambitious cereal development program. After meditating upon Wheat Chex cocktail mix, Post's rice, corn, and wheat cereal Top 3, and a General Mills product called Hi-Pro, Nabisco decided to create the first adult cereal flake made from four grains.

Once the research department perfected the product, finding the right name for it was essential. "One of the first things we tried was to take the first letters of the four grains that were in there—corn, rice, oats and wheat," laughed Bob Schaeberle, future Nabisco chief executive officer. "We could have called it CROW but you're not going to get people to 'Eat CROW' so we came up with the name Team Flakes, since it teamed the four grains."

After Team Flakes, which proved to be a mild success, the concept that captured the imagination of the Nabisco Special Products Division was plastic. Most of the cereal companies, including Kellogg and Post,

---

No More Bull

In 1965 Dave Bull, grandson of Cream of Wheat founder George Bull, ran Nabisco's cereal division and frequently socialized with other industry brass and their wives at various affairs. Once, soon after introducing the new Nabisco cereal Team, Bull was visiting a company plant in Battle Creek when he decided to take the public tour of the Kellogg plant. Bull walked to the adminstration building of the rival company to sign up for the tour. "So I step into this elevator to go take this tour and there's this lady nutritionist from Kellogg that I just sat next to at the Cereal Institute dinner in Chicago a couple of days before," gasped Bull. "She says, 'What are you doing here?' and I squeaked, 'I'm going on a tour!'" Bull said the woman immediately got off the elevator and spread the word. "All the top people at Kellogg came out and said, 'God, Dave, you're some guy trying to . . . you know . . . come in here and see what we're doing . . .' and I said, 'Oh, we would take you through our plant if you wanted' and they scoffed, 'Oh yeah, sure!'" Groaned the rival cereal kingpin, "I guess I got kind of caught there."

had studied the potential of plastic, not as an edible commodity but as a material substitute for the standard cardboard cereal box. At Nabisco, special product honchos Craig Carragan and Ed Breeding decided to get into plastic, throwing caution, and a few tons of Wheat Honeys, to the wind.

"The idea was everybody had premiums in products," remembered Carragan. "Why don't we do it the other way around?" Carragan and Breeding decided to create plastic cereal containers in the shape of Disney characters, for which Nabisco already had the licensing rights. Called puppets, the Wheat Honeys–filled figurines were about a foot high and shaped like Mickey Mouse, Donald Duck, and Winnie-the-Pooh. "Tied in with Disney as it was, everybody thought it was a super idea at the time," recalled Bob Schaeberle.

In the days before shrink wrapping, the packaging concept had one fatal flaw: the screw-cap opening was placed on the bottom of the cereal-filled containers. "We put them in stores all over test areas and kids got so excited they'd grab it off the display or shelf and dump the product all over the floor," said Carragan. "It was really funny to hear back from some of these stores being flooded with wheat puffs because they'd scream, 'Get those damn things out of here!'" laughed Schaeberle. "'And damn the people who designed 'em!'"

As the supply of puppets was dumped in land fills, Craig Carragan and Ed Breeding were brainstorming for new product ideas on the golf course one warm day in the late 1960s when an idea clicked. "Why don't we take a freeze-dried cream and coat a cereal?" said Carragan. Within a few months, the company had created a rice flake coated with vanilla freeze-dried ice cream—"I came up with the name Rice Cream Flakes," claimed Carragan. The tasty stuff was test marketed in Buffalo, where it caught fire with consumers and captured 2 percent of the ready-to-eat market despite the relatively high cost per box of thirty-nine cents.

"It was a damn good product but we couldn't get enough ground freeze-dried ice cream," explained Rand Plass, a Nabisco executive. "Our supplier, Oregon Freeze-Dried Foods, was going out of business and no one else was really making any freeze-dried ice cream at the time." Soon after the ice cream fizzle, Breeding "left Nabisco with a bitter taste in his mouth," sighed his buddy Carragan.

In 1968, Nabisco decided the key to expanding its share of the ready-to-eat cereal market was in the acquisition of hardware. Specifically, the Special Products Division bought a Wanger x150, a half-million-dollar high-powered extruder used primarily to produce dog food. "Whether it's for dogs or kids, the product was made pretty much the same way," said Chuck Allen, a Nabisco executive. "It goes through a die, it's gelatinized, and it explodes under heat."

The first proposed cereal was a jelly-filled peanut-butter puff, which seemed a natural for the kiddie set. Project manager Plass turned to Nabisco's agency, New York–based William Esty for marketing concepts. Plass worked with Tony Jaffe, the cereal veteran who wrote Trix rabbit spots for six years and came up with the slogan for the "Wack-wack-wackiest" cereal, Banana Wackies. Jaffe's suggestion to Plass was to call the peanut-butter-and-jelly puffs Jelliphants.

Despite the promising marketing concept, things didn't extrude according to plan. The Wanger x150 squirted out marbley brown logs instead of perfectly formed puffs. "We just couldn't make the Wanger do what we wanted it to do," sighed Plass, "but it tasted very good."

In 1971, the gang at the Special Products Division received instructions to create a few other new presweetened cereals. Nabisco management made the request, not because they were impressed with the division's past performance, but because the company had a lot of excess capacity at its new cereal-manufacturing plant in Naperville, Illinois.

The division responded with OOOBopperoos, a blueberry cereal pitched by a hip blue kangaroo in sunglasses, and presweetened corn puffs called Normans. After two years of work on the cereals, the Special Products Division launched test markets in four selected cities. Unfortunately, a strike at the manufacturing plant halted production. Brand manager Toby Decker and manufacturing manager Cece Lundy made an emergency trip to Naperville and worked out an arrangement whereby Nabisco was allowed to make just enough OOOBopperoos and Normans to meet the demands in the test markets.

Decker found that the shelves in one of the test markets were low on product. "I wrote an internal memo to the senior product manager in New York," he recalled. "Somehow it got out to the district sales manager, who wrote a letter back saying, 'Mr. Decker doesn't know how to run a test market.' He was really pissed."

Kids liked the taste of both cereals, but once the initial surge of interest was over, repeat sales fell off and the company withdrew the products. "I was upset," admitted Decker. "I put six months of my life— with no social life, really—into Normans and OOOBops . . . that's a lot of freakin' time."

Things weren't going all that well for Wheat and Rice Honeys, the brand reincarnations of the first presweetened cereal Ranger Joe. "Once we moved from Chester to Naperville," confided Plass, "we were running the puffing guns frantically. That gave a more *charred* taste to our product." The product also suffered from the same problem that destroyed the original cereal. The individual sugar-coated puffs still had a bad habit of melding together into a brick inside the package.

The Nabisco men in the Special Products Division tried desperately to save Wheat and Rice Honeys, renaming them Pooh's Great Honey Crunchers with disappointing results. "Special Products Division was insignificant to Nabisco," explained Craig Carragan. "We only had about 3 percent of the cereal market at best." In 1975, with the price of sugar rising and an anti-sugar consumer movement sweeping the country, the last incarnation of Ranger Joe, Klondike Pete's Crunchy Nuggets, was unceremoniously withdrawn from the market. "One of the things that strongly influenced the company was . . . its sensitivity to the issue of sugar in cereal. So there was a strong tendency to stay away from presweetened products."

"There was always the question of where was the limit on how much sugar you can put in before it becomes a confection," admitted former General Mills vice president Jim Fish, reflecting on the presweetened stampede of the 1960s and 1970s. "Activists were already saying, 'These aren't cereals, they're confections to be sold as candies not cereals.'"

"When sugar became bad news for children and their teeth, everybody pulled back," recalled Jack Keil. "The heyday of children's cereals was prior to that."

The Cereal Reformation

19

Ultra-Trash Backlash

It was the long, hot summer of 1970, one of the darkest hours of America's political soul. As the slaughter in Vietnam continued and the Nixon administration began spinning a Watergate web of political intrigue, some of the nation's most powerful leaders gathered on Capitol Hill to launch a series of highly publicized congressional hearings concerning one of the most pressing topics of the day. The subject of this intense political activity was nothing less than breakfast cereal.

Breakfast of Chumps

The radical leader who captured the imagination of America's food revolutionaries was a forty-five-year-old engineer named Robert F. Choate. "It is apparent that humans are viewed not as beings to be nourished but suckers to be sold," Choate told the attentive congressmen, while a nation of cereal crunchers hung on his words. "Your children's food habits are being formed by Madison Avenue cartoonists, not by nutritionists. Tony the Tiger, Fred Flintstone and Cap'n Crunch are the food educationalists of today. Ten times per hour, using wiles that mother never thought of, they advise your children to equate sugar with health and snacks with happiness."

Choate proved that hell hath no fury like a bureaucrat scorned. The scion of a wealthy New England publishing family, Choate left the comfortable enclave of Boston to study engineering at the University of California. He went to work in Phoenix, where he designed housing for low-income families and was swept up in the philosophical tide of the war against poverty. Still firmly attached to his Republican roots, Choate returned to Washington in 1966. Three years later, Choate served as President Nixon's point man at the White House Conference on Food and Nutrition. The conference served as Choate's breakfast epiphany, transforming him into a nutritional Don Quixote, fighting the windmills of the cereal industry.

"I watch the TV commercials on Saturday morning and really get mad," Choate testified before congress. "The industry brainwashes children into demanding the least worthwhile products. . . . To make matters more idiotic, some of the biggest advertising appropriations are devoted to competing products from the same firm."

Choate saved his greatest anger for an attack on what he called America's "nutritional literacy." "Nutrition doesn't snap, crackle, or pop," he told the American people, warning that American children were "programmed to demand sugar and sweetness in every food."

As a further indictment of breakfast cereal, Choate performed what he called "an engineer's analysis" on sixty different cereals, ranking them according to their content of nine nutrients. He declared that fifty-seven of the sixty cereals "fatten but do little to prevent malnutrition." Choate declared that rats fed on a diet of ground-up cereal boxes mixed with sugar, milk, and raisins were healthier than rats fed on the cereals the boxes contained.

Choate reserved particular scorn for Nabisco's Shredded Wheat, the lowest-ranked cereal on his list, declaring that the crunchy wheat pillows contained nothing more than "empty calories—a term thus far applied to alcohol and sugar."

"We were shocked," recalled Bob Schaeberle, who was an executive with Nabisco at the time. "They overlooked the fact that Shredded Wheat is wheat, and wheat has a lot of nutrients."

Others in the industry shared Schaeberle's concern. James P. McFarland, chairman and chief executive officer of General Mills, appeared at the hearings and handed out Breakfast Squares to the congressmen. As the political leaders munched on the dry, chalky high-protein brownies, McFarland explained how difficult it was to sell nutrition.

The Kellogg Company joined the fray with a blistering press release. "Civil engineer Choate's theories and so-called formula might be meaningful for digging a mine shaft, but they are completely valueless as a yardstick for measuring the nutritional value of any type of food."

The nation turned a deaf ear to the cereal defenders. "Soggy Report on Cereal," screamed newspaper headlines. Bumper stickers pronounced that "Jack Armstrong Died of Malnutrition"—no doubt from eating his beloved Wheaties, which Choate dubbed "the breakfast of chumps."

As the congressional hearings wound up, food industry executives increased their anti-Choate rhetoric, calling the cereal critics lunatics, hucksters, dupes, zealots, anti-intellectuals, and quacks. But some members of the breakfast establishment had a broader vision. "The food industry doesn't know it yet, but they are going to thank Choate one day," commented one far-sighted food executive, "the day they realize more nutritious food can be more profitable."

Sure enough, the immediate result of the Choate hearings was to boost sales of Special K, Kaboom, and Total, the three cereals described by Choate as "best from a nutritional standpoint." Nabisco reacted to the trouncing of Shredded Wheat by introducing a "no salt, no sugar" advertising campaign in 1971. "We went from something in the $40 million range to well over $100 million in less that a year," recalled Nabisco executive Rand Plass. "By the time Choate held his second set of hearings, two of his best-rated cereals were Shredded Wheat and Spoon Size Shredded Wheat because of the nutritional information we had put on the label."

FTC Baloney-Enriched Yum-Yums

Other activists were more concerned about cereal premiums than the cereal itself. "I became an expert at making the small into the large by the simple use of lenses," said commercial director Peter Israelson. "I could turn a one-inch toy into a Godzilla-style monster so kids thought they were getting these huge premiums when, in fact, you could hardly find them in the box."

Federal regulators moved in on the deceptive ads, forcing the cereal companies to display the actual size of the cereal premiums on packages and television. The government took further steps to protect consumers against premiums with the passage of the Consumer Product Safety Act in 1972 and the Consumer Product Safety Commission Improvement Act in 1976, legislation that forced manufacturers to meet stringent safety requirements in designing toys. After passage of the legislation, strings, rubber bands, tiny wheels, and other once-standard elements of cereal premium design were outlawed. "When the consumer safety law was passed we had three projects in progress," said premium manufacturer Leon Levy, president of Taico Design Products, Inc. "They were all canceled in one week. It was a loss of a whole year and twenty million pieces. It was a substantial part of our business."

"This is not a humorous business," observed Manny Winston, a Chicago-based premium supplier. "Kids are basically cavemen in formation. The idea of singling out premium toys is absurd when there are literally a thousand things of greater potential hazard in any household."

CEREAL BOMBER

Cereal premiums were serious business—at times, a little too serious. In the late 1960s, Chicago-based designer Leon Levy came up with the idea of making a plastic popsicle-stick building toy that would serve as a premium for a proposed Cap'n Crunch ice cream on a stick. "I made helicopters, bridges, and all kinds of constructions to photograph for the instruction book," remembered Levy. "I got the purchase order for two million sticks, the brochure and the cancellation of the project in the same day. It was heartbreaking."

Quaker Oats, the company that turned down the idea, did refer Levy to the top marketing men at Popsicle and Good Humor. The toy designer immediately loaded his samples into a black artist's case marked with a big "Fragile: Do Not Drop" sign and rushed to O'Hare Airport to catch a flight to New York. "I got stopped at the gate by a couple of security guys who were sure I was carrying a bomb onto the plane," laughed Levy, who admitted that his appearance "fit the profile" of a terrorist. "They drew their guns and took me down to a concrete bunker and stood over me and said, 'Now, open the box!'"

The consumer and regulatory activism swirling around breakfast cereal in the early 1970s caused the Federal Trade Commission to take notice of the industry. The FTC was created by Congress in 1914 to protect Americans from big business. By the early 1970s, the FTC was itself a big business with a budget of $17 million, a staff of 1,300, and a reputation that was terrible. "A self-parody of a bureaucracy, fat with cronyism, torpid through an inbreeding unusual even for Washington," was how the original Nader's Raiders characterized the federal agency in a report released in 1969.

With the rising tide of consumer activism and the controversy stirred up by *The Nader Report* on the Federal Trade Commission, the 500 lawyers at the agency realized they had to do something about something or risk losing their jobs. Breakfast cereal seemed like the perfect thing to do something about. "I didn't pick the auto industry or the petroleum industry because they have too much political clout," explained Charles Mueller in 1970 when he was an FTC staffer. "The cereal industry didn't have the political clout to muddy the water."

It wasn't the first time anti-big-business forces in the federal government had attacked the cereal industry. In 1915, the U.S. government brought suit against the Quaker Oats Company for alleged violation of the Sherman Anti-Trust Act. The prosecuting attorneys claimed that Quaker, which controlled 90 percent of the oatmeal industry at the time, was seeking "to lay a nation's breakfast table under tribute." On April 19, 1916, the court held for Quaker.

Unlike the classic anti-trust oatmeal suit of 1916, the suit filed fifty-six years later by the Federal Trade Commission against the ready-to-eat cereal industry was cut from untried theoretical cloth. In charges that were described by *Fortune* magazine as "novel, even mysterious," the government claimed that Kellogg, General Mills, General Foods, and Quaker had broken Section 5 of the Federal Trade Commission Act by indulging in "unfair methods of competition." The government accused the cereal companies of having formed a "shared monopoly" without ever having made an agreement—sort of a conspiracy without a conspiracy. As FTC staffer Charles Mueller said at the time, "The case is a test to see if you can get at the enormous consumer overcharge without having to prove they had a meeting."

The FTC claimed that the unspoken cereal conspiracy resulted in consumer overcharges of more than $1.2 billion between 1958 and 1972. FTC lawyers told the nation that if they were successful in their suit, they would save American consumers $128 million a year by busting up the cereal trust into smaller companies. In addition, business theoreticians surmised that if the FTC won the cereal suit, almost a third of the U.S. economy would be declared illegal.

The hearing began on April 28, 1976, four years after the original complaint was filed against the cereal companies. What the FTC intended as high courtroom drama quickly degenerated into bizarre verbal goulash, described by one observer as "a muddle of untested economic theory, garbled fact, and contradictory testimony."

When the FTC alleged that cereal makers "produce basically similar ready-to-eat cereals, and then emphasize and exaggerate trivial variations such as color and shape," a Kellogg executive testified that Frosted Mini-Wheats was an "innovation" because "it was more elongated than anything else on the market."

After six years of such legal wrangling, the government's case began to fall apart. Try as they might, the three different sets of FTC lawyers who worked on the case just could not convince the judge that the intensely competitive ready-to-eat cereal business was noncompetitive. In February 1978, one of the government's own experts took the witness stand and recommended that the suit against Quaker Oats be dropped. It was.

In January 1982, after ten years of courtroom maneuvering and more than 40,000 pages of testimony, the FTC voted to drop the case entirely. The investigation of the cereal industry had cost the American taxpayers some $20 million, an amount that William F. Buckley suggested would have been better spent in creating and marketing the government's own cereal, "FTC Baloney-Enriched Yum-Yums."

Barbarians at the Bowl

During the 1980s the Reagan administration's laissez-faire economic and social policies allowed corporate America to gorge itself at a breakfast of the vanities. Reflecting the current pro-business climate, cereal companies decided to feed money-hungry yuppies just exactly what they wanted—money.

In 1986, General Mills launched a million-dollar "Treasure Hunt" promotion, sticking a dollar bill in one out of every twenty boxes of Cheerios. Television ads pictured the Cheerios Kid and Sue gleefully stuffing money into boxes of cereal. "Finally, Cheerios put something in the package I can use," commented one satisfied consumer.

Not to be outdone in the "greed is good" promotion category, a convoy of Brink's trucks with armed guards pulled up to the Ralston Purina plant in Battle Creek in the winter of 1987. Its mission: ensure safe passage of the first batch of Almond Delight cereal to supermarkets in the Midwest. The gimmick was created to promote an Almond Delight premium—the first 4.3 million boxes of the cereal were stuffed with money, one-, five-, fifty-, or five-hundred-dollar bills as well as Irish punts, Bulgarian levas, Brazilian cruzeros, and Bolivian pesos.

Wall Street financiers were as attracted by the money at the bottom of the cereal box as the average consumer. Frederick Ross Johnson began his career selling lightbulbs in Canada. By 1980 he had worked his way up the corporate ranks to become the head of the large food company Standard Brands, creator of what one analyst called "some of the most celebrated failures in the food industry" (including Smooth 'N Easy, an instant gravy shaped like a stick of butter).

Soon after taking over the leadership of Standard Brands, Johnson focused his acquisitive eye on the Nabisco logo, an oval and cross with two bars that had represented the triumph of the spiritual over the material world in medieval Italy. Johnson triumphed over Nabisco and Standard Brands by engineering a $1.9 billion stock swap between the two companies that landed him atop the combined corporate entity, Nabisco Brands.

Not content with his new position, Johnson began to work on a deal with Tylee Wilson, the chief executive officer of R. J. Reynolds tobacco, the makers of Camel cigarettes. The resulting $4.9 billion merger between Nabisco Brands and Reynolds took place in 1985. Johnson realized that, when it came to selling consumer goods, the merger was a good fit. A company that could sell a product that allegedly caused cancer could sell just about anything. Johnson also recognized the irony that Nabisco products such as Shredded Wheat, created for the good of humanity's stomach, were now owned by the "death merchants" who sold cigarettes. "Mom and apple pie meet the skull and crossbones," joked Johnson.

A few years later, Johnson sailed away from RJR Nabisco on a $53 million golden parachute, his payoff for losing a $25 billion bidding war for control of the company, the leveraged buyout transaction that was celebrated in the book *Barbarians at the Gate* and the movie of the same name. Shortly after the RJR Nabisco corporate potlatch, General Foods, the company created from the New-Age health ideas of C. W. Post, disappeared under the corporate cloud of another cigarette manufacturer, Philip Morris. The New York–based makers of the world's most popular cigarette, Marlboro, paid $11 billion for Kraft, which had previously purchased General Foods and its Post cereal division.

In 1993, Philip Morris Companies increased its presence in the cereal aisle by purchasing Nabisco's cold-cereal business for $450 million. Consumer advocates raised anti-trust concerns, and the New York State Attorney General filed suit to block the acquisition. Michael Pertschuk, a former Nader Raider and FTC chairman, lamented, "By the year 2000, there will be two consumer goods companies in the U.S. RJR Nabisco will be selling all the consumer goods west of the Mississippi, and Philip Morris will be selling all the consumer goods east of the Mississippi."

Bran Craze

While federal regulators and the most brilliant minds on Wall Street spent the late 1980s battling over their positions at the breakfast table, American consumers paid much more attention to the words of Wilford Brimley. The elderly, grumbly, phlegmatic actor with a walrus mustache appeared in television advertisements for the Quaker Oats Company and insisted that eating oatmeal was "the right thing to do."

Wilford Brimley's rise from the short-running sit-com *Our House,* to a position as America's most-trusted cereal pitchman paralleled the rise in popularity of a scratchy, indigestible substance known as bran. Bran is the skin or husk of cereal grains, a substance equally rich in dietary fiber and in nutritional controversy. "Put back the bran!" shouted spiritual nutritionist and whole-grain bread baker Sylvester Graham in the 1840s. "Bran does not irritate, it titillates!" lectured John Harvey Kellogg, who spent a decade in a courtroom "bran war" with his brother, W. K. Kellogg, eventually losing the right to market Kellogg's All-Bran.

There were those who battled against bran. "To the consuming fire we consign thee—BRAN," wrote dietician Margaret Sawyer in 1927. "Ten thousand dieticians have wept over thee in vain." In 1961, *Consumer Bulletin* warned its readers that "bran is relatively high in atomic bomb fallout, strontium 90."

In 1984, the Kellogg Company stirred up a bran-filled controversy with a breakthrough promotional effort. Working closely with the National Cancer Institute, Kellogg launched a national print and television ad campaign linking bran with the fight against cancer. One of the television ads for All-Bran cereal showed a couple at breakfast. "I just read about new reports from the National Cancer Institute," a sensitive, New-Age husband told his wife. "Some studies suggest a high-fiber, low-fat diet may reduce the risks of some types of cancer."

The ad created a marketing sensation. It was the first time since passage of the Food, Drug and Cosmetic Act in 1938 that a food manufacturer had linked a product with a claim for disease prevention. The Federal Trade Commission praised the campaign, and consumers ate it up, boosting the sales of Kellogg's All-Bran by 41 percent.

The bran trend was propelled further in 1987 with the publication of the book *The Eight-Week Cholesterol Cure* by Robert E. Kowalski. In the book, which spent a year on the *New York Times* best-seller list, Kowalski claimed that a low-fat diet including three oat muffins a day saved his life. When studies appeared in the *Journal of the American Medical Association* touting the virtue of reducing cholesterol through diet, including the consumption of oat bran, the cereal business began to feel its oats.

General Mills introduced Total Oatmeal in July of 1987. In a quick reaction, Quaker Oats launched a $12 million advertising and marketing campaign featuring Brimley sitting next to children in breakfast nooks, telling viewers that eating oatmeal was the right thing to do. In

1987, there was a 23 percent increase in shipments of all oat cereals, and Quaker Oats sales surged upward by 25 percent.

By 1989, the fiber fad launched by Kellogg had turned into a health sales stampede. A third of the 3.6 billion dollars in yearly food advertising carried some sort of a health claim. Boxes of Total cereal informed consumers that vitamins and minerals helped resist infection, promote wound healing, aid digestion, and improve bone marrow. All-Bran boxes included a "fiber insurance" policy with guidelines for a high-fiber, low-fat diet. The barrage of health claims caused the *Wall Street Journal* to comment that cereal makers had made their section of the supermarket "sound more like a drug store."

Sales of oat-bran products topped $5 billion in 1989, as store shelves were stuffed with oat-bran doughnuts, oat-bran milk shakes, oat-bran waffles, oat-bran muffins, oat-bran fettucine and rotelli, oat-bran enriched potato chips, oat-bran pretzels, oat-bran beer, even an oat-bran aphrodisiac—all of which were advertised as reducing the risk of heart disease and cancer.

General Mills and its best-selling oat-based cereal Cheerios (originally Cheerioats) saw its sales increase dramatically as a result of the oat boom. The executives at Kellogg watched in horror as the bran craze they had started turned against them. The company began a mad scramble to jump on the oat bandwagon and offered its oats-come-lately cereal Common Sense Oat Bran with a five-dollar rebate coupon for a cholesterol screening. Horst W. Schroeder, the president of the company and heir apparent as CEO and chairman of the board, suffered under the strain as competitors shaved points off the Kellogg market share— points that were each worth $75 million in sales. The West German, who introduced Americans to Mueslix, became dictatorial, hid information from company officials, and pushed big-time losing cereals like Pro-Grain and S. W. Graham, named after the original bran promoter. On September 15, 1989, the Kellogg Company shook the upper echelons of American business by firing Schroeder, whose career foundered in an ocean of oats.

By the end of the 1980s, the oat-bran craze had gotten so out of hand that government officials began to take action. "A 'fiber war' is going on out there," warned Dr. Frank E. Young, a commissioner at the Food and Drug Administration. "The grocery store has become a Tower of Babel," proclaimed Health and Human Services Director Dr. Louis Sullivan, "and consumers need to be linguists, scientists, and mind readers to understand the many labels they see."

While the Food and Drug Administration struggled to come up

with new federal labeling regulations to counteract the health-claim trend in advertising, the National Association of Attorneys General launched its own effort to bring governmental control to the cereal box on the state level. The Iowa attorney general began legal actions against Kellogg, seeking to stop the company from claiming that Frosted Flakes were "good for you." In New York, Attorney General Robert Abrams successfully convinced Kellogg not to run ads for Rice Krispies that claimed vitamin B gave consumers increased energy and vigor.

But the real knock-down cereal fight was in Texas. The charge was led by Jim "Mad Dog" Mattox, the attorney general who was locked in a bitter primary race for the governorship of the state. "We're in the middle of an oat-bran craze in this country that was primarily started by Quaker in order to sell its products," claimed Mattox. "Consumers have been duped."

Mattox filed suit against Quaker in the fall of 1989, seeking a temporary restraining order against Quaker advertising. In the suit, Mattox contended that Quaker pitched oatmeal as a drug substitute, urging people to "self-medicate with Quaker Oats" rather than seek the help of a doctor for high cholesterol or heart problems.

A year later, "Mad Dog" was on the prowl once again. This time the substance that threatened the Lone Star State wasn't oats but flea wort. Grown primarily in India, flea wort, better known as psyllium, contained 80 percent soluble fiber compared to the 10 percent soluble fiber found in oat bran. Cereal makers, trying to ride future fiber trends, fixed on flea wort as the next big cholesterol-fighting thing.

Mattox embargoed sales of the psyllium-based cereals Benefit, created by General Mills, and Heartwise, introduced by Kellogg, until the manufacturers could substantiate their health claims for those cereals. When consumers realized that psyllium was the basic ingredient in the laxative Metamucil, the flea wort fad faded, and both Benefit and Heartwise disappeared from the market.

While state attorneys general filed suits and cereal researchers struggled to discover even more exotic fibers, the Washington bureaucracy finally made a move. After reviewing 47,000 public comments, Congress passed the Nutrition Labeling and Education Act in 1990. Two years later, on December 2, 1992, the government approved 5,800 pages of food labeling regulations. The regulations not only specified definitions for such technical terms as "healthy," "light," "fresh," "less," and "more," but required industry to standardize billions of labels on more than 250,000 different products by May 1994, at a cost of some $2 billion. "The Tower of Babel in food labels has come down,"

KOSHER CEREAL

In addition to the issues of nutrition, safety, and value, the religious symbolism of the cereal box has also been a focus of consumer activism. In 1987 an advertising campaign for General Mills' Count Chocula cereal included an image of Bella Lugosi taken from the 1931 film *House of Dracula*. The cereal company overlooked the fact that Lugosi wore a six-pointed medallion on his chest, a Star of David, the symbol of Judaism. When Jewish activists complained about the imagery, General Mills recut the television advertising but refused to recall four million boxes of the cereal, arguing that the blasphemous art work did not present a health hazard. "We are not anti-Semitic," said General Mills spokesman William Shaffer. "Our interest was merely to use Dracula's likeness in a fresh and entertaining way."

In a separate religious incident, a rabbi visited the Post plant in Battle Creek every year in order to inspect the facility. The rabbi's visit was necessary to qualify Post cereals as kosher, a dietary endorsement that meant millions of dollars a year in sales. One year the cereal-inspecting rabbi rode up one of the 150-foot grain towers on a continuously moving ladder. To ride the lift back down, the rabbi had to step over a wide gap back onto the ladder. "He was up there for a while before he mustered the courage to just step onto that thing and grab ahold of it," recalled Bob Traverse. "Of course everybody got a big kick out of it. . . . 'You know, this poor guy was up there for four hours, ha-ha-ha!'" In 1994, the kosher cereal market heated up as Boston entrepreneur Marcia Smith began marketing a kosher cereal made from matzoh meal under the corporate brand name T. Abraham.

announced Sullivan, "and American consumers are the winners."

By the time of the passage of the food-label regulations, the oatmeal bubble, which had been largely responsible for its creation, had already burst. In January of 1990, a group of Harvard researchers published an article in the *New England Journal of Medicine* that claimed that oat bran did little to lower cholesterol. Dr. Frank M. Sacks, who led the study, said, "People shouldn't delude themselves into thinking oat bran will do much for cholesterol."

The report caused a sharp drop in Quaker stock. "Bran bashing" became the rage in the media, as the sales of hot and cold cereals declined precipitously. It did not matter that eighteen months after the Harvard study, the *Journal of the American Medical Association* and other leading journals published at least three major studies supporting the opposite conclusion. The bran craze was over.

Wilford Brimley, the cereal prophet of the go-go eighties, continued to pitch oatmeal in the get-tough nineties. But like the character he played in the film *Cocoon,* Brimley was transformed from a lethargic old grump into an active rowdy. In his ads of the early nineties, Brimley left the confines of the breakfast table to glorify oatmeal while riding horses and digging post holes. Heralded as "a legitimate, honest-to-god cowboy" by ad man James Jordan, whose firm created the Brimley campaign, the new, active buckaroo Brimley pitch was designed to appeal to those who were more interested in cowboy fantasies than regularity.

Cereal Savanarola

One of the most powerful cereal reformists to arise from the activist climate of the 1960s was an attractive, dynamic housewife named Peggy Charren. Charren began her political career in 1968, when she sat down to watch television with her four-year-old child and decided that she didn't like what she saw. Instead of turning off the tube, Charren, who had once worked for a television station in New York City, chose to take on the advertising establishment and formed the advocacy group Action for Children's Television, Inc.

When consumer research in the late 1960s established that children could not distinguish ads from programming and that children who saw ads for sweetened cereal tended to equate sugar with good nutrition, Charren joined with members of the Center for Science in the Public Interest, a group formed by associates of Ralph Nader, in an all-out attack on the $600-million-a-year being spent to pitch cereal to children.

The anti-cereal brigade brought their complaints to Michael Pertschuk, who was chosen by President Jimmy Carter to head up the Federal Trade Commission in 1977. Charren and her "militant mothers" told Pertschuk that cereal advertising directed at children was "unfair" and thus subject to FTC control. Pertschuk, who had earned his political spurs as Ralph Nader's principal legislative facilitator, was sympathetic to the cause. "Commercialization of children has crept up on us without scrutiny or action," Pertschuk declared, ignoring the fact that cereal companies had targeted their advertising toward children since the days of Babe Ruth. "It is a major, serious problem. I am committed to taking action."

After a lengthy investigation, Pertschuk's staff came up with three proposed actions: a total ban on advertising on programs seen by children under the age of eight, a ban on advertising for highly sugared foods for anyone under the age of twelve, or a requirement that advertisers pay for public-service nutrition ads.

The recommendations stirred up a video hornets' nest. Pediatricians and dentists supported Peggy Charren's group. "Censorship," declared newspaper writers, who lived on ad revenues. One editor claimed that the recommendation threatened "to turn us all into children," while the *Washington Post* accused the FTC of trying to act like the "national nanny." When cereal companies started running nutrition ads showing cereal alongside fruit, milk, and orange juice as "a good part of a good breakfast," Charren was chagrined. "It's almost worse than having no disclaimer at all," she sighed.

The debate was muted by passage of the FTC Improvement Act in 1980, which eliminated the FTC's power to rule on "unfair" advertising. The movement to regulate cereal advertising quickly lost steam. The FTC's final report on the issue concluded that food advertising did indeed harm children, while admitting that it was nearly impossible to do anything about it.

But neither Peggy Charren nor the cereal marketers gave up the fight for the pre-teen consciousness. In 1984 the Federal Communications Commission eliminated its already weak restrictions concerning children's programming. Frito Lay created *Yo! It's the Chester Cheetah Show!* based on the Cheetos character, while Kraft, the company that owned Post cereal, developed *Cheesasaurus Rex*, history's first attempt at creating drama from a plateful of macaroni and cheese. Other cartoon characters like G.I. Joe and Rainbow Brite marched straight from their television cartoons onto the cereal box.

Charren and her cohorts successfully lobbied the FCC to issue a decision that banned live or animated television hosts from pitching products on their own programs. Charren further urged passage of a bill to limit the amount of television advertising aimed at kids. Her first bill was vetoed by President Reagan. On July 23, 1990, the House voted in favor of a bill to limit the number of ads on children's programs and to require the FCC to consider the amount of educational programming that a broadcaster presents as part of the license-renewal process.

In 1992, satisfied with the passage of the new television ad bill and a policy statement from the FCC stating that children must be treated as "special members of the viewing audience," Peggy Charren ended her twenty-four-year career as a consumer advocate and closed the doors of Action for Children's Television. "It was never our idea to sanitize the superheroes and reduce the art of animation to its present standards," said Peggy Charren to those that claimed her organization took the life out of children's television programming. "The broadcasters are responsible for what's on the air today, not Action for Children's Television."

20

Baby Boomer Breakfast

As with most messages that hit a responsive chord, the attacks on the cereal industry in the early 1970s echoed a broader movement in the country. The period witnessed the birth of the ecology movement as the Woodstock generation headed back to the land. Many carried with them the best selling *Tassajara Bread Book*, which described bread baking as a "ripening, maturing, baking, blossoming process," a sentiment that echoed Sylvester Graham's belief in the spiritual potential of whole grains.

While the cereal establishment struggled with increased government regulation and the anti-processing crusade of the counterculture, one entrepreneur carved out a niche in the small-is-beautiful breakfast category.

Johnny Granola Seed

In 1965 Layton Gentry, an affable, fiftyish, self-described "freelance baker," set out to create a healthful breakfast cereal. Slaving in his small kitchen, as Post and the Kellogg brothers had slaved before him, Gentry came up with a concoction of rolled oats, wheat germ, sesame seeds, unsweetened coconut, oil, sea salt, and brown sugar. He called his culinary creation Crunchy Granola.

Gentry traveled around the country, offering people tastes of his Crunchy Granola and looking for a partner to manufacture the product. He found a corporate soul mate in Collegedale, Tennessee, at the offices of Sovex, Inc. The Goodbrad family, which ran the company, bought Gentry's recipe for $3,000 and added Crunchy Granola to the list of products it sold primarily to health-food stores. A few years later, Gentry sold the granola rights for the western United States to Lassen Foods of Chico, California, an outfit run by Wayne Schlotthauer.

"I felt to do things right, there should be small plants in several locations manufacturing it," Gentry told the news media. He believed that the Goodbrads and the Schlotthauers would follow the path of dietetic righteousness. After all, they were Seventh Day Adventists and vegetarians, just like Dr. John Harvey Kellogg who had called his first cold cereal creation Granola back in 1881.

Still, the man dubbed "Johnny Granola Seed" by *Time* magazine was worried. "I really think that if the big companies got their hands on it that it would become a bad word," sighed Gentry about Granola, before he drifted off bearing his breakfast food to Australia, Western Canada, Hawaii, and beyond.

It didn't take long for big companies to realize that the small Seventh Day Adventist health-food makers were shipping out millions of pounds of Crunchy Granola per month. Jim Matson experienced a granola revelation when he noticed the red-and-white plastic bags of Lassen granola quickly disappearing from a St. Louis health-food store. Known for his previous marketing successes with the diet drink Tropical Sego and the diet pudding Spoon-Up, the thirty-six-year-old executive with Pet Incorporated decided that granola offered his company the perfect way to break into breakfast.

"There was a retreat to a simpler style of life," he later recalled. "I figured that people didn't want to give up a hell of a lot, but they did want to withdraw from the confusion all around them." To help in this withdrawal, Matson and the ad firm Workshop West came up with a product that they felt would appeal to the people who participated in the first Earth Day, a product that would evoke the feeling of America's rustic past. They called the first corporate granola Heartland Nature Cereal.

"Remember how it was, America? Before cities swallowed us up," voiced the television ads for Heartland Nature Cereal over old black-and-white photographs of fishing trips and family picnics. "Most of us lived on the land. We were simple, natural people. And for us, the seasons spun so slowly that we could watch our own food grow. . . ." At the end of the ad, the simple, natural television audience heard the tag line, "You have a taste for Heartland."

America did indeed have a taste for Heartland. Packaged in sepia-tone boxes, Heartland was introduced nationally in 1972 and captured 2.3 percent of the cereal market by the first quarter of the following year, a phenomenal success for any new breakfast cereal—unheard of for a product introduced by a company new to the cereal game.

The rest of the cereal pack fought a game of granola catch-up. In 1972, Quaker introduced 100% Natural cereal. Kellogg followed suit with Country Morning. General Mills rolled out Nature Valley. Even Colgate-Palmolive, the consumer products company best known for toothpaste, got into the act with its own breakfast cereal, Alpen. By the end of 1973, the new "naturals" had captured 10 percent of the cereal market.

The old naturals weren't doing so badly either. Grape-Nuts, C. W. Post's creation, was repositioned as a new-age edible in a television advertising campaign featuring Euell Gibbons, the author of *Stalking the Wild Asparagus*, a best-selling guidebook to edible plants. "It was one of those brilliant and rare occasions when an advertising agency reaches into the up-to-the-minute culture to seize on someone who was a natural spokesman for a product," observed advertising executive Leslie J. Stark. "He was a cultural icon of the time."

MAKING NATURE LOOK NATURAL

The advertising agency of Benton & Bowles went to unnatural lengths to make Grape-Nuts pitchman Euell Gibbons look natural. Up against a production deadline, the agency needed to find a lush field of winter wheat and big blooming sunflowers. Location scouts found the winter wheat in Ocala, Florida, but the nearest sunflowers were growing 250 miles away.

Undaunted, the production crew dug up 30 large sunflower plants at 10 P.M. one evening, potted them in garbage pails, drove the 250 miles to the wheat-field location, replanted the flowers, built a ramshackle wooden fence, ran through a technical production rehearsal, and waited for the sun to rise. Just before dawn, Euell Gibbons arrived at the scene from an air-conditioned trailer parked close by. In the commercial, the guru of wild plants talked about the relationship between sunflowers and Grape-Nuts before munching on a bowl of the cereal. "We had to shoot the spot in record time," remembered commercial producer Les Stark. "The sunflowers began to wilt in front of our eyes."

In another spot, Gibbons made his Grape-Nuts pitch from a canoe. The man who had once stalked the wild asparagus had long ago hung up his hiking boots. "He was so frail that we actually had a prop man lying flat in the canoe holding Euell Gibbons upright by the legs," recalled Stark, "to make sure he wouldn't topple over."

With his weathered features, Gibbons managed to convince viewers that Grape-Nuts was as natural as dandelions. His pitch for the cereal that "tastes like wild hickory nuts" was as sincere as it was effective. "He really liked the product," recalled Stark. "I don't think that he would have endorsed any product that he did not honestly believe in."

Granola saw its share of the cereal market fade as consumers showed a decided preference for granola snack bars over granola-filled breakfast bowls. For aging love children who still felt the need for a righteous breakfast food in 1991, Bob Weir and Mickey Hart of the rock band the Grateful Dead introduced Rainforest Crisp and Rainforest Granola, cereals that Weir claimed would make "eating breakfast an environmentally responsible act." The cereals were the brainchild of former Grateful Dead manager Sat Santosh Singh Khalsa, who realized that "if we really want people to read our message, we should put it on a cereal box, because everyone reads cereal boxes at breakfast."

Freakies

One of the ad agencies that reflected the disco era of the 1970s was New York-based Wells, Rich, Greene. "It was a young, brash, loud agency tooting its own horn," explained Wells copywriter Bob Moehl. "People were willing to take risks."

When Ralston Purina decided to buck the reformist tide and risk creating a sugar-coated cornflake in 1972, they turned to Wells for marketing help. Twenty-six-year-old copywriter Jackie End was given the assignment. "I remember as a kid I loved monsters," recalled End, one of the first women to create a major cereal ad campaign. "And monsters seemed to be the classic attraction for kids so I came up with this name, Freakie Flakes." When Ralston dropped the flake idea in favor of an extruded puff, "they just called them Freakies," said End.

For the "crunchy, sugary" puffs, End created a clan of creatures based on the characters at her ad agency. "An ass-kisser in personnel was Goody-Goody, Cowmumble was sort of me—a soft-voiced female who was always trying to improve herself. Gargle was a British copywriter. . . . Hamhose was based on a very shy cat I had. Grumble was the manager of the creative department. Snorkledorf was a guy at the agency who was very good looking and he knew it." The leader of the Freakies gang was Boss Moss, a character based on creative director Charlie Moss.

In her gentle, humorous ad copy, End sent her Freakies on a search for the Freakies Tree, the source of a never-ending supply of

Freakies. Having found the tree, the Freakies made their home in seven duplexes nearby. "And the plumbing is completely copper, how lucky!" said Gargle.

Ralston gave the go-ahead for the Freakies characters. Horrible looking creatures covered with bumps who looked like the seven dwarves after an encounter with a toxic-waste dump, the Freakies starred in a series of memorable ads animated by Disney veteran Preston Blair. "They were very bizarre commercials," said Moehl. "They weren't written around a story line, but the kids didn't seem to mind."

Launched in 1973, Freakies was a huge success, briefly capturing more than 2 percent of the ready-to-eat cereal market. Once the spots were broadcast, Jackie End's colleagues caught on to the source of her inspiration. "Everybody got a kick out of it," laughed End. "[Agency head] Mary Wells loved it. In fact, she wanted me to make up a Freakie for her and I did—Nifty-Nifty, but we never got to introduce her."

After the initial Freakies rush, children tired of the cereal. "They did a little research to find out what the problem was," remembered Freakies animator Jack Zander, "and the frank answer was, they tasted terrible. Kids, after one box, didn't go back." An attempt to revive Freakies as Space Surfers in 1987 without Jackie End fell just as flat.

"I was really unhappy with what they did to the Freakies," complained End who has received mail addressed to "the Creator" from Freakies fans. "They were my babies."

As the hippie movement faded in the 1970s and supermarket trade journals announced the "return of sugar," two Ralston vice presidents, Pat McGuiness and Tom Caskenett sat in a St. Louis bar for a drink after work. The two noticed how many patrons played the Donkey Kong video game nearby. "We'll have to make a cereal based on that," chuckled one to the other. A few months later, Donkey Kong Cereal took America's supermarkets by storm and launched Ralston on a character-licensing binge.

Ralston took a new tack on the fifty-year-old practice of grafting well-known characters onto the cereal box. Instead of aiming for the long haul, Ralston chose to go for the quick hit, purchasing the rights to make cereals based on "borrowed equities" like toys and movies as well as "food analogs" like Cracker Jack that were already popular with kids.

"These cereals were in and out in six months," laughed Bob Moehl. "Ralston had a certain number of shapes and a certain number of flavors they could manufacture so the cereals were frighteningly uniform. It was the packaging and the theme and the advertising that changed to protect the innocent!"

In charge of licensing for Ralston was Blair Entenmann. "He was a cereal madman, I mean he was nuts," said Moehl. "He'd look at toilet paper in the john and wonder how you could license Charmin for a cereal."

Entenmann's enthusiasm led to a bewildering assortment of cereals, everything from Nintendo Cereal Systems to Barbie. "We usually paid the licensor a $125,000 cash advance," confided Entenmann. "Over the thirteen- to fourteen-week life of the brand, royalties might run $700,000 for the average license like Dunkin' Donuts, up to a million for the real successful ones like Ninja Turtles or Ghostbusters."

To help boost sales, Ralston went so far as to shrink wrap prizes onto box fronts. Recalled one supermarket worker, "I saw a housewife eighty-sixed from the store for swiping a 'free' Addams Family flashlight off a box. She screamed holy terror as she was led away!"

Other cereal manufacturers screamed at the losses they suffered trying to emulate Ralston's licensing strategy. General Mills poured out $20 million to advertise and promote Pac-Man cereal, and took a big loss on Strawberry Shortcakes. E.T. was an even bigger disaster for Big G. Sighed Dancer ad man Howard Courtemanche, "They banked on the Spielberg sequel and the sequel never came." When Post couldn't land Kermit the Frog or Miss Piggy from Jim Henson, it followed Smurf Berries with a cereal based on the Swedish Chef, a Muppet so obscure that the product's arrival in the supermarket went as unnoticed as its demise. Kellogg introduced C3PO cereal, hoping the force from the *Star Wars* films would be with them. It wasn't.

"They didn't know what they were doing," laughed Ralston's Blair Entenmann, who later bought a house in Minneapolis from a perplexed Big G cereal brand manager. Recalled Entenmann, "When he found out that I was the Ralston license guy, he says, 'We're still trying to figure out how Ralston made money at that [game]!'"

Quaker entered the market with a cereal based on the A-Team's big-hearted tough guy, Mr. T. "That was probably the biggest launch we ever had," recalled Quaker salesman Stan Austin, "and the sales force couldn't believe were were doing it." Max Lomont, Quaker vice president for package design, agreed. "I hated the damn thing. It was just the wrong image for Quaker . . . I mean, that man is an animal . . . a violent person." Despite management reservations about the star, Mr. T cereal was a huge success with as many as 250 cases melting down a week in a high volume supermarket. "We were told that if Quaker could keep it on the market a year, they'd make a million dollars," recalled Austin. "And it stayed on the market seven or eight years. They really got their money out of that one."

The volatility of the market eventually caught up with Ralston. Tie-ins with movie flops like *The Jetsons* proved costly. World Federation Wrestling Super Stars cereal was pulled from shelves when a steroid scandal tarnished wrestling's image. G.I. Joe Action Stars failed because the puff shapes had nothing in common with the commando characters. "Little hand grenades or pistols would have worked," mused Entenmann, "but then mothers would have rebelled." Morning Funnies brand had too much fruit flavor, a quality control problem that torpe-doed a novel marketing idea. Groaned the Ralston man, "You'd open the box and the aroma would just about knock you over." Continued Entenmann, "Once we had a lot of neat sayings like, 'The higher the peak, the longer the life' . . . but after bombs like Nerds and Batman, we said, 'Up like a rocket and drops like a rock.'" In 1993, Ralston saw its sales for cereals based on licensed characters plummet from $30 million to $13 million. In that same year, the company announced it was with-drawing completely from the character-licensed cereal business. "We used to joke that the box tasted better than the cereal," laughed Ral-ston's former licensing czar, Blair Entenmann.

Pig in the Python

After their costly experiments with super-fad cereals, the cereal compa-nies redoubled their efforts to create products and advertising geared toward the aging baby boomers. Cereal marketers who followed this group of consumers, some eighty million strong from cradle to grave, referred to the market segment as "the pig in the python," a population bulge slowly working its way up the demographic timeline.

"The most interesting thing going on is that they have been target-ing this group for the last thirty years," said Jim Gillmore, an ex-Burnett creative director and a professor of advertising at Michigan State Uni-versity. "Nobody is really into the kid thing anymore, at least not at Kel-logg. They are advertising on network news shows and stuff like that 'cause they're going after a target that's forty years old."

Cereal marketers who treated adults like big kids got great results. Burnett began the trend in the 1980s with the nostalgic "Great Day" campaign for Kellogg's Corn Flakes. The agency decorated Corn Flakes boxes with pictures of television stars from yesteryear, including Don Knotts from *The Andy Griffin Show* and Tony Dow from *Leave It to*

Beaver. "It was pretty weird making money being on a box of Corn Flakes," said Dow. "Not my idea of a creative endeavor."

One of the most effective marketing campaigns of the 1980s involved the disappearance of Cap'n Crunch. "Kids thought he was a stupid looking dork," recalled Max Lomont, Quaker's vice president for package design. "He'd been in the same form doing the same thing for nearly thirteen years." In 1984, Quaker decided to refurbish the Cap'n's image. The company decided to have the old salt disappear and then reemerge in a new form. To accomplish this, Lomont and his co-worker Jerry Perkins devised the "Where's the Cap'n?" promotion, in which the likeness of Cap'n Crunch was stripped from the package in favor of an outline and a big question mark.

For three months, a blitz of TV ads prodded kids to win a million-dollar prize by sending in the Cap'n's whereabouts on a boxtop or calling up an 800 number. "And boy did it work," recalled Lomont, who watched Crunch sales soar. The campaign grew so popular that it even made *Saturday Night Live*. Over news file footage of a rubber body bag being dragged out of high weeds, "Weekend Update" anchorman Dennis Miller announced that "the partially decomposed body of Cap'n Crunch was discovered in a Pennsylvania drainage ditch. Erie County officials say the semi-nude body may have been sexually assaulted."

When they saw the success of the baby-boomers-as-kids marketing ploy, the executives at General Mills pushed their advertising men to beat Kellogg at its own game. One of Big G's most memorable aging baby boomers campaigns was devised by ad man Sherman Hemsley. Hemsley's "ten bowls to equal a bowl of Total" campaign made a serious point in a humorous way. General Mills hired a number of celebrities to participate in the campaign. The most popular was Richard Mulligan, silver-haired star of TV's *Soap* and *Empty Nest*.

"We did this one commercial out in L.A. where we built a supermarket set," recalled Howard Courtemanche. "He [Mulligan] is standing there with a box of Shredded Wheat in a shopping bag. We shot him from the waist up, and there was a compressed air tube running into the bag. Suddenly twelve boxes would go up through the tube and fly out the bag, and we'd joke 'You'd have to eat twelve boxes of Shredded Wheat to get the vitamins and mineral nutrition in one box of Total.'" According to Courtemanche, Mulligan was "a real riot" but at about the time the aging actor married and divorced a much younger woman, his relationship with Total was terminated.

PORN FLAKES

Since the 1960s, Kellogg has co-sponsored the Miss America beauty pageant and splashed the toothsome crown winner on the fronts of Corn Flakes boxes as the contemporary Sweetheart of the Corn. In 1984, at the NAACP convention, Kellogg handed out special-edition Corn Flakes boxes featuring twenty-one-year-old Vanessa Williams, the first black Miss America. Although the pretty package claimed to be a lasting reminder to "freely pursue life, liberty and happiness," Kellogg choked when *Penthouse* printed nude photos of Williams taken several years before. Not only did Miss America appear naked, but as the *New York Times* delicately put it, she simulated "sexual relations with another woman." Williams was forced to give up her crown and her place on the Corn Flakes box. Kellogg destroyed the packages it had produced with her picture, but not before plant workers in Battle Creek pilfered hundreds of curiosities as souvenirs. "It's a natural tendency to want to bury those things," said John Long, who retired from working on Kellogg's advertising a year before the debacle. "My own feeling about it is, a guy like me would have caught it. . . . I kept their skirts clean for years."

Coupon Crazy

"The competition in this business is as brutal as pro football," complained one Kellogg executive as early as the 1960s. "It's loaded with linebackers—men who size up the competition and react quickly to enemy strategy."

By the early 1990s, the cereal business was more competitive than ever. Companies employed hidden cameras to study the relationship between the elusive shopper and the cereal aisle. An associate professor at the Harvard Business School created a virtual supermarket for market research, scanning images of Cheerios, Shredded Wheat, and Cap'n Crunch boxes into a computer to allow virtual shoppers to pull the packages off a shelf, turn them around, and examine them. Tourists to Battle Creek were disappointed to find that manufacturers in the

Cereal City had ended the eighty-year tradition of the cereal-plant tour. The reason given by the companies—industrial espionage.

Nowhere was the cereal competition felt more keenly than at Kellogg, the last big-time cereal maker that still relied on breakfast for the bulk of its business. In 1987 Kellogg sued Grey advertising and Post cereals for misrepresenting the number of raisins in Kellogg's Raisin Bran. A year earlier, it sued the planning committee for the 1988 Summer Olympics to enjoin them from using a mascot similar to Tony the Tiger. The description of the tension at Kellogg was reminiscent of the tension surrounding the workaholic W. K. Kellogg himself. "There is a marine-like atmosphere there," noted one analyst. "No one smiles, everyone is intense and serious."

Kellogg long looked to its overseas markets as the most promising area for future growth. "Our future," said Lyle Roll in the 1960s when he was chairman of the company, "is pointed toward educating the world about breakfast." The rest of the world did indeed need education. In the 1940s, when Kellogg first introduced free cartons of cornflakes in France, one housewife complained, "*Alors!* What use are they? No matter how hard I scrub, they make no suds."

By the end of the 1960s, Kellogg had twenty-five overseas plants serving up more than 9 billion bowls of cereal a year to 150 countries. By 1991 over 50 percent of Kellogg's sales came from its overseas operations. In that same year, the same television ad for Frosted Flakes ran in twenty-two countries, with slight variations. In Germany, for example, Tony the Tiger's "Gr-r-reat!" became "Gr-r-rossartig!" A few years later, the company announced plans to open cereal-production facilities in Latvia and Bombay. "It is quite substantial," commented one Latvian housewife after trying Corn Flakes. "Normally I have boiled macaroni with milk and sugar. But I'm planning to buy some of these. The crispiness is different from what we're used to."

Kellogg could not escape the cereal war, even by moving to foreign shores. In 1989 General Mills joined with the world's largest food company, Nestle, to create Cereal Partners Worldwide. Relying on Nestle's marketing channels to distribute General Mills cereal, Cereal Partners Worldwide announced plans to compete with Kellogg all over the globe, beginning with an effort to sell Honey Nut Cheerios and Golden Grahams in France, Spain, and Portugal.

Back in the United States, the battle between Kellogg and Big G came down to the ultimate issue—price. As the cost of some cereals approached five dollars per box, as much per pound as shrimp or steak, cereal manufacturers distributed more than twenty-five billion coupons a year in an attempt to lure price-conscious shoppers. "The cereal companies' biggest problem is getting all those station wagons with families in them to drive in," observed former Burnett ad man John Long, "and they do that with coupons."

The coupon frenzy was nothing new to the American consumer. "Scarcely a middle-class or wage-worker's family may be found," wrote political economist I. M. Rubinow in 1905, "where some kind of coupons are not saved and some kind of free prize not expected." In 1897, the federal government passed laws prohibiting packing coupons into product containers, laws that were later struck down. Nearly one hundred years later, 60 percent of the consumers who bought cereal used a coupon. And anyone who did not use a coupon when buying a box of Cheerios, Frosted Flakes, Total, or other name-brand cereal was being seriously overcharged.

Consumers began to react to the high prices of brand-name cereals even before the price hikes of the early 1990s. According to Dr. Ronald W. Cotterill of the Food Marketing Policy Center at the University of Connecticut, 40 percent to 50 percent of the price of a name-brand cereal represented the cost of manufacturing, the rest "advertising, promotion, and profits." Added to the wholesalers' cost was a retail markup of 18 percent per package. In the late 1980s, sales of private-label cereals surged, as consumers lunged for knock-off cheerios, corn-flakes, and cocoa krispies. Noticing the trend, grocer's placed their private-label brand cereals next to the brand-name product, breaking three decades of industry-inspired shelf management, which grouped manufacturers' products together on the aisle.

Though analysts doubted that private-labels product would ever take up more than 10 percent of the cereal market, brand-name salesmen reacted quickly to the cost-consciousness trend. Instead of giving money away as they had in the go-go eighties, Kellogg emphasized the good value of their product. A series of folksy TV ads featured a policeman, a crusty down easter, and a peppy young woman, all of whom testified to the value of Kellogg cereal with the slogan "four bowls for a buck." Shortly after launching the good value ad campaign, Kellogg once again raised its prices.

Finally, in the spring of 1994, General Mills called a halt to the coupon craze. "There is tremendous cost associated with printing, distributing, handling, and redeeming coupons," announced Stephen W. Sanger, president of General Mills, in the *New York Times*. "Because of this inefficiency the 50 cents the consumer saves by clipping a coupon can cost a manufacturer 75 cents. It just doesn't make sense."

General Mills slashed its promotional budget by $175 million and cut prices on its best-selling cereals by thirty to seventy cents per box. Though Kellogg chose to maintain its prices and continue the coupon barrage, General Mills believed that it would win market share by relying on the one characteristic of cereal that has been most responsible for its popularity over the last century—its relatively low price.

21

Cereal Vérité

At the turn of the century, rumors that breakfast cereals "were extensively adulterated with worthless materials" led the government to make scientific inquiries. "The materials used in preparing the cereal breakfast foods," reported a study prepared and published by the U.S. Department of Agriculture in 1906, "are wholesome grains or some of their more valuable products . . . the addition of bran, corn cob, corn stalk, etc., sometimes said to be adulterants is purely imaginary."

When this study appeared, many believed that it would prove to be the last word on the nutritional content of breakfast foods. Far from it. Over the course of the twentieth century tens of thousands of scientists, consumers, researchers, and market analysts have spent millions of dollars in a search for the answer to the ultimate cereal koan: are breakfast cereals good for you or not?

Rat Chow

Cereal flakes, puffs, and granules have been pounded, chewed, chemically broken down, and reconstituted in an effort to uncover the health mystery at the bottom of the cereal bowl. But no creature has made a greater sacrifice to the understanding of human breakfast nutrition than the rat.

Rats are a lot like humans, digestively speaking. They rely on the same sorts of nutrients and they process foodstuffs in much the same way as humans. Because of this biological similarity, rats have long been a laboratory favorite for the testing of food products and have contributed an enormous amount to what people know or do not know about nutrition.

One of the first major studies to bring rats to the breakfast table was conducted in the late 1920s by Dr. George Cowgill of the Yale University School of Nutrition. Dr. Cowgill published a paper in the *Journal of the American Medical Association* in 1932 entitled, "Studies on the Effects of Breakfast Cereal Intake." "The use of whole grain cereals," concluded Dr. Cowgill, "so as to furnish as much as 84 percent of the calories of the diet is compatible with excellent growth, reproduction, lactation, and general physiologic well being in the rat."

The Yalie rats were later joined by other non–Ivy League rodents who offered up their digestive systems in the search for the truth about cereal. In the 1940s the valiant efforts of one rat pack helped researchers prove that the puffing process destroyed nutrients. Other rats made the ultimate cereal sacrifice, suffering a painful death after a multi-week diet of 40% Bran Flakes, Kix, Grape-Nuts, Grape-Nuts Flakes, and Puffed Wheat. Recalling these experiments in a series of articles published in 1962, the magazine *Consumer Bulletin* recommended hamburgers over breakfast cereal and warned that not only were cereals not nutritious— they could be downright deadly. "Grains used in flour and cereal man-ufacture are often dangerously contaminated with poisons or filth" the magazine reported.

No group has placed more faith in the rat than Consumers Union, the nation's preeminent consumer advocacy group and publisher of *Consumer Reports*. In fact, the first issue of *Consumer Reports*, published in 1936, featured a box of breakfast cereal on the cover and recom-mended the nutritious but commercially short-lived cereals Milkoata, Milkwheata, and Milkorno.

In 1975 the *Consumer Reports* investigative team returned to the breakfast table, this time accompanied by a hired squad of 264 rats to help assess the nutritional content of various cereals. The researchers kept the rats on a strict diet of breakfast cereal and water with the fol-lowing results: The rats that ate Maypo, Cheerios, and Special K did rather well. Those that ate Sir Grapefellow, Baron Von Redberry, Total, or more than a dozen other cereals survived, but developed minor problems such as nervousness and gray hair. The real losers were the rats that ate Product 19, Quisp, Pink Panther Flakes, or some of the other twenty-one cereals that caused "rickets, edema, tremors, emaciation, dehydration."

Consumer Reports believed so strongly in its rat research that it told its readers to disregard the dietary information on cereal labels, recom-mending instead that the federal government employ a legion of rats to establish a cereal-rating system based on "animal growth rates." *Con-sumer Reports* also pointed out that rats were part of a cereal breakfast in any case, as cereals contained extraneous matter including "the hair of rats and other animals, and fragments of weevils, thrips, aphids, borers, parasitic wasps, moths, mites, bettles [sic], flies and spiders."

In 1981, *Consumer Reports* hired 570 more rats to test fifty-seven dif-ferent varieties of cereal. This round of tests proved that Maypo, Instant Quaker Oats, Cheerios, and other top-rated cereals "did sustain the rats relatively well without the considerable help that milk might have provided." Surprisingly, Total, Most, and Product 19 ranked among the least nutritious of the cereals. Though the magazine still emphatically urged the use of rats as the only meaningful way to test the nutritional value of cereal, the research revealed a mystery. "When we tested Spoon Sized Shredded Wheat five years ago, it was low rated," the magazine admitted. "Our tests of regular-sized Shredded Wheat this year place it at the top group. . . . Why? We just don't know."

An even bigger mystery unfolded five years later when the rats disappeared from the *Consumer Reports* cereal rating. America's leading consumer-information writers had replaced their rodent guinea pigs with a rating system that relied on the nutritional information found on the cereal labels, the same labels the magazine had earlier criticized as being untrustworthy. The ratless rating system ranked Nabisco Shredded Wheat, Spoon Size Shredded Wheat, and Shredded Wheat 'n Bran as the most nutritious cereals, which was odd, considering the fact that a decade earlier *Consumer Reports* had condemned these cereals, claiming that they gave rats rickets. "Consumers Union came under a great deal of criticism from professional nutritionists, consumer groups, and the food industry for our use of animal testing in evaluating food products," explained Constance Corbett, testing director for the foods division of *Consumer Reports*. "In our opinion, their arguments against animal testing far outweighed its advantages."

The cereal companies were never much concerned about the eating habits of the breakfast rats. Executives poked fun at the methodology, laughing at the image of hundreds of rodents huddled over tiny bowls with tiny spoons. In 1982, Art Schulze, a General Mills vice president joked, "We passed around a memo recommending that we start advertising in such periodicals as *Good Mousekeeping, Rodent Track,* and *Mouse & Garden.*"

The real concern that cereal companies had about rats was how to keep them out of their grain silos. In the 1970s when General Mills perfected a way of keeping rats out, the company wanted to splash the news across the country in major television ad campaign. "Terrific," said Dancer ad man Leo Stuchkus. "You try to advertise that and they'll say, 'All this time you didn't tell us that rat feces were in the oats?'"

Years of rat research have yielded no definitive answers as to the question of whether or not breakfast cereals are good for you. The only definitive conclusion that can be drawn from these tests is that laboratory rat chow is a healthy and nourishing food for rats. But how many humans would be willing to eat rat chow for breakfast? Even Ralston Purina, makers of lab block rat feed, would probably not take the plunge.

GNAWING PROBLEMS

In 1986, General Mills created Clusters cereal, a presweetened combination of bran flakes, nuts, and honey. Working on the concept that the cereal would appeal to serious nut lovers, the advertising team of Donna Weinheim and Cliff Freeman came up with the concept of a Clusters-stealing squirrel.

General Mills management expressed concern about the new campaign, arguing that squirrels would be repulsive to consumers because rodents are pests. The senior executive with the final okay on the project was particularly anti-squirrel, since he had a chimney at his home and constantly battled invading squirrels with a rake. Eventually, however, he gave the green light.

Once production began, the creators of the first Clusters commercial ran into difficulties with the talent. The star squirrel was supposed to shinny up the side of a bookcase and stand next to some books. Instead of doing this, the squirrel spent eight hours darting around the expensive sound stage, until it finally collapsed from heat exhaustion. The understudy squirrel came out for his big chance, looked at the bookcase and performed the part flawlessly on his first take. "Everybody exploded in applause," recalled ad man Howard Courtemanche.

Despite the fact that the Clusters squirrel campaign was tremendously popular, General Mills hesitated for years before allowing the squirrel to appear on the cereal package, fearing that the image of a cereal-stealing rodent would degrade their product.

Sugar-Coated Vitamins

Other rat-based nutritional discoveries have proven to be equally equivocal. In the early 1920s Dr. Harry Steenbock at the University of Wisconsin relied on the good old rat to perfect the process he called irradiation. He discovered that vitamin D could be activated in cereals by exposing them to ultraviolet rays. When he fed the irradiated cereals to sick rats, he found that the vitamin D-enriched food cured the rodents of rickets.

Quaker Oats was the first cereal company to commercialize the vitamin enrichment discovery. The company licensed the Steenbock process in 1926, one year after the food scientist's experiments were published. In the 1930s, millions of tons of Quaker Oats and Mother's Oats passed under ultraviolet irradiating lights to enrich them with vitamin D, which became known as "the sunshine vitamin." Other cereal manufacturers began to fortify their cereals with vitamins about the same time. By the mid-1930s, General Mills was producing so much vitamin D that it set up an entire company, Sun-A-Sured, Inc., to peddle the sunshine vitamin to other food companies and even to the makers of vitamin tablets.

During World War II, the U.S. government established recommended daily allowances for vitamins and encouraged the addition of vitamins to food products, believing that a well-nourished citizenry was a vital component of the national defense. Since that time, the generally accepted wisdom about enriching foods with vitamins and minerals has devolved into a nutritional morass of contradiction and inconsistency.

The U.S. Food and Drug Administration (FDA) proposed limiting the amount of minerals and vitamins that could be added to cereals or sold over the counter. At one point, the FDA warned that if the popularity of vitamin enrichment increased, "the supposed malnutrition we now suffer as a nation may be replaced by a condition of overnutrition. The danger then will be consuming toxic levels of vitamins." The FDA managed to pass regulations limiting the amount of the vitamin folic acid that can be added to food, but attempts to regulate more closely the practice of vitamin enrichment as well as the sale of over-the-counter vitamins has been halted on several occasions by a barrage of consumer criticism.

But the question remains, are cereals with vitamin and mineral additives good for you or not? California has a law limiting the amount of vitamin A that can be added to foods, to protect consumers from vitamin A toxicity. "Eat your additives, they're good for you," wrote Dr. Frederick Stare, the founder of the Department of Nutrition at Harvard's School of Public Health and a consultant to the Cereal Institute. "I am convinced that food additives are far safer than the basic natural foods themselves." A Michigan State University nutritionist who grew up eating natural foods on an Iowa farm echoed Stare's beliefs. "Now I have prematurely gray hair, wear glasses, and all my teeth filled. I had undulant fever as a child from drinking raw milk, and I've had major surgery for cancer," she noted. "So, I'm delighted that milk is pasteurized, and that our food supply is of consistent, safe quality."

Consumer Reports sits squarely on the fence. In its 1975 rat-at-the-breakfast-table experiments, the magazine made the point that "a cereal can be stuffed with just about every nutrient for which daily requirements have been established and still not be able to support the lives of test animals." In its 1986 cereal ratings, the magazine backed way off its condemnation of vitamin supplements, recommending that consumers "may want to consider them" in choosing the most nutritious cereal.

Although the value of fortifying breakfast cereal with vitamins is still in doubt, there is no doubt that sometimes the cereal companies have run into problems with additives. In 1988, Kellogg doused some 30,000 packages of Rice Krispies with excessive amounts of iron. The company recalled the product, warning consumers that the heavy metal cereal had an off flavor. Later that same year, Kellogg overfortified 28,000 packages of Frosted Mini-Wheats, bathing them with an enormous dose of vitamin A. The company again recalled the product, warning that consumers might experience a tingling or burning in the mouth after eating the vitamin-drenched Mini-Wheats.

In 1994, General Mills learned that it had been selling cereals containing traces of the unauthorized chemical Dursban for more than a year. After trying to sell the pesticide-enriched cereal overseas, the company decided to destroy 50 million boxes of Cheerios, Lucky Charms, Kix, Franken Berry, Reese's Peanut Butter Puffs, and five other brands, as well as fifteen million bushels of oats, an additive purge that cost the company some $88 million.

While everyone agreed that the pesticide Dursban was not a good thing to eat for breakfast, a swirl of controversy continues to revolve around the most publicized ingredient in breakfast cereal—sugar. Everyone knows that sugar rots your teeth and makes you fat. Or does it?

"Overuse of most confections and sugar plummes," warned an English health advocate in the year 1600, "rotteth the teeth and maketh them look black." Though consumers have criticized sugary foods for hundreds of years, it is carbohydrates, not just sugar, that encourages the formation of dental cavities. Bacteria in the mouth thrive on carbohydrates. The more they thrive, the more acid they produce. The acid they produce eats away at tooth enamel, creating holes, or cavities, in the teeth. Because these bacteria consume any type of carbohydrate, it is incorrect to believe that sugar, any more than bread or raisins, will cause tooth decay. In fact, the first issue of *Consumer Reports*, published in 1936, warned consumers that "eating too much oatmeal and bread . . . increases the amount of tooth decay in children." Studies in the 1970s by the National Institute of Dental Research supported the fact that sugar is not the key factor in tooth decay, noting that in breakfast cereals, "a lot of sugar may be no worse for the teeth than a little sugar."

As far as the question of sugar and weight gain is concerned, *Consumer Reports* noted in the 1980s that there is no direct link between sugar cereals and obesity. In fact, the magazine stated that "an ounce of presweetened cereal contains pretty much the same number of calories as an ounce of unsweetened cereal." "What's wrong with sugar as part of any good meal?" wrote Harvard nutritionist Dr. Frederick Stare. "Not a thing."

After almost a century of research, and the scientific analysis of billions of crunchy mouthfuls, the consumer has been left with nothing more than a question mark regarding the nutritive value of breakfast cereals. Perhaps the only conclusion that can be drawn from the rat-infested, vitamin-enriched, sugar-coated evidence is the same one reached by *Consumer Reports* in 1986: "Eating any of the cereals would certainly provide better nutrition than eating no breakfast at all." There it is. The bottom line. Nutritionally speaking, breakfast cereal is better than nothing at all.

Cereal Sanctus

"There is more cant and pure buncombe spoken and written about matters of diet than about any other department of hygeine," proclaimed the *Literary Digest* in 1922 quoting the *New York Herald*. "A great many human beings have lived to a hale old age simply by eating food that agreed with them and not too much of it. That is about all the prescription the average healthy individual needs to give to the choice of diet."

Truer words were never written. However, Americans have a passionate desire to believe in cant and pure buncombe, rather than reasonable advice about their diet. "There is a class of minds much more ready to believe that which is at first sight incredible, and because it is incredible, than what is generally thought reasonable," wrote Oliver Wendell Holmes in 1842.

American consumers want an easy, convenient, one-shot (preferably exotic) solution to their personal problems and are willing to gobble down vitamin C, oat bran, fish oil, Tiger's Milk, Slim Fast, seaweed, grass squeezings, carrot juice, and urine in an attempt to gain weight, lose weight, increase energy, decrease stress, or cure whatever else ails them. Promoters of the $10-billion-a-year diet industry play to the gullibility of the American consumer, as do government regulators and professional consumer advocates whose campaigns against sugar, palm

Cereal boxes have not only provided eye opening reading material for millions of sleepy readers, they have inspired some of America's greatest literary talents. While the poet e. e. cummings dismissed all cereals as "battle creek seaweed," T. Coraghessan Boyle made the cereal scene in Battle Creek the setting for his celebrated novel *The Road to Wellville*. "The Breakfast of Champions," the Wheaties slogan first coined in 1933, was the title of a number-one best-selling novel by Kurt Vonnegut. In the Vonnegut story, a waitress used the phrase to congratulate anyone at the Mid City Holiday Inn who ordered a martini.

One of the most eloquent meditations on the cereal phenomenon was penned by John Updike in 1961.

ON THE INCLUSION
OF MINIATURE DINOSAURS
IN BREAKFAST CEREAL BOXES

A post-historic herbivore,
I come to breakfast looking for
A bite. Behind the box of Brex
I find *Tyrannosaurus rex*.

And lo! beyond the Sugar Pops,
An acetate *Triceratops*.
And here! across the Shredded Wheat,
The spoor of *Brontosaurus* feet.

Too unawake to dwell upon
A model of *Iguanodon*,
I hide within the Raisin Bran;
And thus begins the dawn of *Man*.

oil, flea wort, or bran do little more than add to the hysteria surrounding the simple truth about nutrition. The key to a healthy diet is to eat a wide variety of foods in limited portions. Period.

Given the insatiable interest in the workings of the American stomach, it is surprising how little common sense Americans have about the foods they eat. After a lengthy survey, the Wheat Food Council announced in 1991 that most consumers did not realize that Wheaties were made out of wheat. Kellogg dumped a Sweetheart of the Corn ad campaign when the marketing managers discovered that consumers didn't relate Corn Flakes to corn. It is doubtful that the labeling laws enacted in 1994 will do much to cure this overpowering consumer ignorance. As advertising pioneer Albert Lasker once noted, "The average consumer wouldn't understand a government standard if he bumped into it in broad daylight."

The cereal industry is not to blame for this situation, any more than the fashion industry is to blame for neckties, pre-ripped jeans, bell bottoms, or platform shoes. In the words of Dr. Charles Edwards, a former FDA commissioner, America's nutritional problems stem from "our national penchant for fads."

The one encouraging fact is that there is no great, monolithic cereal conspiracy. Cereal executives with their multi-million-dollar advertising campaigns, scientific-marketing analysis, and billions of coupons, are just as clueless as the average American consumer and the government about what is healthy, what is unhealthy, and what will sell. As David Bull, Nabisco's former cereal chief, once admitted, "Kids are so unpredictable that even with all our sophisticated research tools we still have no way of knowing what is really going to appeal to them."

The key point to remember in discussing nutrition and breakfast cereal is that when people buy cereal, they aren't buying a nutritional commodity. They are buying a dream. The dream factor is why so many well-intentioned consumer advocates and government regulators have had such a frustrating time controlling what appears to be a simple, almost childish commodity. It is impossible to regulate a dream, or put a limit on how much dreams are worth. "The cereal business is like a circus, with lots of acts going on at the same time," said a senior ad man to Post executive Kent Mitchell. "You charm the people and dazzle them a bit, but behind all of that, it's essentially the same product."

Every spoonful of Lone Ranger Cheerios or Shirley Temple Wheat Puffs or Michael Jordan Wheaties is much more than food. It is a bit of edible entertainment, a sugary communion wafer allowing the consumer to enter into the sacred realm of a particular grain god. For a few moments of contemplative munching, the cereal eater is able to transcend the mundane world of burned toast, car pools, and unfinished homework to enter a world of health, happiness, and fantastic prizes.

Today, in this era of the corporate food empire, where Grape-Nuts and Marlboros are interchangeable in the minds of middle managers, there are certain individuals who hark back to the spiritual roots of the cereal dream, and the quirky individuals who set out to nurture the American soul and heal the American stomach.

Seventh Day Adventists continue the spiritual and dietary work begun by Sister White and her protegé John Harvey Kellogg in 1866. Today the church operates America's largest Protestant health-care network. In Battle Creek, next to a fieldstone building once owned by Dr. Kellogg, a group of Seventh Day Adventist doctors, nurses, and nutritionists operate a psychiatric care and alcohol substance abuse treatment center, offering the latest medical technology in a smoke-free, alcohol-free, vegetarian environment.

Garth "Duff" Stoltz, security supervisor at the Adventist-founded health facility, has organized Health and Heritage, Inc., to preserve the legacy of Dr. John Harvey Kellogg and the Battle Creek Sanitarium, the institution that did the most to bring cold cereal to the American breakfast table. "If Dr. Kellogg was alive today, he'd be doing pretty much the same thing as he was back then," observed Stoltz as he told a visitor about electric light baths, mechanical chairs, and the mysterious fire that once burned down the San. "Many of the ideas we have about good health today started at the San. Back then, people thought they were just kind of kooky."

But what does the future hold? Will the product that has been endorsed by Babe Ruth, Maria Rasputin, Bullwinkle, and Wilford Brimley prove popular in the twenty-first century? According to one advertising executive, "Trends in cereal follow people's dietary beliefs." Like the Jew, the Muslim, the Hindu, the Catholic, and the Seventh Day Adventist, the breakfast eater in the new millennium will favor certain foods and consider other foods taboo. It will be the challenge of the cereal manufacturer to react quickly to the ever-changing prejudices of the world's palate and provide consumers with sugar, vitamins, or whatever else they might want. For the consumer, the challenge will be to maintain a healthy skepticism toward the hype-filled products that line the cereal aisle, the point on the American commercial spectrum where health meets Hollywood. Ultimately, Americans are what they eat. And the chances are good that Americans will be eating lots of breakfast cereal in the millennia to come.

Acknowledgments

This book reflects the more than eleven years of research into the cereal industry by the authors. We each began the project independently, with interests in post-war advertising and the founding fathers, respectively. After a chance 1991 meeting in Battle Creek, in which we compared notes and realized that we were chomping into the same story but from opposite ends, we decided to pool our efforts and go for the Big Book. When it comes to an eight-billion-dollar industry with enormous influence stretching over more than a century, two heads are better than one.

Since current employees of the cereal companies were generally unwilling or unable to cooperate with such a candid undertaking, much of the story was pieced together from interviews with retirees and individuals no longer affiliated with the manufacturers or their agencies. The majority of these people were not only eager to talk, but flabbergasted that the subject was of any interest to historians, let alone the general public. As these folks suggested their colleagues, bosses, or friends to speak with, the network of sources expanded, resulting in more than 120 hours of interviews (of which 80 hours were taped). It is our great pleasure to thank those men and women whose shared experiences and efforts helped to make this book possible.

Bert Halloviak, archivist of the General Conference of the Seventh Day Adventist Church, shed light on Sister Ellen White and the organization's hold on the Kellogg family; Catherine Youngman, marketing director of U.S. Mills, and Mary Jane Edney provided documents on Uncle Sam Breakfast Food. Historian Richard W. Schwarz brought to life the rivalries between the Kellogg brothers and C. W. Post.

Insight into the history and culture of the Kellogg Company resulted from discussions with Frank Staley, Howard List, the late Don Brown, Willard Culver, Oella Vosberg, Muriel Watkins, Michael Parkes, Elmer Klett, Eugene McKay Jr., Mr. and Mrs. Lyle Wolf, and Jeff Wolf. Special thanks are owed to Mr. and Mrs. James McQuiston, the late Fred Hanke and his wife Joyce, and the late Bill Becke and his wife Anna, who were hospitable as they lit the way. To Kellogg gatekeeper

Diane Dickey and archivist Betty Crilly we owe four pressured hours inside the company archive at the innocent onset of our labors. Allan Miller; Mrs. Vernon Grant; Mary Lynn Norton of the York County Museum; and the Vernon Grant Advisory Committee of Rockhill, South Carolina, have our thanks for supplying fresh biographical material on the Snap, Crackle, and Pop illustrator.

For theories, insight, and introductions into the Leo Burnett Agency, we wish to thank Jim Gillmore, Gordon Minter, Don Tennant, David Freedman, Bob Noel, Orrin Bowers, Carl Hixon, Dick Esmail, Hal Weinstein, Frank Martello, Rudy Behlmer, Bob Mayberry, Chet Glassley, Joel Hochberg, Bill Stratton, Russ Mayberry, Richard Weiner, Emrich Nicholson, Curt Jones, Hooper White, Roy Sandstrom, Nancy Mengel, and Dick Marx. Special thanks are owed to Kensinger Jones, the late Harry Smedley, John Long, Rudy Perz, Don Keller, and John E. Matthews, who kept the hot coffee coming while we absorbed their stories and pored through their files. Others, still working at the agency, we can thank best by protecting their anonymity. You have our sincere appreciation.

For our picture of the studio art operation in Leo Burnett's orbit, we bow our heads to Pete Eaton, Fred Iwen, Joseph Graziano, Tom Gentile, John Faulkner, Mike Hagel, Ted Carr, Barry Birnbaum, Brent Carpenter, Larry Hubbell, and Ross Wetzel, many of whom volunteered artwork in addition to their time.

For the behind-the-scenes glimpse of Kellogg's TV programming, we'd like to thank the following actors and voice talents who responded to our inquiries with alacrity and, in many cases, called back to be interviewed: Jack Larson, Max Baer Jr., Frankie Thomas, Guy Madison, Donna Douglas, Shirley Jones, Larry Storch, Tony Dow, Phyllis Coates, Art Linkletter, Ray Walston, Bob Keeshan, Laraine Day, Mark Wilson, and Thurl Ravenscroft, who graciously roared "You're GR-R-REAT!" at our delighted children.

Bob Richards, Robert Stafford, Jim Fish, Evie Wilson, and Gage Davis Jr. provided revelations into General Mills and the Wheaties mystique, while Jean Toll, Katherine Newton, Julie Hooker, and Larry Fenske have our gratitude for supplying documents and answering many of our questions.

For insight into the relationship between General Mills and its agency Dancer Fitzgerald Sample, we are indebted to Bill Tollis, Gene Cleaves, Leo Stuchkus, Jack Keil, Tony Jaffe, and Howard Courtemanche, many of whom sent scripts and storyboards to flesh out our understanding. Our gratitude also goes to actors Hugh O'Brian and

Clayton Moore, who filled our bowls with Cheerios lore; and to Chuck McCann, whose impersonations made us laugh so hard it was difficult to conduct the interview.

Our handle on Post/General Foods resulted from conversations with and material supplied by Tom Hollingsworth, Max Lomont, Harold Paul, Howard Slutz, Kent Mitchell, Al Clausi, Stan Reesman, Virginia and Ralph Moody, Dick Basso, Greg Bunger, Tom Irwin, and Robert McCarty. Everett Shipley led us through the world of the cereal-display business, while John DiGianni Sr. and John DiGianni Jr. told of designing Post packaging under Frank Gianninoto in the late 1940s. Special thanks are due to Mr. and Mrs. Bill Betts and Bob Traverse, who, on many occasions, invited us to hear their hilarious war stories in the comfort of their air-conditioned living rooms. Elizabeth Adkins and her assistant Stephen Carvell at Kraft/General Foods were models of corporate archivists, patiently retrieving documents and answering our queries—thanks again. The late Art Rush and Dusty Rogers explained Roy Rogers' brush with breakfast food, while Cliff Robertson gener-ously consented to be interviewed on life inside the Post dynasty.

Roy Eaton, Dick Bloede, Gene Schinto, Ed Graham, Peter Israelson, Max Bryer, Ed Hannibal, Leslie J. Stark, Joe Bacal, Chuck Beisch, and John McKendary opened the window onto Benton & Bowles' marriage to Post and, in many cases, shared their memorabilia. Special thanks are due to Bobby Sherman, Jim Nabors, Sheldon Leonard, Marjorie Lord, Ruth Buzzi, and producer Ward Sylvester, who responded to our letters and, in several instances, called back to chew the fat.

For insight into the Quaker Oats Company and its agencies, we thank Stan Austin, Ken Anthony, Harold Lamb, Joe Lipscombe, Jim Knowland, Harold Gottlieb, Ken Mason, Greg Gwynn, Franz Meier, Howard Alport, George Bruce, Tom Taverna, Irwin Darrow, Don DeForest, Dick Jones, Jack O'Grady, Bill Pearce, and Fred Lewis. Spe-cial thanks go to Bob Dobler, Max Lomont, and Mike Barna, who were as hospitable outside the office as they were informative inside. Janet Rankaitis made available documents for our study of the mush maker. Arthur D. Little, Inc.'s role in the development of Cap'n Crunch was explained by food chemists David Kendell and Dr. Marvin Rudolf (who confirmed our suspicion that there is a molecular basis to the sim-ilarity between the smell of Shredded Wheat and fresh urine—unstable nitrogen compounds. Thanks again guys!).

We owe our vision of cereal animation to Bill Hurtz, Ken Walker, Ray Favatta, George Bakes, Hank Ketcham, Adrian Tytla, Bill Melendez,

Chuck McKimson, Tom McKimson, Robert McKimson Jr., Bob Clampett Jr., Jack Zander, Dan Hunn, Eli Feldman, Ed Justin, Gus Jekel, Mike Lah, Chris Ishii, Allen Swift, Scott Shaw!, Friz Freleng, Charles Ulrich, Andy Lederer, Jerry Beck, and Chuck Jones. Faith Hubley graciously spent part of a morning on the phone with us as well as digging deep for old Maypo files. Special thanks are due to Bill Hanna, who drove in from Palm Springs, and Joe Barbera, who took time away from inspecting his earthquake-shattered home, to share their cereal reminiscences with us.

David F. Bull, Webster Bull, Chuck Allen, the late Mrs. Moses Berger, Elliott H. Berger, Craig Carragan, Clarence Joyce Jr., Rand Plass, Toby Decker, Frank Martello, Sheldon Holzer, Tony Jaffe, Eugene McKay Jr. and Bob Schaeberle were indispensable to our understanding of Ranger Joe, Maltex, Cream of Wheat, Malt-O-Meal, Nabisco, and their agencies. Dave Stivers of the Nabisco Archive diligently answered our many information requests, while Larry Campbell and Norma Reed allowed us to don paper hats and booties to tour Nabisco's Naperville, Illinois, plant.

For understanding of Ralston Purina and its agencies, we owe much to Ron Goulart, Jackie End, Manny DeMagistris, Bob Moehl, Bud Arnold, Elmer Richars, Keith Schopp, Charles Claggett, and Blair Entenmann. Our hats go off to Jack Narz for reminiscencing about his years as a Chex pitchman, an exercise, he laughed, "that is a violation of the child labor law."

Our grasp of the cereal premium business flowed from conversations with Manny Winston, Gordon Gold, Tom Tumbusch, David Reed, Dan Witkowski, Scott Galloway, Bob Knetzger, Martha Carothers, and Belena Chapp. Special thanks go to Ed Gleim; Leon Levy; and the late John "Wally" Walworth and his wife Pudge. John Updike has our gratitude for sharing his inspiration for a poem written more than thirty years ago. "I was a dinosaur buff long before the present rage," he wrote. "My only reservation about the inclusion of the miniatures in with the cereal was that somebody might choke on one."

Many people sent documents, video tapes, radio recordings, reminiscences, vintage ads, packages, art work, and newspaper clippings, as well as expressions of support; for that and more we thank Mark Hamill, Cheryl Chambers, Gary Hunter, Frances Thornton, Mark Lambert, Stephen J. Govoni, Ralph Stout, Jim Dean, Mark Arnold, Eleanor Brody, M. G. Norris, Kevin Dilmore, David Gary, George W. Case III, Ken Allison, Roland Coover Jr., Scott Ennis, Phil Arthurhultz, Barry Martin, Howard Bender, Jeff Hoppa, Bill Janocha, Jay Zilber, Chip

Crawford, Judd Hurd, Dave Bastian, Dale Ames, Bill Bruegman, Jerry Cook, Don Phelps, Wes Narron Jr., James Sturm, Ron Schwinnen, Hal Morgan, Joyce O'Hara, Maureen Coral, Robert Koenig, John Fawcett, Rocky Flynn, Ed Curtis, Steve Roden, Bob Pontes, Bob Bostoff, Kerry Tucker, Lou Miano, Dave Newell, John Alutto, Dan Goodsell, Lou Antonicello, Rick Kohlschmidt, Mitch Diamond, David Gutterman, Larry Blodget, Steve Cox, Hal Lifson, Andy Andersen, Joey Green, Jim Clark, Ed Inglis, Tom Lespasio, and many others whose names were misplaced in the chaos of an impending deadline. Thanks again.

For statistical information, we thank Bob Bregenzer at Information Resources, Inc., and Kathleen Brooks at Competetive Media Reporting. John M. McMillin at Prudential Securities and Dr. Ronald Cotterill at the Food Marketing Policy Center, the University of Connecticut at Storrs, provided us with the insights of longtime industry observers, while David Schardt at the Center for Science in the Public Interest helped clarify some of the issues surrounding the nutritional aspects of breakfast cereal. Thanks to Connie Corbett and Sally Moore for helping us trace the evolution of attitudes toward cereal testing at *Consumer Reports*.

For assistance in library research, we thank David R. Smith, Archivist at the Walt Disney Studios; Jane Ratner and Marlene Steel at the Willard Memorial Library in Battle Creek; Ken Price; Darcie Jane Fromholz; and Morgan Wesson, the man with the camera.

At Faber and Faber, the publisher that had the smarts to recognize a Great American Saga when it saw it, we thank Fiona McCrae, who had the uncommon intelligence to hook the book in the first place, and editors Suzanne Summers and Betsy Uhrig, whose red pencils, sensitively wielded, left the manuscript relatively unscathed and, in places, even improved. Finally, thanks to Kris Dahl for her enthusiastic and generous support, which helped get this project from bowl to shelf.

For more information on cereal history and memorabilia collecting, send a self-addressed, stamped envelope to: *FLAKE: The Breakfast Nostalgia Magazine*, P.O. Box 481-Dept. CA, Cambridge, MA 02140.

Bibliography

Sources are listed by chapter in order of appearance.

Introduction
Interviews/Personal Correspondence
Bob Bregenzer, Information Resources, Inc.; Kathleen Brooks, Competetive Media Reporting.

Articles
Austin American Statesman, April 20, 1994.

"Grain Mill Products," *1987 Census of Manufactures,* U.S. Dept. of Commerce, Issued April 1990.

Samuelson, Robert J. "The Great Cereal Wars," *Newsweek,* September 7, 1987.

Sellers, Patricia. "How King Kellogg Beat the Blahs," *Fortune,* August 29, 1988.

Books
Coyle, L. Patrick. *The World Encyclopedia of Food.* New York: Facts on File, 1982.

Crissey, Forrest. *The Story of Foods.* New York: Rand McNally, 1917.

Chapter 1. Manifest Stomachache
Articles
"No-Sex Cereals." *Detroit Free Press,* November 29, 1981.

Books
Armstrong, David, and Elizabeth Metzger Armstrong. *The Great American Medicine Show: Being an Illustrated History of Hucksters, Healers, Health Evangelists and Heroes from Plymouth Rock to the Present.* New York: Prentice Hall, 1991.

Carson, Gerald. *Cornflake Crusade.* New York: Rinehart & Company, 1957.

Deutsch, Ronald M. *The New Nuts Among the Berries.* Palo Alto, California: Bull Publishing, 1977.

Green, Harvey. *Fit for America: Health, Fitness and Sport in American Society.* New York: Pantheon Books, 1986.

Makanowitsky, Barbara Norman. *Tales of the Table: A History of Western Cuisine.* Engelwood Cliffs, New Jersey: Prentice-Hall, 1972.

Money, John. *The Destroying Angel: Sex, Fitness & Food in the Legacy of Degeneration Theory, Graham Crackers, Kellogg's Corn Flakes & American Health History.* Buffalo, New York: Prometheus Books, 1985.

Root, Waverly, and Richard de Rochemont. *Eating in America: A History.* New York: William Morrow, 1976.

Thornton, Harrison John. *The History of the Quaker Oats Company.* Chicago: University of Chicago Press, 1933.

Zacks, Richard. *History Laid Bare: Love, Sex and Perversity from the Ancient Etruscans to Warren G. Harding.* New York: HarperCollins, 1994.

Chapter 2. Apocalypse Chow

Interviews/Personal Correspondance

Richard W. Schwarz; Garth "Duff" Stoltz; Eugene McKay Jr.; and Bert Halloviak, archivist of the General Conference of the Seventh Day Adventist Church.

Articles

"Battle Creek Home of Health Cranks and Coffee Substitutes says Julian Street in Collier's." *Battle Creek Daily,* July 14, 1914.

Carson, Gerald H. "Early Days in the Breakfast Food Industry: Part 1." *Advertising & Selling,* issue unknown, 1950s.

Carson, Gerald H. "Early Days in the Breakfast Food Industry: Part 2." *Advertising & Selling,* issue unknown, 1950s.

Carson, Gerald H. "Salesmanship: How It Built Breakfast Food Industry and Our City." *Sales Management,* April 1, 1955.

"No-Sex Cereals." op. cit.

Books

Armstrong, David. op. cit.

Carson, Gerald. op. cit.

Deutsch, Ronald M. op. cit.

Green, Harvey. op. cit.

Lowe, Bernice Bryant. *Tales of Battle Creek.* The Albert L. and Louise B. Miller Foundation, 1976.

Major, Nettie Leitch. *C. W. Post: The Hour and the Man.* Washington, D.C.: Judd & Detweiler, 1963.

Massie, Larry B., and Peter J. Schmitt. *Battle Creek: The Place Behind the Products, An Illustrated History.* Woodland Hills, California: Windsor, 1984.

Money, John. op. cit.

Powell, Horace B. *The Original Has This Signature—W. K. Kellogg.* Englewood Cliffs, New Jersey: Prentice-Hall, 1956.

Schwarz, Richard W. *John Harvey Kellogg, M.D.* Nashville: Southern Publishing Association, 1970.

Root, Waverly. op. cit.

Zacks, Richard. op. cit.

Chapter 3. The Original Grape-Nut

Interviews/Personal Correspondence

Fred Hanke, John Swartout, Willard Culver, Post Battle Creek Plant Manager, Richard W. Schwarz, Dick Basso, Virginia and Ralph Moody, James McQuiston, Cliff Robertson, and Bert Halloviak.

Articles

Carson, Gerald H., "Part 1." op. cit.

Carson, Gerald H. "Part 2." op. cit.

Carson, Gerald. "Salesmanship" op. cit.

"The Grape-Nuts Story." *The Post Box,* May, 1955.

"Post's Influence Still Felt After 75 Years of Growth." *The Post Box,* January, 1970.

"Light, Camera, Action—Take One!." *The Post Box,* January, 1970.

Books

Carson, Gerald. op. cit.

Eaves, Charles Dudley, and C. A. Hutchinson. *Post City, Texas: C. W. Post's Colonizing Activities in West Texas.* Austin: Texas State Historical Society, 1952.

Lippen, John K. *Recollections of Early History of the Cereal Industry in Battle Creek,* unpublished manuscript. Battle Creek, Michigan, 1947.

Lowe, Bernice Bryant. op. cit.

Major, Nettie Leitch. op. cit.

Massie, Larry B. and Peter J. Schmitt. op. cit.

Wright, William. *Heiress: The Rich Life of Marjorie Merriweather Post.* Washington, D.C.: New Republic Books, 1978.

Chapter 4. Great Cereal Rush

Interviews/Personal Correspondence

Richard W. Schwarz, Dick Basso, Virginia and Ralph Moody, Max Bryer, James McQuiston, Mary Jane Edney, Clarence Joyce Jr., and Catherine Youngman.

Internal Reports and Memos

Miscellaneous 1- to 2-page company histories and press releases from the Uncle Sam Breakfast Food Company, 1908 to present.

U.S. Patent Office Application for Uncle Sam Breakfood Food, February 28, 1908.

Articles

"Food Boom Has 50th Anniversary." *Battle Creek Enquirer.* January 1, 1951.

Froman, Robert. "The Cereal Story." *Collier's,* April 12, 1952.

Carson, Gerald H. "Part 1." op. cit.

Carson, Gerald H. "Part 2." op. cit.

Carson, Gerald H. "Salesmanship." op. cit.

"Early Competition Came and Went." *Kellogg News,* April, 1956.

"Millions Love 'Em." *Kellogg News,* June, 1957.

Elsner, David. "A Small Cereal-Maker Has a Tough Struggle in a Big Guys' World." *Wall Street Journal,* April 26, 1977.

South, Amy. "Arrival of 20th Century Brought Industrial Boom to Battle Creek." Battle Creek Enquirer. June 2, 1977.

"U.S. Mills Uses Off-Shelf Displays in Marketing Bran, Cereal." *Midlands Business Journal,* September 16, 1977.

South, Amy. "Cereal Is What Put the Wolverines on Top—So the Ad Said." *Battle Creek Enquirer,* November 20, 1977.

Frisbie, Al. "Omaha's U.S. Mills Bucks Giants." *Omaha World-Herald,* June, 1985.

Quinn, James. "U.S. Mills' New Owner Will Expand Omaha Operation." *Midlands Business Journal,* May 16, 1986.

"100 Years of Bland Breakfast." (Middletown, New York) *Times Herald-Record,* May 31, 1992.

Books

Armstrong, David. op. cit.

Cahn, William. *Out of the Cracker Barrel: The Nabisco Story from Animal Crackers to Zuzus.* New York: Simon & Schuster, 1969.

Carson, Gerald. op. cit.

Fox, Stephen. *The Mirror Makers: A History of American Advertising and Its Creators.* New York: William Morrow, 1984.

Green, Harvey. op. cit.

Lippen, John K. op. cit.

Lowe, Bernice Bryant. op. cit.

Massie, Larry B. op. cit.

Nelson, Neal N. *Battle Creek Plant History,* Ralston Purina Company. Unpublished manuscript: Battle Creek, Michigan, 1966.

Strasser, Susan. *Satisfaction Guaranteed: The Making of the American Market.* New York: Pantheon Books, 1989.

Chapter 5. Battle Creek Babylon

Interviews/Personal Correspondence
James McQuiston, Dick Basso, Virginia and Ralph Moody, Richard Schwarz, Muriel Watkins, Willard Culver, Eugene McKay Jr., Fred Hanke, Elmer Klett, Bill Becke, and Frances Thornton.

Articles
"Competition." *Kellogg's Square Dealer.* January, 1913.

"W. K. Kellogg, Cereal Company Founder, Dies." *Advertising Age,* October 15, 1951.

"W. K. Kellogg: April 7, 1860–October 6, 1951" *Kellogg News,* November, 1951.

Carson, Gerald H. "Part 1." op. cit.

Carson, Gerald H. "Part 2." op. cit.

Carson, Gerald H."Salesmanship." op. cit.

"Cereal Story (Pioneers of Industry Series)." *News Front,* May, 1961.

Eastman, Roy O. "The W. K. Kellogg Story: How To Be Successful Although Self-Effacing." *Advertising Age,* March 6, 1967.

Books
Carson, Gerald. op. cit.

Lippen, John K. op. cit.

Lowe, Bernice Bryant. op. cit.

Nelson, Neal N. op. cit.

Massie, Larry B. and Peter J. Schmitt. op. cit.

Powell, Horace B. op. cit.

Schwarz, Richard W. op. cit.

W. K. Kellogg Foundation. *I'll Invest My Money in People.* Battle Creek: W. K. Kellogg Foundation, 1990.

Chapter 6. Some Like It Hot and Mushy

Interviews/Personal Correspondence

David Bull, Webster Bull, Sheldon Holzer, Charles Claggett, Ron Goulart, Max Lamont, Bud Arnold, Elmer Richards, and Keith Schopp.

Articles

"Cream of Wheat's Cream." *Fortune,* January, 1939.

Carson, Gerald H. "Part 1." op. cit.

Carson, Gerald H. "Part 2." op. cit.

"The Personal Reminiscences of Albert Lasker." *American Heritage,* December, 1954.

Sanchez, Jesus. "Quaker Man's Identity Often Mistaken." *Los Angeles Times,* October 14, 1987.

"Popeye Ads Protested by Quakers." *Battle Creek Enquirer,* April 24, 1990.

Books

Danforth, William H. *I Dare You!* St. Louis, Missouri: William H. Danforth, 1940.

Grayson, Melvin. *42 Million a Day: The Story of Nabisco Brands.* East Hanover, New Jersey: Nabisco Brands, 1986.

Green, Harvey. op. cit.

Gunther, John. *Taken at the Flood: The Story of Albert D. Lasker.* New York: Harper, 1960.

Marquette, Arthur F. *Brands, Trademarks and Good Will: The Story of the Quaker Oats Company.* New York: McGraw-Hill, 1967.

Nelson, Neal N. op. cit.

Slappey, Sterling, editor. *Pioneers of American Business.* New York: Grosset and Dunlap, 1970.

Stivers, David. *The Nabisco Brands Collection of Cream of Wheat Advertising Art.* San Diego: Nabisco Brands, 1986.

Thornton, Harrison John. op. cit.

Chapter 7. Spoon in Tomorrow

Interviews/Personal Correspondence
Jim Fish, Robert Stafford, Charles Claggett, Evie Wilson, Tom Tumbusch, Elmer Klett, M. G. Norris, Gage Davis Jr., John Long, David R. Smith and David Bull.

Articles
"Cream of Wheat's Cream." op. cit.

Reddy, John and Tom Carlile. "Breakfast in Hollywood." *Life,* February 11, 1946.

"A Return of Half a Million Orders Isn't Even Colossal." *Life,* March 14, 1949.

"Ralston Ties on a Bigger Feedbag." *Business Week,* December 3, 1966.

King, Fred. "Jack Armstrong: All-American Boy with Many Premiums." *Collectibles Monthly,* November, 1977.

Tumbusch, Tom. "Long Before the Digital Pedometer." *Rarities: The Magazine of Collectibles,* Winter, 1980.

Wulf, Steve. "Famous Flakes of America," *Sports Illustrated,* April 5, 1982.

Shaw, Russell. "For a Boxtop and a Dime." *Sky: Delta Air Lines Magazine,* October, 1984.

King, Fred. "Jack Armstrong: The All-American Boy, Part Two," *Box-Top Bonanza,* September, 1989.

Robinson, Melbourne with Mario DeMarco. "Buck Jones," *Box-Top Bonanza,* November, 1989.

Norris, M. G. "History of Tom Mix Radio Program," *Box-Top Bonanza,* June, 1990.

"Bobby Benson," *Box-Top Bonanza,* October, 1990.

McWhorter, George. "Tarzan Over Radio," *Box-Top Bonanza,* Number 45, 1991.

Gibson, Richard. "Puffed-Cereal Eaters' High Hopes of Yelling Mush! Are Groundless," *Wall Street Journal,* December 13, 1991.

Books
Crissey, Forrest. op. cit.

Gray, James. *Business Without Boundaries: The Story of General Mills.* Minneapolis: University of Minnesota Press, 1954.

Green, Harvey. op. cit.

Fox, Stephen. op. cit.

Lewis, Agnes L. From Crystal Sets to Television. Unpublished History of General Mills, 1940. General Mills Archive.

Nelson, Neal N. op. cit.

Marquette, Arthur F. op. cit.

Maltin, Leonard. *Of Mice and Magic.* New York: Plume Books, 1980.

Dorfman, Ariel. *The Empire's Old Clothes: What the Lone Ranger, Babar, and Other Innocent Heroes Do to Our Minds.* New York: Pantheon Books, 1983.

Carothers, Martha and Belena Chapp. *A Surprise Inside: The Work and Wizardry of John Walworth.* Wilmington: University of Delaware Press, 1990.

Tumbusch, Tom. *Tomart's Price Guide to Radio Premium and Cereal Box Collectibles.* Radnor, Pennsylvania: Wallace-Homestead, 1991.

Chapter 8. Building a Better Mouth Trap

Interviews/Personal Correspondence

Elmer Klett, Jim Fish, Robert Stafford, Evie Wilson, Allan Miller, Mrs. Vernon Grant, Tom Tumbusch, John "Wally" Walworth, Gordon Gold, Charles Claggett, Ross Wetzel, Manny Winston, David R. Smith, Eugene McKay Jr., and James McQuiston.

Articles

Walker, W. H. "Give the Package a Chance." *Modern Packaging,* September, 1936.

Grant vs. Kellogg Co., 58 Federal Supplement (District Court of the Southern District 1944).

"Design Laboratory Visualizes the Package at Work." *Modern Packaging,* April, 1946.

"Quaker Oats Modernizes a 69-Year-Old Character." *Modern Packaging,* month unknown, 1946.

"About Face: General Foods Introduces the 'Change-over' Package for Post Cereal Family." *Modern Packaging,* September, 1946.

"Premiums: Leading Companies Are Returning to These Time-Tested Stimulants." *Modern Packaging,* April, 1947.

Wharton, Don. "Cereal Story: Condensed from the Minneapolis Sunday Tribune." *Reader's Digest,* February, 1948.

"A Return of Half a Million Orders Isn't Even Colossal." op. cit.

Froman, Robert. op. cit.

Carson, Gerald H. "Part 1." op. cit.

Carson, Gerald H. "Part 2." op. cit.

"Gold Speculators Flock to Quaker's Yukon Land Offer." *Advertising Age,* February 21, 1955.

"Krumbles: 45 Years of Acceptance." *Kellogg News,* May, 1957.

"Health Food Edges Into Big-Time Market." *Business Week,* June 8, 1957.

"Kellogg's Rice Krispies." *Kellogg News,* April, 1963.

Eastman, Roy O. op. cit.

Kueker, Clint. "Hi-Yo Silver! The Lone Ranger." *Rarities: The Magazine of Collectibles,* Winter, 1980.

Shaw, Russell. op. cit..

Smith, Eugene. "The Amazing Kix Atomic Bomb Ring," *Box-Top Bonanza,* March, 1989.

McLain, Kay. "Gold's Gadgets Lived Up to Name." *Cue Magazine,* July 27, 1989.

Baxter, Jeanna. "Gold's Finger on Child's Toy Pulse Beat." *Durham [NC] Morning Herald,* July, 1987.

Patterson, Donald. "Family Put Toy Surprizes Inside." *Greensboro [NC] News and Record,* July 20, 1989.

Futch, Michael. "Mommy, I Want That!" *Fayetteville [AR] Observer/Times,* July 22, 1989.

Elliot, Stuart. "Rice Krispies' Ad Has Vintage Snap," *USA Today,* date unknown, 1989.

Miller, Allan M. "Vernon Grant Biographical Outline," unpublished, April, 1991.
Gibson, Richard. op. cit.

Books
Gray, James. op. cit.

Happy Birthday Kix: From the General Mills' Archives. Minneapolis: General Mills publication, 1978.

Holliss, Richard and Brian Sibley. *The Disney Studio Story.* New York: Crown, 1988.

Lewis, Agnes L. op. cit.

Nelson, Neal N. op. cit.

Marquette, Arthur F. op. cit.

Mosley, Leonard. *Disney's World.* New York: Stein and Day, 1985.

Davis, Gage. *The Life and Perils of One Ronald Gage Davis.* Unpublished memoir, Denver, Colorado. 1989. Collection of Gage Davis Jr.

McCay, Eugene Jr. *Eugene Henry McKay.* Unpublished memoir. Collection of Eugene McKay Jr.

Carothers, Martha and Belena Chapp. op. cit.

Tumbusch, Tom. op. cit.

Vernon Grant Advisory Committee, Rockhill, SC, *Life of Vernon Grant,* unpublished manuscript, 1992. Collection of Allan Miller.

Chapter 9. Dynamite in a Dish
Interviews/Personal Correspondence
Frank Staley, Elmer Klett, Fred Hanke, Guy Madison, Bill Betts, Bob Traverse, Willard Culver, Oella Vosberg, Art Linkletter, Murial Watkins, Eugene McKay Jr., James McQuiston, Mrs. Moses Berger, Eliott Berger, Craig Carragan, Stan Reesman, Kent Mitchell, Al Clausi, Jack Keil, Jim Fish, Rocky Flynn, John E. Matthews, and Bob Schaeberle.

Articles
"Corn Pops—The Pride of Omaha." *Kellogg News,* November, 1950.

"Bunky Stark like Tony the Tiger and Sugar Frosted Flakes." *Kellogg News,* September, 1952.

"Introducing Sugar Frosted Flakes." *Kellogg News,* September, 1952.

"General Manager's Page: New Product." *The Post Box,* March, 1953.

"General Manager's Page: New Competition." *The Post Box,* April, 1953.

"Sugar Smacks: Better Than Puffs of Wheat." *Kellogg News,* August, 1953.

"General Manager's Page: Product Imitation." *The Post Box,* September, 1953.

"Nabisco Purchases Ranger Joe Cereal Company." *Nabisco Magazine,* January/February, 1954.

"Why We've Bought Four Companies." *Nabisco Magazine,* March/April, 1954.

"Sugar Smacks: Omaha Plant Scores Again with These New, Delicious, Sugar-Toasted Puffs of Wheat." *Kellogg News,* April, 1954.

"A Kid's Dream Comes True . . . " *Nabisco Magazine,* January/February, 1955.

"New High-Protein Cereal." *Kellogg News,* May, 1955.

"Post's Newest Product." *The Post Box,* January, 1957.

"Popular Bran Flakes Cereals." *Kellogg News,* June, 1957.

"The New Products Committee." *The Post Box,* July/August, 1957.

"Sugar . . . As You Like It." *Kellogg News,* April, 1958.

"50 Years of Goodness." *The Post Box,* June, 1958.

"Omaha Plant: 15 Years of Progress." *Kellogg News,* September, 1958.

"Battle Creek—Cereal Capital of the World." *Inside Battle Creek,* Brochure #6, published by the Battle Creek Public Schools, 1958.

"Post and C & C Team Up on Our Newest Product." *The Post Box,* March, 1959.

"Kellogg's Cocoa Flavored Krispies." *Kellogg News,* June, 1959.

"Kellogg's OKs." *Kellogg News,* October, 1959.

"Kellogg's Concentrate: New Cereal Most Delicious." *Kellogg News,* October, 1959.

"The Best to You from Kellogg's." *Hello!* (A Leo Burnett Agency Publication), April/May, 1966.

Zalaznick, Sheldon. "The Fight for a Place at the Breakfast Table." *Fortune,* December, 1967.

Chapter 10. Leo the Lion

Interviews/Personal Correspondence

Jack Larson, Kensinger Jones, Phyllis Coates, Don Tennant, Carl Hixon, Orrin Bowers, Elmer Klett, Hal Weinstein, Bill Stratton, John E. Matthews, Don Keller, Dick Esmail, Guy Madison, Gordon Minter, Chet Glassley, Frank Thomas, Art Linkletter, Jim Gillmore, John Long, Bob Noel, Frank Martello, Rudy Behlmer, Bob Mayberry, Russ Mayberry, Joel Hochberg, Emrich Nicholson, Hooper White, Nancy Mengel, Dick Marx, Harry Smedley, Rudy Perz, Max Bryer, Bill Hanna, and Joe Barbera.

Articles

"Kellogg to Sponsor Television Show." *Kellogg News,* March, 1949.

"Kellogg's New TV Feature Is Unique." *Kellogg News,* September, 1951.

"1952 Bicycle Safety Parade Biggest Yet." *Kellogg News,* July, 1952.

"They Breakfasted with the Stars." *Kellogg News,* July, 1952.

"Wild Bill and Corn Pops." *Kellogg News,* month unknown, 1951.

"Guy Madison and Andy Devine Make Big Hit at Home Plant." *Kellogg News,* September, 1952.

"Superman: Kellogg's Newest TV Show Brings Famous Character in Living Rooms." *Kellogg News,* January, 1953.

"TV Stars in Kellogg's 1953 Advertising Program." *Kellogg News,* March, 1953.

"1953 Bicycle Parade." *Kellogg News,* June/July, 1953.

"Godfrey's With Us!" *Kellogg News,* November, 1953.

"Superman in Memphis." *Kellogg News,* August, 1955.

"Leo Burnett Tells 'What I Have Learned' About Writing Ads and the Advertising Business." *Advertising Age,* November 7, 1955.

"Kellogg to Sponsor Big New TV Show." *Kellogg News,* September, 1957.

"Battle Creek—Cereal Capital of the World." op. cit.

"Looking Back: Film Star Tim McCoy Dies in Hospital at 87." *The Big Reel,* September, 1992.

Books

Grossman, Gary. *Saturday Morning TV.* New York: Dell Publishing, 1981.

Fischer, Stuart. *Kids' TV: The First 25 Years.* New York: Facts on File Publications, 1983.

Fox, Stephen. op. cit.

Hall, Jim. *Mighty Minutes: An Illustrated History of Television's Best Commercials.* New York: Harmony Books, 1984.

McNeil, Alex. *Total Television.* New York: Penquin Books, 1984.

Brooks, Tim and Earle Marsh. *The Complete Directory to Prime Time Network TV Shows.* New York: Ballantine Books, 1985.

Marschall, Rick. *The History of Television.* New York: Gallery Books, 1986.

Davis, Stephen. *Say Kids! What Times Is It?: Notes from the Peanut Gallery.* Boston: Little, Brown, 1987.

Tumbusch, Tom. op. cit.

Chapter 11. Galloping Goodness

Interviews/Personal Correspondence

Tony Dow, Max Bryer, Rudy Behlmer, Elmer Klett, Clayton Moore, Hugh O'Brian, Frankie Thomas, Dale Ames, Jack Larson, Guy Madison, Art Rush, Dusty Rogers, Jack Narz, Jim Fish, Robert Stafford, Andy Andersen, Don Phelps, Gordon Minter, Evie Wilson, Bill Betts, Ed Inglis, and Frank Martello.

Articles

"Ranger Joe." *Variety,* December 6, 1950.

"Unmelancholy Dane 'Produces' Corn Flakes." *Kellogg News,* February, 1951.

"General Manager's Page: Wide Coverage." *The Post Box,* January, 1954.

"The Story of Our Prize Winning Float." *The Post Box,* February, 1955.

"Boy Oh Boy! They're Giving Away a Space Ship to Sell Ralston Cereal." *Advertising Age,* October 5, 1953.

"General Manager's Page: Rogers Renewed." *The Post Box,* month unknown, 1955.

"Trick Promotion Gets Fine Send-Off." *The Post Box,* December, 1955.

"Post Wins Again!" *The Post Box,* February, 1956.

"Fury Makes Appearance at P.P.C." *The Post Box,* September, 1956.

"Battle Creek—Cereal Capital of the World." op. cit.

"'The Best to You' from Kellogg's." op. cit.

Moshcovitz, Philip. "Remembering Captain Midnight," *Box-Top Bonanza,* September, 1988.

Rothel, David. "George 'Gabby' Hayes," *Box-Top Bonanza,* November, 1988.

Rothel, David. "Gabby on TV," *Box-Top Bonanza,* November, 1988.

Andersen, Andy. "Greatest 1st Prize Ever Offered!" *Box-Top Bonanza,* January, 1989.

Books

Marquette, Arthur F. op. cit.

Grossman, Gary. op. cit.

Fischer, Stuart. op. cit.

Hall, Jim. op. cit.

McNeil, Alex. op. cit.

Brooks, Tim and Earle Marsh. op. cit.

Carothers, Martha and Belena Chapp. op. cit.

Tumbusch, Tom. op. cit.

Chapter 12. The Carton Club

Interviews/Personal Correspondence
Bob Traverse, John "Wally" Walworth, Dick Weiner, Elmer Klett, Bill Betts, Howard Slutz, Harold Paul, John Long, Stan Austin, Frank Staley, Dick Esmail, Kent Mitchell, Al Clausi, Stan Reesman, Dick Basso, Don Brown, Greg Bunger, Tom Irwin, Everett Shipley, John DiGianni Sr., John DiGianni Jr., Pete Eaton, Fred Iwen, Joseph Graziano, Tom Gentile, John Faulkner, Mike Hagel, Ted Carr, Barry Birnbaum, Brent Carpenter, Larry Hubbell, Ken Jones, James McQuiston, and Ross Wetzel.

Internal Leo Burnett Memos and Reports
Thirteen-page Color TV memo from DeWitt O'Kieffe to Ken Jones, May 11, 1954. Includes extensive exerpts from *Television Magazine* and a condensation of Grey Advertising Agency's article on color TV in inhouse organ, *Grey Matter.*

"Report on TV Workshop Meeting: Drake Hotel—October 15, 1954." Memo from Ken Jones to Plans Supervisory Committee, October 25, 1954.

"Report of NBC Color Clinic, February 18, 1955, NBC Studios in Burbank, California," memo from Norm Jonsson to Ken Jones, March 4, 1955.

Articles
"For Our Visitors." *Kellogg News,* June, 1951.

"The Greatest Packages . . . For the Greatest Name in Cereals." *Kellogg News,* March, 1952.

"New Concept: Every Box a Display." *Business Week,* April 12, 1952.

"General Manager's Page: Package Size Changed." *The Post Box,* August, 1953.

"Send Two Box Tops." *Kellogg News,* May, 1954.

"A New Look: Post Packages Are Brighter and Better!" *The Post Box,* month unknown 1955.

"Baseball Promotion Sells Sugar Crisp." *The Post Box,* June, 1955.

"Eye Catchers!" *The Post Box,* June, 1955.

"Salesmanship Parade: Pony Ride Promotion Scores." *The Post Box,* August, 1955.

"TV Program Tells Kids About Post's [sic]." *The Post Box,* August, 1955.

"Wheaties Gets New Face in 4 Delicious Colors." *Advertising Age,* August 1, 1955.

"Car Promotion Sales GN Flakes." *The Post Box,* November, 1955.

"Trick Promotion Gets Fine Send-Off." op. cit.

"Good Shelf Position Means More Sales." *The Post Box,* January, 1956.

"Store Merchandising: Then and Now." *Kellogg News,* April, 1956.

"Unique P.P.C. Held at City Zoo." *The Post Box,* August, 1956.

"Down in Texas They Still Do Things BIG." *The Post Box,* November, 1956.

"Our New Look in Packaging." *The Post Box,* May, 1957.

"Kellogg's New Package Design." *Kellogg News,* January, 1958.

"Battle Creek—Cereal Capital of the World." op. cit.

"Millions of Cartons and Cases." *Kellogg News,* April, 1960.

Margulies, Walter. "Uneasy Marriage of Color TV and Packages." *Advertising Age,* March 6, 1967.

Elsner, David. op. cit.

"U.S. Mills Uses Off-Shelf Displays in Marketing Bran, Cereal." op. cit.

Frisbie, Al. "Omaha's U.S. Mills Bucks Giants." op. cit.

Talorico, Patricia. "John C. Walworth, Jr., Casper, Popeye Animator." (Wilmington, Delaware) *News Journal,* January 1, 1992.

Books
Grossman, Gary. op. cit.

Fischer, Stuart. op. cit.

Fox, Stephen. op. cit.

Brooks, Tim and Earle Marsh. op. cit.

Hall, Jim. op. cit.

Marschall, Rick. op. cit.

Packard, Vance. *The Hidden Persuaders.* New York: David McKay Company, 1957.
Pulos, Arthur J. *The American Design Adventure.* Cambridge: MIT Press, 1990.

Tumbusch, Tom. op. cit.

Chapter 13. Disney Diaspora
Interviews/Personal Correspondence

Gus Jekel, Bill Hurtz, Don Tennant, John E. Matthews, Dick Weiner, Jack Zander, John Long, Dan Hunn, Ray Favata, Frank Martello, George Bakes, Bob Traverse, Bill Betts, Gene Schinto, Joe Bacal, Ed Graham, Ken Walker, Hank Ketcham, Ken Jones, Adrian Tytla, Leo Stuckhus, Gene Cleaves, Bill Tollis, Tony Jaffe, Jack Keil, Bill Melendez, Mike Lah, Eli Feldman, Chris Ishii, Allen Swift, Jerry Beck, Ross Wetzel, Ted Carr, David R. Smith, Stan Austin, Faith Hubley, Thurl Ravenscroft, Dick Esmail, Gordon Minter, David Smith, Don Keller, Bill Hanna, Joe Barbera, Rudy Perz, and Orrin Bowers.

Internal Memos and Reports
"RE: Tony the Tiger." Memo from T. J. Lux of Kellogg Company to D. E. Fleming of Kellogg Company, July 15, 1965.

Articles
Woolf, James D. "What Sells Groceries is Eating Pleasure." *Advertising Age,* March 18,

"The Maypo Marketing Miracle." *Sponsor,* December 14, 1957.

"'The Best to You' from Kellogg's." op. cit.

"Corn Crackos Cereal Makes Its Debut." *The Post Box,* September/October, 1967.

"Tony the Tiger Credit Incorrectly Assigned." *Ad Age,* January 1, 1976.

"Say, Aren't You Tony the Tiger?" *Kellogg News,* December, 1981.

Books
Fox, Stephen. op. cit.

Price, Jonathon. *The Best Thing on TV: Commercials.* New York: Penguin Books, 1978.

Maltin, Leonard. op. cit.

Gould, Stephen Jay. *The Panda's Thumb* (article entitled "A Biological Homage to Mickey Mouse"), New York: W.W. Norton and Company, 1980.

Hall, Jim. op. cit.

Schickel, Richard. op. cit.

Brooks, Tim and Marsh, Earle. op. cit.

Korkis, Jim and John Cawley. *Cartoon Confidential.* Westlake Village, California: Malibu Graphics, 1991.

Chapter 14. From Hillbillies to Bubblegum

Interviews/Personal Correspondence
Bob Richards, Max Baer Jr., Bill Betts, Jim Nabors, Bob Traverse, Bobby Sherman, Ward Sylvester, Hal Weinstein, Max Bryer, Jim Fish, Robert Stafford, Ray Walston, Shirley Jones, John E. Matthews, Joel Hochberg, Bill Stratton, Bob Noel, Lou Miano, Ed Hannibal, Rudy Belhmer, Sheldon Leonard, Marjorie Lord, Roy Eaton, Peter Israelson, Joe Bacal, Gene Schinto, Stephen Cox, Stephen J. Govoni, Orrin Bowers, Dick Marx, Don Keller, Donna Douglas, Russ Mayberry, Bob Mayberry, Evie Wilson, Jack Keil, Gene Cleaves, and Chet Glassley.

Internal Reports and Memos
Letter from Kellogg advertising director Howard List to Burnett's John E. Matthews on danger posed by Big G's Country Corn Flakes, April 5, 1962.

Matthews, John. 'Smother and Assume: A Strategy for Radio Advertising.' Text of speech delivered to Kellogg management at the Waldorf Astoria Hotel, New York, April, 1965.

Kellogg's Corporate and Brand Images Described, Interpreted and Compared with Leading Competition. Princeton: Opinion Research Corp., April, 1961.

Articles

"Here's Why Frank Sinatra Is the Tarzan of the Boudoir!," *Confidential,* month unknown, 1956.

"Kellogg Nears Decision on $6-7,000,000 Spot TV Buy." *Advertising Age,* June 23, 1958.

"Fall Forecast for TV: Very Bright." *Kellogg News,* August, 1958
"This Fall . . . the Biggest TV Line-up in Kellogg's History." *Kellogg News,* October, 1960.

"Three Television Favorites Will Sell Post Products." *The Post Box,* September, 1963.

"Food is a Bargain." *Kellogg News,* October, 1963.

"Homer and Jethro are Back Again for Kellogg's." *Kellogg News,* April, 1964.

"Four Television Programs Advertising Post Products." *The Post Box,* August, 1964.

Zalaznick, Sheldon. op. cit.

"Post Cereals Rock with Archie's Gang." *The Post Box,* September, 1969.

"'Archies' Make Morning Mealtime More Musical." *The Post Box,* April, 1970.

"Chimp Spins Hits for Post." *The Post Box,* January, 1971.

"Singing Bears." *The Post Box,* December, 1971.

Kantor, Seth. "From Golden Glory: Olympian, Presidential Candidate Ordered to Pay Fines." *Austin American-Statesman.* August 10, 1989.

Owens, Tom. "And They Stay Crispy in Milk." *Legends Sports Memorabilia,* July/August and September/October, 1993.

Miano, Lou. "Doin' the Flake." Unpublished article that includes interview with Gary Lewis. 1992.

Books

Lewis, Agnes L. op. cit.

Grossman, Gary. op. cit.

Fischer, Stuart. op. cit.

Hall, Jim. op. cit.

McNeil, Alex. op. cit.

Beck, Ken and Jim Clark. *The* Andy Griffith Show *Book.* New York: St. Martin's, 1985.

Brooks, Tim and Earle Marsh. op. cit.

Cox, Stephen. *The Beverly Hillbillies: From the Small Screen to the Big Screen.* New York: Harper Perennial, 1993.

Adler, David. *The Life and Cuisine of Elvis Presley.* New York: Crown Trade Paperbacks, 1993.

Chapter 15. Yogi and the Fun Hogs
Interviews/Personal Correspondence

Joe Barbara, Bill Hanna, Joe Bacal, Gene Schinto, Bill Stratton, Don Keller, Carl Hixon, Muriel Watkins, Howard List, Don Brown, Frank Staley, Elmer Klett, Willard Culver, Oella Vosberg, James McQuiston, Bill Becke, Jim Gillmore, Gordon Minter, Don Tennant, Bob Noel, Orrin Bowers, Rudy Perz, Dick Esmail, Frank Martello, John Long, Jerry Beck, John E. Matthews, Joel Hochberg, Curt Jones, Pete Eaton, Fred Iwen, Tom Gentile, John Faulkner, Ted Carr, Barry Birnbaum, Brent Carpenter, Ross Wetzel, Hank Ketcham, Laraine Day, Max Baer Jr., Bob Keeshan, Jack Keil, Tony Jaffe, Mark Wilson, Thurl Ravenscroft, Carl Hixon, Dick Marx, Ross Wetzel, Larry Storch, Gus Jekel, Ed Justin, and Rudy Behlmer.

Internal Memos, Reports, and Correspondence

Lyle Roll application letter to International Playboy Club in Chicago from John E. Matthews, March 2, 1961.

"RE: Kellogg Packages." Memo from Burnett's Lyman White to Burnett's Roy Lang, March 9, 1962.

"RE: Huckleberry Finn Back Panel." Memo from Kellogg Company's A. K. Eddy to Burnett's Roy Lang, March 10, 1965.

"RE: Aunt Sally-cont." memo from Burnett's A. K. Eddy to Burnett's Roy Lang, March 16, 1965.

Articles

"New Cartoon Show in Post's TV Line-up." *The Post Box*, February, 1958.

"Those Lovable TV Characters." *Kellogg News*, October, 1959.

"This Fall . . . the Biggest TV Line-up in Kellogg's History." op. cit.

"Sugar Toasted Oat Cereal—Kellogg's Newest" *Kellogg News*, October, 1960.

"Hey! Hey! Take It From Me, Here's the Best to You on Fall TV!" *Kellogg News*, October, 1961.

"New! Kellogg's Froot Flavored Loops." *Kellogg News*, October, 1963.

Kelly, Patrick J. "(Cereal) Keynote: Something for Everyone." *Printers' Ink*, August 14, 1964.

Maxwell, John C., Jr. "Cereals: Snap, Crackle, Boom." *Printers' Ink*, August 14, 1964.

"200,000 Visitors Take a Trip Through Kellogg's." *Kellogg News*, January, 1965.

"Kellogg's Headache: Finn's Aunt Sally Proves Fictitious." *St. Louis Globe Democrat*, March, 1965.

"New Sugar Stars Have a Caramel Coat." *Kellogg News*, Spring, 1965.

"Whose Sally? Huckleberry Finn." *Kellogg News*, October, 1965.

"Kellogg's Triple Snack New Snack Idea!" *Kellogg News,* month unknown, 1965.

Wortman, Victor. "Cereals: Competition Stiffens As Sales Continue To Rise." *Consuming Advertising,* June, 1965.

Nelson, Robin C. "Cereals Snap, Crackle and Sometimes Lay Bombs." *Printers' Ink,* June 24, 1966.

Hirsch, Arnold S. "From Battle Creek, a Sea of Cereal." *Detroit News Sunday Pictorial,* March 27, 1966.

"'The Best to You' from Kellogg's." op. cit.

Gavin, James M. "3 Man Team Steps in for Burnett." *Chicago Tribune,* June 26, 1967.

Zalaznick, Sheldon. op. cit.

Books
Norback, Peter and Craig Norback. *Great Songs of Madison Avenue.* New York: Quadrangle/The New York Times Book Company, 1976.

Maltin, Leonard. op. cit.

Grossman, Gary. op. cit.

Fischer, Stuart. op. cit.

McNeil, Alex. op. cit.

Hall, Jim. op. cit.

Brooks, Tim and Earle Marsh. op. cit.

Sennett, Ted. *The Art of Hanna-Barbera.* New York: Viking Studio Books, 1989.

Korkis, Jim and John Cawley. op. cit.

Wilson, Mark. *The Magic Land of Allakazam: The Inside Story.* Berthod, Colorado: Magical Productions International, 1992.

Chapter 16. Post Mortem
Interviews/Personal Correspondence

Bill Betts, Bob Traverse, Tom Hollingsworth, Max Lomont, Carl Hixon, Hal Weinstein, John Long, Al Clausi, Kent Mitchell, Gene Schinto, Joe Bacal, Harold Paul, Howard Slutz, Tom Irwin, Everett Shipley, Dick Basso, Greg Bunger, Cliff Robertson, Roy Eaton, Dick Bloede, Ed Graham, Peter Israelson, Max Bryer, Ed Hannibal, Leslie J. Stark, Chuck Beisch, Stan Reesman, Sheldon Leonard, Scott Shaw!, Ruth Buzzi, Tom McKimson, Chuck Jones, Chuck McKinson, Robert McKimson Jr., Friz Freleng, Frank Staley, Joe Barbera, Bill Hanna, Bob Clampett Jr., Rudy Behlmer, and Ed Justin.

Internal Reports

New Dimensions for Cereal Packages. White Plains, New York: General Foods Report, 1964.

Cereal Brand Profiles, White Plains, New York: General Foods Report, 1964.

Articles

"New Cartoon Show in Post TV Line-up." op. cit.

"Bugs Bunny Promotions Found on Cereal Packages." *The Post Box,* June, 1961.

"Cereal Line Appears in Colorful New Packages." *The Post Box,* June, 1961.

Munson, C.L. "Post Cereals Claim Home Run with 400 Million Trade cards." *Battle Creek Enquirer,* month unknown, 1961.

"Post Builds an All-Star Team." *GF News,* April/May 1961.

"TV's Newest Comedy Team to Star in Post Fall Show." *The Post Box,* September, 1961.

"Post Reverses Design Theory with New Cereal Packages." *Food Business,* September, 1961.

"Crispy Critters on Parade in Post Test Market Area," *The Post Box,* April 27, 1962.

"Attractive Premiums Offered Free in Post Cereal's New Promotion." *The Post Box,* December, 1962.

"Count Off in 'Orbit.'" *The Post Box,* January, 1963.

"Post's New Crispy Critters Roars Into National Sales Distribution." *The Post Box,* May, 1963.

"Now Packaged Together by Post—Corn Flakes and Strawberries." *The Post Box,* August, 1963.

"Three Television Favorites Will Sell Post Products." op. cit.

"Compacts Go National: Another Post First for the Consumer." *The Post Box,* February, 1964.

"A Compact Cereal Carton." *Modern Packaging,* April, 1964.

Kelly, Patrick J. op. cit.

Maxwell, John C., Jr. op. cit.

"Say Something Like Linus." *TV Guide,* month unknown, 1964.

"Two Post Cereals Make Their Debut." *The Post Box,* August, 1964.

"Post's Pink Elephants No Joke—With New Crispy Critters Offer." *The Post Box,* April, 1965.

"Yes! We Have Now Bananas." *Kellogg News,* Spring 1965.

"Post Launches Corn Flakes and Strawberries." *The Post Box,* May, 1965.

Wortman, Victor. "Cereals: Competition Stiffens As Sales Continue To Rise." *Consuming Advertising,* June, 1965.

"Post Introduces New Honeycomb" *The Post Box,* June, 1965.

"Just What is Freeze-Drying?" *The Post Box,* July/August, 1965.

Nelson, Robin C. op. cit.

Hirsch, Arnold S. op. cit.

"Corn Crackos Cereal Makes Its Debut." op. cit.

Zalaznick, Sheldon. op. cit.

"Post Cereals Offer Cash Refund in Doctor Dolittle Film Tie-in." *The Post Box,* January/February, 1968.

"Cyclamate Ban Halts Two Post Products." *The Post Box,* October, 1969.

"Yabba Dabba Doo! It's Post Pebbles." *The Post Box,* May/June, 1970.

"Three Products Bow." *The Post Box,* January, 1971.

"Post Pebbles Cereal Introduced Nationally." *The Post Box,* May, 1971.

"Pink Panther Flakes Move Coast to Coast." *The Post Box,* June, 1972.

"Not Superman, But . . . " *The Post Box,* June, 1972.

Boss, Kit. "Who Frosts Those Flakes?" *Detroit Free Press,* June 26, 1985.

Books
Maltin, Leonard. op. cit.

Grossman, Gary. op. cit.

Fischer, Stuart. op. cit.

McNeil, Alex. op. cit.

Hall, Jim. op. cit.

Brooks, Tim and Earle Marsh. op. cit.

Handelman, Michelle and Monte Cazazza. "The Cereal Box Conspiracy Against the Developing Mind," an essay in *Apocalypse Culture,* Adam Parfrey, editor. Los Angeles: Feral House, 1990.

John Pulos, Arthur J. op. cit.

Korkis, Jim and John Cawley. op. cit.

Chapter 17. Psychedelic Cereal
Interviews/Personal Correspondence
Tony Jaffe, Jack Keil, Bill Tollis, Leo Stuckhus, Gene Cleaves, Evie Wilson, Howard Courtemanche, Chuck McCann, Jack Zander, Ray Favata, Dan Hunn, Ken Walker, Chris Ishii, John Long, Jim Fish, Don Keller, Carl Hixon, Hal Weinstein, John E. Matthews, Roy Eaton, Frank Staley, Robert Stafford, Bill Hurtz, Gus Jekel, Bill Melendez, Bob Traverse, Gene Schinto, Joe Bacal, Bill Betts, Tom Hollingsworth, George Bakes, David R. Smith, Mike Lah, Charles Ulrich, Bill Hanna, and Joe Barbera.

Internal Reports
Kellogg's Corporate and Brand Images Described, Interpreted and Compared with Leading Competition. Princeton: op. cit.

Articles
Kelly, Patrick J. op. cit.

Maxwell, John C., Jr. op. cit.

Wortman, Victor. op. cit.

Nelson, Robin C. op. cit.

Hirsch, Arnold S. op. cit.

Zalaznick, Sheldon. op. cit.

"What's New With Our Competitors?" *The Post Box,* September, 1968.

"What's New With Our Competitors?" *The Post Box,* September, 1969.

"Animation: Bill Scott of Tujunga." *Cartoonist Profiles,* November, 1978.

Ulrich, Charles and Karl Cohen. "Jay Ward." *Frostbite Falls Far-Flung Flier,* 1989.

Yarrow, Andrew L. "Jay Ward, 69, the TV Cartoonist Who Created Bullwinkle, Is Dead." *New York Times,* October 14, 1989.

Ulrich, Charles. "The Jay Ward Cereal Commercials." *Frostbite Falls Far-Flung Flier,* September, 1993.

Books
Maltin, Leonard. op. cit.

Grossman, Gary. op. cit.

Fischer, Stuart. op. cit.

Hall, Jim. op. cit.

McNeil, Alex. op. cit.

Brooks, Tim and Earle Marsh. op. cit.

Javna, John. op. cit.

Korkis, Jim and John Cawley. op. cit.

Chapter 18. The Kingdom of Crunch
Interviews/Personal Correspondence

Gus Jekel, Bill Hurtz, Joe Barbera, Bill Hanna, Max Lomont, Tony Jaffe, Rand Plass, Toby Decker, Stan Austin, Ken Anthony, Harold Lamb, Joe Lipscombe, Jim Knowland, Leo Stuckhus, Bill Tollis, Al Clausi, Leon Levy, Manny Winston, Bob Dobler, Harold Gottlieb, Ken Mason, Greg Gwynn, Franz Meier, Howard Alport, Dick Jones, George Bruce, Tom Taverna, Don DeForest, Dick Jones, Fred Lewis, Jack O'Grady, Bill Pearce, Mike Barna, Dr. Marvin Rudolf, David Kendell, David F. Bull, Chuck Allen, Craig Carragan, Clarence Joyce Jr., Sheldon Holzer, Eugene McKay Jr., Bob Schaeberle, Dave Stivers, Larry Campbell, Norma Reed, Jim Fish, Jack Keil, and Charles Ulrich.

Articles

Kelly, Patrick J. op. cit.

Maxwell, John C., Jr. op. cit.

Wortman, Victor. op. cit.

"Rivals—Two New Cereals." *Advertising Age*, February 14, 1966.

Nelson, Robin C. op. cit.

Zalaznick, Sheldon. op. cit.

"What's New With Our Competitors?" *The Post Box*, April, 1969.

"What's New With Our Competitors?" *The Post Box*, April, 1970.

"Orange Crisp Still Puffed But Without the Gun." *The Post Box*, July/August, 1971.

"Animation: Bill Scott of Tujunga." op. cit.

Ulrich, Charles and Karl Cohen. op. cit.

Ulrich, Charles. op. cit.

Books
Marquette, Arthur F. op. cit.

Maltin, Leonard. op. cit.

Grossman, Gary. op. cit.

Hall, Jim. op. cit.

McNeil, Alex. op. cit.

Korkis, Jim and John Cawley. op. cit.

Chapter 19. Ultra-Trash Backlash
Interviews/Personal Correspondence
Leslie J. Stark, Rand Plass, Toby Decker, Bob Schaeberle, Craig Carragan, Fred Hanke, Jim Gillmore, Joel Hochberg, John Long, Jim Fish, Robert Stafford, Bill Tollis, Leo Stuckhus, Jack Keil, Tony Jaffe, Tom Hollingsworth, Max Lomont, Kent Mitchell, Leon Levy, Peter Israelson, Al Clausi, Bob Traverse, Max Bryer, Bob Dobler, Ed Gleim, and John "Wally" Walworth.

Articles
Rosenberg, Ronald. "Entrepreneur Hopes Matzoh Cereal Sells." *Boston Sunday Globe*, March 13, 1994.

"Subcommittee Hears Industry Rebuttal." *The Post Box*, August, 1970.

"A Package of Trouble for Cereal Makers." *Business Week*, August 1, 1970.

"The Breakfast of What?" *Newsweek*, August 3, 1970.

"Breakfast of Chumps?" *Time*, August 3, 1970.

"Clausi Urges Partnership to Deal with Nutrition." *The Post Box*, October, 1970.

"Nutrition Guide Printed on Cereal Boxes." *The Post Box*, November, 1970.

"The FTC Declares War on an Oligopoly." *Business Week*, January 29, 1972.

"Not by Cereal Alone," *Time*, August 17, 1970.

Cross, Jennifer. "Storm in a Cereal Bowl." *The Nation*, August 31, 1970.

"A Gadfly Buzzes Around the Table." *Business Week,* September 26, 1970.

"Cereal Critic Aids His Targets." *Business Week,* October 3, 1970.

"What's Behind Those Cereal Headlines?" *Good Housekeeping,* November, 1970.

Stare, M.D., Frederick J. "Cereals? You Bet!" *Ladies Home Journal,* November, 1970.

"Sales for Year Affected Little as Result of Choate Remarks." *The Post Box,* June, 1971.

"Post Will Defend." *The Post Box,* January/February, 1972.

"Concentrated Cereals." *The New Republic,* February 12, 1972.

"Children's Advertising Standards Set." *The Post Box,* September, 1972.

Huth, William E. "An Ominous Storm in a Cereal Bowl." *Fortune,* July, 1973.

Samra, Cal. "Cereal Industry Doing 'Gr-r-reat.'" *Battle Creek Enquirer,* February 26, 1978.

"Too Many Cereals for the FTC." *Business Week,* March 20, 1978.

"One for Our Side." *Forbes,* April 3, 1978.

Kiechel III, Walter. "The Soggy Case Against the Cereal Industry." *Fortune,* April 10, 1978.

Buckley, Jr., William F. "The FTC's War on Success." *The National Review,* March 21, 1980.

"Congress Restrains Rulemaking for Advertising To Children." *Kellogg News,* August, 1980.

"Monopoly on the Cereal Shelves?" *Consumer Reports,* February, 1981.

"Which Cereal for Breakfast?" *Consumer Reports,* February, 1981.

"Snap, Crackle, Flop!" *Time,* January 25, 1982.

Mitchell, Russell. "The Health Craze has Kellogg Feeling GR-R-Reat." *Business Week,* March 30, 1987.

Wallach, Van. "Cereals Dish Up Gratification in Cash." *Advertising Age,* April 27, 1987.

Weiner, Steve. "Food Fight." *Forbes,* July 27, 1987.

Mayer, Caroline E. "Religious Star on Cereal Pack Causes Concern." *Washington Post,* October 15, 1987.

Miller, Annetta. "America Feels Its Oats." *Newsweek,* July 11, 1988.

"Big G is Growing Fat on Oat Cuisine." *Business Week,* September 18, 1989.

"Snap, Crackle, Stop: States Crack Down on Misleading Food Claims." *Business Week,* September 25, 1989.

"Cereal: Breakfast Food or Nutritional Supplement?" *Consumer Reports,* October, 1989.

Moser, Penny Ward. "How I Made $812 in the Oat Bran Craze." *Fortune,* October 9, 1989.

Miller, Annetta. "Oat-Bran Heartburn." *Newsweek,* January 29, 1990.

Books
Burrough, Bryan and John Helyar. *Barbarians at the Gate: The Fall of RJR Nabisco.* New York: Harper and Row, 1990.

Handelman, Michelle and Monte Cazazza. op. cit.

Pulos, Arthur J. op. cit.

Wight, Robin. *The Day the Pigs Refused to be Driven to Market.* New York: Random House, 1972.

Chapter 20. Baby Boomer Breakfast

Interviews/Personal Correspondence
Jackie End, Blair Entenmann, Jim Gillmore, Roy Sandstrom, Michael Parkes, Max Lomont, David Freedman, John Long, Nancy Mengel, Harry Smedley, Tom Gentile, Mike Hagel, Bob Dobler, Manny DeMagistris, Bob Moehl, Elmer Richars, Keith Schopp, Bill Becke, Jeff Wolf, Tony Dow, Ed Hannibal, Howard Courtemanche, and Fred Hanke.

Articles
"Telling the World About Breakfast." *Time,* March 13, 1964.

"Johnny Granola Seed." *Time,* March 6, 1972.

"Euell Visits GF, Tastes New Recipes." *The Post Box,* December, 1972.

"Naturally." *Newsweek,* April 22, 1974.

"The Story Behind Those 30 Million New Natural Cereal Dollars." *Media Decisions,* May, 1974.

Sherwood, John. "Natural Craze Finds a Place in Cereal Industry." *Battle Creek Enquirer,* November 10, 1974.
Waters, Harry F. "Sugar in the Morning." *Newsweek,* January 30, 1978.

Kaufman, Stan. "Ralston Purina Also Means Hockey, Tuna, Plants, Restaurants." *Battle Creek Enquirer,* February 12,1978.

Klein, Joel. "A Social History of Granola." *Rolling Stone,* February 23, 1978.

"Cereals Approved for Kosher 'K'." *Kellogg News,* February, 1983.

"Move Over, Cap'n Crunch: Pac-Man and His Pals Are Taking Over," *Business Week,* July 18, 1983.

"A New Force at Breakfast." *Kellogg News,* February, 1984.

"Here She Comes—Miss America." *Penthouse,* September, 1984.

"Three Product Lines Introduced" *Kellogg News,* April/May, 1985.

"Operation Frosted Flakes." *Time,* February 10, 1986.

Gibson, Richard. "Kellogg Tries to Blunt the Attacks on Cereal Makers' Health

Claims." *Wall Street Journal,* August 31, 1989.

Gibson, Richard. "Fast Fall: Personal 'Chemistry' Abruptly Ended Rise of Kellogg President." *Wall Street Journal,* November 28, 1989.

Berry, Kathleen M. "The Snap Has Turned to Slog," *New York Times,* November 18, 1990.

McCallum, Matt. "The World of Cereal: Battle Creek Rich in Breakfast History." *Battle Creek Enquirer,* April 19, 1991.

McCallum, Matt. "Playing the Hot Hand in Cold Cereals." *Battle Creek Enquirer,* October 6, 1991.

Bombeck, Erma. "Name, Rank, Cereal Number Tell Who You Are." Syndicated column, November 21, 1991.

Gibson, Richard. "How a Hit Movie Can be Truly Delectable." *Wall Street Journal,* December 16, 1991.

Vierria, Dan. "The Morning Habit." *Sacramento Bee,* February 29, 1992.

McCallum, Matt. "Nerds Not So Flaky: Ralston Cereal Based on TV Character." *Battle Creek Enquirer,* May 28, 1992.

Gellene, Denise. "Cereal Prices on the Rise: Manufacturers Cover High Cost of Promotion." *Los Angeles Times,* June 1992.

Kaley, Nancy. "Seeing Stars at Breakfast." *Battle Creek Enquirer,* October 4, 1992.

Zehme, Bill. "Seinfeld." *Rolling Stone,* July 8, 1993.

Graham, Jefferson Graham. "Sein of the Times." *USA Today,* August 26, 1993.

Rosenberg, Ronald. "Entrepreneur Hopes Matzoh Cereal Sells." op. cit..

Holusha, John. "General Mills to Cut Prices," *New York Times,* April 5, 1994.

Gibson, Richard. "General Mills Inc. Will Slash Prices of Eight Cereals." *Wall Street Journal,* April 5, 1994.

Treaster, Joseph B. "Kellogg Seeks to Reset Latvia's Breakfast Table." *New York Times,* May 19, 1994.

Books

Grossman, Gary. op. cit.

Hall, Jim. op. cit.

McNeil, Alex. op. cit.

Stacey, Michelle. *Consumed: Why Americans Love, Hate and Fear Food.* New York: Simon and Schuster, 1994.

Chapter 21. Cereal Verité
Interviews/Personal Correspondence
Howard Courtemanche, John Updike, Leo Stuchkhus, Kent Mitchell, Al Clausi, Jim Gillmore, John Long, John M. McMillin, Prudential Securities, Dr.

Ronald Cotterill, Food Marketing Policy Center, University of Connecticut, Garth "Duff" Stoltz, David Schardt, Center for Science in the Public Interest, Connie Corbett, and Sally Moore, *Consumer Reports.*

Articles

"What Shall We Eat for Breakfast?" *The Literary Digest,* December 9, 1922.

"Breakfast Cereals." *Consumers Union Reports,* May, 1936.

"Vitamin Content of Breakfast Cereals." *Consumer's Research Bulletin,* May 4, 1945.

"Breakfast Cereals." *Consumer Reports,* May, 1961.

"Breakfast Cereals." *Consumer Bulletin,* November, 1961.

"Breakfast Cereals—II." *Consumer Bulletin,* February, 1962.

"A Further Look at Popular Breakfast Cereals." *Consumer Bulletin,* 1962.

"Breakfast Cereals—III." *Consumer Bulletin,* March, 1962.

"Micro-Biology Lab in Action." *The Post Box,* September, 1969.

"About Rats, Cereals, and You." *Consumer Reports,* June, 1975.

"Which Cereals Are Most Nutritious?" *Consumer Reports,* February, 1975.

"How Good is Your Breakfast?" *Consumer Reports,* October, 1986.

"Raisin a Ruckus: Kellogg Sues Post for Millions Over Ads." *Battle Creek Enquirer,* August 26, 1987.

"Cereals: Which Belong in Your Bowl?" *Consumer Reports,* November, 1992.

Gibson, Richard. "General Mills Ends Bid to Sell Tainted Cereals." *Wall Street Journal,* July 8, 1994.

Feder, Barnaby J. "Oat Problem Still Troubles General Mills." *New York Times,* July 11, 1994.

Books

Fox, Stephen. op. cit.

Herbert, Victor, M.D., J.D. and Stephen Barrett, M.D. *Vitamins and 'Health' Foods: The Great American Hustle.* Philadelphia: George F. Strickly Company, 1984.

Stare, Fredrick and Elizabeth M. Whelan. *Eat Ok—Feel Ok! Food Facts and Your Health.* North Quincy, Massachusetts: The Christopher Publishing House, 1978.

Whelan, Elizabeth M. and Fredrick J. Stare. *The One-Hundred-Percent Natural, Purely Organic, Cholesterol-Free, Megavitamin, Low-Carbohydrate Nutrition Hoax.* New York: Atheneum, 1983.

Young, James Harvey. *The Medical Messiahs: A Social History of Health Quackery in Twentieth-Century America.* Princeton: Princeton University Press, 1967.

Updike, John. *Collected Poems of John Updike 1953–1993.* New York: Alfred A. Knopf, 1993.

Index

About the Authors

Scott Bruce

Scott Bruce is the publisher of *Flake* magazine, which *Newsweek* hailed as a "real journalistic gem." He has appeared on CNN, *CBS Morning News,* and *Entertainment Tonight* talking about cereal. In a previous incarnation, Mr. Bruce was known as Mr. Lunch Box, and appeared on *Today, ABC World News,* and many other TV shows. He has written *Cereal Box Bonanza: The Fifties* (Collector Books, 1995), and *Lunch Box: The Fifties and Sixties* (Chronicle Books, 1988). Mr. Bruce lives with his wife and son in Cambridge, Massachusetts.

Bill Crawford

Bill Crawford is a writer and producer based in Austin, Texas, whose articles on American business and pop culture have appeared in *Texas Monthly, American Way,* the *Sun* and other publications. He is the co-author of two previous books: *Border Radio: Quakes, Yodellers, Pitchmen, Psychics and Other Amazing Broadcasters of the American Airwaves* (Limelight Editions, 1990) and the best-selling *Stevie Ray Vaughan: Caught in the Crossfire* (Little Brown, 1993). Mr. Crawford prefers buttered toast for breakfast.